Las Vegas, Reno, and Lake Tahoe

COREY SANDLER

CB

CONTEMPORARY BOOKS

CHICAGO

To Janice, my fellow traveler

Copyright © 1994 by Word Association, Inc.

All rights reserved

Published by Contemporary Books, Inc.

Two Prudential Plaza, Chicago, Illinois 60601-6790

Manufactured in the United States of America

International Standard Book Number: 0-8092-3507-2

10 9 8 7 6 5 4 3 2

Contents

III Reno, Virginia City, and Lake Tahoe

IV Gambling: Nevada's Leading Industry

Acknowledgments

Dozens of hard-working and creative people helped move my words from the keyboard to the place where you read this book now.

Among the many to thank are Eugene Brissie of Contemporary Books for working with me as we expand the Econoguide series and Dan Bial for his capable agentry. Thanks, too, to Bill Gladstone of Waterside Productions.

Fred Swartz of Graphic Arts Consortium of Nantucket, Massachusetts, once again translated ideas and words into a handsome design. Diane Swartz is our fine artist, and Kim Roaf produced the coupons with style.

Thanks to Dawn Barker of Contemporary Books who gave the text a professional polish, and to Kathy Willhoite who managed the editorial and production processes.

Thanks to the hotels, casinos, restaurants, and attractions that opened their doors to us; special thanks to the companies that offered discount coupons to our readers.

Special thanks go to Janice Keefe who worked long and hard in the Word Association offices to collect and process the discount coupons, and to June Brock, who assisted.

And finally, thank you for buying this book. We all hope you find it of value; please let me know how we can improve the book in future editions. (Please enclose a stamped envelope if you'd like a reply; no calls, please.)

Corey Sandler
Econoguide Travel Books
P.O. Box 2779
Nantucket, MA 02584

Introduction to the Second Edition, 1995

We love Nevada. It is one of the most exciting places we know, from the man-made wonders of The Strip and Glitter Gulch in Las Vegas and the concrete canyon of Hoover Dam to the natural splendors of Lake Tahoe and the Sierra Nevada mountains.

Nevada was, is, and probably always will be the frontier. It is a place where things are different, where old assumptions are challenged, and where new ideas are tried.

That is, after all, why people come to Nevada. There is no Las Vegas in Chicago or Boston or Los Angeles. There is no Lake Mead in New Jersey. There are no snow-capped mountains with ski runs that careen down to an alpine lake in Kansas. And, though Nevada is a relatively young state, there are few places we know of imbued with living history like Virginia City.

But before we go too far down the road, let's start with what this book is *not* about:

• It is *not* a rose-colored view of the world endorsed by the Chamber of Commerce. Not everything in Nevada is wonderful, a good value, or a worthwhile use of your vacation time, and we'll try to help you get the most from your trip.

• It is *not* a guide for the cheapskate interested in sleeping in bus terminals (or motels that look like bus terminals) and eating exclusively at restaurants that use plastic forks. What we mean by "Econoguide" is this: How to get the most out of your trip to Nevada. We'll show you how to get the most out of your time and money on travel, hotels, restaurants, and entertainment.

• It is *not* a guide to making money at the gambling tables. We will, though, offer a cautious guide to casinos, concentrating on how to have fun and not lose more money than you are prepared to donate in the name of fun.

Let's think a bit about the state of Nevada, a place of great contrasts.

The seventh-largest state in the union, it is 38th in population. It is today the fastest-growing state, though it is still very sparsely populated with 1.3

million people across 110,540 square miles, almost all of them concentrated around the urban areas of Las Vegas and Reno.

Winters are extremely cold in the north and west; summers in the south are oven-like. Nevada's highest point is a lofty 13,143 feet at Boundary Peak on the snowy border with California; the lowest is along the Colorado River as it enters the hot and dry desert in the southern tip of the state.

Nevada's economy is focused on mining: mining minerals out of the ground and mining gold and silver out of the pockets of tourists who come to visit in droves. Las Vegas alone draws more than 20 million visitors annually. Fully half of the workers in the state are in the service trades, with 25 percent directly employed by a casino or hotel. In Las Vegas alone, casinos provide more than 102,000 jobs.

One of the great, uncelebrated things about Nevada's tourist centers of Las Vegas, Reno, Lake Tahoe, and Laughlin is that you can find a bathroom, telephone, change booth, or restaurant at any hour of the day or night, any day of the year. You can, of course, also find a casino open at any time.

Join us on an exploration of all sides of Nevada, from the oasis in the desert at Laughlin to the mirage at Las Vegas to the great Western Rest Stop at Reno to the honeycombed mountains of Virginia City and the Comstock Lode to the breathtaking beauty of Lake Tahoe.

Caesars, Las Vegas

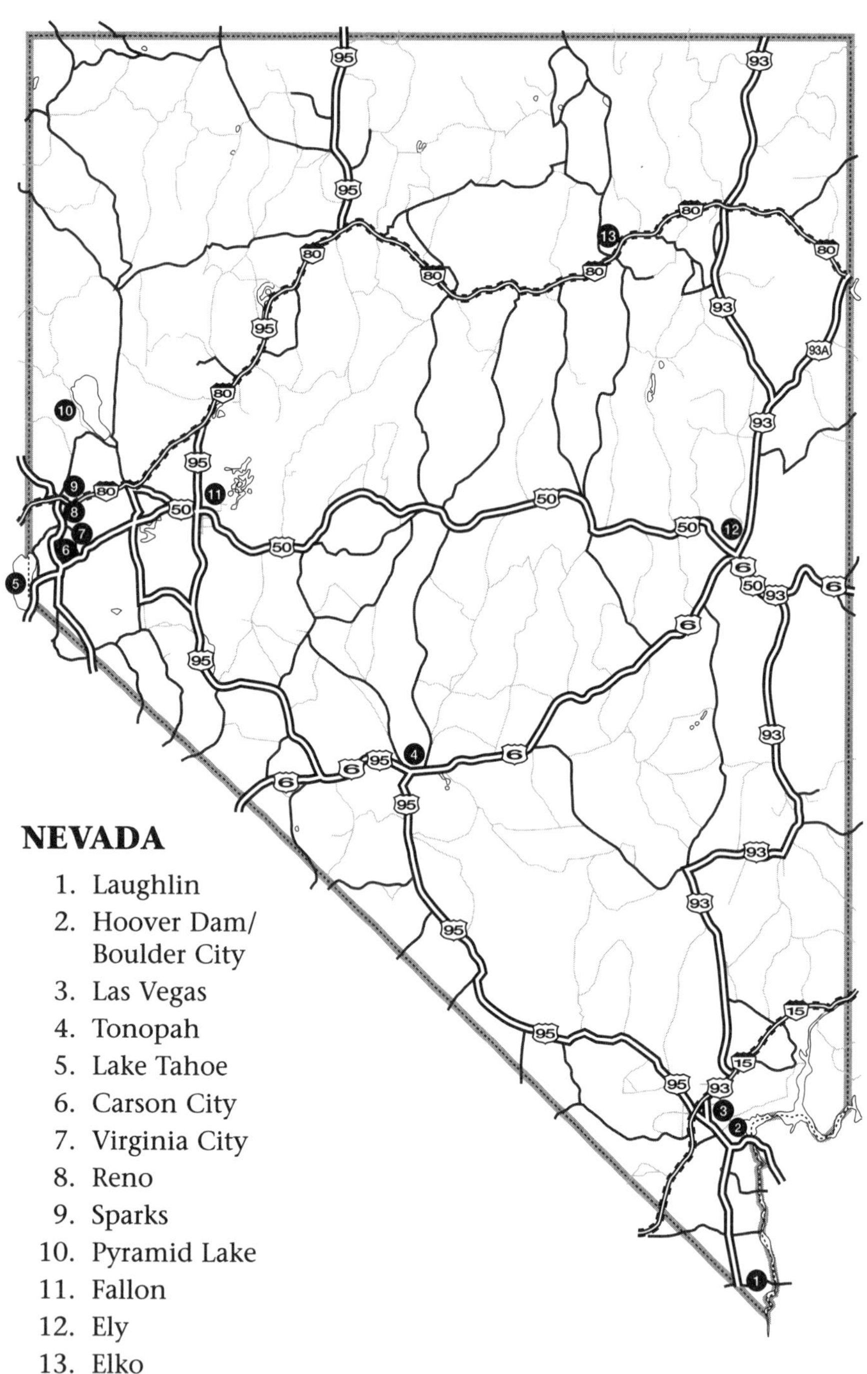

NEVADA

1. Laughlin
2. Hoover Dam/ Boulder City
3. Las Vegas
4. Tonopah
5. Lake Tahoe
6. Carson City
7. Virginia City
8. Reno
9. Sparks
10. Pyramid Lake
11. Fallon
12. Ely
13. Elko

I
Nevada Bound

Chapter 1

A Short and Irreverent History of Nevada

When they spoke of the "Wild West," it was often Nevada they had in mind.

Wild, as in a nearly virgin land when the first white explorers set foot there about the time of the American Revolution.

Wild, as in the extremes of weather from the arid deserts of the eastern part of the state to the high, snowy mountains of Sierra Nevada in the west.

Wild, as in the heady days in the 1850s and 1860s when gold and then silver was discovered south of Reno, and when for a short period of time Virginia City was the richest place on earth.

Wild, as in the early days of Las Vegas at the start of the 20th century when the "anything goes" atmosphere of the railroad town laid the foundation for what would become Glitter Gulch and then The Strip.

Wild, as in the State of Nevada of today, a place that is just slightly ahead of, or behind, or off to one side of anywhere else we know of.

Throughout all of its history, Nevada has been looked upon as a colony for outside interests to exploit. First came the Spanish, then the British and their Canadian surrogates. When the land came under control of the young United States, Nevada was considered little more than a rest stop on the highway to California. When gold and silver were discovered in great quantities in and around Virginia City, much of the wealth was exported out of the state to California and even as far away as England.

The interests that developed much of the early commercial propertie of Nevada were the railroads, and they, too, sent their money west an east. And finally, there was gambling, Nevada's one major homegrow industry. The casinos took off in the 1940s only after organized crime ca italists from New York, Chicago, Miami, Los Angeles, and elsewhere can in and exerted control. Today, the gangsters are mostly gone, but contr

1

of nearly all of the major casinos and hotels rests in the hands of huge stateless corporations.

The River to the Pacific

The region that would one day be Nevada was originally part of the Spanish Empire in the New World. Father Francisco Garcés is believed to have entered the Las Vegas Valley in 1776. Garcés and other priest-explorers were expanding the Old Spanish Trail from the commercial centers of Santa Fe (now in New Mexico) to the missions in southern California. Along the way, they sought to make converts if they could; more than a few Native Americans were killed in skirmishes and by disease.

There was, of course, a significant problem faced by the Spanish: getting through deserts and high mountain passes between New Mexico and California. Sierra Nevada is a Spanish phrase for "Snowy Mountains."

Garcés and others of his time followed the Colorado River into Nevada and did not fully explore the region geologists now call the Great Basin. And in the process, they made some significant errors on their maps and created the myth of what they called the San Buenaventura River, a great waterway that was supposed to cross the Great Basin and empty into the Pacific Ocean. In other words, they were claiming that there was an easy route from east to west that did not require crossing the high mountains. For much of the next half-century, trappers and explorers searched in vain.

In 1825, Peter Skene Ogden explored parts of Nevada from the other direction, on an expedition south from Canada. Working for the Hudson's Bay Company, he discovered the Humboldt River in northwest Nevada in that year. A year later, Jedediah Strong Smith, an explorer and fur trader, followed the Colorado River into southern Nevada—the same entry taken by Garcés 50 years earlier—and soon thereafter the 1,200-mile-long Spanish Trail became firmly established.

Smith, born in 1798 in Bainbridge, New York, went to the West as a young man as a fur trapper and became one of the great pathfinders of our country. His group of 17 set out from the Great Salt Lake in 1826 looking for fur trade routes to California and the Northwest. He crossed the Mojave Desert to Mission San Gabriel, California, near what is today San Diego, and may have been the first nonnative to enter California from the East. Returning eastward the next year, he crossed the Great Salt Lake Desert on an epic journey through the inhospitable, waterless sands.

Another group of explorers sought a way to link the Mormon settlements of Salt Lake City and California, and the trailblazers sought a way to avoid the highest of the Sierra Nevada mountain passes by going south.

In 1829, Rafael Rivera, a young scout for Spanish traders, entered a val-

ley with a patch of tall grass about two miles long and half a mile wide—a desert oasis with a small amount of drinkable water. That valley, called *las vegas* (Spanish for "the meadows") became a regular stopping-off point for travelers on the westward trail.

John C. Frémont, a U.S. Army officer, conducted extensive explorations in 1843 and 1845. In 1848, at the end of the Mexican War, the territory that included what would become Nevada was acquired by the United States from Mexico for $15 million in the Treaty of Guadalupe Hidalgo.

But it took the discovery of gold at Sutter's Mill near Sacramento, California, in 1847 to begin mass migration to the West Coast, and much of the traffic passed through Nevada; over the next seven years, the population of California grew from about 15,000 to 300,000.

In 1849, Mormon settlers established a trading post at Mormon Station (now known as Genoa) in the Carson River Valley, at the base of the Sierra Nevada. In 1855, a colony of Mormon evangelists arrived in the Las Vegas Valley and established the Las Vegas Mission in an attempt to bring their religion to the Paiute Indians. They built a fort—importing some of the wood from mountains as far as 20 miles away—and planted crops. Although they had some success in their assignments, in 1857 the settlers were recalled to Salt Lake City by Brigham Young after the church had a dispute with the U.S. government, and the mission was abandoned.

In the late 1850s, the area around Virginia City, Carson City, and Genoa served as a staging area for settlers about to head over the Sierras to California. The Mormon Station had become a thriving commercial operation after a simple log cabin store had been erected in 1851. Genoa was also the first home of the *Territorial Enterprise* newspaper, which was to become an important element of the developing Western culture.

The relatively quiet status of Nevada as a rest stop on the highway west changed mightily about this time. There had been some minor gold finds in Gold Canyon in about 1850, but the quantity was so relatively small as to be lost in the excitement over the California discoveries.

But in January of 1859, gold and then silver—the Great Comstock Lode—was found on the slopes of Mt. Davidson between Reno and Carson City. By the spring of 1860, a full boom was underway at Virginia City. (One of the miners, James "Old Virginny" Finney, bestowed his name on the rough settlement of tents and cave dwellings of the first miners.)

In 1862, the U.S. Congress granted a charter to the Union Pacific Railroad to build the first transcontinental railroad, stretching from near Sacramento, California, to Missouri, where it would connect to eastern systems.

The mines in and around Virginia City had a lasting impact on the nation, bringing Nevada Territory into the Union as a source of wealth at the start of the Civil War in 1861. Many local mine owners were opposed to statehood, fearing their riches would be taxed to support the war; President Lincoln, who sought Nevada's support in Congress, pushed its statehood, which took place in 1864. Along the way, the riches of the Comstock provided much of the capital for the development of San Francisco.

After the Mormons abandoned their fort in Las Vegas in 1857, a local farmer, Octavius Decatur Gass, acquired the water rights in the valley and moved into the old Mormon fort. Gass, who became a major political force in the area, had come from Ohio in search of gold. The 640-acre site, now referred to as the Las Vegas Ranch, occupied what is now the entire downtown area. A section of the old fort still stands in a city museum.

The next driving force in Nevada was the coming of the railroads. Though the Civil War held most of the attention of a war-weary America, citizens also watched as the Central Pacific and Union Pacific railroads raced east and west toward each other in the construction of the first transcontinental railroad. The CP began on January 1, 1863, in Sacramento, California; the UP broke ground on December 2 of the same year in Omaha, Nebraska. The Central Pacific tracks passed through northern Nevada (Reno, Winnemucca, and Elko) to the meeting point at Promontory Point, Utah, where the Golden Spike was driven on May 10, 1869.

The main line became the lure to additional railroad construction in the state. The Virginia & Truckee Railroad, which serviced the silver and gold mines of Virginia City, was extended from Carson City to the east-west tracks at Reno.

<table>
<tr><td>

Home on the range. Larger mammals native to Nevada include mule deer, pronghorn antelope, bobcat, and bighorn sheep; in some areas wild horses and donkeys can be found. Common smaller mammals are badgers, rabbits, porcupines, muskrats, and marmots.

Desert animal life features various lizards, tortoises, and snakes including the sidewinder rattlesnake. Birds include the thrush, horned lark, Nevada creeper, pheasant, partridge, and sage grouse.

</td></tr>
</table>

At the start of 1905, the final spike connecting a southern railroad route between Los Angeles and Salt Lake City was driven into the desert floor about 20 miles south of what would become Las Vegas. The Tonopah & Las Vegas Railroad sprung up to link mining and ranching operations to the southern tracks.

In 1882, the former Mormon ranch, which covered much of what is now downtown Las Vegas, came into the ownership of the Stewart family. Twenty years later, they sold the property for $55,000 to copper and railroad magnate William Clark, who was also a U.S. senator from Montana. He decided to make Las Vegas a division point for his San Pedro, Los Angeles, and Salt Lake Railroad and not incidentally drive up the value of his land holdings.

And so, on the morning of May 15, 1905, Clark's railroad and the closely linked Las Vegas

Land and Water Company banged the opening gavel for an auction of the Las Vegas Ranch and surrounding lands. The sale was conducted from a temporary structure near the railroad station; the site today is roughly the location of the Union Plaza Hotel at the head of Fremont Street in downtown Las Vegas.

A crowd of more than 1,000 bid feverishly on some 1,200 lots; the action continued into a second day. Spots considered prime property brought as much as $1,750, and the total net was about $265,000.

The Las Vegas Rest Stop

For most of the next quarter-century, the town thrived as a rest stop for travelers on the railroads and also as a commercial center for outlying mining operations.

The wants and needs of the miners were by most sensibilities a bit on the rough side. For many, a trip into what passed for a town was for the purpose of buying basic supplies, obtaining a hot bath, visiting a saloon for some drinking and gambling, and finding a woman for sex; the priorities were not necessarily in that order, either.

As a frontier town, Las Vegas included its share of illegal gaming parlors and a red-light district almost from the start. When the planners for the San Pedro, Los Angeles, and Salt Lake Railroad divvied up the Las Vegas Ranch, they named the area that is now between First and Second and Ogden and Stewart streets (one block in from the main drag of Fremont Street) as Block 16. It was here that the first saloons—many with "cribs" out back—were located.

The Arizona Club was one of the first brick buildings in town and generally considered the class of Las Vegas. An old photograph shows the tiny saloon along a very rough dirt road with a 50-foot-long boardwalk. The sign outside read, "Arizona Club. Headquarters for Fully Matured Reimported Straight Whiskey."

Town officials and the police turned a blind eye to the drinking, entertainment, prostitution, and gambling that took place in Block 16, which soon became known more simply as "The Block." These vices were not exactly illegal, existing in a political netherworld for decades. In fact, the operators of the whorehouses were required to purchase an annual license for their operations, and the employees were subject to weekly medical examinations.

On the rocks. The drinking age in Nevada is 21, and in most of the state there are no closing hours for liquor sales or consumption. Visitors from states with more restrictive laws will be surprised to see other laxities including free drinks at casinos. You don't suppose the casinos (and their partner the state) are happy to see customers loosened up a bit, do you?

<table>
<tr><td>

Can you dig it?
The original foundation of the state was mining, beginning with the gold and silver deposits of the Comstock Lode in 1859. Agriculture developed as the second most important segment of the economy.

Mining today represents about 33 percent of the annual value of goods produced in Nevada—principally gold, barite, silver, and petroleum.

The largest current gold mine is west of Carlin, in northeast Nevada near Elko, although deposits are spread throughout the state; industry mines copper, lead, sand, gravel, mercury, gypsum, tungsten, salt, zinc, magnesium, and manganese.

</td></tr>
</table>

Gambling had been legal in Nevada from the time of its statehood until 1911, when, reacting to a developing conservatism in the country, the legislature outlawed it. Eight years later, the U.S. Congress instituted Prohibition, outlawing consumption of alcoholic beverages.

But that seemed to matter very little in the Wild West of Las Vegas, particularly in Block 16. Bootleggers supplied alcohol, prostitution flourished, and unregulated games of chance continued for the next 20 years.

A Dam Site

The next important event in local history came courtesy of the Federal Bureau of Reclamation when it authorized the construction of the Boulder Dam on the Colorado River, about 30 miles southeast of Las Vegas. The dam was considered necessary to control the Colorado, which regularly flooded both the Imperial Valley in California and the Yuma Valley in Arizona when mountain snows melted each spring, and dried to a near-trickle in the summer.

Bureau of Reclamation engineers investigated more than 70 sites along the Colorado River before choosing Black Canyon for the Boulder Dam.

The dam was to create the 110-mile-long Lake Mead reservoir upstream and allow the controlled release of water down the Colorado River. (During the construction period, the Colorado River was diverted around the site by four huge tunnels, each 50 feet in diameter.)

Construction began in 1930 and took five years to complete. More than 5,000 workers, many of them with families, moved to the area, and Las Vegas once more was the attractive rest stop in the desert.

Not at all coincidentally, the Nevada legislature reestablished legalized casino gambling in 1931, and small casinos began catering to the construction workers. Included in the same session was a liberalization of divorce laws, requiring a short six-week residency for out-of-staters seeking to cast asunder their marriage vows.

And also not incidentally, the huge generators at the dam—renamed as Hoover Dam—produced plentiful, cheap electricity that was essential to the neon signs of Glitter Gulch and The Strip and the air-conditioning within the huge hotels.

The first Las Vegas gaming license was issued in 1931 to the Northern Club at 15 East Fremont St. Two years later, Prohibition was officially ended around the nation, and the consumption of alcohol became legal again.

Block 16, which continued to thrive even when most of its vices became legal, was finally killed off by a different sort of national urgency—World War II. The commander of the Las Vegas Aerial and Gunnery Range, where many thousands of soldiers were training, feared outbreaks of disease and lack of discipline among his troops. Las Vegas officials were informed that unless they cracked down on The Block, the Army would declare all of the city off-limits to servicemen. Almost immediately, the liquor and slot machine licenses of The Block were revoked. Prostitution, which operated as an adjunct to the other forms of entertainment, died off as an organized operation soon afterward.

Prostitution receded into the underworld again for the next few decades, reemerging as a legal industry in 1973 when the Nevada Supreme Court upheld the right of the state's counties to permit the activity. Brothels are legal in several Nevada counties today, and several major brothels operate outside of Las Vegas and Reno.

The first major casinos were established in downtown Las Vegas along Fremont Street, which eventually became known as Glitter Gulch. Joining the Northern in 1932 was the Hotel Apache, with 100 rooms and the first elevator in town. With the exception of the dam workers—most of whom departed by 1936—the attraction of the casinos was almost entirely regional.

The war contributed to the growth of the area, with the establishment of the Aerial Gunnery School and a huge magnesium processing plant, Basic Magnesium, that brought 10,000 workers to a site between Las Vegas and Boulder City.

It was in the 1940s, however, that Las Vegas gained notoriety, and much of the impetus came from organized crime, led by Benjamin "Bugsy" Siegel, Charles "Lucky" Luciano, Meyer Lansky, and others.

Clever businessmen, the gangsters forged links right from the start with Hollywood. This is not to say that the movie stars of the era were directly involved with the gangsters, but there was a definite synergy between the needs of the stars and the operators of the casinos.

Clara Bow (the "It" girl) and Rex Bell, film

Life goes on. Plant life at the lowest desert levels of Nevada includes creosote, mesquite, cactus, and yucca. In the higher northern areas, the predominant plant is sagebrush. On higher mountain slopes and higher elevations can be found juniper, pine, spruce, and fir.

stars of the '20s and '30s, were early adopters of Las Vegas glitz. They built a ranch and were hosts of the town; they brought many later stars, including Clark Gable, Errol Flynn, the Barrymores, and others to town for visits.

Gamblers Get Out of Town

The El Rancho Vegas was founded miles from downtown in 1941, on U.S. 91, then called the Los Angeles Highway. The hotel included 63 bungalows and had riding stables, a showroom and, of course, a casino.

Five years later on the highway (renamed as Las Vegas Boulevard and soon to become known as The Strip) the famous Flamingo hotel opened, and the seeds of modern Las Vegas were sown.

The Flamingo was Bugsy Siegel's lavish dream; at the time of its opening on Dec. 26, 1946 (with Jimmy Durante as the headline act), the hotel was the southernmost hotel on The Strip. (Siegel was executed by business associates in 1947, allegedly because of claims he siphoned money from the building fund for the Flamingo.)

The second big resort out of town was the Last Frontier, which used an Old West theme; guests who flew into town were picked up at the airport in a stagecoach.

One after another, hotels and casinos were built on The Strip, moving farther southward.

In 1966, Caesars Palace opened and launched the era of the opulent gambling palace, and Las Vegas as we know it was born. Las Vegas as a "family" resort accelerated in 1993 and 1994 with the opening of the MGM Grand Adventures theme park and hotel (with a casino, of course) as well as the spectacular Luxor and Treasure Island pleasure palaces.

Chapter 2

How to Buy the Lowest-Cost Airline Tickets and Protect Yourself from the Uncertainties of Modern Travel

The agent at the gate will smile at you and take your ticket, and the flight attendant will point you to your seat without knowing that you paid just $300 for your round trip ticket from Boston to Las Vegas.

The businessman across the aisle will suffer through the same mystery meal, watch the same crummy movie, and arrive at McCarran Airport at the same millisecond you do—and pay $804 for his ticket.

But wait: the couple in front were happily bumped off the previous flight because of overbooking and are discussing where to use the two free round-trip tickets they received in compensation. And up front in first class—where the food is ever-so-slightly better—a family of four is traveling on free tickets earned through Mom's frequent flyer plan.

And me, I've got a cut rate ticket *and* I'm due for a 5 percent rebate on airfare, hotel, and car rental arranged through my travel agent.

In today's strange world of air travel, there is a lot of room for maneuvering for the dollarwise and clever traveler. You can pay an inflated full price, you can take advantage of the lowest fares, or you can play the ultimate game and parlay tickets into free travel. In this section, we'll show you how to do each.

The Econoguide Golden Rules of Travel

There are three golden rules and a handful of corollaries to saving hundreds of dollars on travel: be flexible, be flexible, and be flexible.

Low-season in most of Nevada is generally the late fall to early spring, with the quietest time of the year the weeks around Christmas and New Year's, but not including those holidays themselves.

Watch out for the huge conventions that descend on Las Vegas and grab the premium rooms and drive up the prices of all the rest. And the hotels and casinos of Lake Tahoe sell out—at top rates—during weekends and holiday periods of ski season.

• Be flexible about when you choose to travel, and visit Nevada during the off-season or low-season when airfares, hotel rooms, and other attractions offer substantial discounts.

• Be flexible about the day of the week you travel. In many cases, you can save hundreds of dollars by changing your departure date one or two days in either direction. Ask your travel agent or airline reservationist for current fare rules and restrictions.

• Be flexible on the hour of your departure. There is generally lower demand—and therefore lower prices—for flights that leave in the middle of the day or very late at night.

• Be flexible on the route you will take, or your willingness to put up with a change of plane or stopover. Once again, you are putting the law of supply and demand in your favor. Don't overlook the possibility of flying out of a different airport, either. For example, metropolitan New Yorkers can find domestic flights from La Guardia, Newark, or White Plains. Suburbanites of Boston might want to consider flights from Worcester or Providence as possibly cheaper alternatives to Logan Airport. Suburbanites in California have similar choices.

• Plan way ahead of time and purchase the most deeply discounted advance tickets, which usually are noncancelable. Most carriers limit the number of discount tickets on any particular flight; although there may be plenty of seats left on the day you want to travel, they may be offered at higher rates.

In recent years, most airlines modified nonrefundable fares to become noncancelable. What this means is that if your plans change or if you are forced to cancel your trip, your tickets retain their value and can be applied against another trip, usually for a fee of about $35 per ticket.

> **Light air.** Planes are usually least crowded in midweek and on Saturday afternoons and Sunday mornings.
>
> In general, you will receive the lowest possible fare if you include a Saturday in your trip, buying what is called an **"Excursion Fare."** Airlines use this as a way to exclude business travelers from the cheapest fares, assuming that business people will want to be home by Friday night.

• Or, conversely, you can take a big chance and wait for the last possible moment, keeping in contact with charter tour operators and accepting a bargain price on a "leftover" seat and hotel reservation. You *may* also find that some airlines will reduce the prices on leftover seats within a few weeks of departure date; don't be afraid to check regularly with the airline, or ask your travel agent to do it for you. In fact, some travel agencies have automated computer programs that keep a constant electronic eye on available seats and fares.

• Consider booking a package tour through

an airline or a travel agency. There are enough people traveling to Las Vegas or Reno almost any week of the year to permit companies to buy and resell at a discount blocks of space on scheduled airlines and blocks of rooms at major hotels. There are some very good deals to be had by purchasing a package. However, it is worth the time to deconstruct the package to its various parts: airfare, car rental or bus transfer, hotels, and any meals or entertainment included. Could you do better booking your own trip?

• Take advantage of special discount programs like senior citizens' clubs, military discounts, or offerings from organizations to which you may belong. If you are in the over-60 category, you may not even have to belong to a group like AARP; simply ask the airline reservationist if there is a discount available—you may have to prove your age when you pick up your ticket or boarding pass.

• Consider doing business with discounters, known in the industry as consolidators or, less flatteringly, as "bucket shops." Look for their ads in the classified sections of many Sunday newspaper travel sections. These companies buy the airlines' slow-to-sell tickets in volume and resell them to consumers at rock-bottom prices. Be sure to study and understand the restrictions; if they fit your needs and wants, this is a good way to fly.

• A bit more in the shadows are ticket brokers who specialize in the resale of frequent flyer coupons and other free or almost-free tickets. Are you willing to take a small financial risk to save hundreds or even thousands of dollars on a long trip?

About Travel Agencies

Here's my advice about travel agents in a nutshell: get a good one or go it alone.

A good travel agent is someone who remembers who he or she works for. You. Of course, there is a built-in conflict of interest here, since the agent is in most cases paid by someone else. Agents receive a commission on

Funny hat fares. You may not have to have any affiliation at all with a convention group in order to take advantage of special rates, if offered. All the airline will ask is the name or number of the discount plan for the convention; the reservationist is almost certainly not going to ask to see your union card or funny hat.

Check with conventions and visitors bureaus at your destination to see if any large groups are traveling when you plan to fly. Is this sneaky and underhanded? Yes. But we think it is sneaky and underhanded for an airline to charge hundreds of dollars more for the seat to the left and right of the ones we're sitting in.

Finding a bucket shop. Look for ads for ticket brokers and bucket shops in places like the classified ads in *USA Today*, the "Mart" section of the *Wall Street Journal,* or in specialty magazines like *Frequent Flyer.*

airline tickets, hotel reservations, car rentals, and many other services they sell you. The more they sell (or the higher the price) the more they earn.

I would recommend you start the planning for any trip by calling the airlines and a few hotels and finding the best package you can put together for yourself. *Then* call your travel agent and ask them to do better.

If your agent contributes knowledge or experience, comes up with dollar-saving alternatives to your own package, or offers some other kind of convenience, then go ahead and book through the agency. If, as I often find, you know a lot more about your destination and are willing to spend a lot more time to save money than will the agent, do it yourself.

There is one special type of travel agency worth considering. A number of large agencies rebate part of their commissions to travelers. Some of these companies cater only to frequent flyers who will bring in a lot of business; other rebate agencies offer only limited services to clients.

I use an agency that sends me a check after each trip equal to 5 percent of all reservations booked through them. I have never set foot in their offices, and I conduct all of my business over the phone; tickets arrive by mail or by overnight courier when necessary.

You can find discount travel agencies through many major credit card companies (Citibank and American Express among them) or through associations and clubs.

And if you establish a regular relationship with your local travel agency and bring them enough business to make them glad to see you walk through their door, don't be afraid to ask them for a discount equal to a few percentage points.

Your Consumer Rights

The era of deregulation of airlines has been a mixed blessing for the industry and the consumer. After a period of wild competition based mostly on price, we now are left with fewer, huge airlines and a dizzying array of rules.

The U.S. Department of Transportation and its Federal Aviation Administration still regulate safety issues, overbooking policies, baggage limits and no-smoking rules. Almost everything else is between you and the airline.

Policies on fares, cancellations, reconfirmation, check-in requirements, compensation for lost or damaged baggage, and for delays all vary

Free fare zone.
Although most airlines attempt to prohibit the resale or transfer of free tickets from the original "owner" to a second or third party, the fact is that very rarely are they successful in preventing such reuse. (When is the last time you were asked for some proof of identity in boarding a domestic air flight?)

Still, you do run the risk of losing your ticket and being forced to buy a full-fare replacement en route. Be sure to read and understand the terms of your contract with the broker, and pay for your ticket with a credit card, if possible.

by airline. Your rights are limited and defined by the terms of the contract you make with an airline when you buy your ticket. You may find the contract included with the ticket you purchase, or the airlines may "incorporate terms by reference" to a separate document which you will have to request to see.

Whether you are buying your ticket through a travel agent or dealing directly with the airline, here are some important questions to ask:

Is the price guaranteed or can it change from the time of the reservation until you actually purchase the ticket?

Can the price change between the time you buy the ticket and departure?

Is there a penalty for cancellation of the ticket?

Can the reservation be changed without penalty, or for a reasonable fee?

And, ask your travel agent the following:

Is there anything I should know about the financial health of the airline offering me this ticket?

Are you aware of any significant threats of work stoppages or legal actions that could ruin my trip?

Overbooking

Overbooking is a polite industry term that refers to the legal practice of selling more than an airline can deliver. It all stems, alas, from the unfortunate habit of many travelers of neglecting to cancel flight reservations that will not be used. Airlines study the patterns on various flights and city pairs and apply a formula that allows them to sell more tickets than there are on the plane in the expectation that a certain percentage will not show up at the airport.

But what happens if all passengers holding a reservation do show up? Obviously, the result will be more passengers than seats, and some will have to be left behind.

The involuntary bump list will begin with the names of passengers who are late to check in. After them, airlines must ask for volunteers before

> **The best policy.** If any significant portion of your trip is non-refundable, consider buying trip cancellation insurance from a travel agency, tour operator, or directly from an insurance company (ask your insurance agent for advice). The policies are intended to reimburse you for any lost deposits or prepayments if you must cancel a trip because you or certain specified members of your family become ill. Read the policy carefully to understand the circumstances under which the company will pay.
>
> Take care not to purchase more coverage than you need; if your tour package costs $5,000 but you would lose only $1,000 in the event of a cancellation, then the amount of insurance required is just $1,000. Some policies will cover you for health and accident benefits while on vacation, excluding any preexisting conditions.

bumping any passengers who have followed the rules. Assuming that no one is willing to give up his or her seat just for the fun of it, the airline will offer some sort of compensation—either a free ticket or cash, or both. It is up to the passenger and the airline to negotiate an acceptable deal.

The U.S. Department of Transportation's consumer protection regulations set some minimum levels of compensation for passengers who are bumped from a flight due to overbooking.

If a passenger is bumped involuntarily, the airline must provide a ticket on its next available flight. Unfortunately, there is no guarantee that it will arrive at your destination at a convenient time.

If a passenger is bumped involuntarily and is booked on a flight which arrives within one hour of the original arrival time, no compensation need be paid; if the airline gets the bumpee to his or her destination more than one hour, but less than two hours after the scheduled arrival, the traveler is entitled to receive an amount equal to the one-way fare of the oversold flight, up to $200; if the delay is more than two hours, the bumpee will receive an amount equal to twice the one-way fare of the original flight, up to $400. The compensation is often in the form of credits for future flights; most are transferrable.

It is not considered "bumping" if a flight is cancelled because of weather, equipment problems, or the lack of a flight crew. You are also not eligible for compensation if the airline substitutes a smaller aircraft for operational or safety reasons, and if the flight involves an aircraft with 60 seats or less.

How to Get Bumped

Why in the world would you *want* to be bumped? Well, perhaps you'd like to look at missing your plane as an opportunity to earn a little money for your time. Is a two-hour delay worth $100 an hour to you? How about $800 for a family of four to wait a few hours on the way home—that will pay for a week's hotel plus a meal at the airport.

If you're not in a tremendous rush to get to Nevada—or to get back home—you might want to volunteer to be bumped. We wouldn't recommend doing this on the busiest travel days of the year, or if you are booked on the last flight of the day, unless you are also looking forward to a free night in an airport motel.

Tour Packages and Charter Flights

Tour packages and flights sold by tour operators or travel agents may look similar, but the consumer may end up with significantly different rights.

It all depends whether the flight is a scheduled or nonscheduled flight. A scheduled flight is one that is listed in the *Official Airline Guide* and available to the general public through a travel agent or from the airline. This doesn't mean that a scheduled flight will necessarily be on a major carrier, or that you will be flying on a 747 jumbo jet; it could just as easily be the propeller-driven pride of Hayseed Airlines. In any case, though, a scheduled flight does have to meet stringent federal government certification requirements.

In the event of delays, cancellations, or other problems with a scheduled flight, your recourse is with the airline.

A nonscheduled flight is also known as a charter flight. The term charter is sometimes also applied to a complete package that includes a nonscheduled flight, hotel accommodations, ground transportation, and other elements.

Charter flights are generally a creation of a tour operator who will purchase all of the seats on a specific flight to a specific destination, or who will rent an airplane and crew from an air carrier.

Charter flights and charter tours are regulated by the federal government, but your rights as a consumer are much more limited than those afforded to scheduled flight customers.

Read the Fine Print

You wouldn't buy a hamburger without knowing the price and specifications (two all-beef patties on a sesame seed roll, etc.). Why, then, would you spend hundreds or even thousands of dollars on a tour and not understand the contract the underlies the transaction?

When you purchase a charter flight or a tour package you should review and sign a contract that spells out your rights. This contract is sometimes referred to as the "Operator Participant Contract" or the "Terms and Conditions." Look for this contract in the booklet or brochure that describes the packages; ask for it if one is not offered. The proper procedure for a travel agent or tour operator to follow requires that they wait until the customer has read and signed the contract before any money is accepted.

Second chance. Tour cancellations are rare. Most tour operators, if forced to cancel, will offer another package or other incentives as a goodwill gesture. If a charter flight or charter tour is cancelled, the tour operator must refund your money within 14 days.

Lug-it-yourself. If you are using a scheduled airline to connect with a charter flight, your baggage will not be automatically transferred. You must make the transfer yourself.

Delays may be costly. Charter and tour flights operate independently of other flights. If you are on a trip that combines scheduled and nonscheduled flights, or two unrelated charter flights, you may end up losing your money and flight because of delays.

It may make sense to avoid such combinations for that reason, or to leave extra hours or even days between connections.

Some tour operators offer travel delay insurance that pays for accommodations or alternative travel arrangements necessitated by certain types of delays.

Remember that the contract is designed mostly to benefit the tour operator, and each contract may be different from others you may have agreed to in the past. The basic rule here is: **if you don't understand it, don't sign it.**

Depending on your relative bargaining strength with the provider, you may be able to amend the contract so that it is more in your favor; be sure to obtain a countersignature from an authorized party if you make a change in the document, and keep a signed copy for yourself.

Drop us a card. Keep in touch with your travel agent or tour operator. In many cases they can anticipate major changes before departure time and will let you know. And, many operators will try hard to keep you from demanding a refund if you find a major change unacceptable. They may offer a discount or upgrade on a substitute trip or adjust the price of the changed tour.

The Best way to Book a Package or Charter Flight

If possible, use a travel agent—preferably one you know and trust from prior experience. In general, the tour operator pays the travel agent's commission. Some tour packages, however, are available only from the operator who organized the tour; in certain cases you may be able to negotiate a better price by dealing directly with the operator, although you are giving up one layer of protection for your rights.

Pay for your ticket with a credit card; this is a cardinal rule for almost any situation in which you are prepaying for a service or product.

Realize that charter airlines don't have large fleets of planes available to substitute in the event of a mechanical problem or an extensive weather delay. They may or may not be able to arrange for a substitute piece of equipment from another carrier.

If you are still willing to try a charter after all of these warnings, make one more check of the bottom line before you sign the contract. First of all, is the air travel less expensive than the lowest nonrefundable fares from a scheduled carrier? (Remember that you are, in effect, buying a nonrefundable fare with most charter flight contracts.)

Have you included taxes, service charges, baggage transfer fees or other charges the tour operator may put into the contract?

Is the savings significantly more than the 10 percent the charter operator may boost the price without your permission? Do any savings come at a cost of time? Put a value on your time.

And finally, don't buy a complete package until you have compared it to the a la carte cost of such a trip. Call the hotels offered by the tour operator or similar ones in the same area and ask them a simple question: "What is your best price for a room?" Be sure to mention any discount programs that are applicable, including AAA, airline frequent flyer programs, or other organizations. Do the same for car rental agencies and any other attractions you plan to visit to get current prices.

And, of course, don't overlook the discount coupons for hotels, motels, restaurants, and attractions that are included in this book—that's why they're there.

Airlines Serving Las Vegas

(All area codes are 702 unless otherwise indicated.)

National Carriers

America West Airlines. 798-1715, (800) 247-5692

American Airlines. (800) 433-7300

Continental Airlines. 383-8291, (800) 525-0280

Delta Air Lines. 731-3111, (800) 221-1212

Northwest Airlines. (800) 225-2525

TWA. 385-1000, (800) 221-2000

United Airlines. 385-3222, (800) 241-6522

US Air. 382-1905, (800) 428-4322

Regional Carriers

Aero California. (800) 237-6225

Air Nevada. 736-8900

Air Vegas. 736-3599

Alaska Airlines. (800) 426-0333

Hawaiian Airlines. 796-9696, (800) 367-5320

Skywest Airlines. (800) 453-9417

Southwest Airlines. (800)435-9792

Train Service

Amtrak. The most popular train route into Las Vegas is the **Desert Wind**, which connects to Los Angeles. National information: (800) 872-7245. Reno: 329-8638. Truckee: (916) 582-1623.

Kids in mid-air. If you are flying with children, discuss with your airline or travel agent any special needs you might have. These might include a request for a bulkhead seat to give children a little extra room for fidgeting (although you will lose the storage space underneath the seat in front of you) or special meals (most airlines offer a child's meal of a hot dog or hamburger on request, which may be more appealing to a youngster than standard airline fare).

Be sure to pack a special bag for young children and carry it on board the plane. Extra diapers in the baggage compartment won't help you at all in an emergency at 25,000 feet. Include formula, food, and a snack as well as a few toys and books to occupy young ones.

Changes in altitude at takeoff and landing may cause some children discomfort in their ears. Try to teach them to clear their ears with an exaggerated yawn. Bubble gum or candy, or a bottle for babies can help, too.

Chapter 3
How to Sleep for Less

Negotiating for a Room

Notice the title of this section: I didn't call it "buying" a room. The fact of the matter is that hotel rooms, like almost everything else, are subject to negotiation and change.

Here is how to pay the highest possible price for a hotel room: walk up to the front desk without a reservation and say, "I'd like a room." Unless the "No Vacancy" sign is lit, you may have to pay the "rack rate," which is the published maximum nightly charge.

Here are a few ways to pay the lowest possible price:

1. Before you head for your vacation, spend an hour on the phone and call directly to a half dozen hotels that seem to be in the price range you'd like to spend. (I recommend membership in AAA and use of their annual tour books as *starting points* for your research.)

Start by asking for the room rate. Then ask them for their *best* rate. Does that sound like an unnecessary second request? Trust us, it's not: I can't begin to count the number of times the rates have dropped substantially when I ask again.

[True story: I once called the reservation desk of a major hotel chain and asked for the rates for a night at a Chicago location. "That will be $149 per night," I was told. "Ouch," I said. "Oh, would you like to spend less?," the reservationist said. I admitted that I would, and she punched a few keys on her keyboard. "They have a special promotion going on. How about $109 per night?," she asked.

Not bad for a city hotel, I reasoned, but still I hadn't asked the big question. "What is your best rate?," I asked. "Oh, our best rate? That would be $79," said the agent.

But, wait: "I'm a member of AAA, by the way." Another pause. "That's fine, Mr. Sandler. The nightly room rate will be $71.10. Have a nice day."]

> **Showing your card.** Membership in AAA brings some important benefits for the traveler, although you may not always be able to apply the club's usual 10 percent discount on top of whatever hotel rate you negotiate. (It doesn't hurt to ask, though.) Be sure to request a tour book and Nevada maps from AAA, even if you plan to fly there; they are much better than the maps given by car rental agencies.

> **Room safety.** The small safes available in some hotels can be valuable to the traveler; be sure to inquire whether there is a service charge for their use. We've been in hotels that apply the charge regardless of whether we used the safe or not; look over your bill at check-out and object to any charges that are not proper. In any case, we'd suggest that any objects that are so valuable that you feel they should be locked up should probably be left home.

When you feel you've negotiated the best deal you can obtain over the phone, make a reservation at the hotel of your choice. Be sure to go over the dates and prices one more time, and obtain the name of the person you spoke with and a confirmation number if available.

2. When you show up at your hotel on the first night stop and look at the marquee outside; see if the hotel is advertising a discount rate. Here's where you need to be bold. Walk up to the desk as if you *did not* have a reservation, and ask the clerk: "What is your best room rate for tonight?" If the rate they quote you is less than the rate in your reservation, you are now properly armed to ask for a reduction in your room rate.

Similarly, if the room rate advertised out front on the marquee drops during your stay, don't be shy about asking that your charges be reduced. Just be sure to ask for the reduction *before* you spend another night at the old rate, and obtain the name of the clerk who promises a change. If the hotel tries a lame excuse, like "That's only for new check-ins," you can offer to check out and then check back in again. That will usually work; you can always check out and go to the hotel across the road that will usually match the rates of its competitor.

3. Are you planning to stay for a full week? Ask for a weekly rate. If the room clerk says there is no such rate, ask to speak to the manager: he or she may be willing to shave a few dollars per day off the rate for a long-term stay.

Welcome, Conventioneers

Not all of the visitors to Las Vegas have chosen to go there for recreation. Each year millions are drawn to the spectacular facilities of the Las Vegas Convention Center or the Sands Expo & Convention Center as well as the relatively smaller facilities at many of the major hotels in town.

The conventioneers come to town because of the lure of the casinos and entertainment, but even more importantly, they come because Las

Vegas is one of the few places in the country with a huge capacity for shows as well as an available bank of hotel rooms for attendees.

The biggest Las Vegas conventions include the annual visits of CONEXPO (the Construction Industry Manufacturers Association) in March; the Consumer Electronics Show, usually in January; the National Association of Broadcasters in April; Comdex (the computer industry show) in November; and the International Council of Shopping Centers in May.

Of course, we mustn't overlook the National Pizza and Pasta Association, the American Concrete Pumping Association, the Coca Cola Collectors Club International, the International Carwash Association, and, obviously, the American Ostrich Association, which draws 2,000 people (and, we presume, a few big birds).

The leading convention facility is the Las Vegas Convention Center, at 3150 Paradise Road, about three blocks east of The Strip and adjacent to the huge Las Vegas Hilton Hotel.

Phone bills. Be sure you understand the telephone billing policy at the motel. Some establishments allow free local calls, while others charge as much as 75 cents for such calls. (We're especially unhappy with service charges for 800 numbers.) Be sure to examine your bill carefully at checkout and make sure it is correct.

We strongly suggest you obtain a telephone credit card and use it when you travel; nearly all motels tack high service charges on long-distance calls, and there is no reason to pay it.

Some of the larger conventions need even more space and spill over into the several large halls of the Hilton next door and from there to convention spaces around town.

The Sands Expo & Convention Center is used primarily as the second hall for one show, the annual Comdex computer convention, the largest annual trade show in the U.S. (There's a bit of special interest here: the Sands center is part of the Sands Hotel which is itself owned by the Interface Group, which puts on the Comdex show.)

Another facility that is used for smaller conventions and for occasional special events from the mega-gatherings is the Cashman Field Center, at 850 Las Vegas Blvd. North, just outside of downtown Las Vegas.

Cashman Field Center includes a 1,954-seat auditorium/theater and a pair of exhibit halls that total 100,000 square feet of space. Outside is a stadium that is home to the AAA Las Vegas Stars baseball team April through September.

How to Get a Room During a Convention

For most of the year, finding a place to stay in Las Vegas is not difficult. However, the very largest of the conventions will soak up most of the rooms at the major hotels.

If you are coming to Las Vegas as part of a convention, check with the organizers to see which hotels they may have made special arrangements with. Or, the convention may use the services of the Las Vegas Visitors' Bureau to book rooms.

The advantage of using a group's services include these:

There *may* be less expensive rooms available through the convention group.

The "official" hotel may be the location of the convention itself or on the bus route for shuttle service to the convention hall.

However, there are times when you can obtain a less-expensive or more convenient place to stay by booking directly. Most major conventions, for example, only reserve blocks of rooms at the largest hotels and there may be some rooms available directly; smaller hotels right near the convention halls are sometimes overlooked.

When the town is completely packed because of a convention, you may be able to sweet-talk your way into a room by contacting the lodging bureau handling the group. You don't have to be so bold as to lie, but you may be able to allow them to assume you are with the convention and in dire need of a room.

On the other hand, don't always assume that convention groups will be offered the lowest prices at hotels. On more than one occasion, I have obtained a cheaper price by calling a hotel directly to book a room rather than going through the lodging bureaus.

In addition, though the official hotels for a convention may be packed—and may be charging peak or even above-peak rates—nonconvention hotels may have rooms at low-season bargain rates. For example, during one of the research trips for this book, all of the major hotels were sold out for the CONEXPO show and the few that had rooms were asking $150 to $200 per night. Yet the huge Circus Circus hotel, which was not affiliated with the convention, had plenty of rooms at $39; up The Strip, the independent Center Strip Inn had deluxe rooms with Jacuzzi tubs for $49.

One safe bet in Las Vegas is that downtown hotels will often have available rooms, even during major conventions. Of course, all bets are off during peak Christmas and other holiday times.

Chapter 4

Cars, Trains, and Buses

From the Airport to The Strip and Downtown

You'll know you're in Las Vegas and not Atlanta or Dallas or Podunk the moment you get off your plane. Yep, those are slot machines in the boarding lounge waiting to suck up your first (or last) quarters.

McCarran International Airport is just over a mile from the top of The Strip, and about six miles from downtown Las Vegas.

Taxis cost about $7 to $10 to The Strip or $10 to $15 to downtown, plus tip. Cabs are usually plentiful outside the baggage area of the airport, although long lines may build when a major convention is in town.

An alternative is to take one of the shuttle services. For about $3 to $4 for The Strip or $4 to $5 to downtown per person, you'll share the minibus with as many as a dozen or so others, and the driver will choose the order of the stops. The shuttle service may be appropriate if you are traveling alone and are not in a hurry; otherwise a taxi makes more sense.

A third choice is CAT bus route 20, which leaves the airport and then heads down The Strip. The bus does not enter into the driveways of the hotels, and you may end up on the wrong side of The Strip and have to lug your bags across the road.

Renting a Car

Tens of millions of people come to Las Vegas and other Nevada magnets each year, about half of them by plane. Which means, of course, that the other half arrive by car, bus, or train.

This makes Nevada one of the most competitive markets for car rental agencies in the country. You will find the major rental companies like Avis, Budget, Hertz, and National. You will also find very large operations by companies like Alamo and General. There are also more than a few rental agencies that operate only in Nevada or even just in one of its major cities.

Taxi dancing. Here's a tip for visitors unable to get a cab from the convention center: walk up Convention Center Drive to The Strip and wait for a car at one of the hotels there—with luck you will be able to snare a ride in a taxi that has brought a rider the few blocks you walked from the LVCC.

Be aware that the least expensive car rental agencies usually do not have their stations at the airport itself. You will have to wait for a shuttle bus to take you from the terminal to their lot, and you must return the car to the outlying area at the end of your trip.

Pay attention, too, when the rental agent explains the gas tank policy. The most common plan says that you must return the car with a full tank; if the agency must refill the tank, you will be billed a service charge plus what is usually a very high per-gallon rate.

Other optional plans include one where the rental agency sells you a full tank when you first drive away and takes no note of how much gas remains when you return the car. Unless you somehow manage to return the car with the engine running on fumes, you are in effect making a gift to the agency with every gallon you bring back. We prefer the first option, making a point to refill the tank on the way back to the airport.

Car rental companies will try—with varying levels of pressure—to convince you to purchase special insurance coverage. They'll tell you it's "only" $7 or $9 per day. What a deal! That works out to about $2,500 or $3,330 per year for a set of rental wheels. And the coverage is intended primarily to protect the rental company and not you.

Check with your insurance agent before you travel to determine how well your personal automobile policy will cover a rental car and its contents. And we strongly recommend you use a credit card that offers rental car insurance; such insurance usually covers the deductible below your personal policy. The extra auto insurance by itself can usually more than pay for an upgrade to a "gold card" or other extra-service credit card.

The only sticky area comes for those visitors with a driver's license but no car, and therefore no insurance. Again, consult your credit card company and your insurance agent.

The following are among companies serving McCarran Airport, The Strip, and downtown; check with them for the office nearest where you want to pick up a car (where there is more than one office, we have listed the direct phone number for the airport location). All of Nevada lies within the 702 area code.

Abbey Rent-A-Car. 736-4988
Action Auto Rental. 369-1510
Advantage Rent-A-Car. 386-5775, (800) 777-5500
Agency Rent-A-Car. (800) 321-1972, 798-7795
Airways Rent A Car. (800) 777-9377, 798-6100
Ajax Rent A Car. 798-7200

Alamo Rent A Car. (800) 327-9633, 737-3111
Allstate Car Rental. (800) 634-6186, 736-6147
Avis Rent A Car. (800) 331-1212, 261-5595
Budget Car Rental. (800) 527-0700, 736-1212
Dollar Rent A Car. (800) (800) 4000, 739-8408
Enterprise Rent-A-Car. (800) 325-8007, 795-8842
General Rent-A-Car. (800) 327-7607; 739-1954
Hertz Rent A Car. (800) 654-3131, 736-4900
Montgomery Ward. (800) 367-2217, 736-2279
Payless. (800) 729-5377, 739-8488
Rebel Rent-A-Car. (800) 336-4222, 597-1683
Rent-A-Vette. (800) 372-1981, 736-2592
Sears Car & Truck Rental. (800) 527-0700, 736-8006
Thrifty Car Rental. (800) 367-2277, 736-4706
Value Rent-A-Car. (800) 468-2583, 733-8886

Nevada Commission on Tourism. Capitol Complex, Carson City, NV 89710; 687-3636 or (800) 638-2328.

Lake Mead National Recreation Area. 601 Nevada Hwy., Boulder City, NV 89005; 293-8907.

Nevada Division of State Parks. Capitol Complex, Carson City, NV 89710; 687-4387.

Getting Around in Las Vegas

On the one hand, navigating in Las Vegas is pretty simple. Almost every major hotel and casino is found along Las Vegas Boulevard (better known as The Strip), along Fremont Street in downtown Las Vegas, or on a cross-street to one of those two roads.

Except when there is a large convention in town, taxis are plentiful at the airport and along The Strip, and bus service is adequate. And, although it is not as common as it should be, it is quite possible to walk between and among the clusters of casino/hotels on The Upper Strip and Center Strip.

On the other hand, as you find in reading this book, there is a lot more to Las Vegas than The Strip and Fremont Street. If you've got the time, we strongly recommend you rent a car or take a guided tour to visit some of the great natural and manmade sights of the region.

We find it mind-boggling that a visitor to Las Vegas who will ogle The Mirage or The Luxor or Excalibur can come and go without seeing even more amazing sights like Hoover Dam or Red Rock Canyon. (And, as you will find later in this book, we cannot imagine a trip to Reno that does not include a visit to Lake Tahoe and Virginia City.)

Taxi Services

Cabs, cabs everywhere—except when there is a big convention in town, anytime you are in a hurry, and during one of Las Vegas' rare rainstorms. There are two major taxi companies that all but control the market: Yellow Cab Co. and Whittlesea Blue Cab.

Taxis line up at McCarran Airport to meet most flights. During conventions, taxis usually arrive regularly at the front entrance to the Las Vegas Convention Center. Your next best bet is to wait at the main entrance at one of the major hotels.

Here are the phone numbers of the major local cab companies:

ABC. 736-8444
Ace. 736-8383
Desert Cab. 386-9102
Henderson Taxi. 384-2322
Western. 382-7100
Whittlesea Blue Cab. 384-6111
Yellow-Checker-Star. 873-2000

Mileage to Las Vegas

Atlanta 1,964
Boston 2,725
Carson City 430
Dallas 1,221
Denver 777
Grand Canyon 288
Hoover Dam 25
Kingman 103
Lake Tahoe 470
Los Angeles 282
Palm Springs 280
Phoenix 298
Salt Lake City 433
San Francisco 564
Washington, D.C. 2,393

Barstow 153
Boulder City 24
Chicago 1,772
Death Valley 160
Flagstaff 275
Henderson 13
Jackpot 488
Lake Havasu City 145
Laughlin 93
New York 2,548
Philadelphia 2,468
Reno 440
San Diego 337
Sparks 207
Zion National Park 156

Busing to the Tables

Las Vegas Transit operates bus routes serving much of the metropolitan area. Call 228-7433 for information. The Downtown Transportation Center, at Stewart Avenue and Casino Center Blvd., is the transfer point for many routes, open from 6:15 A.M. to 10 P.M. daily. Riders must request and pay 15 cents for a transfer at the time of paying the first fare.

Fares in 1994 were $1 for adults, 50 cents for senior citizens 65 years and older, and 50 cents for children 6 through 17 years of age.

Here are a few bus routes that service the major tourist areas. Be sure to call to check on hours of operation and possible changes in route:

Strip/Downtown (Route 6). Downtown Transportation Center across Stewart Avenue to Las Vegas Blvd. (The Strip) and south to the Hacienda at the top end of The Strip.

The Strip Express. Express stops only ($1.25 exact fare), OUTBOUND: Downtown Transportation Center, Circus Circus, Caesars Palace, and Excalibur Hotel (rear entrance). INBOUND: Tropicana Hotel, Flamingo Hilton, Riviera Hotel, Downtown Transportation Center.

The Strip Shuttle (Route 13). Las Vegas Convention Center and the Las Vegas Hilton to the Fashion Show Mall and eventually the top of The Strip at the Hacienda Hotel.

The Mall Hopper (Route 14). West entrance of the Fashion Show Mall on The Strip to the Meadows and Boulevard Shopping Malls.

II
Las Vegas

Chapter 5
Welcome, Pilgrim

As far as we are concerned, there are two types of visitors to Las Vegas:

1. Those who have never been there before and are anxious to see if all of the strange and wonderful things they have heard are true, and

2. Those who are returning to Las Vegas to see if things are really as strange and wonderful as they remember.

Either way, a visit to Las Vegas is unlike any other place on earth, with the possible exception of that other fantasy zone called Walt Disney World.

Coming in to Las Vegas

The best way to approach Las Vegas is to fly in on a moonlit, clear night. As your plane descends from points east, you cross hundreds of miles of barren desert that seem as lifeless as the moon. Suddenly, you'll come upon a huge oddly-shaped lake in the desert held back by a tremendous dam, a pale white saucer set on end in a canyon.

Just minutes later you will see on the horizon an island of light, an electric oasis in the desert. About the time the pilot brings down the wheels, you should be able to pick out some of the elements of a skyline like nowhere else on earth: a huge Egyptian pyramid, a Roman garden and amphitheater, a pirate ship, and a gaudy castle constructed of gigantic toy blocks.

Coming in from California and points west, your jet will cross the last wall of mountains and then drop into the Las Vegas Valley. The pilot will hang a right turn over Bob Stupak's stupendous tower and proceed up the length of The Strip to the airport.

Welcome to Las Vegas, pilgrim.

Las Vegas Climate

Las Vegas has two basic weather patterns: sunny and moderate, and sunny and hot.

Las Vegas averages 320 days of sunshine per year and only 4.19 inches of rain. In the summer months from June to September daytime temperatures may top 100 degrees. In the short spring and fall seasons, it usually reaches to the 70s during the day. In the winter, it may drop all the way down to the 50s.

The Econoguide to the Best of Las Vegas

Hotels in Las Vegas

Caesars Palace	Excalibur
Golden Nugget	Las Vegas Hilton
Luxor	MGM Grand
Mirage	Rio
Treasure Island	

Casinos in Las Vegas

Caesars Palace	Circus Circus
Excalibur	Las Vegas Hilton
MGM Grand	Mirage
Rio	Vegas World

Buffets in Las Vegas

Rio
Caesars Palace
Fremont
Bally's

Places to Visit

Hoover Dam
Red Rock Canyon
MGM Grand Adventures
Imperial Palace Auto Museum
Grand Slam Canyon

Chapter 6
The Best of The Strip

MUST-SEE Caesars Palace

Depending on your point of view, this is either one of the unnatural wonders of the world, or one of its greatest exercises in gaudy excess. Either way, Caesars Palace is surely one of the must-see attractions of Las Vegas.

The inside of this sprawling hotel and casino complex includes an incredible amount of detail; the detail may not be accurate, but it certainly is interesting. Think of Caesars Palace as a realization of Hollywood's vision of ancient Rome as seen through the jaded eye of a Las Vegas decorator.

Everything about this place is grand. The Roman Forum casino is a riot of red and gold. The sports book is among the most spectacular theater-like settings at any casino. The various restaurants, including the aptly named Bacchanal, include some of the most opulent settings on The Strip. And the casino employees offer equal-opportunity gawking for both sexes: there are gods and goddesses in short, short togas at most every turn.

And the spectacular Forum Shops at Caesars features more than 70 specialty retailers and restaurants set in a re-creation of the skies of ancient Rome. *See the section about shopping in Las Vegas for full details on this must-see shopping mall.*

It is also an interesting spectator sport to observe the continuing competition between Caesars Palace and its next-door neighbor the Mirage; this is an example of "keeping up with the Joneses" taken to the extreme.

When Caesars Palace was built in 1966, it was set far back from The Strip, partly for zoning reasons in the second wave of construction and partly because at the time it was believed that the new hotels would be destinations in and of themselves and that visitors would drive up the grand driveway to a parking space. The front yard of the hotel is filled

A real fake. The Brahma Shrine on the north lawn of Caesars Palace is a replica of a Buddhist shrine in Thailand. The original was installed more than 30 years ago at the Erawan Hotel in Bangkok to ward off bad luck after the hotel suffered various mishaps during its construction. The statue is credited with fixing the problem.

The Las Vegas version was a gift to the hotel from a Thai newspaper and Hong Kong high roller in 1983. Cast in bronze and plated in gold, the statue is housed in concrete covered with tiny pieces of beveled glass.

Thai-Buddhist tradition associates Brahma with creation. The four faces of the shrine represent the Four Divine States of Mind: loving kindness, compassion, sympathy, and equanimity.

By the way, although Caesars Palace rakes in the coins regularly, this is one small area where Caesars Palace does not hold a house advantage. The money tossed into the shrine is returned to charities in Thailand.

with a mind-boggling collection of strange stuff, including a 20-foot-tall statue of Julius himself, almost two dozen spouting fountains, and a lucky Brahma.

There are also several lengthy people-mover sidewalks intended to suck pedestrians from the curbside of The Strip all the way back to the entrance of the hotel; in 1989 an additional people mover was installed at the far northern corner of Caesars' property. Coincidentally, of course, that put the Caesars moving walkway right next to the moving sidewalk for the new Mirage hotel next door. By the way, the sidewalks move only one direction—into the casino. When you are ready to leave, you'll have to walk to The Strip, or you can call a cab if you have any money left in your pockets.

Hidden from view of casino guests is the Garden of the Gods pool area. It includes, naturally, an Olympic-sized swimming pool that is the centerpiece of the Caesars Garden of the Gods. The garden design was inspired by the Pompeii Baths of Rome.

The bottom and sides of the main pool are covered with imported Carrara marble tiles. On the upper level, a second pool includes three large "lounging islands" installed just below the water's surface so that sunbathers can be cooled by the water while they tan. Fountains spray water to the corners of the pool.

Basic room rates start as low as $95 for a single and $110 for a double room at ordinary periods of the year. Deluxe rooms start at $135 for a single and $150 for a double; superior at $160 and $175. One-bedroom suites begin at $475; two bedrooms start at $610. However, during the quietest times of the year, prices drop into double digits for basic and deluxe rooms. At peak times, prices can double.

Like most other Las Vegas hotels, the quietest time of the year is usually around Christmas, excluding the holiday itself and New Year's Eve. Available rooms at that time are often offered at significantly less than the rack rate. However, Caesars Palace has been working hard to fill up its rooms during slack periods with guests from Asian locations, including Hong Kong.

Olympic Tower. The main tower includes dozens of room types. A typical standard room is the Olympic Square King, which includes marble and mirrors and jacuzzis in each room. Round Kings—featuring round beds—are also available. Standard rooms in the Roman Tower have a rack rate of about $145 per night.

Regular suites rent in the range from about $850 to $1,000 per night, depending on the number of bedrooms. The largest suites can link together eight bedrooms, perfect for the family or high roller traveling with a nanny, bodyguard, chef, or other staff.

Fantasy Suites. It's not that they are free; Caesars prefers to call them "priceless." Suffice it to say that they would cost a small fortune if you were in fact able to rent them; they are offered without charge to invited guests including celebrities, members of royal families, and (of course) the highest of the high rollers visiting Caesars Palace.

We visited a few of the two-story extravaganzas, including the 4,000-square-foot Jupiter Suite, which featured a laser light show in the domed ceiling of the central alcove, glass curtain walls, two bedrooms, five TVs, a karaoke music system, and a pair of servants. The slightly skewed wall sconces were designed by the studio of the extremely skewed Salvador Dali.

There are a total of 10 Fantasy Suites: two in Roman decor, three with

Pompeii Fantasy Suite, Caesars Palace, Las Vegas

Unlike father. On December 31, 1967, daredevil Evel Knievel attempted to jump over the Caesars Palace fountains on a motorcycle; 12 years later, his son Robbie Knievel avenged his father's unsuccessful attempt.

In 1981, an entire race track was created for the first of four Grand Prix auto races on site. In 1991, Wayne Gretzky led the Los Angeles Kings to victory over the New York Rangers in the Palace's first ice hockey event, the NHL's first outdoor game since 1925.

Sport lights. The spectacular Race and Sports Book at Caesars Palace uses 60 panels made up of 1.5 million yellow, red, and green light-emitting diode (LED) panels that display computer-produced data including track conditions, horse and jockey names, and other information.

The largest of the video screens is 32 feet wide by 26 feet high.

Egyptian themes, and five as Las Vegas re-creations of ancient Pompeii. As guests arrive on their interior balconies, they are greeted by a laser show and a fiber optics sky re-creating the night sky as it is believed to have looked on the evening of the birth of Caesar Augustus.

An entire wall of each room is given over to an entertainment system that includes five video screens, two compact disc players, and a karaoke machine. A master control panel can send different music to different rooms. Each of the bedrooms includes an additional large-screen TV. In fact, there's more than two miles of wiring in each suite for entertainment, motorized bedroom and living room draperies, color wheel effects on the ceiling, and other lighting.

Casinos. The 85-acre site includes three casino areas. The main Olympic Casino has more than 1,400 slot machines, 31 blackjack tables, three craps tables, and various other enterprises including the spectacular Olympiad Race and Sports Book with seating for 650. Nearby is the Roman Forum Casino with 615 slots, 30 blackjack tables, nine craps tables, and a keno area. Finally, there is the exclusive Palace Court Casino with three blackjack tables, two baccarat tables, a pai gow table, and a roulette wheel.

The World of Caesar is a presentation in the rotunda at the entrance to the central people mover. Designed to resemble a Roman temple, the World of Caesar includes a miniature city of Rome as it might have looked 2,000 years ago. The hotel spent $2.5 million on just this little bit of decoration. The effect is enhanced with technology including video projection.

The hotel offers a world of fine dining, from one of the most opulent buffets to one of the most sybaritic and expensive feasts in town.

Palatium. One of the best buffets in Vegas. A lovely setting with open-air boundaries just off the spectacular Race and Sports Book. Buffet offerings change from day to day. One evening featured a mountain of crab legs and a huge bowl of shrimp. One indication of class: the shrimp comes pre-peeled.

Palatium, Latin for palatine, takes its name from the second-century meeting place of Rome's first academy of chefs. The term was also used in naming the many royal residences and buildings in the vicinity of Rome's Palatine Hill.

Dining areas are arranged in semi-circles around a double-line service center. The buffet is open for breakfast, lunch, and dinner Monday through Friday; special brunches are served Saturday and Sunday. Dinner includes a variety of breads, an elaborate salad bar, vegetables, and entrees including carved meats and poultry. Ethnic dinners including Italian, Mexican, and Western themes are offered some nights. There is also a sinful dessert section. See hours and prices in the section on buffets in this book.

Palace Court. Classical French cuisine served in a museum-like setting. Guests arrive in a crystal and bronze round elevator or a spiral staircase under a crystal chandelier. The dining area sits beneath a domed stained glass ceiling. Tables are decorated with fine fabric and lit candelabras.

> **Michelangelo's casino.** At the top tier of the portico entrance to the World of Caesar is a marble statue of Apollo, the Greek and Roman god of sunlight, prophecy, music, and truth. According to its makers, it is carved from stone taken from the same quarries that Michelangelo is believed to have used.

> **Private bank.** As you enter the Palace Court, note the small dark room off to the left: the Palace Court Casino is a private gambling room for the highest of high rollers.

Pause for a moment and admire the glorious fruit basket in the glass case at the entrance. It's an edible work of art, constructed out of pulled sugar by a Caesars chef.

The Palace Court, open for dinner only, has entrees in the range of $20 to $40. Some menu items we have seen include: *bisque D'homard a L'Armagnac* (lobster bisque flamed with Armagnac), *papillote de saumon aux asperges* (fresh salmon prepared in a paper pouch with asparagus and sun-dried tomatoes), *cote de veau roti* (veal chop served with roasted leeks and mustard sauce), *maigret de canard au poivre rose* (breast of duck with pink peppercorn sauce), and *carre d'agneau roti a l'ail doux* (roast rack of lamb served with sweet garlic sauce).

Bacchanal. In ancient Rome, they eventually outlawed Bacchanalia, a festival in honor of Bacchus, the god of wine. It seemed that, even for ancient Rome, the parties were becoming drunken, licentious events.

Of course, in modern Las Vegas, almost anything goes. And so there is Bacchanal, which is a re-creation of a Roman feast in the atmosphere of a private villa and a whole lot of fun.

The evening includes a seven-course feast of appetizers, soup, salad, pasta, entree, and flaming dessert; included are three wines, splashed into your

Good reef. The coral reef in the aquarium at the Empress Court of Caesars Palace is a reproduction of an actual reef along the coast of Hong Kong.

chalices by exotically clad "wine goddesses." There are also belly dancers, a smoke and laser light show, and a guest appearance by Caesar and Cleopatra themselves. In the center of the two-tiered dining room is a bronze statue of a vestal virgin pouring water into a marble reflecting pool.

The menu changes with the seasons. Here is one sample fall menu: To start, try garden fresh vegetables with herb dip; shrimp, crab claws, and marinated scallops; cream of chickpeas with legumes; fettuccine Alfredo; Caesar salad, tossed tableside. Choose an entree from one of the following: Cornish game hen; roast duckling with three-color peppercorn sauce; stuffed veal chop with pine nuts; filet mignon; or filet of sole with shrimp florentine. Finally, enjoy a flambéed dessert and fruit plate.

Dinner only, Tuesday through Saturday. Seatings are 6 and 9:30 P.M. daily. The fare in 1994 was $65 per person, including wines and dessert; not included are cocktails, tax, and tip. Reservations: 731-7731.

Empress Court. Named in *USA Today* as one of the top gourmet Chinese restaurants in the country, the kitchen concentrates on Hong Kong–style Cantonese cooking, although there are touches of Malay, Thai, and Indonesian cuisine.

Entrance is via a dramatic staircase that encircles a koi pond and leads

Poolside dining, Caesars Palace, Las Vegas

to a coral reef aquarium at the restaurant's door. Within the kitchen is a more purposeful giant aquarium, stocked with live rock cod, Dungeness crab, lobster, and other seafood that is used in meals. The galley itself includes some extraordinarily hot grills used in preparation of specialties.

The Empress Court menu includes prix-fixe dinners at about $40 to $60 per person, as well as a la carte offerings. Appetizers include crab-meat seaweed rolls, minced squab in crystal wrap, and shrimp with taro. Entrees, generally in the range from about $20 to $48 each, include dou-ble-boiled shark's fin, braised abalone with sea cucumber, sautéed scallops with macadamia nuts, imperial Peking duck, as well as other uncom-mon Chinese fare. Open for dinner only. Reser-vations: 731-7731.

Primavera. A favorite garden spot along-side the Garden of the Gods pool, the menu changes from casual fare for breakfast and lunch to formal Italian dining for dinner.

At the time of our visit, the dinner menu included appetizers of *bresaola con parmigiano* (dried cured beef with parmesan cheese and arugula) and *carpaccio di salmone* (raw salmon very finely sliced with a strawberry vinaigrette). Pasta entrees, in the range of $12 to $20, includ-ed *trenette nere ai calamari* (black noodles with calamari and clams in a natural juice sauce), and *mostaccioli all'amatriciana*. Other entrees, ranging from $20 to $30, included *filetto ai tre pepi* (beef tenderloin with black, green, and pink peppercorns), *pollo cacciatora con polenta* (chicken breast in a sauce of roasted peppers, mushrooms, tomato, and white wine with a side order of cornmeal), or *zuppa di cozze* (New England mussels in a white wine, black olives, capers, and tomato sauce).

One of the specialties of the bar is the Casano-va Cream Fizz, a rich combination of lemon and lime juice with cream and apricot brandy.

Ah'So. Yet another restaurant, this one offer-

Flowery complement. The oil on canvas of Flora surrounded by flowers and classic statu-ary in the Primavera Restaurant at Caesars Palace is a hand-painted reproduction of *Garden of Armida*, by the 19th-century artist Eduoard Miller.

Armless in Vegas. The grounds around Caesars Palace include replicas of some of the most famous statues of antiquity. In front of the fountains at the main entrance of the hotel is a re-creation of the famous *Nike of Samoth-race* statue, sculpted about 300 B.C. by an unknown artist; the original is in the Louvre museum in Paris.

In front of the ellipti-cal pool at the entrance is a copy of the *Rape of the Sabine Woman*; the original was done by Giovanni Bologna in 1583.

Elsewhere you'll find reproductions of Michelangelo's *David* and *Bacchus.* On a more contemporary note, at the entrance to the Olympic Casino stands a statue of the boxer Joe Louis, who worked for the casino as a greeter after he retired from the ring.

Burger palace. Feature films made at Caesars Palace include *Oh God! You Devil*, with the ageless George Burns; *Electric Horseman*, starring Robert Redford, Jane Fonda, Willie Nelson, and Valerie Perrine, and Mel Brooks' *History of the World — Part I.*

Parts of the 1988 Academy Award–winning *Rain Man* starring Dustin Hoffman and Tom Cruise were filmed in a suite at Caesars Palace. Hotel legend includes the story that star Hoffman used to order 200 or so hamburgers every night from the tiny **Post Time** snack bar off the Race and Sports Book for the crew. He apparently knows his chopped meat; the burgers are made from the trimmings of the filets from the hotel's butcher shop.

ing fine dining in a serene Japanese garden. Sushi and sashimi are available with dinners as well as to patrons at the cocktail lounge.

The restaurant offers a prix-fixe six-course menu prepared and served in teppen yaki style at the table (the skills of the chef are part of the entertainment) or shabu-shabu (Chinese fondue-like cooking). Each was priced at $48 in 1994.

Offerings include *miro shiru* (soy bean soup with tofu) or *sumashi* (clear chicken broth with long rice). Appetizer selections feature *tempura* (fried seafood and vegetables) and *sunomono* (a salad of marinated cucumbers with shredded crabmeat). The entree list includes lobster, beef tenderloin, and chicken breast, all served with *yasai* (assorted Japanese vegetables). Open for dinner. A prix-fixe dinner was about $50 per person.

Cafe Roma. A 24-hour restaurant that draws its menu from all around the world. In fact, it's one of the only places we have ever heard of that offers Japanese *miso* broth, Mexican *quesadillas,* New York steak, spaghetti bolognese, Nova Scotia salmon, and more from the same menu. Appetizers are in the range from about $5 to $12, salads from $3 to $14, and entrees from $9 to $15. In keeping with the Las Vegas lifestyle, breakfast is offered around the clock.

But did we mention the all-day Chinese menu? The Cafe doesn't quite have the ambiance of the Empress Court, but we suspect the same kitchen and ingredients are used, and we have long ago learned not to judge a Chinese restaurant by its furnishings. There's an above-average selection of Oriental offerings ranging from $5 to $9 for appetizers and $10 to $28 for entrees.

Nero's. They don't fiddle around in this elegant seafood and steakhouse, open for dinner only. Appetizers can include avocado with lump crabmeat, Scottish smoked salmon, steamed clams, and frog legs Provençale, and range from about $7 to $17. Entrees, which range in price from $26 to $48, include Dover sole, grilled or seared tuna, lamb chops, and more.

La Piazza Food Court. A high-tone food court with offerings from Japanese ramen soups and bento boxes to Chinese stir-fry, Italian pasta and pizza, Mexican specialties, and an All-American deli. There are also ice cream, yogurt, candy, and bakery stands.

Cleopatra's Barge. An actual boat in a small pond; when things really get rocking at this cocktail lounge, the place starts rolling.

And don't overlook the new group of restaurants that were added to the scene with the opening of the Forum Shops at Caesars, including Boogie's Diner of Aspen, Chang—Cuisine of China, La Salsa, Lombardi's, Spago, and the Stage Deli. *You'll discover more about these restaurants in the section of this book about shopping in Las Vegas.*

Omnimax Theatre. Go into space, under the sea, deep into the Grand Canyon, or into an atom in one of the highest-tech movie theaters anywhere. The 386 seats of the Omnimax recline to permit full view of the huge 10-story screen which showcases specially made films such as *To Fly, The Dream is Alive, Grand Canyon—The Hidden Secrets,* and *Africa: The Serengeti.* The films are shot on 70-mm film with a frame size 10 times larger than standard 35-mm media. A nine-channel "sensaround" system engulfs the audience in sound.

Ticket prices are about $6 for adults. Seniors (over 55), juniors (4–12), military personnel, and hotel guests pay $4. Show times vary, but shows typically run hourly from 2 P.M. through 10 P.M. during the week, and from 1 P.M. to 11 P.M. on Friday and Saturday.

Circus Maximus Showroom. The main showroom at Caesars Palace is used for headliner acts and an occasional Broadway production or television show. It is typically set up with more than 1,000 seats; booths are designed in the shape of Roman chariot seats. In a change from Las Vegas protocol of the past, tickets are sold in advance for reserved seats—there is no need to grease the palm of the maitre d' to get a prime spot. However, it is fair to assume that the very best seats will be held by the casino for its "invited guests."

A Brief History of Caesars Palace. The original proposed name for Caesars Palace was Cabana Palace, after developer Jay Sarno's successful Cabana Hotel in Palo Alto, California. Once the design began to take shape, the hotel was renamed as Desert Palace, but it finally opened as Caesars Palace on August 5, 1966.

Sarno, by the way, considered the oval to be a magic shape, believing

> **Check your horse, sir?** The Circus Maximus Showroom at Caesars Palace was used for the scene in the film *The Electric Horseman* when star Robert Redford rode his horse down off the stage and into the casino.

> **Airborne breakfast.** Caesars Palace has installed a "flying kitchen" in one of the tower service elevators permitting delivery of a standard continental breakfast to almost any room in the hotel within eight minutes of a phone call.

Eight-ring circus. The Circus Circus empire has expanded wildly, now including the huge Excalibur Hotel and the Luxor pyramid further up The Strip. The same company also owns Slots-A-Fun, a neighboring coin palace on The Strip, and the Silver City Casino across the road. Other properties include Circus Circus/Reno, Edgewater Hotel & Casino in Laughlin, and the Colorado Belle in Laughlin.

it was conducive to relaxation. The central casino and a number of other rooms took that shape at his suggestion.

In 1969, Caesars Palace was bought by Lum's, a Florida-based fast-food restaurant chain known for, among other things, its hot dogs. In 1971, the tail wagged the dog when Lum's became Caesars World, Inc.

Caesars World includes three gaming resorts: Caesars Palace in Las Vegas, Caesars Tahoe in Lake Tahoe, and Caesars Atlantic City in New Jersey. The company also operates four resorts in the Pocono mountains of Pennsylvania: Caesars Cove Haven, Caesars Paradise Stream, Caesars Pocono Palace, and Caesar's Brookdale.

Caesars Palace, 3570 Las Vegas Blvd. South; 1,518 rooms; 731-7110; (800) 634-6661.

MUST-SEE Circus Circus

From the sublime to the ridiculous: another must-see attraction.

For many of us, our expectations of Circus Circus were molded by the lurid account of Hunter S. Thompson in his gonzo classic, *Fear and Loathing in Las Vegas.* Just about everything Thompson wrote about in that book, including the acrobats tumbling overhead, the motorcyclists roaring around within a ball, and the general atmosphere of a Roman Circus is true— although not quite as wild as he made it out to be.

Circus Circus is one of the great grind joint successes of Las Vegas. It has cheap rooms (including an RV park), cheap meals, and lots and lots of low rollers at the tables. The hotel obviously makes its money on the quantity of action, not the size of the bankrolls at play. (Some wags have called Circus Circus the K-mart of gambling establishments.)

The proprietors were way out in front in their attempts to lure the entire family. Upstairs over the casino floor is an indoor carnival, midway, and video arcade that will entertain (and draw allowance money) from the kids while their parents drop the rent money downstairs.

Most of the rooms are located in two separate towers, connected by a shuttle tram to the main building. Circus Circus often has the least-expensive major hotel rooms in town; the rooms, especially in the main tower, are quite acceptable.

In 1993, Circus Circus opened **Grand Slam Canyon,** a five-acre, $75 million entertainment park that presents a Las Vegas-eye view of the Grand

Canyon, including 140-foot manmade peaks, a 90-foot re-creation of Havasupai Falls, and a river. The entire park is covered by a pink dome called an Adventuresphere.

*See the description of **Grand Slam Canyon** in Chapter 10 of this book.*

Parts of Circus Circus give new meaning to tacky, but it's all part of the peculiar charm of the place. You are sure to want to visit the mezzanine of coin-sucking machines, including pinball, a video arcade, bowling machines, and carnival attractions including coin tosses, dart games, and more.

Restaurants include a **McDonald's.** A food court includes the Circus Circus Pizzeria, which offers 10-inch individual pies for about $2 and unusual offerings like a chicken fajita pizza for about $3.

The **Buffet** is served beneath a red-and-white circus tent ceiling, an assault on the eyes, even by Las Vegas standards.

The **Steakhouse,** open for dinner only from 5 P.M. to midnight, has entrees in the range of $15 to $20 and is generally considered one of the better cuts-of-meat palaces in town. In addition to steaks, you can chow down on lamb chops or broiled lobster tail. And even nicer, it's a dark, quiet, and private sanctuary from the circus.

Exactly the opposite is the garish **Pink Pony** coffee shop just off the casino level. And finally, there is the **Skyrise Dining Room,** serving breakfast, lunch, and dinner, with specialties including French toast or prime rib for $3 to $10. At a recent visit, it offered a steak dinner for $6.95 from 5 to 11 P.M.

Circus Circus Hotel/Casino, 2880 Las Vegas Blvd. South; 2,800 rooms; 734-0410; (800) 634-3450.

MUST-SEE Excalibur

To truly enjoy this place, you've got to buy into the concept: King Arthur's Castle on The Strip, looking as if it were constructed out of a child's toy blocks. It's a place where the staff is drilled to finish conversations with: "Have a Royal Day."

The best approach to the Excalibur is by night. The colors of the 265-foot-tall bell towers and the castle's fairy-tale shape is amazing enough, but even more weird when looked at between the Egyptian pyramid of the Luxor and the tropical gardens of the Tropicana. What a city!

If anything, Excalibur is even more overwhelming inside. The designers seem to have collected all of the missing high ceilings from the older casinos on The Strip and taken them to Nevada extremes. More so than at most other places in Vegas, the Arthurian theme is carried through in almost every detail—the decorations, costumes, restaurants.

In keeping with its orientation toward family visitors, the Excalibur is one of the few casinos in Las Vegas that welcomes cameras: still, movie, and video. (In keeping with state law, though, you must keep children under 21 away from slot machines and gambling tables.)

The Excalibur was holder for several years of the title as the world's largest resort hotel, with 4,032 rooms. Today it is certainly the world's largest resort hotel set inside a castle with a moat, a drawbridge, a jousting tournament, and a western dance hall.

How big is this place? The Excalibur serves an average of about 136,032 guests and 751,388 meals per month, including 330,000 bread rolls, 44,100 Cornish game hens, and 24,000 watermelons.

There are four levels to the hotel; you will enter from the main parking lot or front entrance to Level I, which is, of course, the casino floor and registration desk. An escalator descends to the lower-level **Fantasy Faire,** home of **King Arthur's Arena,** the **Magic Motion Machines,** and **Fantasy Faire** games. Or, you can take an escalator up to Level II, the Medieval Village, home of the **Roundtable Buffet, Wild Bill's Saloon & Steakhouse, Lance-A-Lotta Pasta, Sir Galahad's, Robin Hood's,** and the **Sherwood Forest Cafe.** One more level up takes you to Level III, which includes the **Canterbury Wedding Chapel,** banquet rooms, and the **Camelot** restaurant.

There is, of course, a casino, and it's a whopper: 2,600 slot machines,

Excalibur

68 blackjack tables, six craps tables, six roulette wheels, and more, spread out over 105,000 square feet. The casino includes a central pavilion for high-rolling slot players. The poker room features 18 regular poker tables and two pai gow poker tables.

The Excalibur's 900-seat showroom is unlike any other in Las Vegas. To begin with, the floor of the stage is dirt rather than polished wood, and many of the stars have four legs.

Each afternoon, you can see a family-oriented animal act at the showroom. In 1994, the Excalibur featured **Sooper Dogs**, featuring Moore's Mess O'Mutts, Scooter, The Champion Frisbee Catching Dog, and The Sports Agility Team. All of the animals were rescued by trainer Stacy Moore from shelters and dog pounds.

The frisbee show features Lou Mack and his friend Scooter, an Australian Shepherd. Now six years old and the declared world champion, Scooter moonlights as the team mascot for the San Francisco 49ers.

> **Horse track.** The Excalibur stables are located at the back of the parking lot. The horses for the King Arthur's Tournament are walked to work for the evening show each evening sometime between 5 and 5:30 P.M.

> **Testing the metal.** The swords in King Arthur's Tournament are made of lightweight titanium metal; try as they might, the designers could not find a way to fake the sound of metal hitting metal.

The dog show is presented every afternoon but Wednesday, with tickets priced at $4.95.

The evening program at 6 or 8:30 P.M. is **King Arthur's Tournament**, an original musical production based on the legend of King Arthur. You've got your basic knights in armor, fair maidens in less, and events including a jousting tournament.

The story begins when Merlin the magician satisfies a young boy's wish to be a knight by transporting him back to the Middle Ages and transforming him into Jeffrey, the White Knight. Jeffrey will meet the King, of course, as well as Queen Guinevere, before he battles the treacherous Dark Knight and wins the hand of the beautiful princess. Tickets are $24.95, which includes dinner and tip; they can be purchased up to six days before the show. Check with the hotel for dark days and hours.

When you buy your ticket, you will be assigned to a reserved place. According to insiders, the best seats are up high in the center; in football terms, at the 50-yard line. Avoid the end zones and stay up high to avoid the dust from the horses.

The meal, served on pewter plates, includes a Cornish hen. By the way, they didn't use silverware in medieval times, and neither will you.

The Fantasy Faire level offers carnival games as well as a pair of "dynamic motion simulators" called **Merlin's Magic Motion Machines** that can take riders on a wild ride without ever leaving the room. There are six different "rides," changing during the course of a day, shown in a pair of identical 48-seat theaters. Rides include "Space Race," an outerspace demolition derby directed by George Lucas and "Devil's Mine Ride," a wild and crazy journey through underground caves and caverns. Other experiences include "Desert Duel," a bone-jarring desert race over dirt trails; "The Revolution," a simulation of one of the wildest roller coasters at the Magic Mountain amusement park; and "Runaway Train," a breakneck plunge through tunnels and steep mountain passes on a train with no brakes. Ticket prices are about $3 per ride. Note: You must be at least 42 inches tall and in good health to ride the simulator.

The **Medieval Village** re-creates one vision of an ancient village, with shops, restaurants, strolling magicians, jugglers, and singers. Free 10-minute shows are presented every half hour on the Court Jester's Stage from 10 A.M. to 10 P.M. Many are a bit on the corny side but fun for the youngsters.

The **Fantasy Faire** is an unusual mix of modern video arcade and pinball machines with medieval theme carnival games. If you're into shooting galleries, be sure to check out the Electronic Crossbow (20 shots for 50 cents) with animated, moving figures in the line of fire.

Wedded Biz

Apparently, there are a lot of people who dream of getting married wearing long, flowing velvet robes with swords at their sides and heavy crowns on their heads. There are as many as 50 or 60 weddings a week in the **Canterbury Room** and **Canterbury Gardens**, a small outdoor-like garden. You don't have to dress like King Arthur and Guinevere, either; suit and gown are acceptable. According to the hotel, one of the most memorable weddings took place on Halloween, with all guests in costume.

Excalibur Beds and Breakfasts

Room rates start at $49 for weekdays and $65 to $75 on weekends. There are two pools, one at each tower; plans for expansion include construction of a wall with water slides.

Each of the restaurants at Excalibur is a spectacular exercise in decoration and theme. Some of the food is decent, too.

The **Round Table Buffet** is one of the biggest, if not the biggest buffet room in Las Vegas with 1,446 seats. See the prices and hours in the buffet listings.

Camelot has just 144 seats and reservations are recommended. It is open for dinner from 6 to 10 P.M. Sunday through Thursday, and from 5 to 11 P.M. on Fridays, Saturdays, and holidays. Gourmet entrees range in price from about $13 to $19. Menu items include such items as chicken Guinevere (braised breast of chicken, young potatoes, fresh tomatoes, artichokes, and fresh herbs in a tangy sauce). Also available on one visit was rack of lamb Black Knight (lamb basted with Dijon mustard and finished in the oven with crisp garlic brioche crumbs), and sea bass florentine (poached fresh Pacific sea bass stuffed with cream spinach laced lightly with white wine).

Wild Bill's Saloon and Steakhouse is a large, lively, and loud room that makes mealtime into an adventure (it sounds somewhat like supper at home). Appetizers include chili and fried onions with hot sauce. Entrees, priced from about $10 to $17, include steak, roasted chicken, and a grilled vegetable platter.

Lance-A-Lotta Pasta is a favorite for lunch and light dinner, open from 11 A.M. to 2:30 P.M. daily, and from 5 P.M. nightly. Typical offerings include salads, sandwiches, and Italian sausage heros. Entrees such as lasagna and small pizzas are priced from about $6 to $10. Pizza toppings include bianca (white sauce), scampi shrimp, vegetali (broccoli, sun-dried tomatoes, green peas, and sweet peppers), and Philadelphia (marinated steak, smothered onions, peppers, and sun-dried tomatoes). Desserts include tartufo.

Sir Galahad's Prime Rib House. Open every night for dinner at 5 P.M., the specialties include prime rib from the Traditional English cut to the whopping King Arthur cut, priced from about $10 to $15. Also available are seafood and poultry dishes. Reservations are recommended for the 234-seat eatery.

The Excalibur's 24-hour coffee shop is the **Sherwood Forest Cafe.** Offerings include vegetarian dishes, including omelettes. Entrees and salads range from about $6 to $12 and have included items such as a barbecue platter, ribs, chicken fried steak, orange roughy, and turkey steak.

Excalibur Hotel & Casino, 3850 Las Vegas Blvd. South; 597-7777; (800) 937-7777.

MUST-SEE Las Vegas Hilton

Elvis slept here! In fact, this place is so large that he may still be roaming the halls somewhere, looking for the elevator.

Opened as the International Hotel in 1969, it was for a while the largest hotel in town and still claims the title as the largest convention hotel in the world. In 1994, it reached for another record with the installation of what is said to be the world's largest and tallest freestanding sign, at 362 feet. The Hilton is directly next to the Las Vegas Convention Center, and its own 220,000-square-foot convention facilities and meeting rooms are often used for spillover from shows like the Comdex computer exposition. Its rooms are among the first to sell out for major conventions, too.

The hotel's showroom was the site of the late-model Elvis Presley's glitter-era performances from 1969 until his reputed death in 1977. It also served as the showcase for another Vegas icon, Wayne Newton.

In 1994, the 1,600-seat theater became home of a production of Andrew Lloyd Webber's *Starlight Express,* a musical extravaganza on roller skates. Lloyd Webber is also the author of *Cats, Jesus Christ Superstar,* and *Sunset Boulevard,* among other shows. The show features a cast of 38, outfitted in spectacular costumes and skating in and around the audience including those seated in the center of two "rollerbowls," and others perched on seats directly above the stage.

The three 30-story towers include 3,174 rooms and suites. The 1,500-seat showroom, now used for major shows and boxing matches, has one of the largest stages in Las Vegas. Recreational facilities include a large pool (it actually sits above the ceiling of the main casino), tennis courts, a health club, and a nine-hole putting green.

Parents may be excited to learn about the Hilton's **Youth Hotel,** a separate camplike setting for children from 3 to 18. Supervised by a licensed and professional staff, the Youth Hotel offers indoor and outdoor activities and meals. Overnight accommodations are also available.

The facility is designed to handle up to 101 guests, with overnight accommodations for 24 children in separate dorms for boys and girls, kind of like a large slumber party. The hotel is available to registered guests of either the Las Vegas Hilton or the Flamingo Hilton. Rates per kid are $4 an hour or $25 overnight. The busiest night of the year is New Year's Eve; a recent celebration brought 325 youngsters to the Youth Hotel on that special occasion.

Separate recreation rooms include ping-pong, pool, air hockey, foosball, shuffleboard, a playground, and art supplies. Electronic diversions include movies and the latest video games. Kid-tested meals include such haute cuisine as hot dogs, hamburgers, French toast, waffles, and grilled cheese. Contact the Youth Hotel directly at 732-5706.

There is, of course, a casino, and it is a large

Elvis sighting number one. The "Elvis Suite," an intimate 5,000-square-foot hideaway on the 30th floor of the hotel, was the regular home of the King during his appearances at the Hilton. After Elvis's death, the maintenance staff at the Hilton filled in two bullet holes in the walls and actually redecorated the place! Obviously they have no sense of history.

Bill Cosby, a frequent visitor as a performer in more recent years, helped in the selection of the decorations, which now run to more traditional tastes. Appointments include a large formal dining room and a huge private kitchen.

In any case, we mere mortals cannot rent the suite. It is available only to high rollers and guests of the hotel. The closest most visitors will get to Elvis's old digs is when they visit the Crown Room atop the hotel; the door to the suite is located to the right.

Plans call for the addition of 5,000 more square feet to the Elvis Suite, including a pool.

and attractive field in which to dream. Recent renovations have upgraded the chandeliers throughout. There are 65 game tables and 1,200 slot machines. A sports and race book with more than 50 television monitors and projection screens is one of the most spectacular in town.

Standard room rates start at $85 but can climb sharply—if space is available at all—during conventions. The best rates can be obtained at Christmas time, with the exception of New Year's Eve. Classic Suites on the upper floors are for high rollers only.

> **Elvis sighting number two.** Just outside the showroom doors at the Las Vegas Hilton is a small collection of Elvis memorabilia. Presley made 144 appearances in the showroom, all of them sellouts.

The fanciest restaurant in the building is **Le Montrachet,** which is very French. A wine cellar offers more than 400 varieties. Check out the beautifully sculpted pear in a sugar cage at the entrance. Among the specialties is filet of baby white sturgeon, broiled on mesquite and topped with anchovy butter, for $23.

Barronshire is open from 6 P.M. to 10:30 P.M. every day except for Tuesday; it offers three prime rib cuts: English, Barronshire, and the Barron, for $21 to $25. The meat is served with Yorkshire pudding, mashed potatoes, and creamed horseradish. Dessert on one visit included English trifle, a crystal glass filled with layers of pound cake, fresh strawberries, blueberries, and peach slices, and topped with sauce melba and a dash of sherry with whipped cream.

Andiamo is the home of northern Italian specialties and homemade pasta, offered daily for dinner from 6 P.M. to 11 P.M. There's an impressive espresso and cappuccino counter, and diners can watch the chefs at work behind a glass wall. Specialties include *medaglioni di vitello andiamo* (veal medallions sautéed and served with creamy rosemary sauce and asparagus) for $19.50, and *petto di pollo ai ferri* (grilled chicken breast topped with olive oil vinaigrette sauce, flavored with garlic, oregano, and lemon) for $16.

Benihana Village features two traditional Japanese restaurants, **Hibachi** and the **Seafood Grille.** At Hibachi, chefs chop, slice, and grill your food at your table. The Grille offers barbecued dishes. Dinner is complemented by the animated musical show "Jambirdee" and a fireworks display over the Benihana Musical Waters.

The **Garden of the Dragon** serves gourmet Chinese dishes from 6 to 11 P.M.

The **Hilton Steakhouse** offers charbroiled steak, ribs, fish, and chicken. Open 5 to 11 P.M. and closed Thursdays.

Garden of the Dragon features specialties from Szechuan, Peking, northern, Mongolian, and Cantonese cuisines. Open daily from 6 P.M. to

11 P.M. The house chicken is diced and sautéed with mushrooms, snow peas, bamboo shoots, water chestnuts, and Chinese vegetables for $12.50. Steamed whole fish (whole fresh fish is steamed in Cantonese style and garnished with scallions, ginger, and soy sauce) is $30.

Also available is **MargaritaGrille,** a casual Mexican restaurant, and **Socorro Springs,** a 24-hour coffee shop named for the birthplace of hotel chain founder Conrad Hilton.

The **Buffet of Champions** is open for breakfast during the week from 7 A.M. to 10 A.M. for $6.25; lunch is served from 11 A.M. to 2:30 P.M. for $7.25, and dinner is from 5 P.M. to 10 P.M. for $8.99. A champagne brunch is offered Saturdays, Sundays, and holidays for $8.99.

Las Vegas Hilton, 3000 Paradise Rd.; 3,174 rooms; 732-5111; (800) 732-7117.

MUST-SEE Luxor

The real and imagined treasures of another desert empire come to near-life in the fabulous Luxor, a 2,521-room, 30-story, $300 million pyramid-shaped complex.

Located just south of the Excalibur at the top end of The Strip, the hotel is the latest in a string of Circus Circus resorts.

The designers of the Luxor conceived of it as a simulation of a vast archeological dig where the mysteries of ancient Egypt are revealed as

Architectural cut-away of Luxor

though the interior was a vast excavation site. Replicas of Egyptian artifacts, including a full-sized reproduction of King Tut's tomb, are on display.

As you approach, the hotel appears to be a huge sand-colored pyramid; the rooms of the hotel occupy the exterior steps of the structure. Out front is a huge replica of the Sphinx, the mythical Egyptian creature with a human head and the body of a lion. The figure was often meant to symbolize the pharaoh as an incarnation of the sun god, Ra.

The pyramid, a symbol of eternal life believed by the Pharaohs to be a "stairway to the stars" offers three levels of entertainment. The Hanging Gardens of Babylon occupy the front entrance, while lagoon-like pools and a beach are at the rear entrance.

The main level of Luxor includes the "River Nile" flowing along the perimeter, separating the hotel rooms from the casino. Guests and visitors can take a narrated voyage on the river to view architectural scenes of ancient Egypt. (The original concept had been for the boats to transport guests from the registration desk to the hotel tower elevator lobbies located in the four corners of the pyramid.)

The big top. If you have any doubts about the financial viability of the super resorts of Las Vegas, consider this: according to Circus Circus, the new Luxor's $300 million construction cost was funded entirely by cash flow from the company's various resorts. There is no mortgage.

Boat shop. Across from the check-in desk is an overlook to the boat ride. Note the camouflaged overhead track and the hidden slab beneath. This is not the true secret of the Nile, but actually the entrance to a hidden work area for repair of boats. The slab is lifted and put aside, and then a boat is carried into the work area.

Guests are transported to their floors on unusual inclined elevators moving at a 39-degree angle up the sides of the pyramid, or more conventional vertical lifts.

The rooms themselves have an unusual feature that may be a bit disconcerting to some visitors; the outside window wall is slanted sharply since it is part of the exterior of the pyramid. Other visitors may find the view of the interior atrium a bit dizzying; the interior balconies extend all the way up to the 27th floor, while the top three floors—mostly suites—have interior hallways. And residents of one of the first few floors of the hotel may find a great deal of pedestrian traffic right outside their doors.

The rooms are nicely appointed, from the standard guest room (as low as $59 in off season and more than twice that during conventions and at peak times) to the Jacuzzi Suites (starting at $150) and the spectacular upper-level rooms including the Presidential Suite that rents for several thousand dollars per night.

The real thing. Luxor, on the east bank of the Nile about 315 miles southeast of Cairo, is near the site of Thebes, the capital of ancient Egypt. The temple at Luxor was built by Amenhotep III and dedicated to Amon-Re, king of the gods, the sun god. Nearby are the Valley of the Kings, where the tomb of Tutankhamen was discovered in 1922, the Valley of the Queens, and the magnificent monuments of Karnak.

Within the huge 90,000-square-foot casino area the Egyptian theme is carried through with reproductions of artifacts, columns, and tombs found in the temples of Luxor and Karnak.

The **Sacred Sea Room**, an attractively decorated hideaway, includes entrees priced from about $12 to $26, with dishes including linguine and clams, New York steak, and veal chops.

More adventurous dishes are offered at **Papyrus**. Dishes on a recent visit, priced from about $11 to $21, included spicy Thai shrimp scampi, paniolo steak (grilled pineapple, toasted coconut, and teriyaki sauce), and wok-seared rare salmon with a basil ginger sauce.

The **Pyramid Cafe** has a wide range of salads, priced from about $2 to $9, plus entrees including burgers, grilled Pacific salmon, and fried chicken, priced from about $6 to $14.

The **Millenium High Energy Cafe** is a bright and cheerful open space offering burgers, fajitas, pizzas, and sandwiches, with entrees priced from about $5 to $10.

And there is the **Nile Deli**, which is sort of a New York Jewish delicatessen on the banks of the Nile. Sandwiches, Philly cheese-steaks, reubens, lox on a bagel, and other delicacies are priced from about $5 to $10.

The **Manhattan Buffet** is an open air buffet set in a metropolitan downtown setting. For hours and rates see the section on buffets.

And there is, of course, an ancient shopping bazaar. The hotel features a 1,200-seat oval showroom for a nightly special effects production show.

The third level offers three attractions created by special effects designer Douglass Trumbull (also responsible for the spectacular Back to the Future ride at Universal Studios in Orlando, Florida). *For details, see the section on Las Vegas attractions in Chapter 10.*

Luxor, 3900 Las Vegas Blvd. South, 262-4444, (800) 228-1000.

MUST-SEE MGM Grand

The MGM Grand claimed the mantle as the World's Largest Hotel, Casino, and Theme Park when it opened early in 1994.

It could also advertise itself as the World's Only Hotel Where Guests and Visitors Will Enter Through an 88-foot-tall MGM Lion into a Seven-Story Replica of the Emerald City, Complete with Yellow Brick Road. It is a decidedly strange and somewhat wonderful place, Las Vegas' version of Oz for adults and children of all ages.

The hotel and theme park is located on 112 acres at the northeast corner of Las Vegas Boulevard South and Tropicana Avenue, the former site of the Marina Hotel-Casino and the Tropicana Country Club. The $1 billion project is the largest in the history of Nevada and adds 5,009 rooms, including 744 suites, in a set of 30-story towers.

The biggest lure of this grand experiment is **MGM Grand Adventures,** a 33-acre theme park including rides, shows, themed streets, entertainment, restaurants, and shops. It is all lorded over by King Looey, the lion ambassador of the park. *For details on MGM Grand Adventures, see the section on Las Vegas attractions in Chapter 10.*

The hotel and casino are certainly grand and worth a visit, but the overall tone is down a notch from places like Caesars Palace or the Mirage. It is also one of the few hotel complexes we know of that requires the use of a map.

There are two main entrances to the hotel. The most dramatic is the **Lion Entrance,** which is mostly for use by pedestrians; visitors arriving by car or taxi will probably enter beneath the more formal canopied **Porte Cochere**, a fancy term for carriage entrance.

The Lion Entrance must be seen to be believed. You'll walk between the golden paws of a huge MGM lion; bright lights behind his eyes radiate toward The Strip. An elevated pedestrian crosswalk at the corner connects to the nearby Tropicana, Excalibur, and Luxor. When you walk through the door, you'll be in **Emerald City**, home of a strange little magic show and close to the **Oz Buffet.** You're also within one of four casino areas,

MGM Grand

Some may still be moving east. The first big event at the MGM Grand took place a year before its opening when the hotel/ casino/theme park threw a party to celebrate the "topping off" of the hotel. As a crane lifted the final panel into place on the four emerald green towers, 5,009 balloons—representing each of the rooms in the hotel—were released. Each balloon contained a certificate good for one free night's stay.

one watched over by an animated Good Witch in pink, bestowing a blessing on the slots below. The slots, by the way, can accept folding money as well as tokens; they will eat bills as large as $100.

If you come in through the Porte Cochere, you'll be at the registration desk, which is also worth seeing; a bank of some 60 video monitors behind the clerks displays some spectacular images from sporting events and movies. We enjoyed watching the speeded-up baseball game.

The **Grand Theatre** is a handsome Vegas showroom, wider than deep with a stage about three city buses wide and decorated in red and black. The tables and booths seat about 1,700. The relatively cozy **Hollywood Theatre**, with 630 seats, features headliners.

The **Sports Book**, to the left of the Grand Theatre, has a gigantic screen capable of handling a single event like the SuperBowl, or being split into as many as 12 separate images for various sporting events.

We also mustn't overlook (as if we could) the **MGM Grand Garden** special events center. This arena, modeled after New York's famed Madison Square Garden, offers seating for up to 15,200 for championship boxing. There's nothing very grand about the arena itself, except for its ability to change its configuration for events from ice shows, hockey games, basketball, prize fights, and concerts. According to the designers, it can be transformed from a major exhibition hall to an arena for sporting events or concerts in four hours. The Garden was the site of the much-publicized opening night concerts by Barbra Streisand.

In the hotel, standard rooms are about 446 square feet in size; 744 suites will range in size from 675 to 6,000 square feet. (A bit of perspective here: a typical three- or four-bedroom home is 2,000 square feet or less.)

Standard rooms are decorated in Wizard of Oz, Hollywood, Southern, and Casa Blanca styles. Suites include traditional, Marrakech, Oriental, Bahamian, and Las Vegas designs.

The huge casino encompasses a total of 171,500 square feet, including about 3,500 machines, 165 gaming tables, and a race and sports book. The casino is divided into four themed areas: Emerald City, Hollywood, Monte Carlo, and Sports. The Emerald City dome includes 75-foot-tall emerald crystal spires, a Yellow Brick Road, Wizard of Oz characters, and The Wizard's Secret special effects and magic show.

At the very center of it all is **Wolfgang Puck's Cafe,** a Nevada outpost of the successful California chef's unusual restaurants. You can buy a plain wood-fired pizza for about $7.50, but why would you when you could order a pie with shrimp or with chicken and anchovies. We were drawn to the pizza with smoked salmon and red onions for $14.50.

Most of the other restaurants are in a corridor that leads from the casino to the MGM Grand Garden and the MGM Grand Adventures area.

Leonardo's serves entrees ranging from about $7 to $12 for lunch and about $10 to $20 for dinner. They include pasta dishes and regular-to-extraordinary pizza.

Across the corridor is the **Coyote Cafe,** a transplant from Santa Fe, serving tacos, tortillas, quesadillas, soups, and salads; entrees range from about $7 to $12.

Sir Reginald's Steakhouse offers meat-eater delights including steaks, prime rib, and chicken, priced from about $18 to $30. A signature dish is hobo steak in salt crust, priced at about $45 for a two-person serving.

The Ocean Grille is a small seafood eatery near the Fast Food Court, with entrees priced from about $14 to $25. Outside the doors of the restaurant is a small, pricey seafood bar called **Crack Crab** with offerings including oysters, crabs, and mussels.

Dragon Court is a high-tone Chinese eatery, quiet and off the busy track. The small menu includes braised shark fin and chicken in brown sauce for $30, as well as more ordinary offerings such as beef with oyster sauce for $13.50 and pork chop with black pepper sauce for $15.

The **One-Liners Fast Food Court** features a **Nathan's, McDonald's,** and **Hamada Oriental Express.**

The **Grand Oasis** includes a swimming pool with beach. Nearby is the **Grand Health Club & Spa,** a fitness center including six Jacuzzis.

For children, the MGM Grand features **King Looey's Youth Activity Center,** Las Vegas' second "youth hotel" (the other is at the Las Vegas Hilton) offering supervised activities for children. The center will accommodate children from ages 3 to 12 at its center near the theme park; rates in 1994 were $5 per hour for guests of the hotel and $7 per hour for others. The activity center also offers supervised tours of the MGM Grand Adventures Theme Park. Departing at 11 A.M. and concluding at 5 P.M., the tour is for children from ages 6 to 16 for a fee of $70 for guests and $80 for others.

Also available is the **Wizard's Midway & Arcade,** a 30,000-square-foot center including 33 games of skill and the latest video games. If you've got any stomach left after gambling or visiting the theme park, you may want to try the **G360** virtual reality arcade game; you'll "fly" your craft into a dogfight and then come back to a carrier landing. If you're any-

Real sharks. Of more than 300 species of sharks, only about 12 are considered potentially dangerous to humans. Sharks and rays are among the most primitive of fish, with skeletons made of cartilage rather than bone.

The dorsal (top) spines of triggerfish can be locked into an upright position when needed for a form of sticky defense; if they are threatened, they will withdraw into narrow crevices in the coral and erect their spines to wedge themselves into place.

Another unusual defensive maneuver is performed by pufferfish, which will inflate themselves like a basketball if they are in trouble. An attacker may not be able to get past the spines, and in any case may find the puffed-out fellow too large to swallow.

Inside joke. The "street" outside of Le Bistro and Ristorante Riva bears two authentic-looking European street signs: Via Stefano and Via Elena. They're not real, though: Stefano is named for Steve Wynn, the majordomo of the Mirage, and Elena for his wife Elaine.

thing like the pilots I saw, you'll spend most of the time upside down trying to figure out which way was up.

Bars and lounges include the **Center Stage Lounge, Turf Club Lounge, Flying Monkey Bar, Betty Boop Bar,** and the **Margarita Bar.**

A Bit of History

MGM Grand, Inc., is a publicly traded hotel, casino, and travel company based in Las Vegas. The company also operates MGM Grand Air, a luxury charter airline.

The company's majority shareholder, Kirk Kerkorian, opened his first Las Vegas property, the International Hotel, in 1969. At the time, it claimed the title as the largest hotel in the world with a mere 1,517 rooms. The hotel, considerably expanded, is now owned by Hilton Hotels Corp. and called the Las Vegas Hilton.

The first MGM Grand Hotel opened in 1973 at Flamingo Road, and once again claimed top honors as the largest hotel. After a massive reconstruction after a tragic fire, it was sold to Bally's. Over the years, the company bought—and quickly sold—the Sands Hotel. It also bought the Desert Inn and later sold it to Kerkorian's private holding company.

The latest expansion began with the 1989 and 1990 acquisition and subsequent demolition of the Marina Hotel-Casino and the Tropicana Country Club.

MGM Grand, Inc., 3799 Las Vegas Blvd. South, 734-5110, (800) 634-6753.

MUST-SEE The Mirage

Every desert needs a mirage, although few are quite so phantasmagorical as this one. The Mirage is a sight to behold inside and out, but any description of the hotel has to start with the live volcano out front that spews smoke and fire 100 feet in the air from an artificial lagoon.

When the hotel first opened in 1989, locals were unsure which was more entertaining: the aerial show from the volcano or the continuous fender benders among drivers passing by on The Strip out front.

The manmade, computer-controlled 54-foot-tall volcano puts on a three-minute show every 30 minutes from dusk to midnight, spewing steam, gas-fed flames, and "lava" created with the aid of a sophisticated lighting scheme. The pumping system moves 5,000 gallons of water per minute during the show. For the construction, 1,000 real palm trees were moved to the site; some of the trees nearest the flames, though, are constructed of steel and concrete.

An elevated tram connects the Mirage to its neighboring cousin Treasure Island. The $630 million, 100-acre site has three 30-story towers with 3,054 rooms including one- and two-bedroom suites, eight villa apartments, and six lanai bungalows with private gardens and pools. The top five floors of each tower are reserved for tower and penthouse suites.

The driveway delivers visitors to a white porte cochere with full-length louvered shutters that suggest arrival at a colonial government house. You walk into a 90-foot-high indoor atrium with 60-foot-tall palm trees; a central forest includes tropical orchids and banana trees, an indoor waterfall, and lagoons.

The Mirage, Las Vegas

Behind the hotel's registration desk is a huge 53-foot-long, 20,000-gallon coral reef aquarium stocked with sharks, rays, and other sea life from the Caribbean, Hawaiian Islands, Tonga, Fiji, the Marshall Islands, Australia, and the Red Sea. The aquarium really is worth a look, if you can find the check-in area in the complex maze of the casino.

Public areas are decorated in high-tone marble, teak, and rattan. In the atrium, the bent palm trees are necessarily fake, but they are covered in real bark. Almost every other piece of greenery is real.

The tropical theme is carried through in most of the rooms, featuring lush colors, rattan, and cane. The highest of the high rollers can rent one of six lanai bungalows, each with its own private garden and pool.

The lowest room rates at the Mirage can usually be found bracketing Christmas, when rates fall to as low as $49 for standard rooms; those same rooms can go for as much as $239 at times of highest demand, including during conventions. Penthouse suites rent for $250 to $750.

The Mirage is one of just a few casinos in Las Vegas with $500 slot machines; there is a small nest of them in an alcove near the Caribe Cafe. The slots have a top payoff of $40,000 for a single coin. By the way, if you sit and play the $500 machines for a while, you'll be offered a free catered meal. Of course, they'll want you to eat it at the machines, feeding those expensive tokens all the while.

Nearby is the Salon Privé, a private gambling room for the highest rollers, where tens or even hundreds of thousands of dollars can hang on a single card in blackjack or baccarat, a roll of the dice in craps, or a spin of the roulette wheel. If you want to play, the casino will staff every table in the room in case you change your mind on which game to play.

Color scheming. The original color scheme for The Mirage was almost entirely drawn from a palette of muted earth tones—peach and beige and green. The increasing influx of high rollers from Asia has brought about some redecoration to reds, blacks, and yellows—colors apparently more pleasing to Asian sensibilities. The registration desk—or the keepers of the comp rooms for the guests of the casino—will color coordinate rooms with races.

Speaking of excesses in entertainment, the Mirage is the long-time home of **Siegfried and Roy,** who put on one of the most spectacular and expensive magic and stage shows anywhere. The boys appear 40 weeks per year—if you are determined to see their show, check with the hotel to avoid one of their vacation periods. They sell out almost every one of their 12 shows per week. *See the writeup on Las Vegas showrooms.*

The $30 million production premiered in February of 1990 and grossed more than $80 million in the first two years. The show is presented in the **Theatre Mirage,** a 1,500-seat theater. The production was created and designed by John Napier, the Tony-award winning artist responsible for English and American theatrical triumphs including *Cats, Starlight Express, Les Miserables,* and *Phantom of the Opera.*

There are 27 tigers in the Siegfried and Roy troupe. Not all of them appear in the show, and those that do are given regular times off for good behavior. You can see some of these beautiful creatures through the glass wall at a re-creation of their native Himalayan world near the walkway entrance on the south side of the hotel.

There is, by the way, a hallway that runs from the exhibit area to their cages and the showroom, allowing the animals to be walked to work. We'd suggest you avoid opening unmarked doors in the casino. (Just kidding…we think.)

Another interesting animal exhibit is the **Dolphin Habitat,** a 1.5 million-gallon tank for bottlenose dolphins located out back and open to the public for a nominal fee.

The Mirage also features a collection of some of the best and most attractive restaurants in Las Vegas.

Among our favorites is **Moongate,** a gourmet Chinese restaurant serving spicy Szechuan and subtle Cantonese cuisine in a lovely setting that includes a starfield ceiling, a live cherry tree, and tasteful jade objects and statuary; the hotel reportedly spent $2.5 million on decorations alone. Open for dinner only, from 5:30 to 11 P.M., entrees range from $10 to $38. Among specialties are scallop and shrimp with yellow leek for $30, jade pepper chicken for $15, and Peking duck for $41.

Next door, and sharing the starfield ceiling, is **Mikado,** set in a very elegant Japanese garden. Your chef can prepare teppen yaki dishes of chicken, steak, lobster, or vegetables at your table for $18 to $38. Individual sushi pieces are priced from $4 to $8. A la carte items range from $20 to $34 and include terriyaki dishes. The restaurant is open for dinner only.

No dolphin served here. Dutchess, one of the Mirage's captive dolphins, delivered a bouncing baby calf in 1991; the newborn was three feet long, about half of his expected full-grown size. Each dolphin has its own signature whistle, and it is believed that the mother is able to recognize her own baby by listening for the sound.

By the way, don't feel guilty about ordering a tuna sandwich at the Mirage. The hotel has a "dolphin safe" policy for all of its restaurants. And the hotel also bars the sale of fur in any of its boutiques.

Tiger, tiger. Two or three tigers are usually on display in the habitat at the Mirage at all times, with new groups moved in several times each day.

Boob tube. The casino floor includes high-tech TV monitors advertising various promotions and offering some little bit of entertainment for visitors standing in line for the buffet. (At the time of our visit, the casino also offered one of our least favorite accommodations, a Next Day Tax Refund booth.)

The smallest of the gourmet rooms at the Mirage is **Le Bistro,** with just 90 seats. Very Parisian, with Toulouse-Lautrec-like murals and an attractive pressed-tin ceiling over most of the restaurant except for an exquisite stained glass dome in the center. Specialties we found on one visit, priced from about $20 to $35, included venison tenderloin chasseur, tournedos Diane, breast of duck au poivre, and sea bass grenobloise.

The **Ristorante Riva** was described for us by a hotel official as "an Italian restaurant without a Mob setting." Decorated in peaches and green, it is very Italian and very bright; entrees run from about $15 to $30. Pasta dishes we found included *agnolotti alla grafagnana* (halfmoon pasta with ricotta, spinach, and herbs with marjoram cream). Also offered is *zuppa di pesce cioppino* (shrimp, scallops, lobster, mussels, clams, and squid in a tomato-fish base), and *salmone con carciofi* (salmon with artichokes), *linguine con vongole* (linguine pasta with clams), and *vitello saltimbocca.*

Kokomo is the only full-service restaurant open for lunch. It has an open-air feeling under the atrium. Offerings include burgers, sandwiches, and steaks from $6 to $15.

An interesting alternative for lunch, or for dinner, is the **California Pizza Kitchen** located near the sports bar. They use wood-fired ovens to create some of the strangest—and tastiest—pizzas in town. Pies go for $10 for individual size; also available are salads and pasta dishes. No reservations are accepted, and lines can build during busy times.

The Mirage's **Buffet** is located in an attractive, bright room just off the casino floor. It is officially described as being set in an English garden at Bermuda, although we didn't quite see the connection. The food is good, but it is obvious that the Mirage feels it does not need the lure of a spectacular buffet to bring in the gambling visitors. Breakfast is served from 7 A.M. to 11 A.M. for $5.75, lunch is from 11 A.M. to 3 P.M. for $8, and dinner is from 3 P.M. to 9:30 A.M. for $9.50. A Sunday champagne brunch from 8 A.M. to 9:30 P.M. is priced at $12.50. Children under 10 eat for half price.

The Mirage, 3400 Las Vegas Blvd. South; 3,049 rooms; 791-7111; (800) 627-6667.

MUST-SEE Rio Hotel & Casino

Hot, hot, hot! This is one fun place, a bit of Rio de Janeiro about a mile west of The Strip. It's a place of flowers, flowered shirts, and the hottest cocktail waitress uniforms in town, more of a swimsuit than an outfit, actually. Dancers in pink thong bikinis and dancers with trained birds parade through the casino from time to time.

The original building opened in 1990 and almost immediately was too small; construction of a new 430-room tower was completed in 1994. And in May of 1994, work was begun on a third suite tower with 550 more rooms plus an increase in the size of the **Carnival World Buffet** and a new parking garage.

The Rio is only about a mile from The Strip, although it's not an easy walk because of the highways in the area; you'll need to use a car, cab, or the hotel's shuttle bus to get there.

A new 430-seat showroom opened with **¡Conga!**, an interactive multimedia dinner show.

All of the rooms at the hotel are considered suites, basically one 600-square-foot room with a large bathroom and dressing room. The sleeping area includes a couch. Standard rates in 1994 were about $85 for weekdays and $101 on weekends.

The small pool features a white-sand beach, complete with a volleyball court. A video arcade flanks the casino floor.

Our favorite part of this place, though, is the spectacular **Carnival World Buffet,** which is one of the best values in town. A pretty, bright room right off the casino floor, it offers cooked-to-order Brazilian stir-fry and other quality dishes. Breakfast features made-to-order omelettes, waffles, pancakes, sausage, bacon, fresh salsa, fruit, and variety of fritters. Just when we were ready to waddle on out, we discovered the dessert section, which is the fulfillment of many a sweet tooth's wildest dream: a bakery where you can sample any food by pointing to it.

We visited the buffet again for dinner on a Sunday night and were greeted by a 90-minute line. It was, however, worth the wait. We especially enjoyed the Brazilian stir-fry counter where you get to choose among mushrooms, asparagus, onions, broccoli, bean sprouts, carrots, and tomatoes, plus spices including cilantro, garlic, and ginger; then you choose from pork, lamb, chicken, shrimp, or beef and watch as a chef cooks it all with a special sauce. Other sections of the buffet include international offerings: U.S., Mexican, Chinese, and Italian.

The Rio's newest restaurant is the elegant **Fiore**, near the hotel's Beach Club. it's a quiet sanctuary down a glass-walled hallway; you can eat in the lovely dining room or move out onto the open-air porch. Entrees, priced from about $18 to $34, include veal, chicken, and beef dishes.

Another interesting restaurant is the **All-American Steakhouse.** Luncheon fare includes burgers for $5 to $7 and salads including lobster and avocado for $6 to $11. Dinner selections include pork ribs marinated in a secret sauce

Old money. Be sure to check out the beautiful Caille Brothers Triple Upright slot machine, tucked away in a hallway near Antonio's restaurant at the Rio. This three-in-one machine also includes a music box. Built in 1907, less than ten are known to still exist.

for 24 hours for $9.95, as well as chicken and shrimp dishes. The setting is a small, dark sports bar with pennants on the wall; the walls are open to the casino.

A small food court includes **Sonny's Deli, Pizza and Pasta,** and **Dreyer's** in a bright and airy room with metal chairs and counter service. Pizza by the slice goes for $1.50 to $2.50; whole pies are also available. Pasta with sauce is priced from $4.50 to $6.

Antonio's is a small, quiet eatery with an attractive light wood and marble decor and an impressive espresso machine at the entrance. Entrees include soup and salad and are priced from $15 to $25. A typical offering is *vitello al piccata* (scallops of veal sautéed with lemon, white wine, butter, and shallots). The restaurant is open every day for dinner from 5 to 11 P.M.

The coffee shop, facing the pool area is the **Beach Front Cafe.** Specials include T-bone steak and eggs with all the hot cakes you can eat for $2.99, served from 11 P.M. to 11 A.M. A dinner special, from 4 P.M. to 10 P.M., is steak and lobster tail for $6.49. A nice selection of pies and pastries is also offered.

Rio Suite Hotel & Casino, 3700 West Flamingo Road; 430 rooms; 252-7777; (800) 888-1808.

◆MUST-SEE◆ Treasure Island

Let's give credit where credit is due: extravagant casino developer Steve Wynn, already responsible for installing the town's only active volcano in front of his Mirage resort, was also the first person to realize that what Las Vegas was missing was its own pirate warship. Treasure Island opened with a bang at the end of 1993, just north of its corporate cousin the Mirage; the two hotels are connected by an aerial tram.

The adventure begins with a boardwalk along The Strip and across a lagoon to the front entrance. The front of the resort has been designed as an outdoor theater modeled after Buccaneer Bay, the village in Robert Louis Stevenson's *Treasure Island* classic.

Each hour, the British frigate HMS *The Sir Francis Drake* sails around Skull Point to confront an 80-foot-long replica of the pirate ship *Hispaniola.* "In the name of His Royal Britannic Majesty, King of England and all that he surveys, I order you brigands to lay down your arms and receive a Marine boarding party," the British captain warns. "The only thing we'll receive from you is your stores, valuables, and whatever rum ye might have onboard, you son of a footman's goat," is the pirate's response.

Those are, of course, fighting words. The two ships engage in a cannon battle across the lagoon, complete with explosions, fire, and a spec-

Treasure Island, Las Vegas

tacular sinking ship. Many of the 30 stunt players jump or fall from the rigging into the water below.

This is Las Vegas, after all: the pirates win. (The British captain goes down with his ship—or does he?)

The $430 million Treasure Island resort includes 2,900 guest rooms with 212 suites in three 36-floor towers. All rooms and suites have floor-to-ceiling windows. Standard room rates range from about $45 to $99 and suites are from about $150 to $300.

Other facilities include Pirates Walk, a glittering main street village lined with retail shops, two wedding chapels, and a lavish tropical pool with slide, two cocktail bars, and a snack bar.

The **Buccaneer Bay Club** is a quiet, private room on the second floor off the casino with a view of the pirate battle out front. Offerings, priced from about $14 to $43, on a recent visit included duckling Grand Marnier, Chilean sea bass, spit roasted monkfish, and lobster fra diable.

The Plank is a very elegant and quiet hideaway, with a setting of an educated pirate's booty-filled library. Entrees range from about $13 to $32, including cioppino, mesquite-grilled salmon, and steak with crab meat and béarnaise sauce.

Black Spot Grille. A bit away from the casino, it offers pasta, calzone, burgers, and other such fare, with prices from about $6 to $10.

The **Lookout Cafe** is a high-toned 24-hour coffee shop with dishes such as salmon, halibut, pot pie, and burgers from about $5 to $13.

The three themed buffets, in Italian, American, and Chinese flavors, are in adjoining, attractive rooms. The food is a bit ordinary, though.

For the non-gamblers, there is **Mutiny Bay,** a 15,000-square-foot arcade entertainment center set in an ancient Moorish castle. It includes a bit of Disney-like animated robots, including propositioning pirates, wise-cracking wenches, and various automated animals. In addition to a state-of-the-art collection of video arcade machines (including the most unusual, Ridge Racer, a racing simulator which puts the controls within a *real* red sports car), there is a collection of carnival games, complete with barkers. One favorite entertainment is Castle Climb, which pits three participants in a race to scurry up one of three twisting rope ladders

There is, of course, a casino: a sprawling 90,000 square foot affair.

Entertainment at Treasure Island is built around a permanent 1,500-seat home for the **Cirque du Soleil,** the decidedly strange French-Canadian circus troupe. Cirque du Soleil (French for "Circus of the Sun") is one of the youngest of the great circuses of the world, begun in 1984 in Montreal, Quebec. The genesis was a group of street performers gathered by 24-year-old Guy Laliberte.

What we've got here is a one-ring human circus, without animals, air cannons, motorcycles, and other high-tech trappings of other shows. The emphasis is on strange and wonderful human performances. "Mystère" is the current production.

Treasure Island, 3300 Las Vegas Blvd. South; 2,990 rooms; 894-7111; 800-944-7444.

MUST-SEE Vegas World

If P. T. Barnum was still alive, we think he'd have a little place on The Strip in Vegas. Barnum is long gone, but in his place is Bob Stupak.

Bob Stupak's Vegas World is not the biggest, not the most spectacular, not the most famous—but Vegas World just may be the loudest hotel and casino in town. It is located at the bottom of The Strip, not far from downtown. Developer Stupak runs one of the most iconoclastic casino operations in town.

Have we mentioned Bob Stupak yet? Stupak grew up in a world of gambling; his father ran crap games in Pittsburgh for a living. According to his own autobiography—available at the casino—young Stupak began playing the numbers in third grade. He went on to run crap games in the army. He arrived in Las Vegas in 1972 with bigger dreams and parlayed a few small casinos into one big and splashy one. Stupak has his name on the hotel and on the carpet and his name and picture on the chips. In 1993, financial problems forced Stupak to sell much of his ownership of the property, but his new partners have kept him in place as the front man.

One other preoccupation of Stupak is the space program. There are pictures of the planets and spacecraft on the exterior of the hotel and the casino is decorated in a space theme (including one area with replicas of spacecraft floating overhead). At one time, the casino even displayed an actual piece of the moon in a case. The rock was mounted in a presentation trophy that was inscribed as a present from former President Richard Nixon to Anastasio Somoza, the former president and dictator of Nicaragua. The hotel is officially mum on how Stupak obtained the trophy, but we have to imagine there was a gambling debt involved.

It's actually not all that easy to reserve a room at the hotel, since the place is usually filled with junketeers and members of a nationally advertised vacation club. Something like 90 percent of the guests at Vegas World are there as part of a vacation package, sold mostly by direct mail. The package includes free casino action chips, which can only be used once. If you bet and lose, the chips are gone; bet and win and the payoff is in real money. Stupak is gambling that most visitors will continue to bet with real money instead of merely "washing" the action chips across the table.

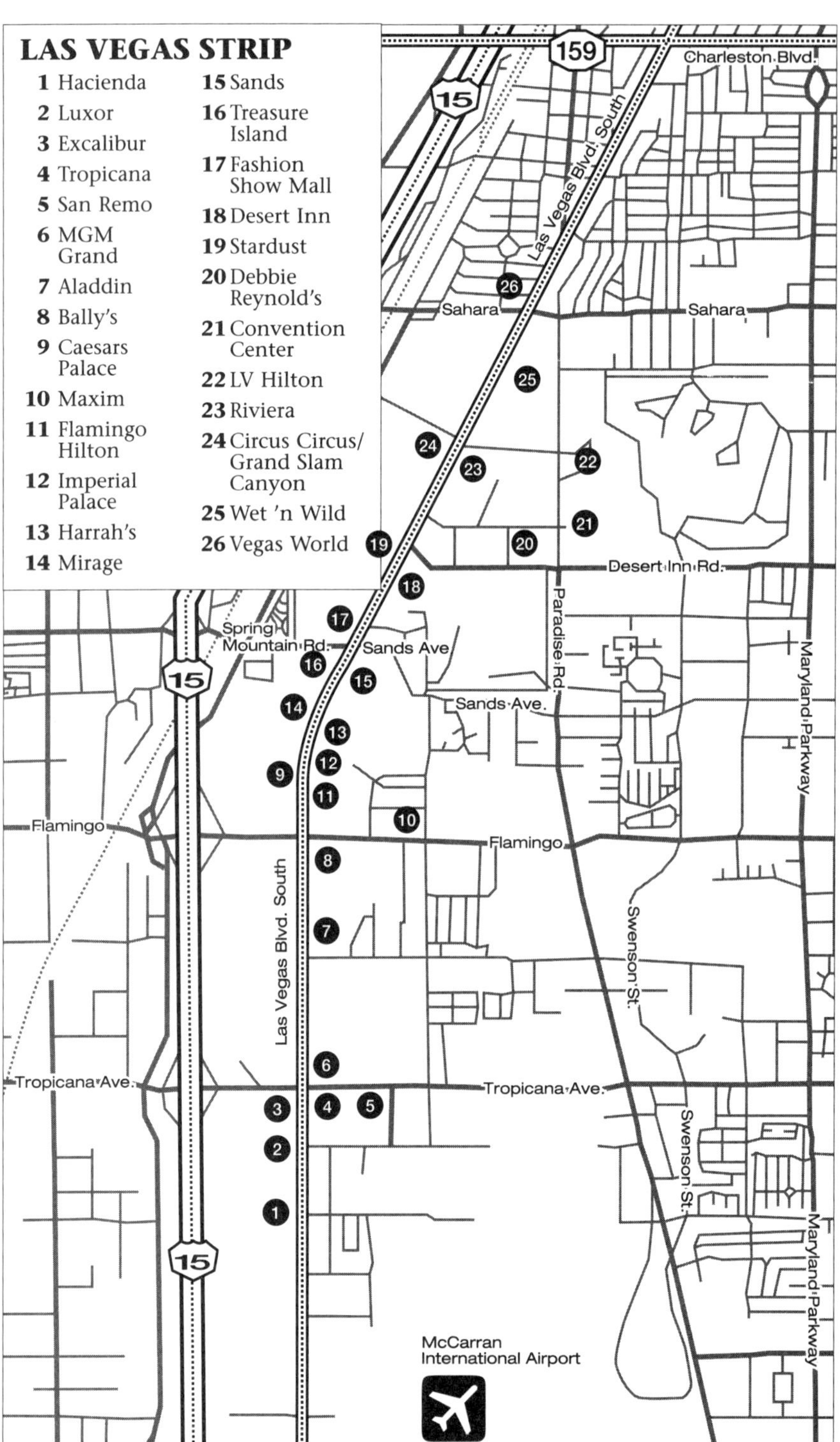

LAS VEGAS STRIP
1 Hacienda
2 Luxor
3 Excalibur
4 Tropicana
5 San Remo
6 MGM Grand
7 Aladdin
8 Bally's
9 Caesars Palace
10 Maxim
11 Flamingo Hilton
12 Imperial Palace
13 Harrah's
14 Mirage
15 Sands
16 Treasure Island
17 Fashion Show Mall
18 Desert Inn
19 Stardust
20 Debbie Reynold's
21 Convention Center
22 LV Hilton
23 Riviera
24 Circus Circus/ Grand Slam Canyon
25 Wet 'n Wild
26 Vegas World
159
15
Charleston Blvd.
Las Vegas Blvd. South
Sahara
Sahara
Desert Inn Rd.
Paradise Rd.
Maryland Parkway
Spring Mountain Rd.
Sands Ave.
Sands Ave.
Flamingo
Flamingo
Swenson St.
Las Vegas Blvd. South
Tropicana Ave.
Tropicana Ave.
Swenson St.
Maryland Parkway
McCarran International Airport

But wait: it gets weirder. In 1991, Stupak announced his latest space adventure: The Stratosphere Tower, a gigantic poured-concrete structure. Construction began soon afterward, but it has proceeded in an on-again and off-again process. For a long time it seemed that Stupak was waiting until he had a few million extra dollars sitting around in his desk drawer before he ordered up a few more feet of the tower.

We don't know if any of the following is true; a lot of it is probably pure hype, but you've got to appreciate the Barnumesque style of it all.

The tower was intended to reach to 1,012 feet when completed, which would have made it the tallest in America. It will be taller than the Leaning Tower of Pisa, the Tower of London, the Great Pyramids, the Washington Monument, Seattle's Space Needle, and the Eiffel Tower. Why, Stupak said, it will even be taller than the Tower of Babel; we haven't the slightest idea how they managed to calculate that.

Construction, though, stalled in 1993; in 1994 Stupak and his new investors stunned Las Vegas with news that he planned to extend it 800 feet more to make it the tallest tower in the world at 1,825 feet, surpassing even the massive CN Tower in Toronto at 1,815 feet. By the way, the tallest building in the world is the Sears Tower in Chicago, at 1,454 feet. New York's World Trade Center is 1,368 feet tall and the one-time benchmark Empire State Building stands a mere 1,250 feet.

Remember, though, that planes taking off or landing on one of the main runways at McCarran Airport proceed up or down the Las Vegas Strip. Stupak ran into opposition from the Federal Aviation Administration, the airline pilots association, and various other groups with his newest plan. As we went to press the whole matter was in the hands of the City Council and an outside aviation expert for study.

We're kind of hoping the thing will be completed in some form or another. Here are a few more details from the original plan for the tower: at the base will be a new 100,000-square-foot addition to the already sprawling Vegas World casino, plus a shopping arcade. Apropos of nothing else, the ground level of the tower was planned to include an African jungle, claimed as the world's largest indoor lion habitat. The lions would roam freely in their environment, and visitors would cruise by overhead on a chairlift ride. About 1,000 feet up, just below observation level, plans called for a fog machine that would create a mist to act as a "movie screen" for a laser light show projected from the tower.

Next up would be four wedding chapels. A 400-seat revolving restaurant on the next level up is planned to include a split-level cocktail bar and balcony lounge. Up one more floor would be an indoor observation deck, topped by an outdoor observation area designed with a glass floor and no visible barriers between visitors and the ground. The plans also called for meeting rooms and a lounge for the highest (literally) of the high rollers near the top.

But, wait: just below the antenna mast at the very tip of the tower, in the original plans, is a Sky Ride that will allow the bravest of the brave to occupy and control their own flight capsules around the top of the tower. On-board instruments will allow thrill-seekers to move up or down or to spin 360-degrees at the end of the support beam.

By the way, Las Vegas is subject to earthquakes, harsh desert winds, and the occasional underground nuclear test in the neighborhood. The designers assure us this has all been taken into account, including computer simulations and wind tunnel testing.

But, back away from the future: here's more about Vegas World as it exists today.

The small showroom at the hotel features a "Memories of Elvis Show" and B-level headliners.

The **El Paso Mexican Kitchens** is a fast food snack bar off the casino floor offering tacos, tamales, and the like for about $5 to $7. **Daisy's Kitchen** is a coffee shop with burgers, sandwiches, and entrees priced from about $4 to $12.

The best restaurant in the house is the small and intimate (60 seat) **Kelly & Cohen's,** open for dinner from 5 P.M. to 11 P.M. daily. It is located just off the casino floor but is well insulated from the hubbub outside its door; reservations are necessary most nights. Offerings, priced from about $15 to $25, include sirloin steak, medallions of beef marsala (slices of filet mignon sautéed with shallots, garlic, and mushrooms, glazed with marsala wine), and seafood offerings.

Bob Stupak's Vegas World, 2000 Las Vegas Blvd. South; 1,013 rooms; 382-2000; (800) 634-6277.

Chapter 7
The Rest of The Strip

Aladdin Hotel & Casino

A once-major hotel gone poof, the Aladdin is valiantly struggling to reinvent itself under new management. Opened in 1966, the hotel at one time was renowned for its huge theater, the 7,500-seat Aladdin Theater for the Performing Arts. Today, it is a sprawling and somewhat disorganized resort tottering on the edge of a descent into low rollerdom. New promotions include a "Country Tonite" show and Bingothons. The country show features a live band and a cast of 12 dancers.

The prime eatery at the Aladdin is the dark and relatively intimate **Fisherman's Port.** Specials on a recent visit, priced from about $15 to $30, include prime rib, steak au poivre, lobster fra diavolo, and fresh catches.

Wellington's Steak House offers beef, seafood, and chicken entrees, priced from $10 to $25. Open 5 to 11 P.M.

The **Market Place Buffet** serves breakfast, lunch, and dinner.

At the 24-hour **Oasis Coffee Shop,** the Late Nighters specials include eggs, sausage, and ham for about $3. Daytime specials on a recent visit included steak and lobster, prime rib, and orange-glazed chicken.

Sun Sun features Chinese, Vietnamese, and Korean cuisine. A complete meal of soup, fried rice, egg roll, selected entrees, and fortune cookie goes for less than $10. Other entrees, priced from about $13 to $20 on one visit included sizzling short ribs with black pepper sauce.

Aladdin Hotel & Casino, 3667 Las Vegas Blvd. South; 1,100 rooms; 736-0111; (800) 634-3424.

Elvis sighting number three. The King married Priscilla Beaulieu at the Aladdin in May of 1967. They met in Germany while Elvis was in the Army.

No short jokes, please. Wayne Newton was a short-time owner of the Aladdin.

Aladdin Hotel, Las Vegas

Alexis Park

This is one of the favorite hotels for visitors to Las Vegas who either don't want to visit the casinos, or who want to be able to find a better-than-decent hotel room without having to navigate through a quarter-mile of flashing neon and jangling slot machines.

The Alexis is half a mile east of The Strip, and any time you need to visit an Egyptian pyramid, a pirate galleon, or an Arthurian castle you can get there from here.

The Alexis includes 500 better-than-average rooms, including many multi-room suites. Several small, pricey restaurants offer gourmet fare. Guests can use a fully equipped health spa and lighted championship tennis courts. Because the hotel does not have the casino to bring in profits, room rates are a bit on the high side for Las Vegas.

Alexis Park Resort, 375 E. Harmon Ave.; 796-3300; (800) 582-2228.

Algiers Hotel

An old-style motor court with rooms centered around a pool, it is located across The Strip from Circus Circus. Nothing fancy but it's a decent place to stay and a good value; once you are into the inner courtyard it is surprisingly peaceful.

If you're a guest, be sure to check out the old black-and-white photographs of the hotel in its hey day; they're located on the wall near the registration desk.

Algiers Hotel, 2845 Las Vegas Blvd. South; 105 rooms; 735-3311.

Bally's

A high-quality joint, very well kept up but without much of an identity of its own. Bally's includes a large convention facility often used for overflow exhibits from some of the larger trade conferences, including the Comdex computer show and the Consumer Electronics Show, so the place really jumps when a big show is in town.

Some of the function rooms and decorations still bear reminders of the former incarnation as the original MGM Grand, with names like the Garland and Gable ballrooms.

In 1994, the hotel underwent another major transformation with the construction of a dramatic moving walkway structure from The Strip to its front door and the installation of a mirrored-glass facade to the main building. Future plans also call for the construction of a monorail that would link Bally's to its corporate distant cousin the MGM Grand a mile up the road.

The nearly 3,000 rooms at the hotel range from standard kings and doubles to Hollywood Suites and the extravagant Royal Penthouse Suites which rent for about $1,500 per night.

The **Big Kitchen Buffet** is one of the more attractive buffet rooms. The daily brunch-breakfast includes eggs, bacon, carved ham, shrimp, herring, and salads. Well isolated from the casino, the only reminder of where you are lies in the keno boards and runners. The buffet is a bit pricey by Vegas standards but worth

Smoky memory. Most of the guests at this huge high-tone hotel and casino have forgotten the images that filled network news shows on November 21, 1980, when the main wing of the MGM Grand burned for several awful hours, killing 84 guests and employees and injuring hundreds of others.

After renovations—including extensive fire detection and fireproofing efforts—the hotel was sold to the Bally Corporation in 1985. Today, Bally's may well be one of the safer hotels in Las Vegas with fire detection, control systems, and alarm systems at every turn. There's even a safety lecture broadcast on the in-house video system.

Behind the curtain. The big production show at the hotel for years is "Jubilee," which is your basic singing, dancing, and variety show with half-dressed girls. For those who want even more, you can purchase a ticket for a backstage tour of the stage, sets, and dressing rooms conducted by a dancer in costume. Check at the box office for details.

Faulty tower. The Landmark Hotel was a landmark of the rise and fall of Las Vegas fortunes.

You would think that this distinctive tower, with its rooftop showroom and prime location directly across the road from the bustling Las Vegas Convention Center where hundreds of thousands of conventioneers gather, would be a license to print money. However, the Landmark was never a success.

Begun in 1961, its developers ran out of money before it was completed, and it stood as a shell of a building for several years. It was finally finished in 1966, and in 1969 it was the sixth Las Vegas hotel purchased by Howard Hughes. Red ink continued to flow and after passing through several hapless owners, it was closed in 1991. Conventioneers eyed its barricaded parking lots and boarded-up casino as they strolled to or from the convention center. In 1994, the property was purchased at auction by the owners of the Riviera; they plan to take down the tower, although some residents planned to object to the removal of the Landmark landmark.

putting on your all-you-can-eat world tour. Brunch is served from 7:30 A.M. to 2:30 P.M. for $5.95; dinner is from 4:30 to 10 P.M. for $10.95.

A special **Sterling Brunch Sunday** is served in Caruso's Restaurant from 9 A.M. to 2:30 P.M. for $22.95.

Barrymore's Steak & Seafood is a simple, elegant, large room decorated in blacks and whites. Specialties include herb marinated chicken breast for about $20. Steaks and filet mignon range from $23.50 to $28 for a 24-ounce porterhouse. If you are a fan of lamb chops, on a recent visit you could order a set for about $26 with your choice of sauce: béarnaise, hollandaise, green peppercorn, horseradish cream or mint jelly. Broiled Lobster Tails went for about $37.50. Appetizers include Black Bean Soup and Oysters Rockefeller.

The *especialidades de la casa* at the Mexican restaurant **Las Olas,** priced from about $10 to $25, include *tampiquena* (skirt steak marinated in spices, grilled in a cheese enchilada) and *zihuatenejo* (salmon broiled with jalapenos and topped with Mexican hollandaise) for $10.95. Also offered are burritos, tacos, enchiladas, tostadas, and fajitas for about $4 to $10. You can wash it all down with a variety of Mexican beers.

A particularly interesting restaurant at Bally's is **Seasons,** with a wide range of American offerings. The menu on one visit included offerings from about $15 to $30 such as ballotine of rabbit in roasted pine nuts and sage, Pacific mahi mahi in lobster sauce, roast rack of lamb in rosemary and garlic, or a grilled veal chop in chantarelle sauce.

Caruso's is a world of Roman/rococo columns and mirrors, more elegant than Rome itself. Specialties, priced from about $15 to $25, included on a recent visit *linguini alla Sangiovannino* (linguini with porcini mushrooms, sun-dried tomatoes, and a dash of cream); *linguini con frutti del mare* (scallops, mussels, clams, and shrimp in a zesty sauce), and *pollo Angelo* (breast of chicken with mushrooms, artichokes, and fresh herbs).

The **Coffee Shop** is open 24 hours and includes a wide range of sandwiches, appetizers, and finger foods. Offerings, priced from about $5 to $15, include chicken wings, Cobb salad, veal cutlet parmesan, and the self-declared Bally's Famous Reuben.

Bally's Las Vegas, 3645 Las Vegas Blvd. South; 2,828 rooms; 739-4111.

Barbary Coast

A small place, almost possible to overlook in the glare of its neighbors, but actually worth a look-see. The Barbary Coast is decorated in a turn-of-the-century San Francisco motif with lots of wood, stained glass, and chandeliers. Dealers wear garters on their arms; cocktail waitresses wear the adornments on their upper legs.

Except for the sign for the McDonald's in the basement, you could almost believe you had been transported back in time. Actually, even the McDonald's sign is constructed from stained glass.

The few rooms at the Barbary Coast are elegantly appointed if you can get a reservation for one; they are mostly kept aside for the regular clientele.

There is no pool, no showroom, and few other amenities except for a pleasant ambiance—which is not a bad thing for a hotel/casino.

Barbary Coast, 3595 Las Vegas Blvd. South; 198 rooms; 737-7111; (800) 634-6755.

Desert Inn

Named after the considerably greener and officially gambling-free hotel in Palm Springs, California, the Desert Inn debuted in 1950. In typical Las Vegas fashion, the grand opening was a blast: ceremonies were made to coincide with the test of an atomic bomb outside of town. The Desert Inn's lure included its lush golf course, a regular stop on professional tours.

Its most famous owner was the reclusive Howard Hughes, who bought the resort in 1967, marking the start of a string of real estate purchases by Hughes.

Deserted again. Look for the new **Desert Kingdom** sometime in 1997, alongside the Desert Inn.

The $750 million, 3,500-room hotel, with a huge 135,000-square-foot casino and convention and meeting space about that large again, will be built by ITT Sheraton, which purchased the Desert Inn in 1993. Early plans call for installation of a 3,000-foot river that visitors can cruise as well as an outdoor attraction visible from the street. The property will be aimed at upper-middle-price visitors.

The Chairman's first office. Frank Sinatra made his Las Vegas debut in 1951 at the Desert Inn; it was the Sands, though, that served as his performing home for many years.

Strike central. The unionized staff members of the Frontier Hotel have been off the job for several years. They've settled into what seems to be a fixture of The Strip with around-the-clock picketing and small huts on the sidewalk. The hotel has remained open through it all; be aware of the situation if your travel agent offers you a special deal there.

Is that a deed in your pocket? Mae West was not only a successful entertainer, but she had a way with real estate, buying half a mile of undeveloped land on The Strip between the eventual site of the Dunes and Tropicana.

Las Vegas high. The official elevation at McCarran International Airport is 2,174 feet, which is low by mountain standards but still nearly half a mile higher than coastal cities like Boston or New York.

Elevations range from 470 feet along the Colorado River in the southernmost section of the state to 13,143 feet atop Boundary Peak on the border with California. The approximate mean elevation is 5,500 feet.

The Desert Inn is now one of the smaller but more posh complexes on The Strip, with just 821 rooms including 92 suites, located across from the Fashion Mall. It was purchased by ITT Sheraton in 1993. The hotel includes five restaurants and the Crystal Room showroom.

There is, of course, a casino with somewhat distracting overhead lighting and mirrors. It is small enough, though, to ignore if you choose.

Rooms are nicely appointed; some near the pool have cabana entrances to the water.

The nice variety of restaurants includes **Howan,** a Szechuan eatery with prix-fixe meals at about $26 per person for appetizer, pot stickers, sweet and sour soup, and *kung pao.* Dishes ordered from the menu range from $10 to $35 for Peking duck. Shark's fin soup is offered for about $22.

La Promenade is a pool-view coffee shop featuring salads and sandwiches. The two finest restaurants at the Desert Inn are **Monte Carlo** and **Portofino,** sharing the same grand glass elevator and marble foyer.

Portofino is a very elegant Italian restaurant. Pasta and other entrees range in price from about $10 to $30 and include *paglia e fieno* (green and white pasta with pancetta, peas, and mushrooms in a rosa cream sauce). Other specialties include *saltimbocca alla romana, osso buco Milanese con risotto* (braised veal shank with rice), *arigosta fra diavolo* (lobster in spicy red sauce over linguine), and *tonna alla griglia Adriatico* (fresh tuna with sweet pepper and a caper sauce).

Monte Carlo offers French cooking in a very elegant peaches-and-cream setting. Entrees range in price from $26 to $35, and include *le vieux favori* (steak Diane flamed in wine sauce with fresh mushrooms) for about $26.

Desert Inn Hotel & Country Club, 3145 Las Vegas Blvd. South; 821 rooms; 733-4444; (800) 634-6906.

The Dunes (Gone but Not Forgotten)

There were no (real) sand dunes in sight, but there was a heck of a golf course out back of this Strip veteran. The hotel and particularly the casino had a checkered past right from the moment of its opening in 1955, with numerous failures and near-failures.

The Dunes is also revered among some aficionados of Vegas for its pioneering contribution to local art: the topless show.

In 1993, the Dunes finally sank beneath the oncoming wave of development by Mirage Resorts. Actually, the hotel collapsed in a spectacular implosion that was part of the grand opening ceremonies for Mirage's Treasure Island hotel and casino; the demolition itself became the dramatic conclusion to a perfectly dreadful made-for-TV movie to promote the Treasure Island (and its publicity-loving chairman Steve Wynn).

In mid-1994, Mirage Resorts and Gold Strike Resorts announced plans to build a 3,000-room, $250 million themed hotel and casino at one end of the 164-acre site; the new property is intended as a low-roller attraction, with room rates projected at between $40 and $50 per night at opening in mid-1996. The deal allows Mirage to go for the low end of the market, while giving Gold Strike—a traditional "grind" operator—its first access to the Las Vegas Strip.

In addition, Mirage said it plans to build a luxury resort at the other end of the Dunes property; details were not announced.

The themes for the hotels have not been disclosed, although at the time of its purchase Mirage said it would turn the 164-acre site into a beach club resort centered around a 14-acre lake and modeled after the famous Fountainebleau Hotel in Miami Beach. The fanciful plans called for using the lake for major water sports events, including jet skiing, waterskiing, windsurfing, and parasailing. Nighttime attractions might include fireworks, boat parades, and cruises.

Among the attractions of the purchase was the fact that the Dunes has four wells on the property that produce over 1,000 acre-feet of non-potable water per year; the precious liquid is used to irrigate the Dunes Golf Course.

At the time of its purchase, the Mirage renamed and relaunched the former Dunes Golf and Country Club, calling it (surprise!) The Mirage Golf and Tennis Club. The course, one of the oldest in Las Vegas, stretches to 7,100 yards from the championship tees for men and 6,000 yards for women. Mirage plans to spend $2 million on redecoration of the clubhouse and installation of a new driving range and four lighted tennis courts.

Greens fees are $90 including cart. Reservations can be made by calling 369-7111.

> **Room service.**
> In Las Vegas, the average hotel room turns over every three or four days.

Dino and the kid. Dean Martin and Jerry Lewis made their Las Vegas debut at the Flamingo in October of 1948; by 1952, their movies made them the top box-office draw in the country.

Like mother. Liza Minelli's first contractual appearance in Las Vegas occurred in 1965 at the Sahara; eight years earlier, her mother Judy Garland had brought her on stage during an appearance at the Flamingo.

Company state. At the start of 1993, the Hilton chain was the largest employer in Nevada, surpassing the state.

Flamingo Hilton

Las Vegas would have to be one of the only places in the world where present owners proudly promote the gangster roots of the founder of the enterprise.

The original Flamingo was the invention in 1946 of Benjamin "Bugsy" Siegel, among the first of many underworld figures to recognize that they could make money from legal gambling at least as easily as they could from illegal activities.

Siegel built his 100-room pleasure palace in a spot that was at the time in the middle of nowhere, six miles south into the desert. He spent an astronomical $6 million and in the process began the world of Las Vegas glitz, a style that has not yet stopped escalating.

Less well known, though, is the fact that Bugsy's Flamingo had a very short life: it closed in January 1947 after just 14 days in business. Bugsy may have been a terrific gangster and certainly was possessed of a showman's vision, but he apparently was not the best businessman.

The hotel reopened later that year under new management, including front men for a different leading light of the underworld, Meyer Lansky. Lansky held onto a hidden interest in the hotel until late in the 1960s.

Still standing well into the 1990s was the Oregon Building, a rather unassuming low structure that included the fourth-floor penthouse once occupied by Bugsy Siegel. Features of the apartment reportedly included a trap door exit to a basement tunnel that leads to a neighboring building.

The Hilton Corporation became the first major hotel chain to "legitimize" the Las Vegas casino market when it purchased the Flamingo in 1971. Since then the company has been adding to the hotel complex almost continuously, building a series of five huge towers with a total of 3,530 rooms. What is called the "final" construction phase will add a 908-room sixth tower, 20,000 square feet of retail shopping, a new 20,000-square-foot buffet, and (of course) an additional 16,000 square feet of casino space. A new rooftop Grand Ballroom will include a glassed-in panoramic view of The Strip, and the rebuilt pool area will have a Hawaiian theme including waterfalls, water slides, and a variety of pools, lagoons, and water sports.

The new construction, alas, required the demolition of Bugsy's suite and the other low-rise garden buildings. According to the Hilton publicists, earlier hopes to make a "historical area" of the Oregon Building's Bugsy Suite had to be scrapped because of architectural complications.

Before the addition, the 50,000-square foot hall included 1,649 slot, video poker, and other gambling machines; 49 blackjack tables; 7 craps tables; two roulette and Big-Six wheels, two mini baccarat; one pai gow poker; and one sic bo table. The Flamingo Hilton also offers six poker tables including Texas Hold 'em and 7-card stud.

The long-running entertainment at the Flamingo Hilton is American Superstars at **Bugsy's Celebrity Theatre.** Impersonators do their best at Elvis, Cher, Little Richard, the Blues Brothers, the Temptations, and other entertainment icons. Tickets are sold at the Flamingo Tickets and Tour Booths in the North Tour Lobby or East Promenade, and are a relative Las Vegas bargain at about $14.95.

Heidi Thompson's imitation of Cher is complete down to the tattoo on her derriere. Men: unless you have an unfulfilled urge to play Sonny Bono, you are advised to stay out of the front rows of the theater.

Flamingo Hilton, 3555 Las Vegas Blvd. South; 3,530 rooms; 733-3111; (800) 732-2111.

Gold Coast

A K-Mart of a casino aimed at the low rollers, hidden behind a tremendous, blank stucco front wall. The Gold Coast features a sea of slot machines including an unusually large number of video poker machines. The Gold Coast sits next door to the Rio, a mile west of The Strip.

The main point of distinction for this hotel is the second floor 72-lane bowling alley (we can only imagine the noise level when all of the lanes are in use). There are also two movie theaters showing first-run movies and a bingo hall. At the back of the casino is a large dance hall featuring country and western high-kicking, with free classes offered. A liquor store sits directly off the casino.

There has been some attempt at creating an old California theme with pressed-tin ceilings and chandeliers, though not anywhere nearly as successfully as at the Barbary Coast on The Strip.

The **Buffet** is an unusually ordinary setting in one of the corners of the casino. Breakfast is served from 7 to 10:30 A.M. for $2.45, lunch is from 11 A.M. to 3 P.M. for $3.45, and dinner is from 5 P.M. to 9 P.M. for $5.45. On Mondays and Tuesdays, the buffet features prime rib; the Friday seafood specialties are salmon, crab legs, and shrimp. A Sunday brunch is served from 8 A.M. to 3 P.M. for $4.45.

Mediterranean offers pasta, veal, and chicken with entrees ranging in price from $4 to $8 in an ordinary room with a keno display on the wall.

Finally, there is **Terrible Mike's** for burgers and hot dogs, and **Kate's Korner** for ice cream and malts.

Gold Coast Hotel & Casino, 4000 West Flamingo Road; 750 rooms; 367-7111; (800) 331-5334.

The Hacienda

When it was built in 1956 near McCarran Airport, this hotel was miles away from the rest of the Las Vegas action. Over the ensuing years, though, The Strip has moved south to encompass the Hacienda; it now finds itself in the reflected gaudy glow of the Excalibur and the new Pyramid.

The Hacienda was, and is, a haven for low rollers. Among its pioneering efforts were some of the first gambling junkets; at one time it maintained its own fleet of 30 airplanes to bring the sheep in to be shorn.

Inside, though, the Hacienda is a pleasant world of southwestern arches and adobe. It is considerably quieter than its neighbors.

The **Charcoal Room** hides behind a massive wooden door, offering prime ribs, steaks, veal chops, chicken, and other steakhouse specialties, priced from about $17 to $30.

The **New York Pasta Company** offers linguine, ziti, fusilli, farfalle, bucatini, and all sorts of other Italian inis and itis with sauce, with prices from about $7 to $13; also available are individual pizzas for $7 to $8.

The **Cactus Room** is an attractive coffee shop with burgers, chicken dishes, and beef dishes priced from about $5 to $10.

The Hacienda's buffet room is one of the prettiest in town, with a window wall facing the mountains.

Hacienda, 3950 Las Vegas Blvd. South; 1,140 rooms; 739-8911; (800) 634-6713.

Harrah's Las Vegas

What was once the largest Holiday Inn in the world is now one of the largest landlocked Mississippi riverboats, or at least so it would seem from the outside. The distinctive exterior covers an attractive hotel and, of course, a casino.

The hotel, which includes 1,725 rooms and suites, is based on a Bourbon Street and New Orleans French Quarter design, with its 450-foot-long Mississippi riverboat facade, complete with 20-story smoke stacks and a 5-story paddle wheel.

The casino offers 1,900 slot and video poker machines and a 200-seat bingo parlor with continuous games from 10:30 A.M. to 1 A.M.

Entertainment includes the 525-seat **Commander's Theatre** where "Spellbound—A Concert of Illusion" has settled in for a long run.

The **Galley Buffet** features at least 35 items. Breakfast is served from

7 A.M. to 11 A.M. for $3.79, lunch from 11 A.M. to 4 P.M. for $3.99, and dinner is from 4 P.M. to 11 P.M. for $5.49.

Claudines presents steak and fresh seafood in turn-of-the-century decor for dinner from 5:30 to 10:30 P.M. Wednesday through Sunday.

All That Jazz offers low-priced breakfasts from 7 A.M. to noon, and Southern-style dinner including ribs, shrimp, and catfish from 5 P.M. to 11 P.M.

Joe's Bayou features Cajun and Southern specialties such as gumbo, jambalaya, blackened red snapper, frog legs, and catfish in a Louisiana bayou setting.

The Veranda Cafe is Harrah's 24-hour coffee shop.

A Bit of Harrah's History

Harrah's Casino Hotels is part of The Promus Companies, the only gaming firm that operates resorts in all five major U.S. casino markets: Las Vegas, Reno, Laughlin, Lake Tahoe, and Atlantic City. The company claims about a 10 percent share of the total U.S. gaming market.

Other hotels in the chain include Harrah's Laughlin, a 1,658-room establishment designed to look like a Mexican village, the only hotel-casino in Laughlin with a private soft sand beach. Harrah's also operates the 565-room Harrah's Reno, the 760-room Harrah's Atlantic City, the Harrah's Lake Tahoe Resort Casino, and Bill's Lake Tahoe Casino. Harrah's began

Harrah's, Las Vegas

School's open. Harrah's is one of several major casinos that offer classes on how to lose more money. Courses, taught by Captain Casino or the Riverboat Gambler take place at various locations in the casino from Monday to Friday.

An able employer. The Imperial Palace has gone out of its way to be sensitive to the needs of the disabled, both in providing employment and in offering adapted accommodations for guests with special needs. The hotel's showroom includes infrared listening devices for guests with hearing difficulties. Available rooms include special features for visitors with a wide range of special needs.

operating two casino riverboats in Joliet, Illinois, and one in Vicksburg, Mississippi, in 1993. Promus was created in 1990 as a spin-off of the Holiday Corp. Holiday sold its worldwide Holiday Inn Hotel chain to Bass PLC of Great Britain and established Promus as a gaming and lodging company. In addition to Harrah's, Promus also owns Embassy Suites, Hampton Inn, and Homewood Suites.

Harrah's Las Vegas Casino Hotel, 3475 Las Vegas Blvd. South; 1,725 rooms; 359-5000; (800) 634-6765.

Imperial Palace

An eclectic place with a mildly Oriental theme, this deceptively large hotel (more than 2,700 rooms) sprawls up, down, left, and right from its location at the heart of The Strip, across from the Mirage and Caesars Palace.

One reason for the chock-a-block disorganization of the place may lie in its origins as a one-man band, the dream of contractor Ralph Engelstad who began by buying the old Flamingo Capri Motel in 1971. Construction has continued almost continually since then.

Today, by Las Vegas standards the IP is a bit on the ordinary side, although it has one distinction that is a secret to many visitors. Hidden away on an upper floor of a parking garage in back is an amazing collection of antique and unusual cars.

Even if you are not the sort to gush over a classic 1928 Cadillac Dual Cowl Phaeton or an antique 1906 Ford Model K Touring Car restored to mint condition, there are other reasons to visit the museum. Concentrate instead on the history of vehicles used by world leaders, or come close to the transportation of some of the greatest stars of the 20th century. *Look for more details on the car collection in the section of this book about Museums in Las Vegas.*

There's a nominal admission charge for the museum, but you can often obtain free passes from casino employees who are stationed at the front entrance of the Imperial Palace. The museum is open every day, late into the night. *You will also find a free pass for two in the coupon section of this book.*

The large casino is a busy place and you may need to drop bread crumbs to find your way back to your room when you try to make your way out. The best rooms can be found in the newer tower; the hotel features an Olympic-size swimming pool and health and fitness center. The long-running show at the Imperial Theatre Showroom is "Legends in Concert" which features re-creations of musical greats, including Elvis (surprise!), the Beatles, Buddy Holly, Liberace, Roy Orbison, Nat King Cole, Marilyn Monroe, and Judy Garland. Legends is presented twice nightly, except Sundays.

The Imperial Palace features a double-handful of restaurants, including the **Teahouse,** a 24-hour coffee shop, and the large **Emperor's Buffet.** Just to make things confusing, there is also a slightly more upscale buffet, for dinner only, called the **Imperial Buffet,** which is served in the Teahouse after 5 P.M.

Standard fare at the Teahouse Coffee Shop includes a steak sandwich or chicken pot pie for about $6 to $8.

Embers, tucked away on the third floor, offers steak, seafood, and Continental dishes in an intimate setting; it is open 5 P.M. to 11 P.M. Wednesday through Sunday with reservations suggested. Menu offerings may include items such as orange roughy sautéed with macadamia nuts for about $15 and Alaskan king crab legs with lemon drawn butter for about $29.

Imperial Palace, Las Vegas

Wild palms. The palm trees of Las Vegas are not from Las Vegas; in fact, they are not indigenous to the United States. They were imported by the early developers of The Strip to give some "class" to the somewhat barren desert. If it makes you feel any better, many of the palm trees of California and Florida are similarly out of place. Some of the palm trees close to the flames at The Mirage's volcano are not native to anywhere on this planet: they are constructed out of fireproof concrete.

Seahouse. A semi-nautical setting with offerings including stuffed mushrooms with crabmeat, and shrimp fettuccine. Entrees priced from about $10 to $20. Open 5 P.M. to 11 P.M. Friday through Tuesday with reservations suggested.

Other self-describing eateries include **Rib House** (5 to 11 P.M. Thursday through Monday), **Pizza Palace** (daily from 11 A.M. to midnight), and **Burger Palace. Betty's Diner** features ice cream, sandwiches, hot dogs, and snacks.

The **Ming Terrace** restaurant features Mandarin and Cantonese cuisine and is open daily from 5 P.M. to midnight. Among out-of-the-ordinary offerings are egg flower soup, black mushroom and sea cucumber stew, and sour cabbage with beef. Entrees range from about $10 to $20.

The various bars in the casino area each bear Japanese names: Geisha, Ginza, Kanpai, Mai Tai, Nomiya, and Sake. Probably the most unusual watering hole in the hotel is the Duesenberg Lounge in the Duesenberg Room of the Auto Collection; aside from the decidedly unusual setting you will also want to check out the antique western bar itself, which is straight out of the Gunsmoke era.

The Imperial Palace is located at the heart of The Strip, across from the Mirage and Caesars Palace. There is a small streetfront casino on The Strip with a set of escalators that can bring you under the hotel entrance driveway to the main casino. Look for various come-ons out front, including cheap popcorn and hot dogs, drink coupons, discounts on shows, and passes to the auto museum.

Imperial Palace Hotel & Casino, 3535 Las Vegas Blvd. South; 2,700 rooms; 731-3311; (800) 634-6441.

Palace Station Hotel & Casino

The Palace is off the beaten track for most visitors, but it's a favorite of Las Vegas locals primarily because of its restaurants. It's no small place, with more than 1,000 rooms and a large and lively casino with 2,200 slots and a 600-seat bingo parlor. Out-of-towners can use the hotel's shuttle bus for free transport to The Strip, about a mile east.

The hotel began simply named The Casino in 1976, the first area operation west of The Strip. It later took on the name Bingo Palace, concentrating on locals for business. In the 1980s, more expansion and a railroad theme was added, and the complex took on its present name.

Fisherman's Broiler was chosen as the best seafood restaurant in Las Vegas in a local newspaper's reader poll four out of five years. Offerings on a recent visit included mesquite broiled mahi mahi, halibut, catfish, red snapper, and other fish for $11 to $15. Landlubbers can also order steak and chicken dishes, priced from about $14 to $18.

The Feast is called an "action buffet" by the management, because many of the dishes are prepared for guests as they wait. These include breakfast omelettes made to order, stir-fry, broiled steaks, and grilled chicken. The Feast often wins "best" ratings from the locals, although on my visits it ranked in the second tier below spectacular offerings like those of the Rio, Caesars Palace, and the Golden Nugget.

The **Guadalajara Bar & Grille** offers authentic Mexican food along with Tex-Mex cuisine and southwestern fare. Specialties, priced from as low as $5 all the way up to $40, include shrimp Guadalajara (shrimp stuffed with cheese, wrapped with bacon, and charbroiled) and crab meat enchiladas. The Guadalajara is also known for its cheap margaritas.

The **Iron Horse Cafe** is opened 24 hours a day. The breakfast special is called the skillet breakfast, served in a cast-iron skillet containing three eggs, ham, sausage or bacon, home-fried potatoes, and all the toast or pancakes you can eat. Iron Horse also serves Chinese food from 11 A.M. to 5 A.M., with graveyard specials nightly from 11 P.M. to 5 A.M.

For lighter fare, there's the **Pasta Palace,** featuring pasta, scampi, veal, and pizza cooked in a woodburning oven. It's open daily for dinner from 5 P.M. to 11 P.M. Nightly specials include steak or lobster dinners.

Palace Station Hotel & Casino, 2411 W. Sahara Avenue; 1,041 rooms; 367-2411; (800) 634-3101.

San Remo

Part of the Ramada group, the San Remo began as a lure to the business traveler and as such delivers decent rooms and service. There is, of course, a casino, too. Recent expansions have added a bit more glitz and a lot more rooms.

The San Remo is located about a block east of The Strip, next door to its corporate flashy neighbor, the Tropicana.

The fancy restaurant at the San Remo is **Le Panache.** Closed Mondays and Tuesdays, gourmet dining is offered from 5 P.M. to 11 P.M. Specials, priced from about $16 to $25, included on a recent visit filet and lobster, porterhouse steak, *cotelette de veau maison* (veal chop stuffed with mushroom duxelle and topped with Montrachet cheese and concasse of tomato), and *crevettes kiev* (large prawns stuffed with herb butter and crab meat). The specialty soup is *le bisque d'homard maison* (lobster bisque, seasoned with french cognac, garnished with lobster meat).

Pasta Remo offers fine Italian dining from 5 P.M. to midnight. Lighter fare, including Italian subs and salads, is available at **Luigi's Deli.**

The **Ristorante dei Fiori** coffee shop and buffet is open 24 hours. At the time of our visit, a prime rib special for $3.95 had a small catch: you had to show a room key from any other Las Vegas hotel and register at the Money Club window. With such deals, though, there is no requirement you gamble.

The **Sushi Bar,** open from 6 P.M. to midnight, offers prix-fixe assortments for $16 to $22. Miso soup is priced at $1.50.

The **Buffet** is available for breakfast from 7 A.M. to 10 A.M. for $3.50, lunch is served from 11 A.M. to 2 P.M. for $5.95, and dinner is from 5 P.M. to 9 P.M. for $6.95. A Saturday and Sunday champagne brunch is offered 7 A.M. to 2 P.M. for $5.95.

San Remo Casino & Resort, 115 East Tropicana Avenue; 711 rooms; 739-9000; (800) 522-7366.

The Riviera

A grand creation intended to bring a touch of the Côte d'Azur to the desert floor, the Riviera collapsed into bankruptcy almost immediately after its opening in 1955. A series of subsequent owners, including the Chicago mob, restored it to health, and there was a tremendous spurt of new construction that culminated in another bankruptcy in 1983. Its latest new owners have given it a major spruce-up since.

The Riviera includes one of the largest casinos in town, at 125,000 square feet. Although there is not much pedestrian traffic on The Strip, the casino does have an open front like some of the downtown joints. Inside is a riot of reds and golds.

The **Rik Shaw** is an ordinary name for a lovely place to eat. A wide variety of entrees range in price from about $10 to $40. Specialties include abalone and black mushrooms for about $40, scallops with asparagus, and shrimp with pine nuts. Appetizers include crabmeat and asparagus soup, about $11, and abalone and chicken soup for about $28.

An overly simple name for a nice place is

> **Odd couple number one.** Marlene Dietrich and Louis Armstrong appeared together at the Riviera in 1962.

> **Citizen Welles.** Orson Welles, a star of radio and cinema, appeared on stage at the Riviera in 1956 with a spectacular magic act.

> **Elvis sighting number four/odd couple number two.** Elvis Presley posed on stage in 1956 in a gold lamé jacket at the Riviera piano while Liberace, wearing Elvis' rocker duds, whipped at a guitar.

> **The chandelier was extra.** Liberace opened the Riviera Hotel in 1955, with a record-setting contract paying $50,000 per week.

Ristorante, a classy Italian eatery decorated with brass, brick, and statuary with a fake skyline of Rome outside the painted "windows." It also has one of the more elaborate espresso machines in town. Specialties, priced from about $16 to $40, include calamari fritti, lobster fra diavolo, chicken vesuvio, veal piccata, and veal francaise.

Kady's Brasserie is a 24-hour coffee shop. Sandwiches and burgers range from about $6 to $8. At the time of our visit, an overnight special offered one pound of snow crab legs for $10, or steak and lobster for $8.88.

Kristofer's offers chicken, steak, filet mignon, or lobster tail for about $20 to $23.

Okay, we get the idea: they like simple names around here. The Riviera buffet is called the **Buffet** and breakfast is offered from 7 A.M. to 10:45 A.M. for $3.95, lunch is from 11 A.M. to 3 P.M. for $4.95, and dinner is from 4:30 P.M. to 11 P.M. for $6.95. Special themes are Mexican on Monday, Italian on Tuesday, Oriental on Wednesday, Hawaiian on Thursday, international on Friday and Saturday, and western barbecue on Sunday.

Riviera Hotel & Casino, 2901 Las Vegas Blvd. South; 2,136 rooms; 734-5110; (800) 634-6753.

Debbie Reynolds Hotel/Casino

Yes, that's Debbie Reynolds, with her very own small hotel, casino, and museum, with a nightly show starring D.R. herself. The 193-room hotel is between the Las Vegas Convention Center and The Strip, the former Paddlewheel Hotel. The hotel's marketing plans attempt to appeal to the mature visitor, presumably including the core of Reynolds' fans.

The **Hollywood Movie Museum** in the hotel includes Reynolds' private collection of memorabilia including treasures from *The Wizard of Oz,* Marilyn Monroe's "subway" dress from *The Seven Year Itch,* and Elizabeth Taylor's "entrance to Rome" costume from *Cleopatra.* Some of the decorations in the lobby are props from films.

> **Filmography.** Debbie Reynolds appeared in 32 major motion pictures, from classics like *Singin' in the Rain* and *The Unsinkable Molly Brown* to cult favorites including *Tammy, How the West Was Won* and even *The Singing Nun.* And for those who must know, Ms. Reynolds was born in 1932.

Reynolds appears in the 500-seat Star Theatre Tuesdays through Sundays; on Fridays and Saturdays she hosts a musical and comedy jam session until deep into the night at the **Celebrity Cafe.** Her schedule of appearances in 1995 was expected to include at least half the year; if you are a serious Debbie-phile, be sure to check with the hotel before making plans.

Debbie Reynolds Hotel/Casino/Hollywood Movie Museum, 305 Convention Center Drive; 734-0711; (800) 633-1177.

> **I want to hold your cash.** The Beatles put on a pair of concerts in 1964 under the sponsorship of the Sahara, but held at the large Las Vegas Convention Center. Tickets for the show averaged $4, and the Beatles were paid $25,000 for the appearance.

> **BINGO!** The Club Bingo opened in 1947 across the road from the El Rancho Vegas and featured a 300-seat bingo parlor in addition to more ordinary games. It was remodeled and renamed as the Sahara in 1952.

The Sahara Hotel & Casino

Another golden Strip oldie, it opened in 1952 and was an immediate sensation for the size and gaudiness of its gigantic outdoor sign. Actually, it can draw its lineage back to the Club Bingo, which opened in 1947 and featured a 300-seat bingo parlor. It was sold, remodeled, and opened as the Sahara five years later. At the time, it was the first casino visitors would come to as they left downtown for The Strip.

The Sahara was designed with an African theme, including statues of camels out front. Plaster Arabs with camels are still out front, but today the once-grand Sahara seems a bit ground down by the sands of time.

There's a sprawling casino, twisting and turning here and there and including a collection of old-style reel slot machines. The African theme is faintly echoed with waitresses in leopard-skin sarong-like outfits.

The long-running show at the Sahara is "Boy-Lesque," a female impersonation show starring Kenny Kerr; if this is the sort of thing you like, here is a fine example.

The showplace restaurant is **House of Lords,** a private and quiet room decorated in reds and blacks. Entrees, priced from about $21 to $30, include rack of lamb, chateaubriand, prime rib, and lobster tail.

The **Turf Club** offers a range of sandwiches from about $6 to $9 including the lox burger (lox, cream cheese, onion, and tomato on a bagel).

The **Caravan Coffee Shop** offers nightly specials such as New York steak and lobster for $8.88, or New York steak and eggs for $2.95.

The **Oasis Buffet** is upstairs and away from the bustle; the food, though, is spectacularly ordinary.

Sahara Hotel & Casino, 2535 Las Vegas Blvd. South; 737-2111; (800) 634-6411.

Sands

In this one hotel/casino can be seen a great part of the modern history of Las Vegas. The Sands has gone from a shady past to a Hollywood connection to Howard Hughes to a mega-corporation to its current ownership by the sponsor of the huge computer convention that descends on Las Vegas once a year.

The Sands opened in 1952 with 200 rooms. It had been built by Texas gaming entrepreneur Jakie Friedman and an assortment of gangsters from around the country. Also among the owners were Frank Sinatra and Dean Martin who each held significant minority interests. Their business involvement made it natural for them to make the Sands their stage for Las Vegas appearances, and also attracted their friends including the famous Rat Pack.

Opening act. The Sands in 1952 featured Danny Thomas at its debut; also appearing were Billy Eckstine and Jane Powell.

The hotel was purchased by Howard Hughes' Summa Corporation in 1966; soon thereafter there was a falling out with Frank Sinatra, who moved his act to Caesars Palace. In 1981, the hotel was sold to a new Texas owner,

Odd couple number three. Former President Harry S Truman appeared at the piano with Jimmy Durante at the Sands in 1962.

but two years later Summa regained control of the hotel. In 1988, it was purchased by Kirk Kerkorian's MGM Grand, Inc., but in one of the more interesting twists of ownership, two months later the Sands ended up in the hands of the Interface Group, the sponsor of the Comdex computer trade show that virtually takes over Las Vegas for a week each year. Interface added a giant 610,000-square-foot convention center at the back of the Sands property.

The Sands Expo & Convention Center is used primarily for the annual Comdex convention. The first phase built about 615,000 square feet of convention space on one level, plus an underground lot for 1,100 cars; future plans call for enlarging the center to 1,000,000 square feet, which would make it the world's largest single-level convention facility.

In days past, the Copa Room was one of the hangouts for the famed Rat Pack of Frank Sinatra, Sammy Davis, Jr., Joey Bishop, Dean Martin, and Peter Lawford, each of whom also appeared on stage at the Sands.

The premier dining establishment is the **Regency Room,** open from 6 P.M. to 11 P.M. nightly; reservations are suggested. The room is elegantly paneled in wood, with widely spaced tables. Its menu features Las Vegas specialties, priced from about $20 to $32, such as steak Diana, Long Island duckling, veal francaise, and lobster tail and filet mignon. Appetizers include oysters Rockefeller.

The **Garden Terrace** is a California-theme coffee shop with a view of internal gardens. A breakfast buffet and menu are available, featuring selections including omelettes for about $5. Lunch offerings when we visited included tuna salad club with cucumbers, egg, and tomato for about $6. Dinner specials, priced from around $15 to $20, included lamb chops with mint jelly, and a whole Maine lobster buffet, including pasta, side dishes, and salads nightly except Saturday. (In case you're interested, and very hungry, you are limited to three lobsters per person.) Overnight specials included steak and eggs or ham and eggs for $2.99.

The **House of Szechwan,** an attractive, tiny room decorated with mirrors and lanterns, opens at 4 P.M. Appetizer specialties include *gee po gai* (paper-wrapped chicken). Entrees, about $12 to $18 each, include such dishes as *chow siong sin* Double Happiness, (a combination of shrimp and scallops with fresh vegetables in wine sauce) and oyster beef (sliced beef sautéed with scallions, snow peas, sliced mushrooms, and Chinese oyster sauce). Early bird specials are available Monday through Friday.

Sands Hotel Casino, 3355 Las Vegas Blvd. South; 720 rooms; 733-5000; (800) 634-6901.

The Stardust

A venerable establishment, if you are somehow able to overlook an extremely checkered history of involvement by various factions of organized crime. For many years, the hotel was a semi-legit operation of the Chicago mob, a connection which ended with the discovery of a massive "skimming" scandal—the raking off of profits from gaming operations before they were recorded and subject to taxation.

The Stardust was famous for its reproduction of the "Lido de Paris" floorshow, which saved millions on costume expenses for its showgirls, many of whom were dressed only in, err, stardust. The Lido finally departed a few years back, after more than 30 years on stage. The current show is "Enter the Night," which features just a bit more glitz than sex.

There is a Stardust and a Stardust: the newer West Tower building is quite nice; the old strips of low motel buildings at the back of the hotel are generally not the sort of place you'd want to write home about, and the East Tower is somewhere in between.

The classy **William B's Steakhouse** is decorated like an old Chicago steakhouse in black and white. Entrees range from $15 to $20. Specialties include petite filet mignon for $16; king porterhouse for $20, and boneless double center cut pork chop for $16. Veal or chicken dishes are offered with your choice of style of preparation including oskar, marsala, angelo, francaise, parmigiana, piccata, and William B (coated with flour and served with avocado and crab).

The **Tres Lobos Mexican Restaurant and Cantina** is open for dinner only, from Wednesday to Sunday, with entrees priced from $5.95. Food is attractively presented in this lively room just off the casino floor.

On the menu at **Ralph's Diner** they say: "If it is not on the menu—ask. We'll see." They don't say what they'll do, though. Options that are listed on the menu include burgers for about $5 and chili for a bit less.

There's a branch of the **Tony Roma's** chain, offering a full slab of baby back ribs, barbecue chicken and ribs combo, and a half barbecue chicken, priced from about $9 to $16.

Toucan Harry's is an attractive coffee shop decorated with palms and brass. Dinner specials included half orange glazed chicken, fantail shrimp, and steak and lobster for $5 to $8. A 24-hour special is eggs with bacon or sausage for about $4.

The Stardust's **Warehouse Buffet** is one of the better buffets in town, set in a reproduction of a food locker, with huge industrial-sized cans of food stacked about. The food is, thankfully, fresher than that. Breakfast Monday through Saturday is served from 7 A.M. to 10:30 A.M. for $4.95, lunch is from 10:30 A.M. to 3 P.M. for $5.95, and dinner every night is from 4 P.M. to 10 P.M. for $7.95. A Sunday champagne brunch is offered 7 A.M. to 3 P.M. for $6.95.

Stardust Resort & Casino, 3000 Las Vegas Blvd. South; 2,340 rooms; 732-6111; (800) 634-6033.

The Tropicana

An interesting mix of colorful Miami schmaltz and flashy Las Vegas glitz, the Trop is among the favorite "old" hotels on The Strip. First built in 1957, it has had its share of mob intrigue and corruption over the years. It was restored in recent years under the ownership of the Ramada Corporation.

Once all alone at the top of The Strip, now it is almost possible to miss in the flow of the flashy Excalibur, Luxor, and MGM Grand across the road. In 1994, though, they added to the overdose at the corner with a Caribbean Village facade and a new main entrance; in case you still miss the point, a nightly laser light show is presented.

The leaded stained-glass ceiling above the tables in the casino is worth a peek, and lovers of Miami staples such as dancing water fountains and chandeliers will not be disappointed. Machines sit under a blue sky in a forest of bamboo trees. Overall, it's a lively place, well kept up.

In keeping with its tropical theme, there is an emphasis on watery decorations including a five-acre water park with lagoons, spas, waterfalls, and what is claimed as the world's largest indoor/outdoor swimming pool. There are dozens of exotic birds and fish in surrounding cages and pools.

There is even a swim-up blackjack table. The entire area is carefully lit at night, including a laser light show.

Standard rooms are somewhat ordinary, jutting off long, long boring hallways.

The long-playing show at the Trop is the "Folies Bergere," which features $5 million in sets and costumes.

There's an attractive **Food Court** offering ice cream, pizza, hot dogs, and deli specialties.

The **Rhapsody Brunch** is in an elegant setting which includes a sushi bar and a selection of smoked fish. Entrees range from about $18 to $30 and include duckling Chambord (Long Island duckling with black raspberry liqueur). The obligatory Las Vegas appetizer of oysters Rockefeller is available for about $10.

Mizuno is your basic tableside barbecue teppen yaki restaurant. The **Ristorante di Martino** offers Italian specialties in a simple and modern decor. And there is the **El Gaucho Steak House** for meat, chicken, and seafood offerings.

The **Winners Coffee Shop** is a somewhat ordinary place, overly bright under fluorescent bulbs.

Tropicana Resort and Casino, 3801 Las Vegas Blvd. South; 1,910 rooms; 739-2222; (800) 634-4000.

Chapter 8
Glitter Gulch

Downtown Las Vegas is where it all started, and though the flashiest and largest of the casinos have moved south to The Strip, there is still a great deal of life and excitement on Fremont Street.

In fact, it is often the neon splash of Fremont—nicknamed Glitter Gulch—that is used as the picture to represent all of Las Vegas. The lights of the various signs are so bright in the narrow manmade canyon that pedestrians enjoy electric noon at midnight.

While The Strip is (mostly) opulent, Glitter Gulch is (mostly) wide open and a lot of fun. And, according to gambling experts, the downtown casinos pay off a bit better on their slots and many table games including blackjack. Although some of the side streets of downtown are a bit scary, even to the locals, a visitor who parks in one of the casino parking garages off Fremont Street can enjoy a manmade wonder worth a stroll and a visit.

MUST-SEE Golden Nugget Hotel & Casino

Part of the Mirage dynasty, the Golden Nugget is the class of downtown. The lively casino is decorated with a San Francisco theme, painted in white and gold with ornate chandeliers and ceiling fans. The new tower at the hotel is a local landmark with its brilliant gold reflective glass.

Be sure to walk deep into the casino to a display case near the registration desk to check out a few real golden nuggets. The most impressive is the Hand of Faith Nugget, which is claimed to be the world's largest piece of unrefined gold. Weighing in at 875 troy ounces (almost 62 pounds) it was discovered with a metal detector by a young man prospecting behind his trailer home in 1980 near Wedderburn, in Victoria, Australia.

As aficionados of the brewing art, we were most impressed with the central **38 Different Kinds of Beer Bar,** which delivers guess-how-

<table>
<tr><td>

How many kinds?
Available American brands at the 38 Different Kinds of Beer Bar on one visit included Coor's, Anchor Steam, Budweiser, Michelob, Miller, Pete's Wicked Ale, and Rattlesnake. Also available are Australia's Foster's and Red Back; Canada's Labatt's and Moosehead; China's Tsingtao; England's Bass Ale and Watney's Red Barrel; Germany's St. Pauli Girl, Beck's, and Hofbräu; Holland's Heineken, Amstel, and Grolsch; Ireland's Harp Lager and Guinness Stout; Italy's Peroni; Japan's Sapporo and Asahi; Mexico's Bohemia, Carta Blanca, Dos Equis, Corona, Simpatico, Pacifico, and Negra Modelo; the Philippine's San Miguel Pale; Scotland's McEwan's Ale; and Switzerland's Lowenbräu.

</td></tr>
</table>

many-kinds of guess-what. Each of the restaurants at the Golden Nugget is a small gem, too. They include:

Stefano's. A truly lovely small room, well insulated from the casino. Decorated like a real Roman hideaway, only much cleaner and newer. You'll be served by flocks of waiters in long aprons. A few sample offerings from one recent visit: *penne Bolognese* (fluted penne pasta served with veal meat sauce) or *zuppa de pesce "cioppino"* (shrimp, scallops, lobster, and squid in a light tomato fish broth) for about $22.

Lillie Langtrie's. Another lovely room, decorated in gold and mirrors and serving Cantonese fare by way of San Francisco. (Lillie, also known as the Jersey Lily, was an English actress who made her name in the United States with a tour in the 1880s that included the Wild West, becoming the Madonna of her day.)

California Pizza Kitchen. An outpost of the California-based wood-fired pizza chain (another location is within the Mirage on The Strip) it features more than 25 varieties of pizza ranging from the traditional to the unusual (BLT, barbecue chicken, duck sausage, Cajun, and goat cheese toppings among them) in personal sizes priced from about $7 to $10 on regular or honey-wheat dough. We were also intrigued by the possibility of a *moo-shu* chicken calzone.

Golden Nugget Buffet. Breakfast Monday through Saturday from 7 A.M. to 10:30 A.M. for $4.75, lunch is 10:30 A.M. to 3 P.M. for $7.50, dinner is 4 to 10 P.M. for $9.50, and a champagne Sunday brunch is 8 to 10 P.M. for $9.95.

Poker Parlor Snack Bar. Is this mix strange enough for a poker parlor? We think so: teriyaki chicken sandwich, assorted California sushi rolls, or grilled Spam with steamed rice, each for about $4.

Golden Nugget Hotel & Casino; 129 East Fremont Street; 1,907 rooms; 385-7111; (800) 634-3454.

Las Vegas Club

A lively, informal small club with a high mirrored ceiling, the Las Vegas Club holds a special attraction for baseball and blackjack fans.

The casino claims the most liberal blackjack rules in the world; the somewhat complex rules do seem to reduce the house advantage, at least for experienced and knowledgeable players.

Among the special rules are these: you can double down on any of the first two or three cards; you can surrender your original two cards for half your bet; you can split and resplit aces up to two times; you can split and resplit any pair any time you choose, and any hand of six cards totaling 21 or less is an automatic winner. The Las Vegas Club somewhat compensates for its loose rules by dealing cards from a multi-deck shoe, reducing the edge for card counters.

But back to the atmosphere: you'll notice things are a bit different when you see the uniforms worn by the dealers; instead of white shirts and string ties, they are each decked out in baseball jerseys. The cocktail waitresses wear cheerleader outfits.

Take the hint and head toward the back of the casino to examine the great collection of old sports photos and memorabilia—mostly baseball and boxing—near the Dugout Restaurant. Photos on the wall date back as far as the 1920s.

Among the favorite sports stars is former speedster Maury Wills; you'll find his original 1950 minor league contract to the Hornell Baseball Association in upstate New York. He was paid a whopping $150 a month with a $500 signing bonus. Also on display are Wills', shoes from 1962, the year he set a major league record with 104 stolen bases.

(Wills, by the way, had a short career on stage in Vegas; among his appearances was at the Sahara in 1969 where he played saxophone.)

Food service at the Las Vegas Club is better than at the ballpark:

The Dug Out. At a recent visit, the All Star Special was eastern prime rib au jus for about $6. The three-egg hall of fame omelettes go for about $5 and are available in cheese; ham and cheese; and spinach, chili, and cheese varieties.

Great Moments Room. Specialties, priced about $13 to $20, include *scalone,* a combination of abalone and shrimp sautéed and finished with light white wine and garlic sauce, for about

Sky high. North Las Vegas, a few miles beyond downtown, is the home of Nellis Air Force Base. The North Las Vegas Air Show takes place each fall, usually near the end of October, drawing tens of thousands of visitors. Events include all sorts of aircraft, hot air balloons, vintage autos, and various celebrations of Indian heritage.

Truth in advertising. On The Strip heading into downtown, keep an eye out for the tiny Normandie Hotel on the left, a rather jarring pink stucco motor court. On one visit, the sign outside proclaimed, "Elvis Slept Here."

We suspect it was on an off night.

(By the way, the other side of the sign read, "Highly Recommended by Owner.")

$14. Also offered on a recent visit was a julienne of grilled boneless breast of chicken over fresh garden greens with sesame oil and balsamic vinegar, and lemon chicken scallopini.

Las Vegas Club Hotel & Casino, 18 E. Fremont Street; 385-1664.

Binion's Horseshoe Hotel & Casino

One of the eclectic oddities of Nevada, and worth a visit. It's a rambling, dim place semi-decorated in dark browns, blacks, and reds.

Benny Binion was one of Las Vegas' oldtime gambling men who ran a casino, which is quite different from today's business people who own gambling casinos. However, Steve Wynn, the flamboyance behind the Mirage and Treasure Island, was a protégé of Binion in his younger days.

Binion created his Horseshoe in the late 1940s out of two old downtown properties, the Apache Hotel and the Eldorado Casino. Today the casino has absorbed an entire city block.

> **Trivia question.** Who is pictured on a $10,000 bill? The answer: Salmon Chase, Chief Justice of the U.S. Supreme Court under President Lincoln and a major political figure of his time.
>
> Here's an even more obscure question: What is pictured on the back of a $10,000 bill? The answer: nothing. It says in big print: "The United States of America. Ten Thousand Dollars."
>
> And for those of you whose minds run to investment strategies, consider this: if the million dollars in the case was invested in a 10 percent account compounded monthly, it would be earning about $105,000 per year; at the same interest rate over the course of 10 years, the million would have grown to $2.7 million.

Work your way all the way in to the back of the casino and stand for a moment and gawk at the display of a cool million dollars in bills. There are 20 rows and five columns of $10,000 bills mounted between two sheets of thick glass. There's a guard and an alarm system, too. (Another million dollar display—made up of a jumbled mix of coins and bills—can be found at Bob Stupak's Vegas World.)

You can also find the Poker Hall of Fame on the right wall of the casino, with pictures of famous and infamous card players of all time.

Before you leave, go for a ride on the glass-walled elevator for a great view of downtown.

Coffee shop. The overnight special at the time of our visit was a 10-ounce New York strip steak with salad, potato, rolls, and butter for $2. Deeper into the night and into lunch, a chef's salad was offered for about $7.

Seafood Buffet. A downtown favorite, served from 4 to 10 P.M. for about $13, it includes shrimp, crab legs, salmon, oysters, mussels, prime rib, and seven hot entrees. Specials can include catfish and orange roughy.

Binion's Horseshoe Casino & Hotel, 128 E. Fremont Street; 354 rooms; 382-1600; (800) 937-6537.

Jackie Gaughan's Plaza

An attractive and well-kept hotel at the head of Fremont, it was for many years called the Union Plaza as a reminder of the former railroad interests that once controlled Las Vegas and of the railroad station that formerly occupied the spot. The hotel today is still connected to the Amtrak station at one end and the Greyhound terminal at the other.

The hotel was opened in 1971 on the spot where the land auction of 1905 took place. At the time it had the largest casino in Las Vegas, a distinction that has since been passed up The Strip several times.

The Plaza offers a wide range of gambling opportunities, beginning with rarely seen penny slots and nickel progressive jackpot machines and moving upward from there.

The casino also occasionally features one of our least favorite come-ons: an instant tax refund stand. Why don't we like that? Even assuming you come to the desk with a professionally prepared tax return, what you are essentially doing is taking out a short-term loan at a very high interest rate; by some calculations, the cost of the loan can be the equivalent of as much as 100 percent in interest. If you are that hard up for an instant return of your tax refund, you might want to consider whether you really should be spending the money in a casino.

On the third floor of the hotel is an attractive Chinese and Thai hideaway restaurant with the unimaginative name of **Kung Fu Plaza.** Open for lunch and dinner, entrees range from about $8 to $20 and when we visited included hot spicy catfish, honey duck, moo goo gai pan, sweet and sour shrimp, and Mongolian beef.

The signature restaurant at the Plaza is the **Center Stage,** on the second floor of the tower with a spectacular view up Glitter Gulch. The eatery is open from 4:30 P.M. to midnight, with dinners priced from about $10.

The **Plaza Diner** on the first floor serves breakfast, lunch, and dinner 24 hours a day.

Plaza, 1 Main Street; 1,037 rooms; 386-2110; (800) 634-6575.

Lady Luck

One block in from Fremont on Ogden and Third streets, this is one of the livelier places in downtown. Queen of the Lady Luck Showroom at the time of our visit was Melinda, who put on a magic show twice night-

We bet the tables are still busy. The Plaza is the focal point of a Las Vegas tradition on New Year's Eve. Crowds line Fremont Street to watch the fireworks set off behind the hotel.

No day of rest. Sundays are surprisingly busy days at many casinos, bringing out the locals for brunches. It's also a common arrival day for big tour groups.

Elvis sighting number five. The King's first Las Vegas appearance took place at the New Frontier in downtown in 1956, and it wasn't a smashing success. It seemed that the King of Rock 'n Roll's appeal was to younger crowds than were coming to Las Vegas. In 1969 he returned and made the first of a long series of appearances at the International Hotel (now the Las Vegas Hilton).

ly. To be charitable, Melinda's act could be considered second-tier, not in the league with the huge production shows on The Strip. She is a bit prettier than former beau Rich Little, though. The Lady Luck offers a few no-smoking tables, which we like to see, but the overall atmosphere is still pretty clouded.

One of our favorite slot machines in all of Nevada is the parking ticket validation machine at the Lady Luck. The sign reads: "Every 2,000th ticket pays a $25 jackpot."

The **Burgundy Room** offers entrees such as tournedos rossini and fresh halibut. **Marco Polo's** features *osso buco rissoto* and *broiled salmon alla Savoia.*

On Monday nights at the Lady Luck, you might want to check out **Lady Luck Luau,** a $12.95 all-you-can-eat Luau and dance review with dinner beginning at 7 P.M.

The **Brasserie** coffee shop offers specials including a broiled chopped sirloin with soup or salad for about $4, a prime rib dinner for about $5, and a New York steak dinner for about $10. On the lighter side, there is broiled skinless chicken breast or a pita pocket with chicken or beef, sprouts, tomatoes, and cucumbers, each for about $6.

The **Emperor's Room** offers a mix of entrees from about $7, including Asian specialties such as *kung pao* chicken and Mongolian beef.

The **Banquet Buffet** offers breakfast, lunch, and dinner.

Lady Luck Casino Hotel, 206 North 3rd Street; 796 rooms; 477-3000; (800) 523-9582.

Four Queens

By Las Vegas standards, a relatively understated hotel decorated in blue and beige with mirrored ceilings and featuring a small but lively casino.

The hotel was first built in 1964, and supposedly drew its name from the fact that former owner Ben Goffstein had four daughters. Over the years, the hotel has expanded to 720 rooms with twin 19-story towers, and it occupies the entire block at Fremont and Third Street.

Check out **Hugo's,** one of the better eateries in Las Vegas. The meal begins with a make-your-own salad from a tableside cart laden down with offerings from bay shrimp to roasted pine nuts to hearts of palm. Appetizers include the Hugo's Hot Rock Specialty for $21: diners are presented with a sizzling slab of granite and plates of tenderloin medallions, marinated swordfish, breast of chicken, and jumbo shrimp with bowls of herbs and spices; you do the cooking to taste.

Entrees, priced from about $20 to $30 on a recent visit included filet of red snapper with crabmeat and shrimp sauce, *snapper en papillote,* chicken Hugo (in a basil and pine nut cream sauce), New York strip loin in petite and extra thick cuts, and tournedos Hugo (topped with a slice of *pate foie gras,* artichoke hearts, and sauce béarnaise).

At the more-casual **Magnolia's Veranda,** you can try the Four Queens' Dip, a pair of French rolls filled with sliced beef, and swiss cheese served au jus. Also available are a variety of omelettes in real and no-cholesterol versions. Entrees are priced from about $4 to $10. A complete prime rib dinner was offered for $3.95.

Where do they get the coins? The Four Queens claims the title for the world's largest slot machine, duly noted in the *Guinness Book of World Records.* The Queens Machine is 9-feet, 8-inches tall and 18 feet long. Six people can play the slot at the same time.

The Food Court offers a good selection of fast food.

Four Queens Hotel & Casino, 202 East Fremont Street; 720 rooms; 385-4011; (800) 634-6045.

Fremont THE BEST

One of the first "carpet joints" in downtown, it also featured one of the first block-long neon signs in the neighborhood. The joint is always jumping.

Paradise Buffet. The weekend champagne brunch, served Saturday and Sunday from 7 A.M. to 3 P.M., is one of the better deals in downtown. It includes breakfast omelettes and eggs cooked to order, herring, sour cream, smoked salmon, New York strip loin, ham, turkey, and salads. Diners are also offered specialty coffees including amaretto, chocolate mint, hazelnut, and mocha. *See the section on buffets for hours and prices.*

The hotel includes a branch of the **Tony Roma's** chain, open for dinner from 5 P.M. Specialties include prime rib, steak, and chicken with prices starting about $8 for dinner.

The **Second Street Grill** offers American and Pacific Rim specialties priced from about $13 to $20. Offerings on a recent visit included seared ahi tuna steak with cucumber and plum wine vinaigrette, campfire grilled rib eye steak, bamboo steamed Hawaiian snapper, and grilled Szechuan rack of lamb with cabernet plum sauce.

The ground floor **Lanai Express** offers shrimp cocktail for 75 cents, hot dogs, and Chinese offerings.

The **Overland Stage Cafe** offers coffee shop fare including soup and sandwich for about $4. Breakfast is available from 11 P.M. to 11 A.M., with

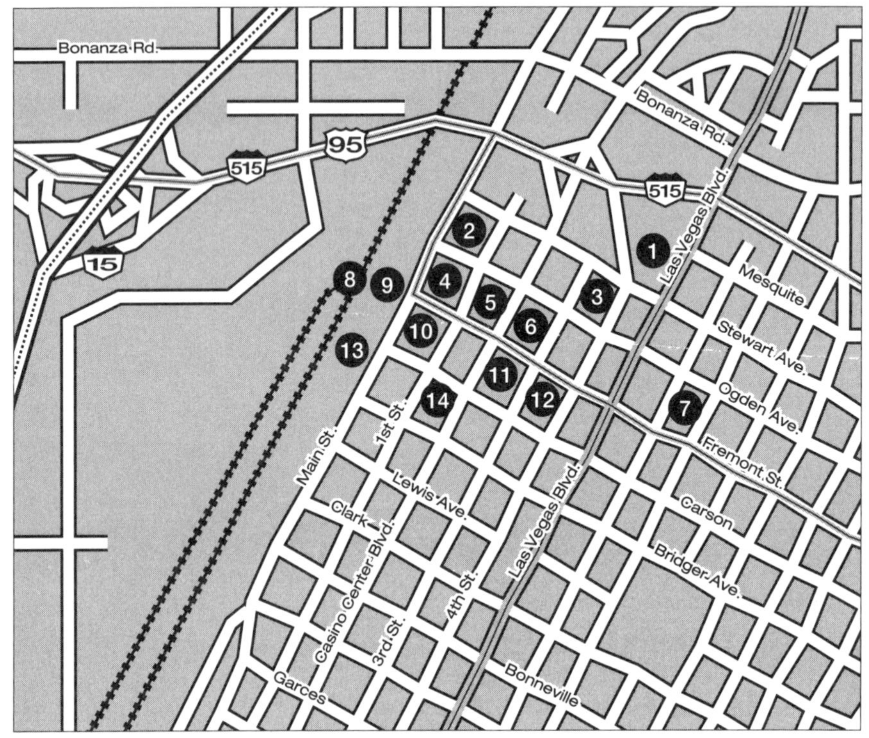

LAS VEGAS DOWNTOWN

1	City Hall	8	Train
2	California	9	Plaza
3	Lady Luck	10	Golden Gate
4	LV Club	11	4 Queens
5	Horseshoe	12	Fitzgerald's
6	Fremont	13	Bus
7	El Cortez	14	Golden Nugget

$2 specials such as three eggs, two pieces of bacon or sausage, potatoes, toast, and jelly.

Sam Boyd's Fremont Hotel & Casino, 200 East Fremont Street; 452 rooms; 385-3232; (800) 634-6182.

Fitzgerald's

If you have any question about whether this place intends to cater to the low rollers or the high rollers, a quick glance at the ubiquitous advertisements for the hotel should tell you: a regular come-on at Fitzgerald's is a free burger at the McDonald's within the casino.

In the core of the casino is a world of Irish green, including what is claimed to be a piece of the Blarney stone, a collection of four-leaf clovers, and a gaggle of leprechauns. In other words, lots of luck.

The other come-on, if you can spot it in the neon glare of Glitter Gulch, is the hotel's 400-foot-tall skyscraper.

Molly's Country Kitchen and Buffet offers a champagne weekend brunch from 8 A.M. to 4 P.M. for $4.99.

Cassidy's offers a weekday luncheon special of soup and salad with bread sticks for about $5; a mix-and-match surf and turf dinner with a choice of prime rib, petite filet mignon, or New York strip sirloin and lobster tail, scampi, or orange roughy goes for about $20.

Fitzgerald's, 301 East Fremont Street; 650 rooms; 388-2400; (800) 274-5825.

El Cortez Hotel

A small corner of this now-sprawling downtown casino and hotel, at the corner of Fremont and Sixth, constitutes the oldest continuously operating original casino in Las Vegas. The El Cortez opened in 1941 as a western-themed casino and hotel with about 80 rooms. A 14-story, 200-room tower opened in 1983.

El Cortez, 600 East Fremont Street; 308 rooms; 385-5200; (800) 634-6703.

Street Casinos

Not all of the casinos in Las Vegas are billion-dollar enterprises with thousands of slot machines and spectacular settings. Some are small, full of character, and populated with characters. Some are so tacky you'll want to take a shower immediately after you make a break for the exit.

The best of the little places can be found in downtown along Fremont Street, which on a busy night becomes an outdoor block party with visitors strolling from one casino to the next.

Las Vegas Chamber of Commerce. 711 E. Desert Inn Road, Las Vegas, NV 89109; 735-1616.

Las Vegas Convention and Visitors Authority. 3150 Paradise Rd., Las Vegas, NV 89109; 892-0711.

(We would be remiss if we did not warn visitors against strolling too far off Fremont Street in downtown; like any big city, some places are relatively safer than others. The casinos and city police concentrate their efforts on the main drag of downtown.)

Here are our four favorite street-level joints in downtown; you can stop in at all of them in a single visit.

Sassy Sally's Casino

Positively jumping with action and a lot of sassy women. This storefront casino is all slots, bouncy music, and special promotions and is one of our favorite places in downtown. You'll know you're there when you are accosted by a man on horseback handing out coupons; actually it's a man inside a walking horse costume, and boy does the horse feel silly.

Walk in to the back left corner for a decent snack deal at the **Belt-Bustin' Bar-B-Que.** Right out on the floor of the casino you can sit at a checkered tablecloth table and chow down on a plate full of ribs, sliced barbecue beef, or a T-bone steak with potato, all for $2 to $4.

Sassy Sally's Casino, 32 Fremont Street; 382-5777.

Pioneer Club

Another open-front downtown casino, it is notable for its frozen yogurt stand within. There's also a Carl's Jr. burger joint.

The Pioneer is the home of the huge animated neon cowboy sign on Fremont Street. Every few minutes he will announce, "Howdy Pardner. Welcome to Downtown Las Vegas." His name, at least among the locals, is Vegas Vic.

Pioneer Club, 25 E. Fremont Street; 386-5000.

Coin Castle

Not quite a castle, but surely a haven for coin players of all denominations. You will likely be accosted on the street with one of many come-ons for free drinks, sweepstakes, and other attractions.

Coin Castle, 15 E. Fremont Street; 385-7474.

Golden Gate Hotel & Casino

There's not much in the way of fancy accoutrements at the Golden Gate, although it is a lively streetfront joint. At the very back is the **San Francisco Shrimp Bar and Deli,** which not surprisingly specializes in shrimp (99 cents for a cocktail) and overstuffed deli sandwiches for $2 to $3.

Golden Gate Hotel & Casino, 1 Fremont Street; 382-6300.

Chapter 9
Las Vegas Showrooms and Nightlife

With a few notable exceptions, some of the best entertainment buys in America can be found in Las Vegas, with lavish stage shows, superstars, and fabulous music. Prices are as low as $15 or $20 for most shows; dinner shows or combination tickets with buffets are not much more.

Why are the prices generally reasonable? In a word, gambling. Las Vegas, Inc., uses the shows and the buffets and anything else they can to try to lure you into the casino. You'll walk past every slot machine and gaming table they can possibly put in your way between the front door and the showroom; then you'll have to walk back past them on your way out.

But let's get one thing straight: you are under no obligation to spend any more money than the price of your ticket. If you don't want to gamble, just stroll on by the tables and the machines and go to the show.

Before you buy your ticket, be sure you understand what's included. A common deal includes two drinks, usually from a selection of house brands; if you prefer a particular brand of alcohol, you'll have to pay extra. Both drinks are usually served before the show begins. Additional drinks and snacks are billed at lounge prices. Some shows offer dinner, again usually from a limited menu (and rarely worth writing home about).

Another important thing to know about Vegas shows: in the past, most of the shows did not offer assigned seating and you were at the mercy of the maitre d'. High rollers, and those who slipped the guy at the door $10 or $20 or more, got the best tables. Over the past few years, though, many of the showrooms have gone over to assigned seats, on a first-come, first-served basis; high rollers still get the very best places. In any case, there are very few really bad seats in the showrooms, which are most often designed to be wider than they are deep with a lot of front row tables.

The least-preferred seats will put you at a long table perpendicular to the stage. You will share your evening with 10 or 12 strangers at the table.

The best seats, although usually not the closest, are the first tier of couch-like booths.

The huge expense of creating, mounting, and promoting entertainment spectacles in Las Vegas generally means that shows will run for extended periods. Be sure to check with hotels for current schedules and prices.

The Econoguide to the Best Shows in Las Vegas

Cirque du Soleil. Treasure Island
Siegfried and Roy. The Mirage
Starlight Express. Las Vegas Hilton
City Lites. Flamingo Hilton
Enter the Night. Stardust Hotel
Folies Bergere. Tropicana Hotel
Spellbound. Harrah's Las Vegas
Splash. Riviera

Production Shows

(All phone numbers are in the 702 area code.)

Aladdin Hotel. Bagdad Showroom. "Country Tonite" country-music comedy dance review. 7:15 and 10 P.M. nightly. Dark Tuesdays. $17.95. Children under 18, $11.95. Combination tickets with buffet available. 736-0111.

Bally's. "Jubilee!" Singing, dancing (some topless), and fantastic production numbers. Did we mention the topless dancers? Mondays and Tuesdays 8 P.M.; Thursdays, Saturdays, and Sundays 8 and 11 P.M. Dark Fridays. $40. 739-4567.

Excalibur. "King Arthur's Tournament." Production show about the Legend of Arthur. Two dinner shows nightly at 6 P.M. and 8:30 P.M. $24.95 with meal. 597-7600.

Excalibur. "Sooper Dogs." Mondays through Fridays 2 P.M., Saturdays and Sundays noon and 2 P.M. Dark Wednesdays. $4.95. 597-7600.

Flamingo Hilton. Flamingo Showroom. "City Lites" variety and comedy show with ice dancers. Dinner show 7:45 P.M. from $29.50, and cocktail show 11 P.M. $21.95, including two drinks. Dark Sundays. Minimum age is seven. 733-3333.

Imperial Palace Hotel. Imperial Theatre. "Legends in Concert" impressions. 7:30 and 10:30 P.M. nightly. Dark Sundays. $17.95, including two drinks. 794-3261.

Jackie Gaughan's Plaza. "David Wright's Hot Rock 'N Country" variety show. 7:30 and 10:30 P.M. Dark Tuesdays. $19.95, including one drink. 386-2110.

Las Vegas Hilton. "Starlight Express." Dark Mondays. Tuesdays, Fridays, Saturdays, and Sundays at 7:30 and 10:30 P.M., Wednesdays and Thursdays at 9 P.M. Ticket prices vary; about $39.50 for adults, $25 for children. 732-5755.

Luxor. "Winds of the Gods." Chariot races, lavish costumes, and exotic animals on stage where they belong. 7:30 and 10:15 P.M. nightly. Dark Wednesdays. Dinner show $39.95; late cocktail show $24.95.

MGM Grand. Grand Theatre. "EFX," a dancing, singing, and special effects spectacle with a cast of 70. 891-1111.

The Mirage. Theatre Mirage. "Siegfried and Roy" magic spectacle. Twice nightly at 7:30 and 11 P.M. Dark Wednesdays. $72.85, including two drinks. Appearances 40 weeks of the year; other headliners appear during breaks. 792-7777.

Rio. Copacabana Showroom. "¡Conga!" dinner show. 6 and 8:30 P.M. $29.95. 252-7776.

Riviera Hotel. Versailles Theatre. "Splash" musical variety. Nightly 7:30 and 10:30 P.M. $27.50, including two drinks. 794-9301.

Riviera Hotel. Mardi Gras Room. "An Evening at La Cage" female impersonators. Nightly 7:30 and 9:30 P.M. Late show 11:15 on Wednesdays and Saturdays. Dark Tuesdays. $12.95; $18.45 with buffet. 794-9433.

Riviera Hotel. "Crazy Girls — Sensuous Passion & Pudgy" adult entertainment. Nightly 8:30 and 10:30 P.M. $12.95, including two drinks. Midnight show Fridays and Saturday. Dark Mondays. 794-9433.

Sahara Hotel. "Boylesque" female impersonators. 8 P.M. and midnight nightly. Dark Wednesdays. $17.50. 737-2878.

San Remo. "Outrageous." Nightly 7:30 and 9:30 P.M.; 11:30 P.M. show on Saturdays. Dark Mondays. $15.95, including one drink. 597-6024.

Sands Hotel. "Hot Stuff" dance revue, 7:30 and 9:30 P.M. Dark Tuesdays. $15.95, including one drink. 733-5453.

Stardust Hotel. "Enter the Night" stage spectacular and laser light show. Nightly 7:30 and 10:30 P.M. Wednesdays through Saturdays; 8 P.M. Sundays and Mondays. Dark Tuesdays. $24.90, including two drinks. 732-6111.

Treasure Island. Cirque du Soleil's "Mystère." 7:30 and 10:30 P.M. Dark Mondays. $42; children under 12 about $21. Two shows nightly. 894-7111.

Tropicana Hotel. Tiffany Theatre. "Folies Bergere" music and dance show, the longest running stage production in Las Vegas. Dinner show 7:30 P.M., $26.95; cocktail show 10:30 P.M., $19.95, including two drinks. Dark Thursdays. 739-2411.

Vegas World. "Memories of Elvis." 6 P.M. nightly. Dark Thursdays. Free. 382-2000.

"King Arthur's Tournament" at Excalibur

Magic Shows

Hacienda Hotel. Fiesta Theatre. "Lance Burton." Nightly 7:30 and 10:30 P.M. $19.95. Dark Mondays. Minimum age for 11 P.M. show is 18. 739-8911.

Harrah's Las Vegas. "Spellbound." Nightly 7:30 and 10 P.M. $21.95, including one drink. Dark Sundays. Minimum age 21. 369-5222.

Lady Luck. "Melinda, First Lady of Magic and Her Follies Revue." Shows at 8 P.M. and 10:30 P.M.; late show for adults only. $19.95, including one drink. 477-3000.

Comedy Shows

Bally's. "Catch a Rising Star" cabaret. Nightly 8 and 10:30 P.M. $12.50. Minimum age 18. 739-4111.

Maxim Hotel. Cabaret Showroom. "Comedy Max." Nightly 8 and 10 P.M. $12.95 with two drinks; $16.95 with buffet. 731-4300.

Riviera Hotel. "An Evening at the Improv." 8, 10, and 11:30 P.M. nightly. $13.95, including two drinks.

Tropicana Hotel. Monte Carlo Showroom. "The Comedy Stop." 8 and 10:30 P.M. nightly. $12.95, including two drinks. 739-2358.

Celebrity Shows

Caesars Palace. Circus Maximus Showroom. Tickets generally start at $40. 439-7110.

Debbie Reynolds. Star Theater. Debbie herself, or other celebrities. Tuesdays through Saturdays 8 P.M.; Sundays, 3 P.M. Dark Mondays. $29.95 with two drinks. 733-2243.

Desert Inn. Crystal Room. 733-4566.

Golden Nugget. Cabaret, Claude's. 386-8100.

Lady Luck. Cabaret. 477-3000.

Las Vegas Hilton. Showroom. 732-5755.

MGM Grand. MGM Grand Garden. Ice shows, sporting events, shows. 474-4000.

"American Superstars" at the Flamingo Hilton, Las Vegas

Off the Beaten Track

We're going to skip right over the strip joints, mud wrestling exhibitions, and table dancing bars….If you want 'em, there are more "adult" and "topless" night clubs in Las Vegas than you could shake a cocktail stick at. You will be assaulted with leaflets and advertisements and personal appeals as you walk along The Strip or downtown. The joints are every bit as crummy inside as they appear from outside, and Las Vegas police advise you to keep a close eye on your wallet and hotel key and anything else of value if you venture within.

There are, though, quite a few alternative and traditional nightclubs and cafes worth visiting in the Las Vegas area. Many of them cater to the locals rather than the tourists, which, depending on your orientation, may be a real advantage.

Lounges

Café Copioh. A quirky dive across from UNLV. 4550 S. Maryland Parkway. 739-0305.

Café Espresso Roma. Another college joint, it features poetry nights on Thursdays and comedy on alternate Saturdays. 4440 S. Maryland Parkway. 369-1540.

The Cave. Call beforehand to find out the weirdness du jour. Nights include erotica for women, hip hop, female impersonators, strippers, leatherware, and more. 5740 W. Charleston. 878-0001.

The Coffee Bar. Espresso, cappuccino, and desserts in a corner of the huge **Basset Book Shop.** Borrow a book and give it a test read. 2323 S. Decatur. 258-0999.

"Legends" at the Imperial Palace, Las Vegas

Goodtimes. Disco fever, on what is claimed to be Las Vegas' only stainless steel floor—which sounds quite plausible. Thursday nights are for trash disco, in costume. 1775 E. Tropicana Avenue. 736-9494.

Nightclubs

Favorites. An eclectic mix—call for the latest—that can include an 18-piece brass band or punk rockers, or both. 4110 S. Maryland Avenue. 796-1776.

The Hard Rock Cafe. The Las Vegas outpost of the national chain, it's a loud place decorated with memorabilia of the rock 'n roll pantheon. Go for drinks or dinner. 4474 Paradise Road. 733-8400.

Hurricane. Not for the sensitive of hearing or sensibilities. Call for scheduled events. 1650 E. Tropicana Avenue. 798-3883.

The Metz. An elaborate, multi-level dance club. 3675 S. Las Vegas Boulevard (between the Tropicana and Aladdin Hotels). 739-8855.

Shark Club. A high-tech club with a four-sided video screen and surrounding sound. 75 E. Harmon Avenue. 795-7525.

Cheyenne Saloon and Dance Hall. Country music and restaurant with a hardwood dance floor. 310 N. Rancho at Cheyenne. 645-4139.

The Country Club Music Hall. Dance hall and restaurant; open 24 hours. 3785 Boulder Highway. 641-5800.

Fremont Street Reggae and Blues. Live bands. 400 E. Fremont Street. 594-4640.

G.O. Nutz. Country fun saloon. 4424 West Spring Mountain Road at Arville. 368-6800.

Idle Spurs Tavern. Rodeo bar. 1113 S. Rainbow Boulevard at Charleston. 363-7718.

Play It Again Sam. Eat, drink, and be moody in a recreation of Rick's Café Americain from *Casablanca*. 4120 Spring Mountain Road. 876-1550.

"Starlight Express" at the Las Vegas Hilton

Chapter 10

Mama Don't Allow No Gambling 'Round Here: Area Attractions

Okay, we know that Las Vegas *is* a show all by itself, but there is more to life than casinos, showgirls, neon lights, buffets, casinos, showgirls, shopping malls, exploding volcanos, battling pirate ships, and Egyptian pyramids. Did we mention casinos and showgirls?

Although you sometimes have to squint through a forest of slot machines and neon lights to see it, there is life outside of the casinos of Las Vegas that has nothing to do with gambling and sex. Hidden to most visitors to Las Vegas is a wide variety of cultural and outdoor activities. With the developing role of the town as a lure for the entire family, the other attractions of the area will become more important.

Hardly qualifying as cultural highlights, but still a lot of fun are pleasure palaces including **MGM Grand Adventures, Grand Slam Canyon**, and **Wet 'n Wild.**

MGM Grand Adventures

MGM Grand Adventures is without doubt the best theme park in Las Vegas. It's also the only one. So, I won't devote a lot of space to comparing it to mega-parks like Walt Disney World, Disneyland, Universal Studios Hollywood, Universal Studios Florida, or even to the Disney-operated Disney-MGM Studios in Orlando. Except to say that MGM Grand Adventures is one notch below the major leagues, but a lot better than most amusement parks.* And there are no slot machines or blackjack tables in the park, at least not yet.

MGM Grand Adventures is worth a day or an evening, especially if you have children in tow. It's all part of the effort by many of the

> * If you're a fan of theme parks, you might want to pick up a copy of *Econoguide 1995— Walt Disney World, Epcot, and Universal Studios Florida*, also by Corey Sandler and published by Contemporary Books.

casinos in Las Vegas to give families a reason to come to town.

Surprisingly, because of MGM's identification as a movie studio, there's not much of a cinema theme to the park. (A legal dispute with Disney over the Orlando park, which is very much based on movie themes, may be the reason.)

In any case, there are eight "areas" in the tightly packed park: **Casablanca Plaza, New York Street, Asian Village, French Street, Salem Waterfront, Tumbleweed Gulch, New Orleans Street,** and **Olde England Street.** You'll find restaurants, including **Benninger's Gourmet Coffees, Hamada Orient Express, Mamma Ilardo's Pizzeria, Kenny Rogers Roasters, Hildegard's Ice Cream Parlour, The Cotton Blossom, Nathan's Famous,** and **Burger King** scattered around.

As you descend the escalator into the park from the MGM Grand, you'll arrive in Casablanca. Given a choice, most people go to the right, and that is the general flow around this park—a counterclockwise tour. Therefore, if the park is very busy you might want to go against the flow and head to the left. Our tour here, though, will discuss the rides as most people will come to them.

The first big ride is **Lightning Bolt,** an indoor roller coaster on an outerspace adventure. That certainly sounds like the famous Space Mountain ride at Disneyland and Walt Disney World, but the Disney touch is missing. There's almost no buildup to the adventure, and the space theme is merely hinted at; the ending, which features a landing in Las Vegas at night, is almost possible to miss. And the ride is very short, about a minute.

If you're in the mood to remember your trip forever, you can purchase a souvenir picture taken as you swooped about. We didn't.

Next up is **Deep Earth Exploration,** a more polished (and cinematic) simulator adventure that takes you aboard Gopher 1 for a voyage deep into the earth's core, and then back up out an erupting volcano.

The **Backlot River Tour** is a very hokey simulation of a studio tour; there are no real production facilities at MGM Grand Adventures. Instead you'll see scenes sort of reminiscent of famous movies, including swamp creatures, a Vietnam War helicopter firefight, and other scenes. Bits and pieces of the outside world, including a nearby motel balcony, intruded on the view of some of the "sets." What made our particular tour very enjoyable was the hitchhiker we picked up at the loading dock; an actress playing the part of Betty Boop sat down beside us and took the tour, staying in character all the way through. Try as we might—and we tried—we were unable to break her out of the role.

From the backlot tour, you'll move on to **Parisian Taxis,** which is a bumper car ride with a few French street signs.

Haunted Mine is, well, a haunted mine. It does a better job of set-

MGM GRAND ADVENTURES LAS VEGAS

Special Features
12 Central Park Wedding Chapel
8 Grandmosphere

Arcades
27 Quick Draw
28 Shooting Gallery
36 Les Boats

Theatres
14 King Looey Theatre
26 You're In The Movies
21 Magic Screen Theatre
24 Rio Grande Cantina
18 Pirate's Cove

Themed Areas
5 Casablanca Plaza
9 New York Street
39 Asian Village
37 French Street
32 Salem Waterfront
25 Tumbleweed Gulch
19 New Orleans Street
15 Olde England Street

Food Establishments
6 Benninger's Gourmet Coffees
11 Trolley Treats
16 Burger King
38 Hamada Orient Express
31 Kenny Rogers Roasters
23 Hildegard's Ice Cream Parlour
30 The Cotton Blossom
22 Nathan's Famous
34 Mamma Ilardo's Pizzeria

Retail Shops
10 Harry's China Shop
13 Backstage Collectibles
35 Backlot Heirlooms
33 Hollywood Clothiers
29 Old West Supply Company
20 Bayou Toys
17 Behind the Scenes Craft Co.
1 Kodak Photo Products Center
4 Casablanca General Store
2 Photoplay Gallery
3 King Looey's Hollywood Memorabilia
7 Studio Souvenirs

ting up the atmosphere for the ride, but this is still no Disney Haunted Mansion—oops, there I go again making comparisons. Let's just say that this is a PG-rated moving spook ride, a little bit better done than your local Jaycee Halloween Funhouse.

Are you ready to go **Over the Edge?** It's a pleasant little journey through a nostalgic old saw mill with quaint scenery and rustic charm. (Did someone say, Thunder Mountain Railroad?) This log flume ride takes you up

King Looey at MGM Grand, Las Vegas

in the air over a corner of the park and down into two wet dropoffs.

You're now at the top of the map, and ready to visit **You're in the Movies**, a show familiar to veterans of studio tours but always amusing. Participants are drawn from the line about 15 minutes before the show and given small parts to play in a series of scenes from television and movie classics. Their actions are electronically combined with video and presented on the big screen for the rest of the audience to see. On the day of my visit a Rhett and Scarlet were chosen for a scene from a *Gone With the Wind*-like film (sort of Rhett meets the Three Stooges), a vampire was cast for a menacing pizza delivery, a Cleopatra and an Anthony were selected for a romantic vamp, and various children and other monsters were cast.

Magic Screen Theatre turned out to be one of the most enjoyable spots in the park. The large theater alternates between presentations of **The Three Stooges**, a combination of live-action look-alikes and vintage video clips for an appropriately nyuk-nyuk show, and **Kaleidoscope,** a very entertaining black light puppetry and live performance show that should enthrall children of all ages.

Behind the Magic Screen building is the largest ride at the park, **Grand Canyon Rapids.** This is your basic raft ride (four to six per boat) through rapids and down a "blasting tunnel" drop; this is definitely a wet ride.

Nearby in **King Looey Theatre** is **The Cartoon Show,** a demonstration of animation and based on the park's own theme character.

And then there is the **Dueling Pirates** show, a stunt performance that will entertain the kids pretty well. It does, though, suffer a bit by comparison to the (free) outdoor battle fought in the lagoon outside Treasure Island down on The Strip.

If you're on the lookout for souvenirs of MGM Grand Adventures or Hollywood collectibles the park contains stores including **Backstage Collectibles, Backlot Heirlooms,** and **Hollywood Clothiers.** Other shops include the **Behind the Scenes Craft Co.,** offering glass, leather, wood, pottery, and wax works. In Tumbleweed Gulch you'll find the **Old West Supply Company.** And at New Orleans Square, there is **Bayou Toys.**

You must be at least 36 inches tall to ride Parisian Taxis or the Backlot River Tour, and 42 inches or taller for Grand Canyon Rapids, Over the Edge, and Lightning Bolt.

The park is outdoors, and nights and winter days can be chilly. Check with the park for operating hours. In the off-season, the park usually closes at 7 P.M.; in what was expected to be a busy summer, the park was scheduled to remain open until 10 P.M. Admission in the early summer of 1994 was $18.95 for adults and $13.95 for children from 4 to 12; prices are subject to change and may be higher in the busy summer season. The park may also offer discount rates for admission late in the day.

Luxor

The hollow interior of the Luxor pyramid houses three attractions created by special effects designer Douglass Trumbull (also responsible for the spectacular Back to the Future ride at Universal Studios in Orlando, Florida). The theme for the mini-park is a three-part adventure more or less set in the time of King Tut and the more contemporary rediscovery of his tomb in Egypt.

Episode 1, **In Search of the Obelisk,** is a 15-minute simulation that includes a runaway elevator into the tomb (not quite as wild as the new Twilight Zone Tower of Terror at the Disney-MGM Theme Park in Orlando) and then a frenzied chase sequence within a pyramid with some interesting special effects. The second episde, **Luxor Live?**, involves guests in a 30-minute "live" broadcast that combines actors and video effects in a television studio setting. Voyagers visit the future in a 17-minute cosmic time machine using high-tech movie and computer imagery for the third episode, **The Theater of Time.**

The attractions, presented as three separate shows, can be visited as part of a multi-ticket pass for about $13, including the river ride and the museum exhibit that replicates parts of King Tut's Tomb. Or, you can purchase individual tickets for elements of the show. The rides open at 9 or 10 A.M.

The Luxor attractions are entertaining for the technology they employ, but the story line is rather muddied. During 1994, some changes were made and more may be in the offing.

On the lowest level of the Luxor is **King Tut's Tomb and Museum,** a re-creation of part of the treasure chamber found by explorer Howard Carter in 1922. And finally, there is the **Nile River Tour** by boat around the circumference of the pyramid; it's a pleasant break from the casino, although you can see it from the water.

Grand Slam Canyon

Only in Las Vegas could they come up with something like this: **Grand Slam Canyon,** a five-acre indoor entertainment park that presents a Las Vegas–eye view of the Grand Canyon, including 140-foot manmade peaks, a 90-foot re-creation of Havasupai Falls, and a river. The entire park, attached to the **Circus Circus Hotel and Casino** is covered by a pink space-frame dome called an Adventuresphere.

The park includes the world's only indoor double-looping roller coaster. If you're not already dizzy from the gambling, the neon, the buffets…then you are ready for the **Canyon Blaster** at Grand Slam Canyon. I'm not sure I was ready, but I went for a ride anyway; I survived but I'm having a hard time reading the notes I took. You'll know this is a serious ride as you walk around the Adventuresphere; you'll feel the floor shake beneath your feet as the cars rumble by. This is a ride that emphasizes speed and twists and turns over height; its track circles in and around much of the sphere. There are two loops, two corkscrews and some interesting views of the hotel and The Strip if you keep your eyes open.

The **Rim Runner** is a three-and-a-half-minute indoor water flume ride, with much of the raft ride in the dark. "This is a wet ride. You will get soaked," warn the signs. In case you are not fully prepared, the gift shop sells disposable ponchos for a dollar or two.

Other attractions include the **Twist 'n Shout Slide,** a dry plunge; youngsters are permitted to ride on an adult's lap. You can participate in **Hot Shots Lazer Tag** or ride in a **Magic Motion** simulator, like the ones at the Excalibur Hotel.

The first year for the park was a rough one, with its offerings greatly overshadowed by the excitement of the MGM Grand Adventures and Luxor; in the spring of 1994, there was an early overhaul of the park, and several new attractions were added, including **Canyon Cars** (bumper cars), **Thunder Birds** (plane ride), the **Cliff Hangers** net climb, the **Sand Pirate** swinging ship, **B.C. Bus,** and several high-tech **R-360** and **AS-1** motion simulators.

Grand Slam Canyon is open every day and into the night; check with Circus Circus for operating hours. Admission to the park is free, and various ticket plans have been in effect at different times of the year. They have included an all-rides ticket, as well as a general admission ticket plus individual ride tickets. The busiest times at the park are weekends and holidays, with nighttime crowds larger than during the day.

Wet 'n Wild

For a cooling antidote to a hot day on The Strip, try Wet 'n Wild, located between the Sahara Hotel/Casino and El Rancho Hotel.

The park, which operates from about April 1 to October 1 of each year, added a pair of new wet and wild attractions recently: the **Bomb Bay** and the **Banzai Banzai.** Bomb Bay is about as close as you are likely to get to a free fall; think of it as a bungee jump without the bungee. One person at a time slips into a bomb-like capsule at the top of a 76-foot-high water slide which is then moved into a vertical position with the lucky occupant standing almost straight up inside. Then the bottom drops out and the rider drops nearly straight down the watery chute.

The Banzai Banzai is a double-slide water coaster, allowing a pair of riders to race each other down to a 120-foot-long runway pool at the bottom. There are, of course, a few slightly less wild but wet rides, too.

Wet 'n Wild, 2600 Las Vegas Blvd. South; open in season; call 737-7873 for hours and rates. *Discount coupon in this book.*

Museums

Barrick Museum of Natural History. UNLV's collection includes a selection of lizards (leopards, chuckwallas, Gila monsters), snakes (rattlers, desert boas, red racers), and spiders (the poisonous brown recluse and black widow) guaranteed to make your skin crawl, as well as an impressive display of arrowheads. On the campus of UNLV at 4505 S. Maryland Parkway; open weekdays; 739-3381.

Boulder City Hoover Dam Museum. Historic artifacts of the construction of Hoover Dam. 444 Hotel Plaza in Boulder City; 294-1988.

Clark County Heritage Museum. A collection of local and area history, including railroad rolling stock and memorabilia; Heritage Street, a collection of historic homes in a park setting; and a time line from prehistoric to current times. Located in the former Boulder City railroad depot; open daily except holidays, 9 A.M. to 4:30 P.M.; 1830 South Boulder Highway; Henderson; 455-7955.

Guinness World of Records Museum. If Las Vegas is not quite weird enough for you, you might want to try out this strange collection. Part of an expanding chain of exhibits under license from the famous recorder of world records and strange accomplishments, the museum includes models and replicas that inform about such things as the largest number of hard-boiled eggs eaten at one sitting, the smallest ridable bicycle, the largest

The Guinness World of Records Museum

human being, the world's oldest man, and much more. Where else could you learn about the world's greatest shallow dive (from 28 feet into 12 inches of water), the world's loudest snorer, or the human lightning rod?

The museum is open every day at 2780 Las Vegas Blvd. South, on The Strip north of Circus Circus and across from Wet 'n Wild and the Sahara Hotel/Casino; call 792-3766 for hours and information. *Discount coupon in this book.*

Imperial Palace Antique Auto Collection. With more than 200 antique and classic cars, one of the most impressive collections anywhere.

One corner of the museum is a room full of 25 or so Duesies worth more than $50 million; classic Duesenberg cars including Jimmy Cagney's 1937 Model J. More contemporary and a bit more flashy is Liberace's pale cream 1981 Zimmer Golden Spirit, complete with candelabra. There is, of course, an Elvis car: a pale blue 1976 Eldorado. Also on display is a 1938 Cadillac V-16 touring sedan (with backseat bar) owned by W. C. Fields.

Presidents Row includes John F. Kennedy's 1962 Lincoln Continental "Bubbletop," Lyndon Johnson's 1964 Cadillac, Dwight Eisenhower's 1952 Chrysler Imperial, Harry S Truman's 1950 Lincoln Cosmopolitan, Franklin D. Roosevelt's 1936 V-16 Cadillac, and a 1929 Cadillac that transported Herbert Hoover.

From the darker side of history are vehicles including Al Capone's 1930 V-16 Cadillac, Adolf Hitler's 1936 Mercedes-Benz 770K, Benito Mussolini's 1939 Alfa Romeo, and Emperor Hirohito's 1935 Packard.

And in keeping with the generally offbeat atmosphere of Las Vegas, also

The Imperial Palace Auto Collection

on display is Howard Hughes' 1954 Chrysler, which comes equipped with an elaborate air purification system in the trunk intended to protect Hughes from the germs that afflict we mortals.

The oldest cars on display include an 1897 Haynes-Apperson, a two-cylinder, four-seat surrey that ran on naptha; and an 1898 LaNef, a three-wheeler with tiller steering. Rare cars include a few Tuckers, a 1903 Lenawee, and a 1913 Stanley Steamer bus.

There's a nominal admission charge for the museum, but you can often obtain free passes from casino employees who are stationed at the front entrance of the Imperial Palace. The museum is open every day, late into the night. Listed prices are $6.95 for adults and $3 for children from 5 to 12. *You will also find a free pass for two in the coupon section of this book.*
Open daily; 3535 Las Vegas Blvd., South; 731-3311.

Las Vegas Art Museum. Free admission. Three galleries with displays of local and national artists. Within Lorenzi Park, 3333 Washington Avenue; 647-4300

Las Vegas Natural History Museum. A nice collection of dinosaurs, including the skull of a T-Rex. Open daily; 900 Las Vegas Blvd. North; adults $5, children (4 to 12) $2.50; 384-3466.

Las Vegas Southern Nevada Zoological Society. 1775 N. Rancho; 382-5437.

Liberace Museum. "Mr. Showmanship" is gone, but much of his collection of costumes, pianos, candelabras, and cars remains in this museum. Some of his outfits were wilder than those worn by showgirls on The Strip, including a suit made of ostrich feathers. 1775 E. Tropicana Avenue; 798-5595; adults $6.50, children (6 to 12) $2. Monday to Saturday 10 A.M. to 5 P.M.; Sunday 1 P.M. to 5 P.M. *Discount coupon in this book.*

Lied Discovery Children's Museum. A hands-on place for youngsters, including Toddler Towers, a model of the Space Shuttle, a kid-operated radio station, a collection of computer toys, and more. Tuesday to Saturday 10 A.M. to 5 P.M.; Thursday 10 A.M. to 9 P.M.; Sunday from noon to 5 P.M. Across from Cashman Field, 833 Las Vegas Blvd. North; adults $5, juniors (12 to 18) $4, and children (4 to 11) $3; 382-5437.

Lost City Museum of Archeology. Artifacts and interpretations of Pueblo Grande de Nevada, the so-called Lost City of the Anasazi Indians, who occupied the area for about 1,200 years until the year 1150. Located in Overton, 60 miles northeast of Las Vegas via I-15, at 721 S. Highway 169; 397-2193.

Nevada State Museum & Historical Society. The history of southern Nevada from the dawn of native culture some 13,000 years ago to the present. Take I-95 to Valley View. 700 Twin Lakes Drive in Lorenzi Park; 8:30 A.M. to 4:30 P.M.; 486-5205.

Searchlight Museum. A small outpost of the Clark County Heritage Museum, it chronicles the history of the former mining town of Searchlight and the story of famed Hollywood fashion designer Edith Head and screen stars Clara Bow and Rex Bell, all of whom were raised there. Searchlight Community Center, 60 miles south of Las Vegas; 455-7955.

Commercial Attractions

Bonnie Springs Ranch/Old Nevada. Located at the southern edge of Red Rock Canyon, it's a rather pedestrian western theme park in a very pretty setting. The area includes a petting zoo, a western street with shops, demonstrations, and the occasional shootout. Hwy. 159, 20 miles west of Las Vegas. Open 7 days a week, with tickets priced at about $6.50 for adults and $4 for children; 875-4191.

Dolphin Habitat. Mirage Hotel, 3400 Las Vegas Blvd. South; open 9 A.M. to 7 P.M. daily; admission $3, children under 3 free; 791-7111.

White Tiger Habitat. Mirage Hotel, 3400 Las Vegas Blvd. South; open 24 hours; free admission; 791-7111.

Ethel M. Chocolate Factory. Free factory tour and botanical garden and cactus display. Yes, there are samples. Between The Strip and Hoover Dam. 2 Cactus Garden Drive, Henderson; call for hours; 458-8864.

Kidd Marshmallow Factory. Sweet satisfaction for the kid in all of us. Tour and sampling area. 8203 Gibson Road; open daily 9 A.M. to 4:30 P.M.; 564-5400.

Omnimax Theatre. A giant dome theater, just off the gambling floor and a better bet for families and adults than most other entertainment on The Strip. The theater has a continuous schedule of spectacular 70-mm films. Caesars Palace, 3570 Las Vegas Blvd. South; 731-7900.

Vegas Chip Factory. Ever wonder where the casinos get their gambling chips? Not here; these are the kind that come in bags and are covered with salt. Free tours working days. 2954 N. Martin Luther King Boulevard; 647-3800.

Cultural Information

Allied Arts Council. 731-5419.
Clark County Library. 382-3493.
Cultural Hotline: Southern Nevada Arts Hotline. 385-4444.
Las Vegas Cultural Community Affairs. 455-8200.
University of Nevada Las Vegas Performing Arts.
  UNLV is a center of culture just two miles from The Strip. Call 739-3801 for information on various events.
Charles Vanda Masters Series.
  Orchestra performance, ensembles, and soloists.
Nevada Symphony Orchestra.

Nevada Dance Theatre.
(Traditionally puts on *The Nutcracker* at Christmas time.)
Nevada Opera Theatre.
Chamber Music Southwest.
University Dance Theatre.
UNLV's University Theatre.
The City of Las Vegas Cultural and Community Affairs Division.
Puts on a variety of events from Shakespeare to jazz.
New West Theatre. A professional troupe, cosponsored by the City of Las
Vegas, putting on shows at the Charleston Heights Arts Center, 800 S. Brush
Street; call 656-5000.
Actors Repertory Theatre. 1824 Palo Alto Circle, Las Vegas 89108; 648-1986.
Community Drama Workshop. 3402 Katmai Drive,
Las Vegas 89122; 458-0069.
Las Vegas Community Theatre. 111 Las Vegas Blvd. South, Suite 214,
Las Vegas 89104; 382-7225.
Las Vegas Little Theatre. 2566 Sherwood, #11, Las Vegas 89109; 731-5958.
New West Stage Company. 3540 W. Sahara, Suite 235,
Las Vegas 89101; 396-6553.
Sign Design Theatre. 3933 Renate Drive, Las Vegas 89102; 873-7446.
Theatre Arts Group. 1612 Metropolitan, Las Vegas 89102; 877-6463.
UNLV Department of Theatre Arts. 4505 S. Maryland Parkway,
Las Vegas 89154; 739-3666.

Dance

Academy of Nevada Dance Theatre. 4634 S. Maryland Parkway, #110,
Las Vegas 89109; 794-2889.
Department of Dance Arts. 4505 S. Maryland Parkway, UNLV,
Las Vegas 89154; 739-3827.
Las Vegas Civic Ballet Association. P.O. Box 159,
Las Vegas 89125; 385-1630.
Nevada Dance Theatre, UNLV. 900 Las Vegas Blvd. North,
Las Vegas 89154; 739-3838.
Nevada State Troupers. 900 Las Vegas Blvd. North,
Las Vegas 89101; 457-2044.
Opus Dance Ensemble of Las Vegas. 1600 E. Desert Inn Road, #209D,
Las Vegas 89109; 732-9646.
Simba Talent Development Center. 3280 Wynn Road,
Las Vegas 89102; 367-6788.
Theatre Ballet of Las Vegas. 3265 E. Patrick Lane,
Las Vegas 89120; 458-7575.

Chapter 11

Local Protocol:
Sex, Marriage, Comps, and Shopping

Sex, Sex, Sex

There, we got your attention, didn't we? That is the philosophy of Nevada, too, and especially Las Vegas. The casinos and hotels and just about everything else in town are tied to sex, from the costumes on the cocktail waitresses, the togas on the greeters at Caesars Palace, and the production shows to the more-directly-to-the-point topless bars.

Getting past the idea of sex as tease, there is also a small but apparently thriving industry in prostitution in much of the state.

Prostitution is perhaps no more common in Nevada than it is in most other parts of the country, and certainly on a par with most convention and entertainment centers. It is, though, legal in several parts of the state, and there are about 36 legalized houses or "ranches" in the state. The industry is centered just outside of Reno and up or down the road from Las Vegas. For the record, the Nevada Supreme Court upheld the rights of the counties to legalize and regulate brothels; Clark County, which includes Las Vegas, and Washoe County, home of Reno, are among the few that do *not* permit brothels.

In Las Vegas, though, the streets are littered with brochures from "escort" services that offer what they describe as "in-room entertainment" and other such euphemisms. And Reno is ringed by special service companies.

Many of the companies masquerade as massage services ("Cathy's College Girls of Reno Hotel Guest Massage Service"), entertainment bureaus ("Plato's Retreat"), or escort services.

Among the brothels are the Cherry Patch Ranch an hour out of Las Vegas, the Mustang Ranch 1 six miles east of Reno in Lockwood, and the Sagebrush Ranch just outside of the state capital in Carson City.

In this day and age it would be very remiss of us not to warn that using the services of a prostitute is a highly dangerous activity. A much safer diversion is to read the Entertainment section of the *Yellow Pages* in your hotel room for a few dirty laughs.

Getting Hitched

Speaking of more socially acceptable forms of expression, the idea of Las Vegas as a wedding—and divorce—mecca dates back to the same "anything goes" mentality that gave birth to the gambling industry and other adventures. The more convoluted and time-consuming the regulations for getting hitched or unhitched in the other states of the union, the more Nevada appealed as a place of convenience.

Today, many states have relaxed their strictures, but Las Vegas and Reno continue to have a thriving industry in weddings, offering the added lure of the grand hotels and casinos. Today, more than 75,000 couples tie the knot in Las Vegas each year.

If you are the sort of person who is impressed by celebrity name-dropping, check out some of the ads or billboards for the various wedding chapels. According to the proprietors, among those who have done the deed at their establishments include Joan Collins, Mia Farrow, Eddie Fisher, Michael Jordan, Jon Bon Jovi, Demi Moore, Dudley Moore, Mickey Rooney, Frank Sinatra, Elizabeth Taylor, and Bruce Willis.

Most of the major hotels offer elegant chapels for ceremonies rang-

"We've Only Just Begun" Wedding Chapel at the Imperial Palace Hotel & Casino

ing from the ridiculous to the sublime. You can get married dressed as King Arthur and Guinevere at the Excalibur, in a toga at Caesars Palace, or as just about anything else at any of a number of chapels. And there are dozens of small establishments that do nothing else but service the needs of the betrothed.

The busier chapels will require reservations, but many of the chapels in Las Vegas can also deal with walk-in customers. There are (honest!) a drive-up wedding window and a chapel on wheels for those in a hurry.

If you are planning to get married in Las Vegas, check with the County Clerk's office for the current legalities; here is a summary of the rules as this book went to print.

Marriages

The prospective bride and groom must appear together at the County Clerk's office to apply for a wedding license.

In Las Vegas, the County Clerk's Office is located in the Courthouse, in the 200 block of South Third Street in downtown; 455-3156. The office is open from 8 A.M. until midnight Monday through Thursday, and from 8 A.M. Friday straight through to midnight Sunday. In addition, the clerk is available 24 hours a day on all Nevada legal holidays. *Fee.* $35.

If you can prove you are 18 years or older, you do not need parental consent. Persons between the ages of 16 and 18 must have the consent of either parent or a court-appointed guardian. Either parent must appear in person, or the applicants must bring a notarized affidavit of consent including the birthdate of the minor and stating the relationship of the party giving consent.

A person under the age of 16 must have a court order from the Nevada District Court as well as the consent of either parent or a legal guardian. The court order will be granted if the court determines that the marriage will serve the best interests of the minor. Pregnancy alone is not an automatic qualification.

Blood tests are not required and there is no waiting period. Divorces must be final in the state where granted. The date of the final decree and the city and state where granted are required.

Civil Ceremonies

If you want to have a quick civil ceremony in Las Vegas you can hop over to the office of the Commissioner of Civil Marriages at 136 South 4th Street, one block from the marriage License Bureau. You can walk in single and stroll out married during the same hours that the County Clerk is open. The fee for a ceremony is $25 Monday through Friday from 8 A.M. to 5 P.M., and $30 for late nights, weekends, and holidays.

You must have at least one witness besides the person performing the ceremony. You cannot count on finding an extra clerk in the office; people have been known to hire strangers from the street.

Chapel Ceremonies

For many visitors, though, a civil ceremony at the commissioner's office is not what it is all about. Instead, they want to do it up in grand (by Las Vegas standards) style at one of the dozens of wedding chapels. You can get just about anything you want, from a choir of Elvis impersonators to a chapel on wheels to a ceremony in King Arthur's Court. Rates vary and reservations are necessary at some—but not all—of the chapels.

Here is a listing of some:

A Chapel by The Courthouse. 203 Bridger Avenue; 384-9099.
Candlelight Wedding Chapel. 2855 Las Vegas Blvd. South; 735-4179.
Chapel of the Bells. 2233 Las Vegas Blvd. South; 735-6803.
Chapel Of Love. 1431 Las Vegas Blvd. South; 387-0155.
Cupid's Wedding Chapel. 827 Las Vegas Blvd. South; 598-4444.
Graceland Wedding Chapel. 619 Las Vegas Blvd. South; 474-6655.
L'Amour Chapel. 1901 Las Vegas Blvd. South; 369-5683.
Las Vegas Wedding Gardens. 200 W. Sahara Avenue; 387-0123.
Little Chapel of the Flowers. 1717 Las Vegas Blvd. South; 735-4331.
Little White Chapel. 1301 Las Vegas Blvd. South; 382-5943.
San Francisco Sally's Victorian Chapel. 1304 Las Vegas Blvd. South; 385-7777.
Silver Bell Wedding Chapel. 607 Las Vegas Blvd. South; 382-3726.
Wee Kirk o' The Heather. 231 Las Vegas Blvd. South; 382-9830.

Here are some of the hotel chapels in Las Vegas:

Bally's Wedding Chapel. Bally's Casino Resort; 892-2222.
Circus Circus Chapel of The Fountains. Circus Circus Hotel/Casino; 794-3777.
Excalibur Hotel Wedding Chapel. Excalibur Hotel & Casino; 597-7260.
Little Church of the West. Hacienda Hotel; 739-7971.
Plaza Chapel. Union Plaza Hotel; 386-2110.
Riviera Royale Wedding Chapel. Riviera Hotel; 794-9494.
Shalimar Wedding Chapel. Shalimar Hotel; 382-7372.
We've Only Just Begun Wedding Chapel. Imperial Palace; 733-0011.

Money, Money, Money

We can't think of very many places on earth more oriented to finding ways to take money out of the pockets of visitors than Las Vegas. And so, the proprietors are also quite accommodating when it comes to helping visitors scratch out every possible penny from its hiding place.

Arriving with foreign currency? No problem. Every major casino will be glad to exchange your francs, pounds, yen, or whatever into cash—or gambling chips. They'll extract a fee in the form of a discount from the actual exchange rate; you will probably get the best deal at a bank.

Travelers checks are no problem at hotels, casinos, restaurants, or stores in Las Vegas; some places may require a photo ID card.

Need to cash a check? No problem for guests at a major hotel, although some establishments may enforce a limit on the amount they will release each day. At the casinos, the cashier will often cash checks for clients known to the casino, or in some way guaranteed by a credit card.

Need a loan? Most casinos will extend "markers" (credit vouchers) to gamblers who apply for such a loan in advance of their visit. Unsecured loans on the spot are more difficult to obtain.

Need a cash advance? Most major casinos have installed automated teller machines that permit withdrawal of cash from bank accounts or as cash advances against credit cards. Bank machines generally work with one of the national syndicates such as Plus, Cirrus, or Instant-Teller. If you choose to take a cash advance, be sure to read the disclaimer on the machine carefully; some systems apply a hefty service charge to the amount of money you are withdrawing, over and above any interest the holder of your credit card will charge.

A notch down on the pecking order are check-cashing businesses which specialize in handling out-of-state personal checks, money orders, and even savings account passbooks. You'll need personal identification, and you can expect to pay a fee that will increase with the complexity of the verification and transfer of funds.

And then there are the pawnshops of Las Vegas, filled with jewelry, cameras, furs, and other items left behind to raise cash. There are more than four pages of listings in the current *Yellow Pages*. If you are that desperate for cash, perhaps you should seek counseling of a different sort than is available in these pages.

Comps

Let's get one thing out of the way: there is no free lunch, not even in Las Vegas.

There are, however, "comp" lunches, breakfasts, dinners, drinks, hotel rooms, shows, airline tickets, and more. That's comp as in complimentary, but as we say, they're not quite free.

The distinction is this: almost all of the casinos in Nevada offer all sorts of freebies to gamblers. They do so because they know that, over the long haul, they will win and you will lose.

The system starts with free drinks for players, which is actually one of the more insidious come-ons in marketing. Not only does it encourage players to sit at the slot machine or at the gaming table, but alcohol dulls the senses and reduces the inhibitions and otherwise aids in the removal of cash from your wallet.

The next step up is the provision of free meals. At a smaller casino, the process might be as simple as this: the pit boss, perhaps alerted by the dealer to your consistent gambling, will drop by and hand you a card good for dinner. It might be a free pass to the coffee shop or the buffet, or you may be "comped" into the gourmet restaurant. Either way, it's a reward for playing at the casino and it also keeps you on the premises before and after the meal.

At larger casinos, the process has become a bit more complicated. Ask the floor manager or the pit boss to "evaluate" your play; he or she may actually chart your bets or may consult with the dealer. Generally, a comp rating will be given based on several hours of play at a consistent level.

And major casinos have begun using various electronic means to track the play of visitors at slot machines; they will issue a magnetically coded card that is placed in readers attached to the slots to record the amount of action. The cards can be cashed in for free meals or shows after a certain amount of play.

(Some casinos have a slightly less sophisticated means of tracking slot players, relying on records kept by change booths or strolling change attendants. There is, of course, more of an opportunity to cheat here; one scheme would be to change a few hundred dollars in bills into coins but only play a small portion of the silver.)

It doesn't hurt to ask one of the supervisors about how you can be evaluated. If you don't like the answer, you can always take your business elsewhere.

It all comes down to the amount of "action" you will provide the casino. Action is the amount of money you will put at risk over a particular period of time. For example, if you bet $25 per hand in blackjack for four hours a day over a three-day weekend, you are giving the casino something like $7,500 in action; at most middle-of-the-road casinos that should be worth a free hotel room for the length of your stay.

There is no official rulebook to the distribution of comps. Smaller casinos more desperate to attract action may be more generous than the bigger places. However, the most spectacular casinos—places like Caesars Palace and the Mirage—offer the most spectacular comps to the highest of rollers. The two-story, 4,000-square-foot Fantasy Suites at Caesars Palace, for example, are described by the casinos as "priceless" because they cannot be rented by guests. They are offered as comps, along with free meals, room service, shows, limousine service, and other amenities to people for whom money must truly hold no meaning.

According to casino insiders, the serious freebies start at about the $25 per hand level for free rooms. "RFB" players, who receive rooms, food, and beverages, generally are $75 to $125 per hand gamblers. The penthouses, limousines, and other perks are usually offered at about the $150 per hand level.

Some hotels are more up-front about their programs than others. For example, the Flamingo Hilton in Reno issues a rate card for players in its Club Flamingo slot system, which uses a magnetic card to record action.

At the Flamingo Hilton in Reno, players can earn rewards ranging from a pair of free passes to the buffet to meals at the coffee shop or food court to admission to the Heavenly Bodies showroom and, for the highest rollers at the slots, free meals at the Top of the Hilton gourmet restaurant.

Playing time is based on six handle pulls per minute (once every ten seconds) using the maximum number of coins for each machine. In other words, if you are playing at a $1 machine, the club payoffs are based on betting the maximum number of tokens—usually five—for that machine. Fewer coins bet or fewer handle pulls per minute will require more playing time.

The quickest way to freebies is to play a $5 machine where you can obtain a dinner buffet, coffee shop, or food court pass for two for one hour of play. (At $30 per pull, six times a minute, this means you are risking $10,800 in hopes of obtaining $20 worth of food.)

More reasonable requirements apply to the 25 cent machines. The Reno Hilton will give the same meals described above to a player who puts in five hours. (That's $1.25 per pull, six times a minute; a mere $2,250 in action.)

By the way, you'd have to play for four and a half hours at the $5 machines or 25 hours at the quarter slots for a pass for two to the Top of the Hilton.

Of course, unless you are completely luckless, you should be able to avoid losing all of your money. Slot machines generally pay back something between 90 and 99 percent of money bet. Remember, though, that this percentage applies over the very long haul and includes the very rare huge jackpot payoffs.

For table players, the Flamingo Hilton Reno offers comp packages that begin with discounts on hotel rooms for visitors willing to put down $10 at a time for four hours a day; free rooms for bettors playing $35 a hand for four hours a day; free room and buffet or coffee shop meals and drinks for $75 bettors, and free rooms, gourmet meals, and drinks for a player betting $100 at a time for four hours a day. If you are willing to bet even more and establish your credentials beforehand, the hotel will offer reimbursements of your airfare to Reno.

If you want to earn comps, keep in mind a few pointers. It is against your own interests to move from casino to casino, since you are diluting your influence. (And don't think that casinos don't know this. That's why they have all of those "clubs" for loyal patrons.) And, if you change from one area of the casino to another, be sure that whoever is evaluating you is aware of where you are going and can transfer supervision.

Note that we have not talked about winning versus losing here. At any particular moment, the casino doesn't really care whether a player is ahead or behind. They know which way the dollars will eventually flow; in fact, if you're ahead of the game, they very much want you to stick around at their casino until the odds start to run the other way.

A Guide to Tipping

Las Vegas, Reno, and Lake Tahoe are very much dependent on the tourist and conventioneer, and tipping is an essential element of the economy. In fact, it has its own name in the casino: toking. You will have an extraordinary opportunity to grease the palms of dozens of strangers on your visit, but it's not necessary to pay everyone you meet.

Here's a guided tour to outstretched hands.

Transportation. The standard tip for **taxi drivers** is in the range of 15 to 20 percent of the fare; you might want to give a little bit more for a driver who helps with the bags or one who puts out his or her cigarette at your request.

Valet parking. A tip of about $1 to $2 is standard.

Bartenders and cocktail waitresses. Most casinos offer free drinks to players at the tables and some extend the privilege to slot players; a tip of 50 cents per drink or $1 per round is standard.

Restaurant servers and room service. Again, a tip in the range of 15 to 20 percent is standard. A sore point among some waiters and waitresses are visitors to buffets who don't leave money for the people who clear away your dishes and bring you drinks.

If you have received a free meal, check to see if your comp includes a gratuity for the staff; if it does not, you should leave a tip equal to 15 to 20 percent of what the bill would have been.

Bell captains and bellmen. The usual rate is about $1 to $2 per bag; give $1 or $2 to a bellman who summons a cab for you.

Bingo and keno runners. A small tip every few cards, and a larger tip with a winning card.

Dealers. A small tip, in the form of cash or a chip a few times an hour is standard. Some dealers might prefer that you place a small bet for them every once in a while, especially if you are winning; ask them how they'd like to be toked. In theory, this will not give you any special advantage at the table, but it might earn you more friendly treatment.

Maids. About $1 per day is standard; more if you have created an unusual amount of work or if extra services have been provided.

Showroom maitre d'hotel. In the past, nearly every casino showroom had a maitre d' out front who determined where each guest was seated. Ignore him and you might end up in the back corner behind the coffee pot; make him happy and you would end up down front and center. The current trend, though, is toward reserved seats at most shows—

especially the more expensive ones. Therefore, tipping the maitre d'—if there is one—is optional.

Shop Till You Drop in Las Vegas

Once you are married, then comes the real excitement: shopping.

If you've got any money left in your wallet—or if you are traveling with a spouse who prefers to gamble on clothing or accessories instead of the roll of the dice—Las Vegas offers several major shopping areas.

Actually, the hottest shopping area for those with dough to blow, or dreams of the same, is connected to one of the most spectacular casinos in Las Vegas, at Caesars Palace.

We'll start with the two largest conventional malls and a major factory outlet shopping center.

Fashion Show Mall

The **Fashion Show Mall,** located directly on The Strip at 3200 Las Vegas Boulevard South, at the head of Convention Center Drive and next to the Mirage, is a large mall with 145 shops, including a wide range of clothing and specialty stores. It is within walking distance of most center-Strip motels and the Las Vegas Convention Center. Valet parking is available. Hours are Monday to Friday 10 A.M. to 9 P.M., Saturday 10 A.M. to 7 P.M., and Sunday noon to 6 P.M. For information, call 369-8382.

Women's Fashions: Abercrombie & Fitch; Ambiance; Benetton; Bullock's; Cache; Casual Corner; Chez Magnifique; Contempo Casuals; Deon's; Evening Classics; Judy's; Koala Blue; Kolonaki; La-dy Ferenc; Laise Adzer; Lane Bryant; Lauren & The Boys; Lillie Rubin; The Limited; Marshall-Rousso; Mondi; Next Door; Petite Sophisticate; Pizazz; Portofino; Private Collections; 5-7-9; Wet Seal.

Shoes: Bally of Switzerland; Bianca; Brass Boot; Cobbie Shop; Florsheim Shoes; Foot Locker; Joyce-Selby; Kinney; Lady Foot Locker; Leeds; Norman Kaplan; Rocky Mountain; Rococo; San Remo.

Cards, Gifts, Toys, and Books: Animal Crackers; Carlan's Gifts; Crystal Palace; Expanding Wall; Fantasia; Gifts of the World; Serendipity Gallery; Waldenbooks; West of Dallas.

Art Galleries: Centaur Sculpture; Gallery of History; Minotaur Gallery.

Apparel, Specialty: American Sock; Banana Republic; Disney Store; Furs by Yolanda; I Love Hats; Koala Blue; Merle Harmon's Fan Fair; Midnight Lace; Miller Stockman Western Ware; North Beach Leather; St. Croix Shop; Units; Victoria's Secret.

Food: Bernie's Bagel; Cafe Capri; Chin's; Ethel M Chocolates; Heidi's Frozen Yogurt; See's Candies; Sweets of Las Vegas; Food Court.

Men's and Family Apparel: Abercrombie & Fitch; Benetton; Brats; Custom Shop Shirtmakers; Camouflage; The Gap; Harris & Frank; JW; Lauren & The Boys; Melwan's; Miller's Outpost; Oak Tree; Schwartz Big & Tall; Shirt Shoppe; Steve Gordon's; Uomo Uomo Sport; Zeidler & Zeidler.

Jewelry: Bailey Banks & Biddle; Chainery; Fashion Shop Jewelry; Gold Factory; Lindstrom Jewelers; Weisfield's; Whitehall; Zales.

Specialty: Abercrombie & Fitch; Antique Emporium; Bag & Baggage; Collegetown USA; Electronics Boutique; El Portal Luggage; Futuretronics; Gallery of Collectibles; Gloria Jean Coffee Bean; La Perfumerie; Lenscrafters; Louis Vuitton; Omni Chemists; Sam Goody's; San Francisco Music Box; Sharper Image; Suncoast Motion Picture; Sun Shade Optique; Tennis Lady Tennis Man; Vignettes.

Department Stores: Bullock's; Dillard's; May Company; Neiman-Marcus; Saks Fifth Avenue.

The Boulevard Mall

The **Boulevard Mall** is a typical suburban sprawl of shops decorated with real plants and palms under an attractive atrium. There's an open, bright feeling—sort of like being outdoors. It is located at 3528 S. Maryland Parkway, at the intersection with Desert Inn Road about five minutes east of The Strip. It claims the mantle as the largest mall in Nevada. Hours are 10 A.M. to 9 P.M. Monday to Wednesday, 9 A.M. to 9 P.M. Thursday to Saturday, and 10 A.M. to 7 P.M. Sunday. Valet parking is available. For information, call 735-8268.

Accessories: Afterthoughts; Carmen Bed Bath & Gifts; Claire's Boutique; Joan Bari; Parklane Hosiery; Sporting Eyes; Sunglass Designs.

Men's Apparel: Chess King; Coda; Harris & Frank; J. Riggings; JW; Oak Tree; Pacific Wave; Structure; Zeidler & Zeidler.

Men's and Women's Apparel: County Seat; The Gap; Going to the Game; Gymboree; Hot Cats; Howard & Phil's Western; Sports Logo; Wilson's Leather Experts.

Women's Apparel: Cacique; Casual Corner; Charlotte Russe; Contempo Casuals; Deon's; Express; 5-7-9; The Gap; Lane Bryant; Lerner; Limited; Next Door; Petite Sophisticate; Switzer's; Victoria's Secret; Wet Seal; Woman's World.

Cards, Gifts, and Specialty: Amy's Hallmark; Bath & Body Works; Country Hutch; Disney Store; Hot Topic; Just a Buck; Nature Co.; San Francisco Music Co.; Sanrio Surprises; Sesame Street General Store; Spencer; Tinderbox.

Services: Glamour Shots; Great Expectations Hair Salon; Kiddie Kandids; Prestige Travel; Stark Express Shoe Repair.

Shoes: Castleby; Dolci's; Famous Footwear; Foot Action; Foot Locker; Kids Foot Locker; Kinney Shoes; Lady Foot Locker; Leed's; Naturalizer; Nine West; Wild Pair.

Miscellaneous: I Natural Cosmetics; Merle Norman Cosmetics.

Food: A&W Hot Dogs; Bain's Deli; Cinnabon; China Star; Ethel M's Chocolates; Everything Yogurt; Flamers; General Nutrition Center; Gloria Jean's Gourmet Coffees; Great Steak and Potato Co.; Hot Dog on a Stick; Hibachi San; Island of Hawaii; JB's Restaurant; La Salsa; McDonald's; Mrs. Field's Cookies; Orange Julius/Dairy Queen; Panda Express; Quiet Corner; Sbarro; See's Candies; Sweet Factory; The Vineyard.

Pets, Hobbies, and Entertainment: B. Dalton Bookseller; Champs Sports; Docktor Pet Center; KayBee Toy & Hobby; Radio Shack; Sam Goody; Software Etc.; Suncoast Motion Picture Co.; Wherehouse Records.

Home Furnishings: The Bombay Co.; Carmen.

Jewelers: Bailey Banks & Biddle; The Chainery; J. Burton Jewelry; Lundstrom Jewelry; Mission Jewelers; Tiffin's Jewelers; Whitehall Jewelers; Zales.

Department Stores: Broadway; Dillard's; Marshall's; JC Penney; Sears; Woolworth's.

Factory Outlets

Las Vegas Factory Stores. Five miles south of Tropicana Ave. off the top of The Strip, the casual mall offers products from some of the best-known brand names. Located at 9155 Las Vegas Boulevard South. Open Monday to Saturday from 10 A.M. to 8 P.M., and on Sunday 10 A.M. to 6 P.M. For information, call 897-9090.

Stores include Adolfo II; American Tourister; Applause; Banister; Barbizon; Blue Wave; Book Warehouse; Cape Isle Knitters; Corning/Revere; Famous Brands Housewares; Famous Footwear; Florsheim Shoe; Geoffrey Beene; Gitano; IB Diffusion; Indian Traders; Leather Loft; Mikasa; Nine West; No Nonsense; Paper Factory; Perfumania; Prestige Fragrance & Cosmetics; Rocky Mountain Chocolate Factory; Toy Liquidators; Van Heusen; Welcome Home; Westpoint Pepperell; Westport Ltd.; and Whims.

Belz Factory Outlet World. I-15 at the Blue Diamond exchange, south of Las Vegas. Open daily 10 A.M. to 9 P.M., and Sunday 10 A.M. to 6 P.M. Call 897-7271.

Stores include Adolfo II; Amity Leather; Afterthoughts; Aileen; Bass Apparel; Blue Wave; Bon Worth; Bruce Alan Bags; Bugle Boy; Burlington Brands; Buxton; Carter's Childrensware; Chez Magnifique; County Seat; Corning/Revere; Crown Jewels; Danskin; Designer Labels for Less; Ducks Unlimited; Ellen Ashley; Hushpuppies; Kitchen Collection; Kitchen Place; Leather Loft; L'eggs/Hanes/Bali; Levi's; Lucia; Music 4 Less; Naturalizer; Nike; Oneida; Osh Kosh b'Gosh; Perfumania; Pfaltzgraff; Prestige Fragrance; Publishers Warehouse; Ribbon Outlet; Ross Simons; Ruff Hewn; Springmaid Wamsutta; Stone Mountain Handbags; Stride Rite; Swank; Toy Liquidators; Trader Kids; Van Heusen; Village Hatter; Westport Ltd.; Whims/Sarah Coventry; and Young Generations.

Other Stores

Here are a few of our favorite stores located outside of shopping malls.

Bookstar. 3910 S. Maryland Parkway; 732-7882. One of the largest and best-stocked bookstores anywhere. And it's open late into the night; stop off on the way to the airport.

Cowtown Boots. 328 W. Sahara; 384-8622. A factory outlet for hand-made leather boots from cowhide to snakeskin to Teju lizard.

Lance Burton Magic Shop. Hacienda Hotel, 3950 Las Vegas Blvd. South; 739-1920. Tricks, gags, books, and lessons.

The Magic Shop. Riviera Hotel. 2901 Las Vegas Blvd. South; 733-1965.

The Magic Mansion. 4702 S. Maryland Parkway; 732-1714. A professional magic shop.

Waldenbooks Superstore. 3783 S. Maryland Parkway; 369-1996. An oversized version of your basic Waldenbooks store; if you can't find what you're looking for at Bookstar across the road, check here, or the other way around.

If you're determined to bring a bit of Las Vegas home with you (and if you've left a bit of money in your wallet or on your credit card) you may want to visit one of several stores that sell gambling equipment. Be sure you investigate state and local laws before you bring back machines.

Gamblers Book Club. 630 S. 11th; 382-7555; (800) 634-6243. They take their games seriously here, offering the biggest collection of gambling arcana we know of, as well as a fine collection of local history, travel, and fiction.

Gamblers General Store. 800 S. Main Street; 382-9903. Slot machines, poker machines, personalized poker chips, and craps tables.

Paul-Son Dice and Card. 2121 Industrial Road; 384-2425. Gambling equipment, including used dice and cards from major casinos.

Hail Caesars!

And then there are the **Forum Shops at Caesars,** which has to qualify as among the most other-worldly, spectacular shopping venues anywhere in the world. In other words, perfectly appropriate for Las Vegas.

The storefront facades and common areas are designed to appear like an ancient Roman streetscape, with huge columns and arches, central piazzas, ornate fountains, and classic statuary.

Overhead, on a barrel-vaulted ceiling, a painted dome emulates the Mediterranean sky. The sky turns from daylight to sunset to dawn to full daylight over the course of two hours. Check it out: the sun rises in the east and sets in the west.

The 240,000-square-foot-mall, built for a mere $100 million or so and opened in 1992 on a site that had been used by Caesars (mostly unsuccessfully) as a race track, has become one of the most successful shopping "streets" anywhere. According to the owners, on a typical day, the mall draws 40,000 visitors; on busy weekends as many as 90,000 show up. To put that into a bit of travel perspective, Walt Disney World on its busiest days around Christmas will draw 75,000 to 80,000 people.

According to a *Forbes* magazine piece a few months after the mall opened, the stores and restaurants have been averaging nearly $3 million in sales per week, or $900 in annual sales per square foot. This compares with the average mall which draws about $158 per square foot. Nevertheless, there have been a few turnovers among stores from the opening; late in 1994, a branch of the Planet Hollywood restaurant chain will arrive.

The Forum Shops were attached onto the north side of Caesars Palace, and the main entrance connects to the main casino. Amazingly, though, there are no casinos within the Forum Shops area itself—although there are a few banks of slot machines right by the entranceway just to ease the transition. It has to be the only place in the world where an actor dressed as Bugs Bunny (at the Warner Bros. Studios store) poses within 30 feet of slot machines.

The Forum area stays open until 11 P.M. most evenings, with some of the restaurants keeping later hours when necessary. When the shops are closed, you can still walk the simulated streets of ancient Rome.

At the entrance to the mall is the **Quadriga** statue, four gold-leafed horses, a charioteer, and five heroic arches, an ancient symbol of great

The Appian Way Shops at Caesars Palace, another shopping area within the resort

achievement. (*Quadriga* is a Latin word for a team of four, and is pronounced *kwod-reye-ja*.) As you look at the fountain, Jupiter is perched up top. Mars faces Gucci. Diana the Huntress checks out Louis Vuitton, and Venus and Pluto keep an eye on the casino.

At the far end of the U-shaped mall is the spectacular **Festival Fountain.** It may look like marble, but it is not; every hour on the hour, starting at 10 A.M., the statuary comes to life.

In the animated tableau, Bacchus, god of merriment and wine, hosts a party. The seven-minute show stars Bacchus, who has already had more than a few sips from his goblet. He enlists the power of Apollo (god of music), Venus (goddess of love), and Plutus (god of wealth) in preparing a party for the guests gathered around his fountain. Plutus will cast his jewels upon the waters of the fountain; Bacchus will summon a laser-drawn chariot to cross the sky above. From the sun, Apollo commands a beam of light that strikes Bacchus' wine goblet to explode it into light.

When the party is over, the statues return to marble-like silence. This high-tech fountain was brought to life by Ron Hays, who produced some of the animated statuary used in the spectacular Pirates of the Caribbean ride at Walt Disney World in Orlando, Florida.

You may want to park the kids at the large video arcade on the lower level of the mall. Free parking is available in the Caesars Palace garage, with valet service offered. By the way, the Forum Shops offer a service that will deliver any packages from Caesars Palace to your hotel—for a fee, of course.

Women's Fashions: Ann Taylor; Bebe; Caché; Express Compagnie Internationale; Plaza Escade; St. John.

Specialty Apparel: A/X Armani Exchange; Beyond the Beach; Boogie's Diner of Aspen; The French Room; Gianni Versace; Gucci; Guess; Nazareno Gabrielli; North Beach Leather; Pollini; Rose of Sharon—Size 14 and Up; Sudachi; Victoria's Secret.

Specialty: Animal Crackers; Antiquities; Brookstone; Caesars World; Crystal Galleria; CyberStation; Davante; El Portal Luggage; Endangered Species; Field of Dreams; Kids Kastle; Louis Vuitton; Magic Masters; Magnet Maximus; The Museum Company; Porsche Design; Roman Times; Sports Logo; Stuff'd; Sungear; Warner Brothers Studio Store; West of Santa Fe.

Men's Apparel: Bernini; Cuzzens; Kerkorian; The Knot Shop; Structure; Vasari.

Jewelry: Bulgari; M.J. Christensen; N. Landau Hyman; Roman Times; Zero Gravity.

Shoes: Avventura; Bruno Magli; Just for Feet; Shoooz at The Forum.

Art Galleries: Circle Fine Art; Galerie Lassen; Minotaur's Forum Gallery; One World; Thomas Charles Gallery.

Food: Bertolini's; Boogie's Diner of Aspen; La Salsa; the Palm; Spago; Stage Deli; Sweet Factory; Swensen's Ice Cream.

Warner Brothers Studio Store. Look up over the entrance for statues of Sylvester the Cat, the Tazmanian Devil, and Daffy Duck—in togas! The inscription over the door reads "Warnerius Fraternus Studius Storius" which is a rough Latin approximation for Warner Brothers Studio Store.

Inside the shop, let your eyes drift upward to spot the Gremlins hiding at the ceiling level. At the back of the store is a video wall showing snippets of classic and current WB movies and cartoons. A pair of computer paint programs allows kids to colorize their own cartoons. Nearby is Marv's Matomic Service, a crawl-through space for kiddies.

And then there are the things on sale: sweatshirts, tees, stuffed animals, toys, and souvenirs with a Warner's theme, for children of all ages. Also on sale is a selection of original cels from WB cartoons with prices ranging from about $100 to $7,000 and more.

Just for Feet. An "interactive shoe store" with more than 100,000 pairs of sports shoes in a 12,000-square-foot space that includes a small basketball court and a treadmill so that customers can try out their footwear in real situations. They've even got tennis shoes for babies.

Magic Masters. A wood paneled room designed to look like Houdini's library. (Check out some of the framed photographs on the wall.) There's a secret door to the left of the counter that leads to a small room where secrets are unveiled to the buyer.

Palm Restaurant. An elegant extension of the famed New York eatery, among its offerings is a $12 prix-fixe lunch menu that includes petite filet mignon, prime rib, or pasta. Dinner offerings include seafood crab cakes for $26, a New York strip steak for $27, and a 36-ounce double steak for two for $57; a variety of salads is also available.

The Econoguide to the Best of
The Forum Shops at Caesars

Warner Brothers Studio Store
Just for Feet
Magic Masters
Palm Restaurant
Spago
Bertolini's
Porsche Design
Antiquities

Spago. Not your average pizzeria. Specialties at the open air cafe which sits under the beautiful artificial Roman sky include spicy chicken pizza with caramelized red onions and chili pesto for $12, Mediterranean fish soup with lobster and couscous for $24, and grilled tuna with tomato-fennel salsa and crisp smoked salmon ravioli for $23.

Bertolini's. The most spectacular setting in the Forum, this "sidewalk cafe" Italian eatery faces the Fountain of the Gods. (It opened as Lombardi's, but changed its name and menu in 1994.) Specialties include unusual pizzas for about $9 and pasta dishes from about $10 to $14. It's the place to see and be seen, although the noise of the water in the fountain can become a bit overbearing.

Porsche Design. "Design is neither form nor function alone, but the synthesis of the two." So says F. A. Porsche, grandson of the legendary automaker Ferdinand Porsche. In 1991, F. A. Porsche was named chairman of the family auto business. His store showcases some of his company's elegantly functional forms including sunglasses, pipes, and shavers.

Antiquities. Not to be missed, this unusual store facing the Festival Fountain is proof of the theory that one man's garbage is another's collectible investment. Where else can you buy a beautifully restored Coke machine, a classic jukebox, or a fortune-telling machine?

The owners of the store include among their treasure mines the backyards of the deep South and the cellars of Brooklyn; recovered items are repaired, repainted, and in some cases improved. Everything works just as it did when the items were new.

On one visit we found a 1942 Wurlitzer Model 950 Gazelle jukebox, the one with colored liquid bubbles and neon. Only 3,400 were ever made, and the unit on display includes more than 300 hours of restoration. It was a bargain at $47,000.

Nearby was a 1940s coin-operated photo booth in working order for $9,800. Other unusual offerings included a restored 1937 Dodg'em bumper car and a Gypsy Grandma Fortune Teller from the 1940s.

Foto-Forum. Here's your chance to put your face on the body you've always dreamed of: a biker babe, a bikini beauty, or Southern belle for the ladies, or perhaps a hockey star, beefcake stud, or Hollywood leading man. The shop uses computer and video wizardry to merge your face with images on file; the result can be a poster, a small portrait, a personalized coffee cup, or just about anything else.

According to the operators, the most popular image for men is (what else could it be in Las Vegas?) Elvis; for women, it's the chance to sit atop a pair of 50-D cups barely contained in a string bikini.

Chapter 12

An Index of Las Vegas and Area Hotels

Standard rooms, non-peak rates

$	$74 or less	**$$$$**	$200 or more
$$	$75–$124	LVBS	Las Vegas Boulevard South
$$$	$125–$199	LVBN	Las Vegas Boulevard North

Las Vegas Strip

Aladdin Hotel & Casino. $$–$$$; 3667 LVBS; 736-0111; (800) 634-3424
Alexis Park. $$$; 375 E. Harmon Ave.; 796-3300; (800) 582-2228
Algiers Hotel. $; 2845 LVBS; 735-3311
Bally's Las Vegas. $$–$$$; 3645 LVBS;739-4111; (800) 634-3434
Barbary Coast. $$; 3595 LVBS; 737-7111; (800) 634-6755
Boardwalk Hotel & Casino. $$; 3750 LVBS; 735-1167; (800) 635-4581
Bourbon St. Hotel & Casino. $$; 120 E. Flamingo Rd.; 737-7200; (800) 634-6956
Caesars Palace. $$–$$$; 3570 LVBS; 731-7110; (800) 634-6661
Carriage House. $$–$$$; 105 E. Harmon Ave.; 798-1020; (800) 777-1700
Center Strip Inn. $–$$; 3688 LVBS; 739-6066; (800) 777-7737
Circus Circus. $–$$; 2880 LVBS; 734-0410; (800) 634-3450
Days Inn Center Strip. $–$$; 3265 LVBS; 735-5102; (800) 828-8032
Desert Inn. $$–$$$; 3145 LVBS; 733-4444; (800) 634-6906
Diamond Inn Motel. $; 4605 LVBS; 736-2565
Econo Inn. $–$$; 3939 LVBS; 736-8031
Econo Lodge. $; 1150 LVBS; 382-6001
El Rancho. $; 2755 LVBS; 796-2222
Excalibur. $$–$$$; 3850 LVBS; 597-7777; (800) 937-7777
Flamingo Hilton. $$–$$$; 3555 LVBS; 733-3111; (800) 732-2111
Frontier Hotel & Gambling Hall. $$; 3120 LVBS; 794-8200; (800) 634-6966
Hacienda. $–$$; 3950 LVBS; 739-8911; (800) 634-6713
Harrah's Las Vegas Casino Hotel. $$–$$$; 3475 LVBS; 369-5000; (800) 634-6765
Holiday House. $; 2211 LVBS; 732-2468
Holiday Inn Las Vegas. $$; 325 E. Flamingo Rd.; 732-9100; (800) 732-7889
Howard Johnson Hotel & Casino. $–$$; 3111 W. Tropicana Ave.; 798-1111, (800) 654-2000
Imperial Palace. $$–$$$; 3535 LVBS; 731-3311; (800) 634-6441
Klondike Motor Inn. $; 5191 LVBS; 739-9351
La Concha Motel. $; 2955 LVBS; 735-1255

Sands Hotel & Casino, Las Vegas

La Quinta. **$**; 3782 LVBS; 739-7457; (800) 531-5900
Luxor. **$$$**; 3900 Las Vegas Blvd. South; 262-4444; (800) 228-1000
Maxim. **$$–$$$**; 160 E. Flamingo Rd.; 731-4300; (800) 634-6987
MGM Grand Hotel. **$$–$$$**; 3799 LVBS; (800) 929-1112
The Mirage. **$$$**; 3400 LVBS; 791-7111; (800) 627-6667
Riviera Hotel & Casino. **$$**; 2901 LVBS; 734-5110; (800) 634-6753
Rodeway Inn. **$**; 3786 LVBS; 736-1434, (800) 228-2000
Sahara Hotel & Casino. **$$**; 2535 LVBS; 737-2111; (800) 634-6666
Sands Hotel Casino. **$$–$$$**; 3355 LVBS; 733-5000; (800) 634-6901
Stardust Resort & Casino. **$–$$**; 3000 LVBS; 732-6111; (800) 634-6757
Sun Harbor Budget Suites. **$**; 1500 Stardust Rd.; 732-1500
Sunrise Fountain Suites. **$**; 3801 LVBS; 434-0848
Tam O'Shanter. **$**; 3317 LVBS; 735-7331; (800) 727-3423
Travel Lodge Center Strip. **$**; 3419 LVBS; 734-6801; (800) 854-7666
Travel Lodge South Strip. **$**; 3735 LVBS; 736-3443; (800) 255-3050
Travel Lodge Strip. **$**; 2830 LVBS; 735-4222; (800) 422-3313
Treasure Island. **$$–$$$**; 3300 LVBS; 894-7111; (800) 944-7444.
Tropicana Resort and Casino. **$$–$$$**; 3801 LVBS; 739-2222; (800) 634-4000
Vacation Village. **$$–$$$**; 6711 LVBS; 897-1700; (800) 338-0608
Vegas World. **$–$$**; 2000 LVBS; 382-2000; (800) 634-6277
Westward Ho Hotel. **$–$$**; 2900 LVBS; 731-2900; (800) 634-6803

Near The Strip

Arizona Charlie's Hotel Casino & Bowling. **$**; 740 S. Decatur Blvd. 258-5200; (800) 342-2695
Best Western Parkview Inn. **$–$$**; 905 LVBN; 385-1213; (800) 528-1234
Blair House Residence Suites. **$–$$**; 344 E. Desert Inn Rd.; 792-2222; (800) 553-9111

Bonanza Lodge Motel. $; 1808 E. Fremont St.; 382-9990
Budget Inn. $; 301 S. Main St.; 385-5560
Comfort Inn S. $–$$; 5075 Koval Ln.; 736-3600
Continental Hotel Casino and Resort. $–$$; 4100 Paradise Rd.; 737-5555; (800) 634-6641
Courtyard by Marriott. $$–$$$; 3275 Paradise Rd.; 791-3600; (800) 321-2211
Fairfield Inn (Marriott). $$–$$$; 3850 Paradise Rd.; 791-0899
Gold Coast Hotel & Casino. $$; 4000 W. Flamingo Rd.; 367-7111; (800) 331-5334
Grand Flamingo. $; 100 Winnick Ave.; 731-6100
Highlander Inn. $; 211 E. Flamingo Rd.; 733-7800; (800) 634-6774
Holiday Royale Apartment Suites. $$; 4505 Paradise Rd.; 733-7676
King Albert. $; 185 Albert Ave.; 732-1555; (800) 553-7753
King 8 Hotel & Gambling Hall. $$; 3330 W. Tropicana Ave.; 736-8988; (800) 634-3488
Meadows Inn. $; 525 E. Bonanza.; 366-0456
Motel 6. $; 195 E. Tropicana Ave.; 798-0728
Moulin Rouge. $; 900 W. Bonanza Rd.; 648-5054
Nevada Palace Hotel and Casino. $–$$; 5255 Boulder Hwy.; 458-8810; (800) 634-6283
Palace Station Hotel & Casino. $$; 2411 W. Sahara Ave.; 367-2411; (800) 634-3101
Paradise Resort Inn. $$; 4350 Paradise Rd.; 733-3900
Plaza Suite Hotel & Casino (Howard Johnson's). $$; 4255 Paradise Rd.; 369-4400; (800) 654-2000
Quality Inn Hotel & Casino. $–$$; 377 E. Flamingo Rd.; 733-7777; (800) 634-6617
Quality Sunrise Suites. $$; 4575 Boulder Hwy.; 434-0848
Ramada Las Vegas Inn. $–$$; 1501 W. Sahara Ave.; 731-3222; (800) 228-2828
Residence Inn by Marriott. $$–$$$; 3225 Paradise Rd.; 796-9300; (800) 331-3131
Rio Suite Hotel & Casino. $$–$$$; 3700 W. Flamingo Rd.; 252-7777; (800) 888-1808
Sam's Town Hotel & Gambling Hall. $; 5111 Boulder Hwy.; 456-7777; (800) 634-6371
San Remo Casino & Resort. $$–$$$; 115 E. Tropicana Ave.; 739-9000; (800) 522-7366
Santa Fe Hotel & Casino. $–$$; 4949 N. Rancho Dr.; 658-4900; (800) 872-6823
Sheffield Inn. $$; 3970 Paradise Rd.; 796-9000; (800) 632-4040
St. Tropez. $$–$$$; 455 E. Harmon Ave.; 369-5400; (800) 666-5400
Super 8 Motel. $; 4250 Koval Ln.; 794-0888
Town Hall Hotel & Casino. $; 4155 Koval Ln.; 731-2111; (800) 634-6541

Las Vegas Convention Center

Best Western Mardi Gras Inn. $$–$$$; 3500 Paradise Rd.; 731-2020; (800) 634-6501
Convention Center Lodge. $–$$; 79 E. Convention Center Dr.; 735-1315
Desert Paradise. $–$$; 465 E. Desert Inn Rd.; 735-5112; (800) 634-6635
D.I. 500 Motel. $$; 505 E. Desert Inn Rd.; 735-3160
Las Vegas Hilton. $$–$$$; 3000 Paradise Rd.; 732-5111; (800) 732-7117
Paddlewheel Hotel & Casino. $$; 305 Convention Center Dr.; 734-0711; (800) 782-2600
Royal Hotel & Casino. $; 99 Convention Center Dr.; 735-6117
Somerset House. $; 294 Convention Center Dr.; 735-4411
Villa Roma. $–$$; 220 Convention Center Dr.; 735-4151; (800) 634-6535

Airport Area

Airport Inn. $–$$; 5100 Paradise Rd.; 798-2777; (800) 634-6439
Best Western McCarran Inn. $$; 4970 Paradise Rd.; 798-5530; (800) 626-7575
E-Z 8 Motel. $–$$; 5201 S. Industrial Rd.; 739-9513

Downtown and Area

Ambassador East Motel. $; 916 E. Fremont St.; 384-8281
Apache Motel. $; 407 S. Main St.; 382-7606
Arrowhead Motel. $; 2403 LVBN.; 399-9043

Aztec Inn. $; 2200 LVBS; 385-4566
Best Western Main St. Inn. $–$$; 1000 N. Main St.; 382-3455; (800) 851-1414
Best Western Marianna Inn. $–$$; 1322 E. Fremont St.; 385-1150; (800) 356-5329
Binion's Horseshoe. $$; 128 E. Fremont St.; 382-1600; (800) 622-6468
California Hotel Casino. $$; 12 Ogden Ave.; 385-1222; (800) 634-6255
City Center Motel. $; 700 E. Fremont St.; 382-4766
Convention Inn. $$; 735 E. Desert Inn Rd.; 737-1555; (800) 845-5564
Crest Budget Inn. $; 207 N. 6th St.; 382-5642; (800) 777-1817
Daisy Motel. $; 415 S. Main St.; 382-0707
Days Inn. $–$$; 3227 Civic Center Drive; 399-3297
Days Inn Downtown. $–$$; 707 E. Fremont St.; 388-1400; (800) 325-2344
Downtowner. $; 129 N. 8th St.; 384-1441; (800) 777-2566
El Cid Motel. $; 233 S. 6th St.; 384-4696
El Cortez. $–$$; 600 E. Fremont St.; 385-5200; (800) 634-6703
El Morocco. $–$$; 2975 LVBS; 735-7145
Ferguson's. $; 1028 E. Fremont St.; 382-3500
Fitzgerald's. $–$$; 301 E. Fremont St.; 388-2400; (800) 274-5825
Four Queens Hotel & Casino. $$; 202 E. Fremont St.; 385-4011; (800) 634-6045
Gold Spike Hotel/Casino. $; 400 E. Ogden Ave.; 384-8444; (800) 634-6703
Golden Gate. $–$$; 111 S. Main St.; 382-3510; (800) 426-0521
Golden Inn. $; 120 LVBN; 384-8204
Golden Nugget. $$–$$$; 129 E. Fremont St.; 385-7111; (800) 634-3454
Hotel Nevada. $; 235 S. Main St.; 385-7311; (800) 637-5777
Jackie Gaughan's Plaza Hotel. $; 1 S. Main St.; 386-2110; (800) 634-6575
Lady Luck Casino Hotel. $$–$$$; 206 N. 3rd St.; 477-3000; (800) 523-9582
Las Vegas Club Hotel & Casino. $$; 18 E. Fremont St.; 385-1664; (800) 634-6532
Lee Motel. $; 200 S. 8th St.; 382-1297
Main St. Station. $; 300 N. Main St.; 387-5333
Nevada Hotel & Casino. $; 235 S. Main St.; 385-7311; (800) 637-5777
Ninth St. Motel. $; 117 N. 9th St.; 384-1908
Ogden House. $; 651 Ogden Ave.; 385-5200
Par-A-Dice Inn. $; 2217 E. Fremont St.; 382-6440
Queen of Hearts Hotel. $; 19 E. Lewis Ave.; 382-8878; (800) 835-6005
Rainbow Vegas Hotel. $–$$; 401 S. Casino Center Blvd.; 386-6166; (800) 634-6635
Sam Boyd's Fremont Hotel & Casino. $; 200 E. Fremont St.; 385-3232; (800) 634-6182
Shalimar Hotel & Casino. $; 1401 LVBS; 388-0301
Showboat Hotel, Casino & Bowling Center. $–$$; 2800 E. Fremont St.; 385-9123;
  (800) 826-2800
Town Palms. $; 321 S. Casino Center Blvd.; 382-1611
Travel Lodge Downtown. $; 2028 E. Fremont; 384-7540; (800) 255-3050
Union Plaza. $–$$; 1 Main St.; 386-2110; (800) 634-6575

Laughlin, Nevada

Colorado Belle. (800) 458-9500
Edgewater. (800) 634-6154
Flamingo Hilton. (800) 352-6464
Gold River. (800) 835-7903
Golden Nugget. (800) 237-1739
Harrah's. (800) 447-8700
Pioneer Club. (800) 634-3469
Ramada Express. (800) 272-6232
Riverside Resort. (800) 227-3849

Chapter 13

Eating Your Way Across Las Vegas

Las Vegas' Favorite Food Buffets

Comedian Gary Shandling offered us the best reason we've ever heard for the popularity of buffets in Las Vegas. He told us of an unlucky visitor who had dropped $800 at the tables and found himself at an all-you-can-eat buffet at the casino. "By God, I am going to eat $800 worth of food if it kills me!"

The history of buffets in Las Vegas may go back to the town's origins as a provisioning center for miners and railroad workers. Bars would compete for business by offering the proverbial "free lunch" for customers who kept their glasses full.

Today's casinos, of course, view the buffet in somewhat the same way. They figure if they can lure you into their doors with the offer of an inexpensive meal you are quite likely to stop to play the tables or the slot machines on your way in or out. The casinos try to encourage this as much as they can by placing the buffets at the back of the casino. The casinos also try to find ways to encourage all-night gamblers to stick around for breakfast.

In case you were wondering, The Excalibur reports that each month it goes through 50,500 heads of lettuce; 27,000 pounds of bacon; 18,000 gallons of milk; 5,400 gallons of Pepsi; 330,000 bread rolls; 44,100 Cornish game hens; 24,000 watermelons; 15,000 pounds of hamburger meat; 9,600 pounds of ham; and 1,500 flats of tomatoes.

Whatever the reason for the buffets, it is true that *some* of the offerings represent the best values for food anywhere we know of. The best of the buffets offer top-quality meals in attractive settings for a mere fraction of the price of a sitdown restaurant. (The worst of the buffets are spectacularly ordinary and unattractive, but still represent better values than McD's or the neighborhood greasy spoon.)

In general, the best meals are the dinner buffets and the weekend brunches; a few casinos offer spectacular, cholesterol-laden breakfasts. As you might expect, the more popular buffets can build lengthy lines; the best strategy is to eat a bit early—before 8 A.M. for breakfast and before 6 P.M. for dinner. Prices are subject to change. Call to check hours. Most buffets offer lower rates for children. Soft drinks, coffee, and tea are included with most meals; alcoholic drinks are extra.

Here's our Econoguide Best Picks:

Econoguide's Best Buffets in Las Vegas

Carnival World Buffet. Rio Suite Hotel & Casino

Palatium. Caesars Palace

The Buffet. Golden Nugget

Big Kitchen Buffet. Bally's

Aladdin Hotel. Market Place Buffet. Breakfast 7:30 to 10:30 A.M., $4.95; lunch 10:30 A.M. to 3 P.M., $5.95; dinner 4 to 10 P.M., $6.95.

Alexis Park. All-you-can-eat fajita and salad bar. 4:30 to 9 P.M. Wednesday, Friday, and Saturday, $6.50; Sunday brunch 10 A.M. to 3 P.M., $9.50.

Arizona Charlie's. Wild West Buffet. Breakfast 7 to 10:30 A.M., $2.80; lunch 11 A.M. to 3:30 P.M., $3.27; dinner 4 to 10 P.M., $4.67.

Bally's. Big Kitchen Buffet. Brunch 7:30 A.M. to 2:30 P.M., $6.45; dinner 4:30 to 10 P.M., $11.95. sterling brunch Sunday, Caruso's Restaurant, 9 A.M. to 2:30 P.M., $29.95.

Binion's Horseshoe. Seafood Buffet. 4 to 10:30 P.M., $12.94.

Bourbon Street. Weekday lunch 11 A.M. to 2 P.M., $3.95; dinner Monday to Thursday 5 to 9 P.M., $4.95. Friday through Sunday dinner 5 to 9 P.M., $5.95. Bloody Mary brunch weekends 8 A.M.-2 P.M., $5.95.

Caesars Palace. Palatium Buffet. Breakfast Monday to Friday 7:30 to 11 A.M., $7; lunch 11:30 A.M. to 2:30 P.M., $8.59; dinner 4:30 to 10 P.M., $12.75. Palatium Brunch Saturday 8:30 A.M. to 2:30 P.M., $12.75. Champagne brunch Sunday 8:30 A.M. to 2:30 P.M., $14.50.

Circus Circus. Big Top. Breakfast 6 to 11:30 A.M., $2.29; lunch noon to 4 P.M., $2.99; dinner 4:30 to 11 P.M., $3.99.

Continental. Florentine Room Buffet. Breakfast 7 to 10:45 A.M. $2.95; lunch 11 A.M. to 2:45 P.M. $3.95; dinner 4 to 10 P.M., $5.95. Crab Leg Buffet daily 4 to 10 P.M., $9.95.

Sheraton Desert Inn. Weekend champagne brunch, Crystal Room. Sunday 9 A.M. to 2 P.M., $10.95.

El Rancho. Buffet. Steak nightly 5 to 10 P.M., $5.95; weekend brunch from 8 A.M. to 3 P.M., $3.25.

Excalibur. Round Table Buffet. Breakfast 7 to 11 A.M., $3.49; lunch 11 A.M. to 4 P.M., $4.49; dinner, 4 to 10 P.M., $5.79. Weekends 9 am to 1 P.M., $7.95.

Fitzgerald's. Molly's Country Kitchen & Buffet. Breakfast 7 to 11 A.M., $3.99; lunch, 11:30 A.M. to 4 P.M., $4.49; dinner 5 to 9 P.M., $5.99. Champagne brunch weekends 8 A.M. to 4 P.M., $4.99.

Fremont. Paradise Buffet. Weekday breakfast 7 to 10:30 A.M., $3.95; lunch 11 A.M. to 3 P.M., $4.95; dinner nightly except Tuesday, Friday, and Sunday, 4 to 10 P.M., $7.95. Champagne brunch Sundays 7 A.M. to 3 P.M., $6.95. Seafood Fantasy Tuesday, Friday, and Sunday 4 to 10 P.M., $11.95.

Gold Coast. Breakfast Monday to Saturday 7 to 10:30 A.M., $2.45; lunch 11 A.M. to 3 P.M., $3.45; dinner 4 to 10 P.M., $5.45. Sunday 8 A.M. to 3 P.M., $4.45.

Golden Nugget. The Buffet. Breakfast Monday to Saturday 7 to 10:30 A.M., $4.75; lunch Monday to Saturday 10:30 A.M. to 3 P.M., $7.50; dinner 4 to 10 P.M., $8.75. Champagne brunch Sunday 8 A.M. to 4 P.M., $9.50.

Gold Strike Inn. Lunch Monday through Friday 11 A.M. to 4 P.M., $3.95; dinner Monday through Friday 4-10 P.M., $3.49.

Hacienda. El Grande Buffet. Monday through Saturday. Breakfast 7 to 11 A.M., $3.95; lunch 11:30 A.M. to 3 P.M., $4.95; dinner 5 to 10 P.M., $6.95. Sunday brunch 8 A.M. to 3 P.M., $6.95.

Harrah's Las Vegas. Galley Buffet. Breakfast 7 to 11 A.M., $3.99; lunch 11 A.M. to 4 P.M., $4.49; dinner 5 to 10 P.M., $6.95.

Imperial Palace. Imperial Buffet, Teahouse Coffee Shop. Monday through Friday 7 A.M. to 2:30 P.M., brunch $5.95. Saturday, Sunday, and holiday champagne brunch 8 A.M. to 2:30 P.M., $6.50; prime rib dinner buffet nightly 5 to 9:30 P.M., $7.95.

Imperial Palace. Emperor's Buffet. Breakfast 7 to 11:30 A.M., $3.99; lunch 11:30 A.M. to 4 P.M., $4.49; dinner 5 to 10 P.M., $4.99.

Lady Luck. Breakfast 6 to 10:30 A.M., $2.49; lunch 11 A.M. to 2 P.M., $3.99; dinner featuring prime rib, crab, and shrimp 4 to 11 P.M., $6.99.

Las Vegas Hilton. Buffet of Champions. Breakfast weekdays 7 to 9:30 A.M., $5.99; lunch weekdays 11 A.M. to 2 P.M., $7.99; dinner 5 to 10 P.M., $11.99. Champagne brunch Saturday, Sunday, and holidays 8 A.M. to 2:30 P.M., $9.99.

Luxor. Manhattan Buffet. Breakfast, $3.95; lunch, $4.95; dinner, $6.95.

Maxim. Daily brunch buffet. 10 A.M. to 3 P.M., $4.95; evening buffet 4 to 10 P.M., $5.95. Weekend champagne brunch 9 A.M. to 3 P.M., $6.95.

MGM Grand. Oz Buffet. Breakfast 7 to 11 A.M., $4.95; lunch 11 A.M. to 4 P.M., $5.95; dinner 4 to 10 P.M., $7.95.

Roundtable Buffet at the Excalibur

The Mirage. Breakfast 7 to 10:45 A.M., $6.96; lunch 11 A.M. to 2:45 P.M., $9.10; dinner 3 to 9:30 P.M., $10.97.

Nevada Palace. German Buffet, Sunday 4 to 9 P.M., $5.95. BBQ buffet Monday 4 to 9 P.M., $5.95.

Palace Station. The Feast. Breakfast 7 to 11 A.M., $3.95; lunch 11 to 2 P.M., $4.95; dinner 4:30 to 10 P.M., $7.95. Champagne brunch Sunday 7 A.M. to 3:30 P.M., $6.95.

Rio. Carnival World Buffet. Breakfast 7 to 10:30 A.M., $3.95; lunch 11 A.M. to 3:30 P.M., $5.25; dinner 3:30 to 10 P.M., $7.95. Weekend brunch 7 A.M. to 3:30 P.M., $6.95.

Riviera. World's Fare Buffet. Breakfast 7 to 10 A.M., $4.95; champagne brunch 10 A.M. to 3 P.M., $5.95; dinner 4:30 to 11 P.M., $6.95. Seafood Fair Friday 4:30 to 11 P.M. $11.95; prime rib Saturday 4:30 to 11 P.M. $6.95.

Sahara. Oasis Buffet. Breakfast Monday through Friday 7 to 11 A.M., $4.95; lunch 11 A.M. to 2:30 P.M., $5.95; dinner daily 4 to 10:30 P.M., $6.95. Sunday brunch 8 A.M. to 2:30 P.M., $6.95.

Sam's Town. Uptown Buffet. Weekday brunch 8:30 A.M. to 2:30 P.M., $3.95; Dinner Monday through Thursday 4 to 9 P.M., $6.49; dinner Friday through Sunday 4 to 9 P.M., $6.95. Weekend champagne brunch 8 A.M. to 2:30 P.M., $5.95.

San Remo. Ristorante del Fiori Buffet. Monday through Friday breakfast 7 to 10 A.M., $5.25; lunch 11 A.M. to 2 P.M., $6.25; dinner 5 to 9 P.M., $7.25. Champagne brunch weekends, 7 A.M. to 2 P.M., $7.25.

Sands. Breakfast 7 to 11:30 A.M., $3.99; lunch 12 to 3:30 P.M., $4.99; dinner 4:30 to 10:30 P.M. for $6.99.

Santa Fe. Lone Mountain Buffet. Monday through Saturday breakfast 7 to 10 A.M., $5.25; lunch 11 A.M. to 2 P.M., $6.25; dinner 5 to 9 P.M., $7.25.

Showboat. Captain's Buffet. Lunch weekdays 10 A.M. to 3 P.M., $4.45; dinner Monday, Tuesday, and Thursday 4:30 to 10 P.M., $6.45; seafood Wednesday and Friday 4:30 to 10 P.M., $7.45. Weekend brunch 8 A.M. to 3 P.M., $5.45; dinner 4 to 10 P.M., $6.45.

Stardust. Warehouse Buffet. Breakfast Monday through Saturday 7 to 10:30 A.M., $4.95; lunch 10:30 A.M. to 3 P.M., $5.95; dinner every night 4 to 10 P.M., $7.95. Sunday champagne brunch 7 A.M. to 3 P.M., $6.95.

Treasure Island. Breakfast 7 to 10:45 A.M., $4.99; lunch 11 A.M. to 3:45 P.M., $6.99; dinner 4 to 11 P.M., $8.99.

Tropicana. Rhapsody Brunch. Sunday only 9:30 A.M. to 2 P.M.. $20.95.

Vacation Village. Upstairs Buffet. Monday through Friday lunch 11 A.M. to 3 P.M., $4.95; dinner every day 3 to 10 P.M., $5.95; Sunday champagne brunch 9 A.M. to 3 P.M., $5.95.

Westward Ho. Lunch 11 A.M. to 4 P.M., $3.50, dinner 4 to 8 P.M., $4.50.

Restaurants

ENTREE PRICES ONLY

$	Inexpensive (Up to **$**10)	**$$$**	Expensive (**$**20 to **$**40)
$$	Moderate (**$**10 to **$**20)	**$$$$**	Deluxe (**$**40 and over)
LVBS	Las Vegas Blvd., South (Strip)	LVBN	Las Vegas Blvd., North

You can get just about anything you want at a Las Vegas restaurant. In this section, we'll give some details about many of the more interesting restaurants in town. Most restaurants are open for lunch and dinner; weekend hours may vary. Be sure to call and confirm hours and check to see if a reservation is necessary.

American *(Strip or Nearby)*

Alias Smith & Jones. 541 E. Twain Ave., 732-7401. **$$**

All American Bar & Grille. Rio Hotel/Casino, 252-7767. Mesquite-grilled steaks and seafood. **$$**

All That Jazz. Harrah's Las Vegas Casino Hotel, 3475 LVBS, 369-5000. New Orleans atmosphere. Prime rib, crab legs, catfish, and steamed shrimp. Closed for dinner Wednesday and Thursday. **$$**.

American Cafe. Algiers Hotel, 2845 LVBS, 735-3311. **$$**

Bally's Steakhouse. Bally's Las Vegas, 3645 LVBS, 795-3990. Steaks, chops, and seafood served in a New York club atmosphere. **$$**

Barronshire. Las Vegas Hilton, 3000 Paradise Rd., 732-5111. Closed Mondays. English style, featuring prime rib carved at your table; also fish and chicken entrees. **$$**

Big Dog's Cafe & Casino. 6390 W. Sahara Ave., 876-3647. **$-$$**

Big Mama's. 3765 LVBS, 597-1616. Big Mama McWhorter's southern, Cajun, Creole, and barbecue recipes. **$$**

Boogie's Diner. Forum Shops at Caesars. A '50s diner in re-created glory. **$-$$**

Cafe Roma. Caesars Palace, 3570 LVBS, 731-7110. **$$**

California Pizza Kitchen. The Mirage, 3400 LVBS, 791-7111. **$-$$**

Caribe Cafe. The Mirage, 3400 LVBS, 791-7111. **$$**

Clay's Texas Pit BBQ. 414 N. Eastern Ave., 399-7911. **$-$$**

The Coachman's Inn. 3240 S. Eastern Ave., 731-4202. Prime ribs and sandwiches. **$$**

The Coffee Shop. Bally's Las Vegas, 3645 LVBS, 736-4111. **$-$$**

Country Inn. 2425 E. Desert Inn Rd., 731-5035. **$**

Country Inn. 1401 S. Rainbow Blvd., 354-0250. **$**

El Gaucho. Tropicana Hotel, 3801 LVBS, 739-2376. Steak, ribs, and lobster. **$-$$**

42nd Street Deli & Cafe. 3735 LVBS, 795-2010. **$$**

Gates Bar-B-Que. 2710 E. Desert Inn Rd., 369-8010. A Kansas City-style barbecue joint; raucous and fun. **$-$$**

Iron Horse Cafe. Palace Station Hotel & Casino, 2411 W. Sahara. 367-2411. **$-$$**

Jeremiah's Steak House. 171 East Tropicana, 736-3044. **$$-$$$**

Jerome's. 4503 S. Paradise Rd., 792-3772. San Francisco atmosphere, featuring pasta and seafood. Butcher paper tablecloths and crayons provided. **$$**

Kiefer's. 105 E. Harmon Ave., 739-8000. Penthouse restaurant in Carriage House apartment complex with view of The Strip. Veal, steak, and seafood specialties. **$$**

La Promenade. Desert Inn Hotel & Country Club, 3145 LVBS, 733-4580. **$-$$**

Marie Callenders. 600 E. Sahara Ave., 734-6572. American right down to the apple pies; just like the other couple hundred in the chain. **$-$$**

Marie Callenders. 4875 W. Flamingo Rd., 365-6226. **$-$$**

MarketPlace Restaurant. Alexis Park Resort, 375 E. Harmon Ave., 796-3300. **$-$$**

Oasis Coffee Shop. Aladdin Hotel & Casino, 3667 LVBS, 736-0111. **$-$$**

The Palm. Forum Shops at Caesars, 732-7256. The Vegas branch of the venerable New York steak and seafood house; casual and fun. **$$$**

Peppermill Lounge. 2985 LVBS, 735-4177. **$-$$**

The Pink Pony. Circus Circus Hotel Casino, 2880 LVBS, 734-0410. **$-$$**

Rafters. 1350 E. Tropicana Ave., 739-9463. Fresh seafood, served in an intimate winery-like setting. **$-$$**

Ralph's Diner. Stardust Resort & Casino, 3000 LVBS, 732-6111. **$-$$**

Ristaurant dei Fiori. San Remo Casino Resort, 115 E. Tropicana Ave., 739-9000. **$$**

Sadie's Southern. 505 E. Twain Ave.,, 796-4177. Closed Monday. **$-$$**

Sherwood Forest Cafe. Excalibur Hotel/Casino, 3850 LVBS, 597-7777. **$-$$**

Skyrise Dining Room. Circus Circus Hotel/Casino, 2880 LVBS, 734-0410. **$-$$**

Socorro Springs Cafe. Las Vegas Hilton, 3000 Paradise Rd., 732-5111. **$-$$**

TGI Friday's. 1800 E. Flamingo Rd., closed Sundays, 732-9905. **$-$$**

Tony L's. 4801 S. Eastern Ave., 736-7211. **$-$$**

Tony Roma's. 520 E. Sahara. 733-9914. Steak, seafood, and pasta chain. **$$**

Tree House Coffee Shop. Maxim Hotel Casino, 150 E. Flamingo Rd., 731-4300. **$-$$**

Veranda Cafe. Harrah's Las Vegas Casino Hotel, 3475 LVBS, 369-5000. **$-$$**

William B's. Stardust Hotel/Casino, 732-6111. **$$**

American *(Downtown and Out of Town)*

California Pizza Kitchen. Golden Nugget, 129 E. Fremont St., 385-7111. **$–$$**

Carson Street Cafe. Golden Nugget, 129 E. Fremont St., 385-7111. **$$**

The Dugout. Las Vegas Club Hotel & Casino, Downtown Casino Center, Main and Fremont, 385-1664. **$–$$**

Green Shack. 2504 E. Fremont, 383-0007. The oldest continuously operating restaurant in Las Vegas, virtually unchanged since 1932 when it was converted from a Union Pacific bunkhouse. Fried chicken, fish, and more. **$**

Hugo's Cellar. Four Queens Hotel/Casino, Fremont Street, 385-4011. A local institution; fine steaks, seafood, and fowl. **$$–$$$**

Marie Callenders. 4800 S. Eastern Ave., 458-2127. **$–$$**

Mount Charleston Inn Hotel. 2 Kyle Canyon Rd., Mt. Charleston, 872-5500. Quail, rabbit, game, and other down-home specialties in a mountain chalet. Check driving conditions in wintertime. **$$**

Mount Charleston Lodge. Mt. Charleston, 872-5408. Check for hours and driving conditions. **$–$$**

Redwood Bar & Grill. California Hotel, 12 Ogden Ave., 385-1222. Steaks, ribs, and seafood in a comfortable English inn–like setting. **$$**

Skye Room. Binion's Horseshoe, 731-7731. **$$**

Asian/Middle Eastern *(Strip or Nearby)*

Bamboo Garden. 4850 W. Flamingo Rd., at Decatur, 871-3262. No lunch Sunday. **$$**

Beijing. 3900 Paradise Road, 737-9618. No lunch Sunday. Vegetarian specialties and unusual seafood dishes complement standard fare. **$$**

Cathay House. 5300 W. Spring Mountain Rd., 876-3838. A great panoramic view of The Strip. Dim sum carts. **$$**

China Doll Restaurant. 2534 E. Desert Inn Rd., 369-9511. **$–$$**

China First. 1801 E. Tropicana Ave., 736-2828. Closed Monday. **$$**

China Star. 3582 S. Maryland Pkwy., 732-1608. Luncheon buffet. **$–$$**

Chinese Garden. 5485 W. Sahara Ave., 876-5432. **$–$$**

Chin's. Fashion Mall, 3200 LVBS, 733-8899. A decidedly modern and elegant Chinese restaurant. **$$**

Chung King. 3400 S. Jones Blvd., 871-5551. A neighborhood Chinese eatery. **$–$$**

Emperor's Table. 4670 S. Decatur Blvd., 876-9588. **$–$$**

Empress Court. Caesars Palace, 3570 LVBS, 731-7110. A most elegant Hong Kong–style Cantonese restaurant, including abalone, jellyfish, shark's fin, and bird's nest soups using rare spices from the Orient. Closed Tuesday and Wednesday. **$$$**

Garden of the Dragon. Las Vegas Hilton, 3000 Paradise Rd., 732-5111. Szechwan, Peking style, Northern, Mongolian, and Cantonese. Overlooking the Oriental gardens of Benihana. **$$–$$$**

Hakase. 3900 Paradise Road, 796-1234. Sushi, teppen yaki tableside Japanese cooking. Closed Monday. **$$–$$$**

Hamada of Japan. 598 E. Flamingo Road, 733-3005. Sushi, teppen yaki tableside Japanese cooking or menu items. **$$–$$$**

HoWan. Desert Inn Hotel & Country Club, 3145 LVBS, 733-4547. Authentic Mandarin, Szechwan, and Cantonese. Closed Monday and Tuesday. **$$$**

Iron Horse Cafe. Palace Station Hotel & Casino, 2411 W. Sahara. 367-2411. **$–$$**

Lotus of Siam. 953 E. Sahara Ave., 735-4453. Lunch buffet Monday through Friday; dinner Saturday and Sunday. Thai specialties. **$–$$**

Ming Terrace. Imperial Palace Hotel & Casino, 3535 LVBS, 731-3311. **$$**

Moongate. The Mirage, 3400 LVBS, 791-7111. A lovely room with elegantly presented Oriental dishes. **$$–$$$**

Rik Shaw. Riviera Hotel and Casino, 2901 LVBS, 734-5110. **$$**

Saigon. 4251 W. Sahara Ave., 362-9978. A very ordinary storefront restaurant with very extraordinary Vietnamese cooking. **$–$$**

Shalimar. 3900 Paradise Road. 796-0302. Authentic Indian Tandoori chicken and meat, curries, unusual rice, and vegetarian specialties. Closed Sunday. **$$**

Shalimar. 2605 S. Decatur Blvd., 252-8320. A branch of the restaurant described above. Closed Sunday. **$$**

Silver Dragon Restaurant. 1510 E. Flamingo Rd., 737-1234. **$–$$**

Sun Sun. Aladdin Hotel & Casino, 3667 LVBS, 734-0111. Chinese, Vietnamese, and Korean specialties. **$$**

Szechwan Restaurant. 3101 W. Sahara, 871-4291. Szechwan, Mandarin, Shanghai, and Cantonese cuisine. **$$**

Asian/Middle Eastern *(Downtown and Out of Town)*

Emperor's Room. Lady Luck Casino Hotel, 206 N. 3rd St., 477-3000. Closed Sunday and Monday. **$–$$**

Fong's Garden. 2021 E. Charleston Blvd., 382-1644. An old-line, old-style family Chinese restaurant. **$–$$**

Seoul B-B-Q. 953 E. Sahara Ave., 369-4123. Ribs and fish and kimchi (pickled cabbage) that will clear your sinuses for months to come. **$$**

Cajun

Joe's Bayou. Harrah's Las Vegas Casino Hotel, 3475 LVBS, 369-5000. Cajun and New Orleans–style seafood and other specialties. **$$**

Palace Court Restaurant, Caesars Palace, Las Vegas

Continental *(Strip and Nearby)*

Alpine Village. 3003 Paradise Road, 734-6888. Country-style German and French specialties. **$$**

Bacchanal. Caesars Palace, 3570 LVBS, 731-7110. An opulent seven-course Roman feast that will provide tales of near-debauchery that will last for years. Closed Sunday and Monday. **$$$$**

The Bistro. The Mirage, 3400 LVBS, 791-7111. **$$–$$$**

Bootlegger Ristorante and Lounge. 5025 S. Eastern Ave., 736-4939. An old family eatery with a lot of character. Closed Monday; no lunch Sunday. **$$–$$$**

Cafe Michelle. 1350 E. Flamingo Rd., 735-8686. A sidewalk cafe featuring Caesar salad, seafood, pasta, chicken, and veal dishes. **$$**

Camelot. Excalibur Hotel, 3850 LVBS, 597-7777. Seafood, escargot, pasta dishes, rack of lamb, and beef wellington in a Vegas version of a medieval castle. **$$–$$$**

Da Vinci's. Maxim Hotel/Casino, 160 E. Flamingo Rd., 731-4300. **$$**

Embers. Imperial Palace Hotel & Casino, 3535 LVBS, 731-3311. **$$**

Flamingo Room. Flamingo Hilton, 733-3131. **$–$$**

GiGi. Ballys Casino Resort, 3645 LVBS, 739-4111. Closed Monday and Tuesday. **$$–$$$**

House of Lords. Sahara Hotel, Closed Tuesday and Wednesday. **$$$**

Kokomo's. The Mirage, 3400 LVBS, 791-7111. A Continental restaurant with seafood specialties, in a rain forest within a Las Vegas casino; we're not sure what it all has to do with a city in Indiana of the same name. **$$–$$$**

Monte Carlo. Desert Inn, 3145 LVBS, 733-4524. Very French. **$$$**

Le Montrachet. Las Vegas Hilton, 3000 Paradise Rd., 732-5111. Closed Tuesdays. **$$$**

Le Panache. San Remo Casino & Resort, 115 E. Tropicana Ave., 739-9000. Closed Monday and Tuesday. **$$–$$$**

Palace Court. Caesars Palace, 3570 LVBS, 731-7110. Among the best Continental fare on The Strip. **$$$**

Pamplemousse. 400 E. Sahara Ave., 733-2066. Closed Monday. A changing, fresh menu of French country specialties. **$$–$$$**

Kokomo's Restaurant at the Mirage, Las Vegas

Pegasus. Alexis Park Resort, 375 E. Harmon Ave., 796-3300. Seafood, veal, beef. **$$$–$$$$**

Regency Room. Sands Hotel, 733-5000. **$$**

Rhapsody. Tropicana Hotel, 3801 LVBS, 739-2440. Closed Tuesday through Thursday. **$$–$$$**

Seasons. Bally's Las Vegas. 739-4561. **$$$**

Second Story. 4485 S. Jones Blvd., 368-2257. French and continental cuisine. Enclosed porch. **$$$**

Continental *(Downtown and Out of Town)*

Andre's French Restaurant. 401 S. Sixth St., 385-5016. A re-created French country home. No lunch weekends. **$$–$$$**

Aristocrat Restaurant. 850 S. Rancho Rd., 870-1977. No lunch on weekends. A quality, small Continental hideaway. **$$–$$$**

Burgundy Room. Lady Luck Casino Hotel, 206 N. 3rd St., 477-3000. A comfortable, pleasant room and menu. **$$**

Elaine's. Golden Nugget Hotel and Casino, 129 E. Fremont St., 385-7111. A beautiful setting and exceptional (and quirky) menu including seafood specialties. Closed Tuesday and Wednesday. **$$–$$$**

The Great Moments Room. Las Vegas Club. 18 E. Fremont St., 385-1664. **$$–$$$**

Delicatessens *(Strip and Nearby)*

Champions Deli. Desert Inn Hotel & Country Club, 3145 LVBS, 733-4513. **$–$$**

Derby Deli. Harrah's Las Vegas Casino Hotel, 3475 LVBS, 369-5000. **$–$$**

Jerusalem Kosher Restaurant & Deli. 1305 Vegas Valley Drive., 735-2878. Closed Friday evening, Saturday. Open Sunday for lunch and dinner only. **$$**

Le Montrachet Restaurant at the Las Vegas Hilton

Kady's Brasserie. Riviera Hotel & Casino, 2901 LVBS, 734-5110. **$–$$**
Luigi's Place. San Remo Casino & Resort, 115 E. Tropicana Ave., 739-9000. Italian sandwiches featuring premium cold cuts, cheeses, and trimmings. **$–$$**
Park Deli. 3900 Paradise Rd., 369-3354. No breakfast Saturday; closed Sunday. **$–$$**
Stage Deli. Forum Shops at Caesars, 893-4045. Imported lox, stock, and barrels from New York. **$$**

German *(Strip and Nearby)*

Old Heidelberg. 604 E. Sahara Ave., 731-5310. **$$**
Swiss Cafe. 1431 E. Charleston Blvd., 382-6444. **$$**

Italian *(Strip and Nearby)*

Amici Ristorante Italiano. 6120 W. Tropicana. 222-0384. Northern Italian cuisine. **$$**
Andiamo. Las Vegas Hilton, 3000 Paradise Rd., 732-5111. Northern Italian cuisine. **$$**
Battista's Hole In The Wall. 4041 Audrie St., 732-1424. A classic, comfortable family Italian restaurant. **$$–$$$**
Bertolini's. The Forum Shops at Caesars, 735-4663. **$$**
Cafe Picasso. 2605 S. Decatur, Suite 110 at W. Sahara, 367-3007. Outdoor patio in season. **$$–$$$**
Cangemi's. 4213 W. Sahara Ave., 876-5698. **$$**
Carluccio's Tivoli Gardens. 1775 E. Tropicana Ave., 795-3236. Closed Monday. Liberace's sequinned ghost is everywhere. **$$**
Caruso's. Bally's Las Vegas, 3645 LVBS, 739-4111. Northern and Southern Italian. **$$**
Cipriani Restaurant. 2790 East Flamingo. 369-6711. Closed Sunday. **$$–$$$**
DiMartino & Sons. 2797 S. Maryland Pkwy., 732-1817. A friendly family spot. **$$**
Fisherman's Port. Aladdin Hotel & Casino, 3557 LVBS, 735-0111. Fresh seafood and special chicken, veal, pork, and pasta entrees. **$$**
Fratelli's Ristorante. 3311 E. Flamingo Rd.,, 458-5555. Nightly entertainment. **$$**
Georgio's. 1020 E. Desert Inn Rd., 735-1170. **$$**
La Strada Restaurant. 4640 Paradise Rd., 735-0150. **$$**
Lance-a-Lotta Pizza. Excalibur Hotel, 3850 LVBS, 597-7777. **$–$$**
Manfredi's Limelight. Tropicana at Eastern Ave., 739-1410. **$$**
Olive Garden. 1547 E. Flamingo Rd., 735-0082. A national seafood and Italian chain that offers a bottomless salad bowl at your table. **$$**
Olive Garden. 1361 S. Decatur Blvd., 258-3453. **$$**
Parma Ristorante. 1750 S. Rainbow Blvd., 258-0680. **$$**
Pasta Palace. Palace Station Hotel & Casino, 2411 W. Sahara, 367-2411. **$–$$**
Pasta Remo. San Remo Casino & Resort, 115 E. Tropicana Ave., 739-9000. Unlimited house salad. **$–$$**
Piero's. 355 Convention Center Drive, 369-2305. Quality Italian pasta, seafood, and meat specialties in an intimate room. Across from the Convention Center. **$$–$$$**
Pizza Palace. Imperial Palace Hotel & Casino, 3535 LVBS, 731-3311. **$–$$**
Portofino. Desert Inn Hotel & Country Club, 3145 LVBS, 733-4495. **$$–$$$**
Primavera. Caesars Palace, 3570 LVBS, 731-7110. Quality Northern and Southern Italian food in an attractive poolside setting. **$$–$$$**
Ristaurante Riva. The Mirage, 3400 LVBS, 791-7111. **$$–$$$**
Ristorante Italiano. Riviera Hotel & Casino, 2901 LVBS, 734-5110. **$$–$$$**
Romeo's Ristorante & Lounge. 2800 W. Sahara Ave., 873-5400. Closed Sunday. Northern Italian. Attractive dining area and outdoor cafe. **$$–$$$**
The Shark Club. Cosmos Uptown Restaurant & Piano Bar, 75 E. Harmon Ave., 795-7527 or 739-0330. Closed Monday. Nightclub open all night through breakfast. **$$–$$$**
The Sicilian Cafe. 3510 E. Tropicana Ave., 456-1300. No lunch weekends. **$$**
Spago. Forum Shops at Caesars, 369-6300. A truly eclectic, trendy, and generally satisfying eating experience under the electronically changing Roman sky. Very busy on

weekends and when conventions are in town. **$$–$$$**
That's Amore. 3310 Sandhill Rd., 435-5889. **$$**
That's Italian. 4601 W. Sahara Ave., 873-8055. Closed Sunday. **$$**.
Vincenzo Ristorante. 610 Naples Dr., 737-5755. **$$**
Vineyard Restaurant. 3630 S. Maryland Pkwy., 731-1606. **$–$$**

Italian *(Downtown and Out of Town)*

Cosmos Underground Italian. 32 E. Fremont St., 382-0330. Closed Monday. **$$**
Pasta Pirate. California Hotel Casino, 12 Ogden St., 385-1222. **$–$$**
Stefano's. Golden Nugget Hotel and Casino, 129 E. Fremont St., 385-7111. Singing waiters; the food and room are tuneful, too. **$$–$$$**

Japanese *(Strip and Nearby)*

Ah'So. Caesars Palace, 3570 LVBS, 731-7110. Sushi and sashimi, sold either in the lounge or to dinner guests. The preselected, six-course dinner ($47.50) is prepared and served in teppen yaki style at your table. **$$$$**
Benihana Village. Las Vegas Hilton, 3000 Paradise Rd., 732-5111. Two traditional Japanese restaurants (hibachi and robata), each with different atmosphere. The food is classy; the entertainment, which includes a show starring animated stuffed birds and electronic fireworks, is straight out of Disney World. **$$–$$$**
Kabuto Japanese Restaurant. 324 W. Sahara Ave., 388-1203. **$$–$$$**
Mikado. The Mirage, 3400 LVBS, 791-7111. **$$–$$$**
Mizuno Teppan. Tropicana Hotel, 3801 LVBS, 739-2713. Australian lobster, Gulf shrimp, gourmet steak served in teppen yaki style tableside. **$$–$$$**
Nippon. 101 Convention Center Drive, 735-5555. No lunch Saturday. Closed Sunday. Sushi bar, sashimi. **$–$$**.
Sakura Garden. 324 S. Sahara Ave., 384-3524. Closed Sunday. **$$**
Sushi Bar San Remo. San Remo Casino, 115 E. Tropicana Ave., 739-9000. **$$**
Teru-Sushi. 700 E. Sahara Ave., 734-6655. Closed Sunday. **$$**

Mexican *(Strip and Nearby)*

El Chollo Paradise. 4080 S. Paradise Rd., 359-5334. **$$**
Garcia's Mexican Restaurant. 1030 E. Flamingo Rd., 731-0628. **$$**
Garcia's Mexican Restaurant. 2575 S. Decatur Blvd., 876-6191. **$$**
Guadalajara Bar & Grille. Palace Station Hotel & Casino, 2411 W. Sahara, 367-2471. **$$**
Las Holas. Ballys Las Vegas, 3645 LVBS, 739-4111. **$$**
Macayo Vegas. 1375 E. Tropicana Ave., 735-1898. A local chain. **$–$$**
Macayo Vegas. 1741 E. Charleston Blvd., 382-5605. **$–$$**
Macayo Vegas. 4457 W. Charleston Blvd., 878-7347. **$–$$**
Macayo Vegas. 3752 LVBN, 644-1020. **$–$$**
Paco's. Las Vegas Hilton, 3000 Paradise Rd., 732-5111. Closed Wednesday and Thursday. **$–$$**
Ricardo's. 2380 E. Tropicana Ave., 798-4515. Local chain. **$–$$**
Ricardo's. 4300 Meadows Lane (Meadows Mall), 870-1088. **$–$$**
Ricardo's. 4930 W. Flamingo Rd., 871-7119. **$–$$**

Moroccan *(Strip and Nearby)*

Marrakech. 3900 Paradise Rd., 736-7655. Six-course French Moroccan meal, an array of domestic and imported wines, and full bar. With a belly dancer, of course. **$$–$$$**

Seafood *(Strip and Nearby)*

Fisherman's Broiler. Palace Station Hotel & Casino, 2411 W. Sahara, 357-2411. Seafood specialties. Inexpensive luncheon seafood buffet. **$$**

Fisherman's Port. Aladdin Hotel & Casino, 3667 LVBS, 736-0111. **$$–$$$**
Neros Steak and Seafood Restaurant. Caesars Palace, 3570 LVBS, 731-7110. **$$–$$$$**
Seahouse. Imperial Palace Hotel & Casino, 3535 LVBS, 731-3311. Closed Wednesday and Thursday. **$$–$$$**

Steakhouses *(Strip and Nearby)*

Beef Barron. Flamingo Hilton, 733-3502. **$$–$$$**
Cattlemen's Steak House. 2645 S. Maryland Pkwy., 732-7726. **$$–$$$**
Cavalier Restaurant. 3850 E. Desert Inn Rd., 451-6221. **$$–$$$**
Charcoal Room. Hacienda, 739-8911. **$$$**
Claudine's Steak House. Harrah's Las Vegas Casino Hotel, 3475 LVBS, 369-5000. Closed Monday and Tuesday. Onion soup to die for; steaks, chops, and more. **$$–$$$**
Diamond Lil's. Sam's Town, 454-8009. **$$–$$$**
Dickinson's Wharf. 953 E. Sahara Ave., 732-3594. **$$–$$$**
El Gaucho. Tropicana Hotel, 3801 LVBS, 739-2376. **$$–$$$**
Embers. Imperial Palace, 794-3261. Closed Monday and Tuesday. **$$–$$$**
Ferdinand's Steak House & Saloon. 5006 S. Maryland, 798-6962. Cajun blackened fish, sausage, and jalapeno hush puppies. **$$–$$$**
Flame. 1 Desert Inn Rd., 735-4431. Pick your own meat for breakfast, brunch, lunch, and dinner. Seafood and chicken specialties, too. **$$**
Golden Steer. 308 W. Sahara Ave., 384-4470. Pounds of steak and ribs; also game, fish, and poultry in a western atmosphere between The Strip and the Convention Center. **$$–$$$**
Hilton Steakhouse. Las Vegas Hilton, 3000 Paradise Rd., 732-5111. Prime steaks and fresh seafood prepared over mesquite wood. **$$–$$$**
Kelly & Cohen Restaurant. Vegas World, 2000 LVBS, 382-2000. **$$–$$$**
Kristofer's. Riviera Hotel & Casino, 2901 LVBS, 734-5110. **$$$**
Philip's Supper House. 4545 W. Sahara Ave., 873-5222. **$$–$$$**
Play It Again, Sam. 4120 Spring Mountain Rd., 876-1550. **$$–$$$**
Port Tack. 3190 W. Sahara Ave., 873-3345. **$$**
Rib House. Imperial Palace Hotel & Casino, 3535 LVBS, 731-3311. **$$**
Rosewood Grille. 3339 LVBS, 792-6719. **$$$**
Ruth's Chris Steak House. 3900 Paradise Rd., 791-7011. **$$–$$$**
The Sandpiper Restaurant. 3311 E. Flamingo Rd., 458-5555. **$$**
Sir Galahad's. Excalibur Hotel, 3850 LVBS, 597-7777. **$$**
Steakhouse. Bally's Hotel/Casino, 739-4661. Closed Sunday and Monday. **$$–$$$**
The Steak House. Circus Circus Hotel/Casino, 2880 LVBS, 734-0410. Award-winning steakhouse, offering prime rib, lamb chops, lobster, fish, chicken, and steaks broiled over mesquite. The celebrity portraits on the wall are not movie stars but dinner steers. **$$**
The Tillerman. 2245 E. Flamingo Rd., 731-4036. **$$**
Tony Roma's. Stardust Hotel/Casino, 732-6500. **$$–$$$**
Yolie's Brazilian Steakhouse. 3900 Paradise Rd., 794-0700. Unusual menu of marinated meats, sausage, and poultry cooked over wood-fired rotisserie that is part of the entertainment. **$$**

Steakhouse *(Downtown and Out of Town)*

Binion's Steak House. Binion's Horseshoe, 128 E. Fremont St., 382-1600. Victorian-style decor, specializing in huge steaks and prime ribs. **$$**
Cassidy's Steak House. Fitzgerald's, 382-6111. **$$**
Nick's Supper Club. 15 Lake Mead Drive, Henderson, 565-0122. Summer closed Sunday and Monday; winter open 7 days. Lunch and dinner. **$$–$$$**
Tony Roma's. Fremont Hotel/Casino, 200 Fremont St., 385-6257. **$$–$$$**

Chapter 14

Sports and Recreation

Spectator Sports

Las Vegas Stars Baseball. The Las Vegas Stars, the AAA farm club of the San Diego Padres in the Pacific Coast League, one step below the majors, play a 140-game season from April through September with home games at Cashman Field, with 9,334 permanent seats and 3,000 bleachers in the outfield. Fans can also have dinner at the Club Level Restaurant and watch the game from there.

Games begin at 7:05 P.M. Monday through Saturday and at 6:05 P.M. on Sunday. Prices are field level, $6; plaza level, $5; reserved, $4.50; and general admission, $4. Seats in the air-conditioned Club Level Restaurant are $7.50. Children and seniors can purchase general admission tickets for $3. For ticket information call 386-7200, or call Ticketmaster at 474-4000.

The Stars are one of the most successful minor league franchises; they drew more than 430,000 fans in the 1993 season. In typical minor league fashion, there are many special promotions at games, including firework nights, "Catch or Splash" competitions, "Pitch for Cash" games, and "Dizzy-Dizzy" contests.

In 1994, other teams in the PCL and their major league affiliations were the Albuquerque Dukes (LA Dodgers), Calgary Cannons (Seattle Mariners), Colorado Springs Sky Sox (Colorado Rockies), Edmonton Trappers (Florida Marlins), Phoenix Firebirds (SF Giants), Salt Lake Buzz (Minnesota Twins), Tacoma Tigers (Oakland A's), Tucson Toros (Houston Astros), and Vancouver Canadians (California Angels).

At the start of the 1994 season, the Las Vegas Stars were coached by former major leaguer Russ Nixon; one of the coaches is Marty Barrett, a former infielder for the Boston Red Sox and Las Vegas native. Among the present-day stars who played for the Stars in the past are Roberto and Sandy

Alomar, Carlos Baerga, Joey Cora, Ozzie Guillen, John Kruk, Tony Gwynn, Benito Santiago, Kevin McReynolds, and Shane Mack.

In recent years, the Stars have brought in major league teams including the Chicago Cubs, Oakland Athletics, San Diego Padres, and Houston Astros during spring training in late March or early April.

UNLV Runnin' Rebels. The nationally ranked college basketball team plays home games at the Thomas and Mack Center. Tickets can be very hard to get for some matchups. Call 739-3761.

Rodeo. The National Finals Rodeo is held in December.

Las Vegas International Marathon. February. 876-3870.

World Firefighters Games. May. 434-1046.

Las Vegas Cutting Horse Annual. September. 385-5257.

Health Clubs

Many of the major hotels have small health clubs for guests or can offer special arrangements for use of a commercial club. Following are some of the largest clubs that cater to short-term visitors; call to check on hours and availability of day or short-term passes.

Family Fitness Centers. West: 3055 S. Valley View, 368-1111. East: 2605 S. Eastern, 641-2222. North: 3141 N. Rainbow, 656-7777.

Gold's Gym. East: Flamingo and Sandhill, 451-4222. West: Sahara and Decatur, 877-6966.

Goodbody's Fitness Center. 6080 Burnham Avenue, 798-8111.

Harrah's Casino Hotel. 3475 Las Vegas Boulevard South, 369-5007.

Las Vegas Sporting House. Racquetball, squash, tennis, and volleyball courts; indoor and outdoor running tracks. Open 24 hours. 3025 Industrial Road (behind Stardust Hotel), 733-8999.

Racquetball

Caesars Palace. 731-7110.

Las Vegas Athletic Club East. 1070 East Sahara Avenue, 733-1919.

Las Vegas Sporting House. 10 racquetball and two squash courts. Open 24 hours. 3025 Industrial Road (behind Stardust Hotel). 733-8999.

Bowling

Gold Coast Hotel & Casino. 72 lanes. Open 24 hours. 4000 W. Flamingo Road. 367-4700.

Sam's Town Hotel Gambling Hall & Bowling Center. 56 lanes. Open 24 hours. 5111 Boulder Highway. 454-8022.

Santa Fe Hotel & Casino. 60 lanes. 4949 Rancho Drive. 658-4900.

Showboat Hotel, Casino & Bowling Center. 106 lanes. Open 24 hours. 2800 Fremont Street. 385-9153.

Horseback Riding

Bonnie Springs Old Nevada. Seven days a week through Red Canyon. Highway 159 West of Las Vegas. 875-4191.

Mt. Charleston Riding Stables. Seven days a week, on Mt. Charleston. Highway 157 North of Las Vegas. 872-7009.

Ice Skating

Santa Fe Resort. The only public ice skating arena in southern Nevada, with an NHL regulation-size rink. Figure skating and hockey lessons and leagues. 4949 N. Rancho Drive. 658-4900.

Roller Skating

Crystal Palace. 4680 Boulder Highway, 458-0177.
Crystal Palace. 3901 N. Rancho Drive, 645-4892.
Crystal Palace. 4740 S. Decatur, 253-9832.
Playland Skating Center. 1110 E. Lake Mead Drive, Henderson, 564-2790.

Skiing

Lee Canyon. Mount Charleston. 646-0008.

Vertical	Elevation	Lifts
1,030	9,320	3

Base: 8,290 feet. Summit: 9,320 feet. A secret to many winter visitors to Las Vegas is that there is a ski hill less than an hour north of The Strip. Lee Canyon is not to be confused with one of the Sierra Nevada monsters in and around Lake Tahoe, but it does offer decent skiing from about December through April. The resort offers shuttle bus service from Las Vegas, and you can rent equipment, from ski pants and jackets to skis, boots, and poles.

Lee Canyon is predominately an intermediate hill, with about 15 percent beginners' slopes and 5 percent expert terrain.

Miniature Golf

Funtazmic. 4975 Polaris Avenue, west of I-15. 795-4386.
Scandia Miniature Golf & Family Fun Center. 2900 Sirius Road. 364-0070.

Golf Courses

Angel Park Golf Club. Two courses. 100 S. Rampart Boulevard. 254-4653.
Black Mountain Golf and Country Club. 501 Country Club Drive, Henderson. 565-7933.
Boulder City Municipal Golf Course. 1 Clubhouse Drive, Boulder City. 293-9236.
Calvada Golf and Country Club. Red Butte, Pahrump. 727-4653.
Craig Ranch Golf Course. 628 W. Craig Road. 642-9700.
Desert Inn Country Club. 3145 Las Vegas Boulevard South. 733-4444.
Desert Rose Golf Course. 5843 Club House Drive. 438-4653.
Mirage Country Club. 3650 Las Vegas Boulevard South. 369-7111.
Las Vegas Golf Club. 4349 Vegas Drive. 646-3003.
Legacy Golf Club. 130 Par Excellence Drive. 897-2187
Los Prados Golf and Country Club. 5150 Los Prados Circle. 645-5696.
North Las Vegas Community Course. 324 E. Brooks Ave., North Las Vegas. 649-7171.
Painted Desert Country Club. 5555 Painted Mirage Way. 645-2568.
Peppermill Palms Golf Course. 1134 Mesquite Boulevard, Mesquite. (800) 621-0187.
Royal Kenfield Country Club. 1 Showboat Country Club Drive. 434-9009.
Sahara Country Club. 1911 E. Desert Inn Road. 796-0016.
Sun City Summerlin Golf Club. 9201-B Del Webb Boulevard. 363-4373.

Tennis

Aladdin. Three illuminated outdoor courts on the hotel's upper story pool deck. Dawn to 10 P.M. Priority to guests. 736-0111.
Alexis Park. Two lighted courts. Priority to hotel guests. 6 A.M. to 8 P.M. 796-3300.
Bally's. Ten outdoor courts, five illuminated. Reservations only. No fee to guests, minimal to others. Dusk to dawn. 739-4111.

Caesars Palace. Four outdoor courts. Guests and public welcome. Lessons available. Dawn to dark. 731-7786.

Desert Inn. Ten outdoor courts, five lighted. Open to the public. Lessons and rentals available. 733-4577.

Flamingo Hilton. A new tennis complex will be available after the completion of construction of a new entranceway at the hotel. 733-3344.

Frontier. Two outdoor courts, lighted. No fee for guests. 794-8200.

Hacienda. One illuminated court. 8 A.M. to 11 P.M. Reservations for hotel guests. 739-8911.

Hot Springs Tennis Club. Four outdoor courts, lighted. 361-5683.

Las Vegas Hilton. Six illuminated courts on pool deck. Hilton guests only. 732-5111.

Plaza. Four outdoor courts, all lighted. Rentals available. 386-2110.

Riviera. Two courts, both lighted. Guests first, others welcome. Reservations only. 734-5110.

Sports Club - Las Vegas. Two outdoor courts, lighted. Reservations required. 733-8999.

Studio 96. Ten indoor courts, four outdoor courts, lighted. 735-8153.

Sunset Park. Eight illuminated courts. $2 per hour. 7 A.M. to 11 P.M. 455-8200.

Tropicana. Four outdoor courts, lighted. No fees for guests. Reservations recommended. 739-2381.

Twin Lakes Racquet Club. Eight outdoor courts, lighted. Open to the public. Reservations required. 647-3434.

Bicycle Rentals

Bikes USA. 1537 N. Eastern Avenue. 642-2453.

Blue Diamond Bicycles. 14 Cottonwood Drive, Blue Diamond. 875-4500.

City Streets Bike Tours. Bicycle rentals for Red Rock Park and Mt. Charleston, maps, and equipment. 596-2953.

Parks and Scenic Areas

Floyd Lamb State Park. 9200 Tule Springs Road. 486-5413.

Hoover Dam. 293-8367.

Lake Mead Recreation Area.
> **Boulder Beach:** 293-1891.
> **Callville Bay:** 565-8958.
> **Cottonwood:** 297-1464.
> **Las Vegas Wash:** 565-9111.
> **National Park Service:** 293-8096.

Lee Canyon. Mount Charleston in Toiyabe National Forest, northwest of Las Vegas on Highway 95 to Highway 156. 646-0008.

Spring Mt. Ranch. Blue Diamond. 875-4141.

Valley of Fire. Overton. 397-2088.

RV Parks

Boomtown Hotel Casino & RV Resort. I-15 and Blue Diamond. 263-7777, (800) 588-7711.

California Hotel-Casino & RV Park. California Hotel and Casino, 1st and Ogden Avenues in downtown. 388-2602.

Circus Land RV Park. Circus Circus Hotel and Casino, 500 Circus Circus Drive. 794-3757.

Good Sam-Hitchin' Post Camper Park. 3640 N. Las Vegas Boulevard. 644-1043.

Hacienda Camperland. Hacienda Hotel, 3950 Las Vegas Boulevard South. 739-8214.

KOA Kampgrounds. 4315 Boulder Highway. 451-5527.

Sam's Town RV Park. Sam's Town Hotel, 4040 S. Nellis Boulevard. 454-8056.

Silver Nugget Casino & RV Park. Silver Nugget Casino, 2240 Las Vegas Boulevard North, North Las Vegas. 649-7439.

Chapter 15

Journeys North of Las Vegas: Mount Charleston, Lee Canyon, Red Rock Canyon, and Valley of Fire

As we've noted, Las Vegas is a lot more than just green felt, computer-controlled volcanic eruptions, and mock Egyptian pyramids. Few things make that point more clearly than a journey a few miles north of town along I-95.

Just past downtown the trappings of Las Vegas fall away quickly, yielding to the near-barren Mojave Desert. On the plateau to the right is the huge Nellis Air Force Base, and beyond that are two of the area's less-well-known attractions: the Nellis Air Force Range that runs for almost 125 miles from Las Vegas to near Tonopah, and the Nevada Test Site, a nuclear weapon testing area included within the range.

Nellis is generally off-limits to civilians, except for occasional open houses. Visitors can tour the home of the famed Thunderbirds aerial demonstration team on Tuesdays and Thursdays at 1:30 P.M. The 90-minute tour includes a film about the flyers, a museum, and a visit to a hanger to see an F-16. Call 652-4018 for information.

The top secret status of the Nellis base and the vast size of the area have regularly spawned all sorts of interesting rumors about goings-on in the area, including reports ranging from testing of strange military aircraft (including the Stealth bomber) to detailed reports of military experiments on captured UFOs and their alien crews. We got that last tidbit, by the way, from Elvis, who has his hideaway on the range.

Going to Dreamland

And then things get really weird. About 120 miles northwest of Las Vegas is a huge government military installation that officially doesn't exist. There are several very long runways and dozens of hangars and buildings, but according to FAA pilot charts and U.S. Geological Survey topographic maps, it just ain't there.

The installation, at Groom Lake, is known to some as Dreamland; old government maps call it Area 51. When officialdom is pushed to the wall, they will acknowledge the existence of something called a "remote test facility."

According to *Popular Science,* which published an investigation of the air base in 1994, every weekday 10 to 12 Boeing 737 jets depart from special terminals operated by defense contractor EG&G Corp. at McCarran Airport, or in Palmdale, California. The planes, painted white with a broad red stripe down their lengths, make low-level 30-minute flights to Groom Lake with an estimated 1,500 to 2,000 employees.

This explains a lot, doesn't it? As if Las Vegas wasn't already one weird place, consider the fact that 50 or so miles north and west of town is the neighborhood nuclear test site.

From its start in the depths of the Cold War in 1951 through today, there have been nearly 700 tests of nuclear bombs. At first, the explosions were conducted in the atmosphere and it was not an unusual sight to see a mushroom cloud cresting over downtown Las Vegas. Since the 1960s, the explosions have taken place underground.

The Nevada Test Site at Yucca Flat is part of the huge Nellis Air Force Range. The test site is 1,350 square miles, about the size of the entire state of Rhode Island. In case you had your heart aglow in anticipation of a tour, though, we're sorry to disappoint you: the entire area is off-limits.

What goes on there? According to unofficial observers, the base has been used for projects from testing of the ultrasecret SR-71 spyplane in the 1960s to flight tests of Soviet Sukhoi Su-22 and MiG-23 fighters somehow obtained by the military to training for the F-117A Stealth attack planes. And, there are those who maintain that the U.S. government has captured UFOs and maintained them at the base.

There is not much chance of taking a sightseeing trip to Dreamland, though. About as close as you can get is up in the hills near the tiny town of Rachel (population about 100). The Bureau of Land Management property outside the base is patrolled by sheriff's deputies; closer in is the boundary of the base itself, which is guarded with detection devices, video cameras, and signs warning "Use of Deadly Force Authorized."

The Air Force is attempting to expand its property by taking another 4,000 acres of BLM land near Rachel to make it more difficult to peer into the base.

By the way, if you go to the trouble of driving to Rachel (I-15 north to Route 93 north, picking up Route 375 westbound near Ash Springs), you'll find the Little A'Le'Inn (pronounced "alien"), its walls covered with UFO memorabilia and a large photo of the base that doesn't exist.

Natural Wonders

On the left side of I-95 and The Strip, heading out of Las Vegas, are two expeditions worth taking. Note: we would suggest you fill up the gas tank in your car before heading out on a tour; gas stations are few and far between.

Red Rock Canyon. Here is an extraordinary world of rusty red cliffs, Joshua trees, yucca plants, and sagebrush; just as other-worldly and much more real than the nearby manmade canyons of Las Vegas. It's heaven for hikers, perfect for picnickers, and a delightful drive even if you never leave your car.

Take I-15 to the West Charleston exit and drive west on Charleston Avenue toward the hills. About 10 miles out of town, Las Vegas is a garish memory and Red Rock Canyon is a garish reality. The sandstone cliffs, towering 2,000 feet above the desert floor, are an artist's palette of red, orange, yellow, pink, purple, and brown.

Check at the Bureau of Land Management Visitor Center on Red Rock Road to pick up hiking, bicycling, climbing, or general nature brochures. Marked hiking trails range from about two miles to a 14-mile tour to the top of the escarpment. There's also a 13-mile one-way driving loop with pulloffs at some of the more spectacular views, with even more "Oohs" per mile than on the Las Vegas Strip.

> **Beep-beep.** The roadrunner rarely flies, but will make a short hop into the air when necessary to escape from danger or to pounce on a meal, including lizards, snakes, insects, and squirrels—these juicy foods are the primary source of moisture for the roadrunner.

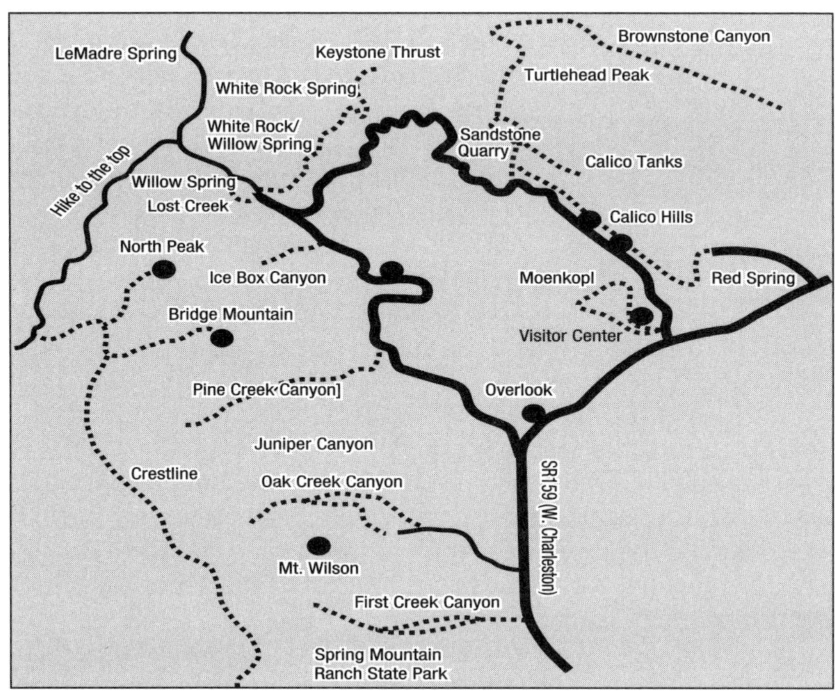

Red Rock Canyon

Don't be a burro. Heed the warning signs against feeding the wild burros in the area; they bite. The state puts teeth into the warning with a $25 fine for unauthorized feedings.

Roll of the dice. In 1942, actress Carole Lombard was killed when her DC-3 airplane slammed into Mount Potosi southwest of Las Vegas in the Spring Mountains. She was returning from a war bonds rally in the midwest to Los Angeles and husband Clark Gable.

In remembrance of the popular Miss Lombard, an orange butterfly with black spots peculiar to the local hills was named the *Carole's fritillary*.

The name holds Las Vegas significance: fritillary comes from the Latin *fritillus*, meaning dice box.

For much of the past 600 million years, the land that is now Red Rock Canyon was the bottom of a deep ocean basin; the western coast of North America was in present-day western Utah.

A rich variety of marine life in the waters left behind deposits of shells and skeletons more than 9,000 feet thick, which were eventually compressed into limestone and other carbonate rocks.

About 225 million years ago, movements in the earth's crust caused the seabed to slowly rise. Streams entering the shallower waters left behind mud and sand which later became consolidated into shales and marine sandstones.

Large bodies of salt water became cut off from the sea and eventually evaporated, leaving behind salt and gypsum. The exposure of the sediments to the atmosphere caused some of the minerals to oxidize, changing their colors to red and orange.

Beep, beep! One of the most famous residents of the Red Rock Canyon is the roadrunner. And yes, this chicken-sized bird really does streak across the desert on foot. (And though there are coyotes, too, we are not aware of a local franchise for the Acme Dynamite Company.)

Another stage in the geologic history of Red Rock Canyon occurred about 180 million years ago when the area became an arid desert. A giant dune field stretched eastward to Colorado, with sand more than half a mile deep in some areas. The shifting sands left behind curved and angled lines known as "crossbeds" that were eventually cemented into sandstone in combination with calcium carbonate and iron oxide; this is the source of some of the red rock cliffs.

Most recently, some 65 million years ago, a thrust fracture in the earth's crust drove one crustal plate over another, placing the older gray carbonate rocks of the ancient ocean above the younger tan and red sandstone below. Red Rock Canyon is part of the Keystone Thrust Fault, a huge system that extends north in Canada.

Over thousands of years, at least four and possibly several other Native American cultures occupied the Red Rock area. They were drawn because of the relative abundance of water in the canyon, which includes more than 40 springs and catchment basins. Archaeologists have found roasting pits and a historical sandstone quarry.

For information, call the Red Rock Canyon Visitors Center at 363-1921.

Mount Charleston. About 20 miles north of town, after a long jaunt along a flat desert floor, look for Nevada Route 157 branching off to the left. From here you will begin a long, steady climb. The road is one of the more dramatic ones we know of: for much of the early part of the climb you are able to look straight into the face of the mountain ahead of you.

Mount Charleston is a serious hill, reaching to 11,919 feet, the principal peak of the Spring Mountain Range. Much of the surrounding area is part of the Toiyabe National Forest.

The trip is an interesting exploration of the effect of elevation on climate and plant and animal life. The yucca, Joshua trees, and creosote bushes are able to survive the intense heat and lack of rain at the desert floor. A bit further up the road you'll find junipers, scrub pine, and sagebrush. Higher up the mountain the vegetation gives way to bristlecone pines that are adapted to the extremes of cold and wind on the mountain.

About 10 miles up the road is the **Mt. Charleston Hotel,** an old-timey mountain lodge (okay, so it's less than 10 years old; it still feels real) with beam ceilings and a large open fireplace. Rooms range from ordinary to extraordinary, including a few suites with fireplaces. The **Canyon Dining Room** is an attractive place to eat, especially on a moonlit night. Call 872-5500 for information.

At the very end of Kyle Canyon road is a stunning resort area, first developed by the Civilian Conservation Corps during the depression and now offering vacation homes, campgrounds, and picnic areas.

Route 158 branches off to the right, just before the Mt. Charleston Hotel. This is a stunning, twisty mountain road that traverses a ridge over to Lee Canyon Road (Route 156). Turn left, into the mountain and climb for another four miles to reach the **Lee Canyon Ski Area.**

Lee Canyon benefits from its elevation—a lofty 8,290 feet at the base and 9,320 feet at the peak—and its meteorological conditions. As a mountain oasis in the desert, it gathers a

Hot and cold. The climate of Nevada varies greatly, with tremendous extremes between the desert floors and mountain tops.

In the south, summers are generally long and hot and winters short and mild; at Las Vegas the average annual temperature is 66 degrees.

In the north, summers are short and hot and winters are long and cool; at Reno, the average annual temperature is 49 degrees.

Nevada is the driest state in the U.S., with average annual rain of just four inches in the southeast. The wettest parts of the state are the Carson Sink and the Sierra Nevada mountains of the northeast.

> **Something to glow about.** Another improvement to the Nevada economy—if not its environment—is the Nevada Nuclear Waste Repository at Yucca Mountain about 100 miles from Vegas. Due for an off-limits opening sometime around the year 2000, the repository is planned as a waste dump for the radioactive garbage from nuclear weapons, power plants, and other assorted reactors around the nation.
>
> This permanent improvement has to be able to remain untouched for 10,000 or so years, which just may outlast The Strip.

> **Rocking the treetops.** More than 45 species are peculiar to Red Rock Canyon. Larger animals in the area include bighorn sheep, cougars, wild horses, and burros; other smaller creatures include kit foxes, coyotes, and bobcats.
>
> The river areas are home to more than 30 species of reptiles and amphibians.

fair amount of natural snow. Many of the trails are also covered with snow-making equipment. However, the season is extremely variable. In a good winter, skiers can schuss from as early as Thanksgiving to as late as early spring; in a dry or warm season, the slopes can turn to mud very quickly.

The ski hill itself has a respectable vertical drop of 1,030 feet served by three chairlifts. None of the 11 trails would qualify as a scary double-diamond expert slope; the predominance of the trails are decidedly intermediate, with a separate, wide beginner's slope that has its own chairlift. A pleasant lodge with a sun deck sits at the bottom of the hill; rental equipment is available at the lodge or at one of several sporting goods stores in Las Vegas. Ski Lee runs its own charter bus service to the mountain from town. The area participates in the Ski Wee program for youngsters between 4 and 12 years of age.

For information, road and ski conditions call 593-9500; 872-5462 for information about ski lessons; and 646-0008 for bus reservations.

An alternate route to Mount Charleston is to go past Route 157 and continue on I-95 for about 14 miles to Route 156. This road goes directly to the Lee Canyon Ski Area; from there you can also cross over the upper trail (Route 158) and descend on Route 157.

Valley of Fire State Park. A bit farther up the road, but a bit wilder than Red Rock Canyon, this park includes spectacularly colored desert sandstone that has been sculpted by the wind and rain into fantastic shapes. You'll also find ancient petroglyphs (prehistoric rock drawings) on canyon walls; they are believed to date back more than 2,000 years to the time of the Anasazi. Check in at the visitor station for maps and information or call 397-2088.

The Valley of Fire is about 50 miles northeast of Las Vegas, off I-15; you can make a loop that connects to the top of Lake Mead and down to Boulder and the Hoover Dam for a nice day trip.

Chapter 16

Journeys South of Las Vegas:
Hoover Dam, Boulder City,
Lake Mead, and Laughlin

Hoover Dam

If they had a casino at Hoover Dam, it would be a building that would rival Luxor, Excalibur, Caesars Palace, and MGM Grand combined. They don't, of course, and though nearly 700,000 visitors a year come to visit this incredible monument to our attempts to exercise control over our environment, this means that nearly 20 million other visitors to Las Vegas don't make the 40-mile trip south. There ought to be a law....

The Colorado River, which flows 1,400 miles from the Rocky Mountains in Colorado to the Gulf of California is one of the great geological forces in the west, creating natural wonders including the Grand Canyon.

In the early days of settlement, the Colorado was the source of great respect and fear. Early settlers attempted to divert some of its waters for irrigation purposes. They were defeated by the tremendous seasonal changes from steady flow to summertime trickle to wild flooding in the spring as mountain snows melted.

Steam-powered riverboats navigated the Colorado River upstream from its mouth in the late 1800s, able to reach as far north as the Mormon settlement of Callville part of the year.

One of the most difficult parts of the 600-mile trip was passage through the Black Canyon rapids. Crews had to use a system of winches and cables strung through ring bolts anchored in the canyon walls.

It took a disastrous flood in California's Imperial Valley in 1905 to begin the move to finally tame the river. In that year, early spring flash floods washed away small earthen dams which had been created to divert water from the river to the Imperial Canal. The heavy water flow changed the course of the river and caused it to flow for the next two years into the Imperial Valley and the large Salton Sea east of San Diego, increasing the size of that body of water from 22 to 500 square miles; to this date the

Nowheresville. The massive construction project of Hoover Dam takes on an even greater scope when you realize that at the start of the project Black Canyon was an isolated stretch of river with few roads and no support facilities. The nearest town of any significance was Las Vegas, which was still a small rest stop for the railroads. The huge influx of workers changed Las Vegas forever, setting it on its current course as a gambling and entertainment mecca.

High way. The two-lane highway atop the dam connects Nevada and Arizona. By the way, Nevada is in the Pacific time zone, and Arizona is one hour later in the Mountain time zone.

Salton Sea has not fully retreated to its turn-of-the-century size, covering about 300 square miles today.

The first task for the construction crews when they began in April of 1931 was to deal with the water already passing through the canyon. Four huge diversion tunnels, nearly 60 feet in diameter, were dug out of the walls of the canyon to the left and right of the eventual location of the dam. A year-and-a-half later they were ready to send the Colorado River through the tunnels and leave dry the dam's base.

More than 5,000 men worked day and night in a continuous pour of concrete that took two years—a total of 4.4 million cubic yards of concrete for the dam and supporting structures. Although there is a commonly held belief that some of the 94 workers who died in the course of the dangerous construction project are entombed within the concrete, dam tour guides will tell you otherwise.

The dam itself is described as an arch-gravity structure. Still the highest concrete dam in the Western Hemisphere, it rises 726 feet above the bedrock of Black Canyon. It is 660 feet thick at its base and 45 feet thick at the top, with a span of 1,244 feet across the canyon.

The dam was completed in 1935, two years ahead of schedule, which has to be a record for a government project. The diversion tunnels were closed in February of 1935, and Lake Mead began to form behind the dam. The first power generator began operation in 1936; the 17th and final generator went on line in 1961.

The dam cost about $175 million to build at the time, and the cost has been repaid through revenues from the generation of power and the supply of water. The energy distribution from the dam, as set by contracts among the states, sends about 19 percent of the power to the state of Arizona, about 25 percent to Nevada, 28 percent to the Metropolitan Water District of Southern California, and the remainder to various municipalities in California including Los Angeles.

The Lake Mead reservoir which built up behind the dam extends for 110 miles and usually stores about 2 years of average Colorado River flow, which is released as needed for irrigation and power generation. Water in the lake irrigates more than one million acres of land in the United States and half a million acres in Mexico.

The generators produce about 4 billion kilowatt-hours of energy per year, enough for 500,000 homes. The gravity-fed generators are non-polluting, and of course, water flow is a renewable resource.

Another effect of the dam is to clear the once-muddy waters of the Colorado for much of its downstream passage and within Lake Mead itself.

Tours of the dam are conducted by the Bureau of Reclamation daily except for Christmas, and more than 700,000 pass through each year. The tour passes down through the body of the dam to the generating stations and out onto the walkway near the diversion tunnels at the base.

Work was continuing in 1994 on the construction of an impressive new visitor's center, cantilevered out from the rock wall of the canyon on the Nevada side. Critics have pointed out that the visitor center will cost more than the original price tag for the dam itself.

Stop off at the **Alan Bible Visitor Center** on Lakeshore Drive (Route 166 just past the junction with U.S. 93) for information about Lake Mead and Hoover Dam.

Boulder City

Boulder City is a planned community created by the U.S. Bureau of Reclamation as housing for some of the construction workers for the dam and for administrative offices. The construction of the town coincided with a period of architectural design and government master planning; the result was a designed town with a great deal of un-Nevada-like greenery and parks. Think of it as a U.S. government-approved oasis in the desert.

The feds continued to own and operate the town, controlling almost every detail until 1960 when it gave up dominion and the town was incorporated. Only then was alcohol permitted to be sold; today, Boulder City continues as the only city in Nevada that bans public gambling.

The **Boulder City/Hoover Dam** Museum is worth a visit to ogle the impressive collection of construction photos. The museum is located at 441 Nevada Highway. Call 293-1823 for hours and information.

Lake Mead

It seems odd to speak of a fabulous outdoor wonderland like Lake Mead as a creation of man, but so it is.

Before Lake Mead was formed when the diversion tunnels of Hoover Dam were closed in 1935, this area was almost untouched by humans. Indian tribes once inhabited some of the canyons. Explorers like John Wesley Powell went deep into the Grand Canyon and other areas; the first foreign settlers included fur trappers, Mormon settlers, and prospectors.

You can't get there from here. The Shivwits Plateau can only be reached by unpaved roads from the north; check with park rangers for information on access.

Anson Call established a Mormon colony in 1864 with a trading post to service emigrants on their westward passage along the Colorado River. Callville was abandoned five years later, although the walls of part of the settlement were still in place when the entire region—including many ancient Indian sites—was flooded by the developing lake. It is a good question whether Hoover Dam could have been built under today's historic preservation and environmental impact laws.

Lake Mead National Recreation Area includes the 110-mile-long Lake Mead, the 67-mile-long Lake Mohave, which backs up behind the smaller Davis Dam at Laughlin, the surrounding desert, and the isolated Shivwits Plateau in Arizona, which connects into the Grand Canyon National Park. Together, the two huge (274 square-mile) lakes sparkle in one of the driest, hottest places known to man.

In summer, daytime temperatures rise above 100 degrees regularly. From October to May, temperatures range from the 30s to the 50s.

Plan to include a stop at the Alan Bible Visitor Center, four miles northeast of Boulder City on U.S. 93. Travel south from Las Vegas on Route 93/95 and stay on Route 93 at the split. The visitor center offers maps and information on services in the park.

Down the drain. Nearly all of the state's streams and rivers drain internally into lakes or into dry lake beds, called playas or sinks. The major exception is the Colorado River.

The Humboldt rises in the northeast and flows west to disappear into the Humboldt Sink; and the Walker, Carson, and Truckee Rivers rise in the Sierra Nevada and flow east to the Walker, Carson, and Pyramid Lakes. Many other streams are dry for most of the year, filling their banks only in the spring with snow melt, or after the rare summer rain.

You can also go to the park headquarters at the intersection of Nevada Highway and Wyoming Street in Boulder City, or visit one of the many park ranger stations.

Reservations are necessary for most lodging and many services in the summer. Campsites are available, for a fee, on a first-come first-served basis; some have time limits for stays. Each camp area includes picnic tables, grills, water, restrooms, and a trailer sewage dump; no utility hookups are provided.

Back country camping is permitted along the shore on both lakes and in designated sites along unpaved back country roads.

Outside of the parks you can find hotels, restaurants, and services in Las Vegas, Boulder City, Henderson, Laughlin, Searchlight, and Overton in Nevada; Bullhead City and Kingman in Arizona; and Needles in California.

Park Facilities

Lake Mead	Distance from Visitor Center (miles)	Services
Boulder Beach	2	L T C M R F S
Las Vegas Wash	10	C M R F S
Callville Bay	27	C M R F S G H
Echo Bay	49	L T C M R F S G H
Overton Beach	63	L T M R F S G
Temple Bar	50	L T C M R F S G H

Lake Mohave		
Willow Beach	22	L T M R F S G H
Cottonwood Beach	54	L T C M R F S G H
Katherine	81	L T C M R F S G H

L = Lodging; **T** = Trailer village (fee); **C** = Campground;
M = Marina; **R** = Restaurant; **F** = Food;
S = Sewage dump; **G** = Gasoline; **H** = Houseboat rentals

Animal Life in the Lake Mead Area

Living things have to be very hardy to survive in the temperature extremes of the desert and the annual rainfall of less than six inches.

The creation of Lake Mead dramatically changed the ecology of the region, bringing waterbirds, fish, and aquatic plants. In the surrounding desert, more than 1,000 bighorn sheep live along the mountain ridges; they are among the few desert animals active in the heat of the day. Other creatures include lizards, squirrels, rabbits, insects, and spiders.

The desert blooms year-round, but some of the flowers are so tiny that it is easy to miss them. A winter rain can cause a brief but glorious overnight bloom of wildflowers on the desert.

Fishing

In Lake Mead, the most sought-after fish is striped bass, which can reach 50 pounds and more. In Lake Mohave, especially in the upper reaches in Black Canyon, rainbow trout is the most popular. Other species include largemouth bass, channel catfish, black crappie, and bluegill.

Nevada and Arizona share jurisdiction over the two lakes. You must have a state fishing license to fish from shore. To fish from a boat, you must have a license from one state and a special use stamp from the other. Licenses and stamps are available at most marinas.

Lake Mead information. Write to: Superintendent, Lake Mead National Recreation Area, 601 Nevada Highway, Boulder City, NV 89005-2426. The phone number is 293-8907.

Swimming

Both lakes are clear and clean for swimming. Water temperatures across most of the two lakes average about 78 degrees in spring, summer, and fall. The coldest water is usually found in the northern portion of Lake Mohave. Lifeguard beaches can be found in summer at Boulder Beach on Lake Mead and at Katherine on Lake Mohave.

Boating

Boaters can get to some spots inaccessible to cars and can roam the entire 274 square miles of water of Lake Mead, including the narrow steep gorge of Iceberg Canyon. Around the lake, many secluded coves are formed by fingers of the desert jutting out into the water; these are among the most popular campsites.

Sailboarding, a relatively new sport, is increasingly popular on the lake. Participants generally prefer near-shore areas with stronger breezes.

There are six privately operated marinas along Lake Mead and three on Lake Mohave, each offering services and supplies year-round. Free public launching ramps and parking areas (parking limited to seven days) are found at each site.

Several companies offer boat tours, including a paddlewheel vessel departing daily from the Lake Mead Marina. In summer, a tour through Boulder Canyon departs from Callville Bay every day. On Lake Mohave, one-day raft trips are offered through the slow-moving waters of Black Canyon from Hoover Dam to Willow Beach.

Boulder City Chamber of Commerce. 1497 Nevada Highway, Boulder City, NV 89005; 293-2034.

Boulder City Visitor Center. 100 Nevada Highway, Boulder City, NV 89005; 294-1220.

Water proofing. Before going out on the water, call 736-3854 or monitor marine radio channel 162.55 for National Weather Service forecasts. High winds can arrive suddenly, building up waves as high as six feet; lightning storms pose particular hazards to boats on open water. If you are caught in a storm, seek shelter in a protected cove.

Hiking

The best hiking months are October through May. Temperatures the rest of the year make for furnace-like conditions. You can explore on your own or join an escorted tour lead by naturalists. Always carry one gallon of water per person per day and let someone know where you are going and when you expect to return.

Health Considerations

The desert includes several dangerous species, including rattlesnakes, scorpions, and Gila monster lizards. All of these will likely leave you alone if you do not disturb them. Wear sturdy boots to protect your feet.

A microscopic amoeba common to some hot

springs can cause a rare infection that can become fatal; do not dive or submerse your head in springs and streams. A toxic plant called oleander is common in the area, and hikers are advised not to eat unknown plants or drink water from ditches.

Lake Mead Resorts and Recreational Facilities

Boulder Beach Store. 290 Lakeshore Road, Boulder City. 293-1891. Snack bar, public showers, grocery store.

Callville Bay Resort. Callville Bay. 565-8958. Cafe/lounge, marina, small boat rentals, houseboat rentals, trailer village, RV sites, showers, laundry, auto/boat gas, dry boat storage, store.

Echo Bay Resort. Overton. Reservations (800) 752-9669. 394-4000. Restaurant/lounge, marina, boat rentals, houseboat rentals, trailer village, RV sites, hotel, showers/laundry, auto/boat gas, store, dry boat storage.

Lakeshore Trailer Village. 268 Lakeshore Road, Boulder City. 293-2540. Trailer village with RV sites, dry boat storage, showers, and laundry.

Lake Mead Resort. 322 Lakeshore Road, Boulder City. 293-3484. Call 293-2074 for lodging reservations only, or (800) 752-9669 for other reservations. Restaurant/lounge, marina, boat rentals, store, dry boat storage, boat gas, and motel.

Lake Mead Cruises. Boulder City. 293-6180. Scheduled and charter sightseeing tours on the *Desert Princess* paddlewheel boat from Lake Mead Marina to Hoover Dam.

Las Vegas Bay Marina/Las Vegas Boat Harbor. Henderson. 565-9111. Restaurant/lounge, marina, boat rentals, dry boat storage, store, boat gas.

Overton Beach Resort. Overton. 394-4040. Snack bar, boat rentals, moorings, fuel dock, auto/boat gas, store, showers, laundry, trailer village, RV sites, dry boat storage, summer jet-ski rental.

Temple Bar Resort. Temple Bar, Arizona. (602) 767-3211. Reservations (800) 752-9669. Restaurant/lounge, motel, trailer village, dry boat storage, store, marina, boat rentals, showers, laundry, auto/boat gas, RV sites.

Canoe/Raft Services

Down River Outfitters. Boulder City. 293-1190. Canoe/raft delivery and retrieval.

Jerkwater Canoe Co., Inc. Topock, Arizona. (602) 768-7753. Canoe delivery and retrieval.

Tincanebitt Taxi. Meadview, Arizona. (602) 564-2424. Boat/raft retrieval.

Lake Mohave Resorts and Recreational Facilities

Black Canyon, Inc. Boulder City. 293-3776, (602) 767-3311. Raft tours from Hoover Dam to Willow Beach.

Cottonwood Cove Resort. Cottonwood Cove. 297-1464. Cafe, marina, boat rentals, houseboat rentals, auto/boat gas, dry boat storage, store, showers, laundry, motel, trailer village, RV sites.

Lake Mohave Resort. Bullhead City, Arizona. 754-3245. Reservations (800) 752-9669. Restaurant/lounge, store, motel, auto/boat gas, marina, boat rentals, houseboat rentals, trailer village, RV sites, showers, laundry, dry boat storage.

Willow Beach Resort. Willow Beach, Arizona. 293-3776 or (602) 767-3311. Reservations (800) 845-3833. Restaurant/lounge, marina, houseboat rentals, showers, laundry, auto/boat gas, store, motel, trailer village, RV sites, dry boat storage.

Laughlin

The burgeoning community of Laughlin, and its shadow community of Bullhead, Arizona, across the Colorado River, is unique in Nevada in at least two respects. First, it is among the few major settlements that has no real history of its own other than as a gambling resort. There wasn't even a rest stop there! Secondly, the place was named by and for its founder, who still operates a major casino there.

The man behind the town is Don Laughlin, who made his grubstake with a small-time Las Vegas bar and casino. He had the foresight to develop a stretch of sand in Sandy Point at the southeastern corner of the state, on the border with Arizona and not far from California. The resort mostly draws from Arizona and California, but it's about a 90-mile drive from Las Vegas, if you want to check it out.

Laughlin's first operation, the Riverside Casino, was established in 1967 and quickly became a rest stop of its own, drawing visitors from its neighboring states. Within a few years, there was enough of a draw at the community, now renamed Laughlin (allegedly by a postmaster) to attract a number of other major casinos and hotels.

Today, Laughlin ranks third among Nevada resorts in gaming revenue, behind Las Vegas and Reno and ahead of Lake Tahoe. From 450 rooms in 1983, Laughlin now offers more than 10,000 rooms.

Laughlin is different from Reno and Las Vegas in another way, with a real connection to the beauty of the area. Among other things, most of its casinos are designed with windows that let in sunlight and views of the Colorado River flowing in front of the buildings.

Across the river is **Bullhead City,** where many of the casino workers live and where there are some non-casino hotels. One bridge (built by Don Laughlin) and a second across the Davis Dam span the river. In addition, numerous ferry boats ply the waters. At the far north end of the town is Davis Dam and Lake Mohave which backs up behind it.

Don Laughlin's Riverside Resort & Casino. The start of it all, today offering 660 rooms, a three-screen movie theater, five restaurants…and a casino. Restaurants include the Gourmet Room, featuring continental and American dishes from chateaubriand to rack of lamb to steak and lobster specials, open for dinner only; the Prime Rib Room, offering beef carved at your table and an all-you-can-eat salad, potato, and dessert bar; the Riverview Restaurant, a 24-hour coffee shop; the East Buffet, offering breakfast, lunch, and dinner, and special Friday night seafood and Saturday and Sunday champagne brunches; and the West Buffet, open daily for dinner.

Across the river in Bullhead City, the Riverside runs the River Queen Motel which includes a 600-space RV park; the two hotels

Henderson Chamber of Commerce. 100 E. Lake Mead Drive, Henderson, NV 89015; 565-8951.

Henderson Convention Center. 200 Water Street, Henderson, NV 89015; 565-2171.

are connected by 24-hour ferry service. Rooms go for as low as $19. Call 298-2535, (800) 227-3849, or (602) 763-7070.

Colorado Belle Hotel & Casino. Here's your basic 608-foot-long three-deck Mississippi River gambling boat, only it's on the Colorado and it has never gone and will never go, anywhere. There are 206 rooms in the "boat" and another 1,082 in a more conventional structure nearby.

Restaurants include The Orleans Room, specializing in seafood, steaks, and pasta; Mark Twain's, offering barbecued chicken and ribs; The Paddlewheel 24-hour coffee shop; and the Captain's Food Fair, offering a breakfast buffet, lunch and dinner specials, and a Friday night seafood buffet.

The Colorado Belle is owned by Circus Circus Enterprises, the most successful gaming company in the state. Call 298-4000 or (800) 458-9500 for reservations.

The Edgewater Hotel/Casino. Next door to the Colorado Belle is a corporate cousin, a 1,450-room budget behemoth. Restaurants include the Hickory Pit Steak House, open for dinner and serving steaks, seafood, chops, barbecued ribs, and chicken; the Garden Room, a 24-hour coffee shop including a one-pound prime rib special; the Bountiful Buffet is said to be Laughlin's largest buffet with a trio of 90-foot serving lines, and the Winner's Circle Deli. Room rates are generally in the range from about $27 to $499. Call 298-2453 or (800) 677-4837.

Flamingo Hilton. A flashy Las Vegas–like resort with 2,000 rooms. As with other Hiltons in Nevada, there is a move toward accommodating young visitors with a video arcade and the Flamingo Funland carnival open during the summer season.

Restaurants include Alta Villa, open evenings for fine Italian dining from Friday to Tuesday; Beef Barron, a steak house open for dinner; the Flamingo Diner, a 24-hour '50s-style diner; and the Training Table Buffet for breakfast, lunch, and dinner. Rates start at about $29; for information call 298-5111 or (800) 352-6464.

Golden Nugget Laughlin. An opulent tropical-theme resort, including an indoor rainforest and more ferns than a Los Angeles singles bar. The hotel is part of the Mirage Resorts chain and is a mini-version of the Las Vegas showpiece. Visitors enter through an arcade adorned with animatronic singing birds into a tropical atrium. The hotel has 300 rooms. Eateries include Jane's Grill, featuring a mesquite grill and wood-fired oven pizza; the River Cafe, a 24-hour diner; and the Bountiful Buffet. Open for breakfast, lunch, and dinner with a special Friday night seafood buffet. Call 298-7222 or (800) 950-7700.

Sam's Town Gold River Gambling Hall & Resort. A 1,003-room riverside box nearby to the Emerald River Golf Course. Restaurants include Sutter's Lodge, a fine dining establishment featuring continental and American cuisine in a Yosemite hunting lodge setting; Pasta Cucina, a moderately priced Italian restaurant; Cafe Victoria, a garden cafe for breakfast, lunch, and dinner; Aunt B's Snack Shoppe, a 24-hour coffee shop, and the Opera House Buffet. For information call 298-2242 or (800) 835-7904.

Harrah's Casino Hotel. A little bit of Mexico along the river, a 958-room outpost of the Harrah's chain. Restaurants include William Fisk's for steaks, seafood, and continental cuisine in a southwestern setting; La Hacienda, offering fine Mexican and American dishes; the Colorado Cafe, a 24-hour coffee shop; the Del Rio Buffet; and Gringo's Grill for hamburgers. For information call 298-4600 or (800) 447-8700.

Pioneer Hotel and Gambling Hall. Eateries include Granny's Gourmet Room for fine dining; Granny's Old-Fashioned Champagne Brunch; the Boarding House Restaurant offering menu items or buffet; and the Fast Draw Snack Bar. Call 298-2442 or (800) 634-9469 for information.

Ramada Express Hotel Casino. A 406-room railroad theme hotel, including a full-size train that circles the property. Eateries include The Steakhouse; The Dining Car Coffee Shop; the Whistle Stop snack bar; and The Round House Buffet for breakfast, lunch, and dinner. For information call 298-4200 or (800) 272-6232.

Laughlin Chamber of Commerce.
Box 2280, Laughlin, NV 89029; 298-2214, (800) 227-5245.

Laughlin Visitor Center.
1555 S. Casino Drive, Laughlin, NV 89029; 298-3321.

Laughlin Area Attractions

Davis Dam. Self-guided tours weekdays from 9 A.M. to 4 P.M.

Grapevine Canyon. Indian petroglyphs and a year round stream, located seven miles from Davis Dam west on Highway 163.

Katherine's Landing. A Lake Mohave resort and marina with boat slips, boat rentals, launch ramp, and sandy beaches with barbecues and picnic areas. (602) 754-3245.

Colorado River Boat Tours. Fiesta Queen and Little Belle paddlewheel boats offer daily 90-minute tours of the Colorado River. Call 298-1047 or (800) 228-9825 for information.

Oatman. Authentic western ghost town and historic gold mining area with museums, shops, and eateries. Gunfighters stage weekend show-downs on the town's main street, on historic Route 66, approximately 30 miles southeast of Laughlin.

III
Reno, Virginia City, and Lake Tahoe

Chapter 17

The Biggest Little Chapter in This Book: Reno

We're not at all certain what it means, but welcome to a place that calls itself "The Biggest Little City in the World." That's the slogan on the famous arch that crosses Virginia Street in downtown.

We do know that Reno is an unusual place, even by Nevada standards, because of the interesting mix of activities available to the visitor. There are, of course, the casinos in Reno and nearby Sparks; they range from ultra-modern corporate creations with all of the amenities to iconoclastic, small establishments with a great deal of individual character.

What is there to see within a few hours drive from Reno?

North:
> Spectacular **Pyramid Lake,** a high desert lake with unusual geological formations, is 33 miles northeast of Reno.

South:
> **Virginia City,** the living ghost of what was once the richest place on Earth, and one of the most fascinating places we know of for the amateur historian.
>
> **Carson City,** the historic state capital.
>
> **Lake Tahoe,** one of the most beautiful Alpine lakes in the world. At the southern tip of the lake are the new casinos of **Stateline,** which sit between spectacular snow-capped mountains and the lake. From there you can head north, pausing to admire **Emerald Bay** on the California side.
>
> Some of the greatest ski hills in the world, including **Heavenly** and **Kirkwood.**
>
> World-class summer outdoor activities including boating, swimming, and horseback riding from sites around Lake Tahoe.

West:
> **Donner Pass** and remote **Donner Lake,** the site of the tragic attempt to cross the Sierra Mountains in the winter of 1846.
> More great ski mountains, including world-famous **Squaw Valley.**

East:
Sparks, a historic Nevada town.

Reno and Lake Tahoe Average Temperatures

The climate in the Reno/Tahoe area can vary greatly by elevation and location. The overall climate is very arid; the Reno area receives very little precipitation, with an average of about an inch per month. Snowfall can vary greatly, from about six inches per month from December to February to measurements by the yard in some mountainous areas.

Although the highways and major roads are plowed and sanded as necessary for safe driving conditions, many mountain passes are subject to closing because of poor visibility, ice or blowing, and drifting snow. Drivers must use snow tires in the winter and are generally advised to carry tire chains to cross mountain passes.

Reno/Sparks Average Temperatures

	High	Low		High	Low
Jan	45	19	Feb	50	24
Mar	54	27	Apr	63	32
May	70	39	Jun	79	45
Jul	89	50	Aug	87	47
Sep	81	41	Oct	70	33
Nov	56	24	Dec	48	21

Road and Weather Information:

> **California Dept. of Transportation Road Reporting Service,** (916) 653-7623.
> **Nevada Dept. of Transportation Road Reporting Service,** 793-1313.
> **Nevada Weather Service,** 793-1300.
> **Reno-Sparks Convention & Visitors Authority,** (800) 752-1177.

The area enjoys warm and dry days in spring, summer, and early fall, turning crisp though sunny for much of the winter. Nights turn cool year-round and sweaters or light jackets are usually appropriate. Sweaters and coats are needed in the winter. In ski season, ski clothing is acceptable in most casual restaurants and all casinos.

About Reno

The site of present-day Reno was settled about 1858 and was first known as Lake's Crossing. The town grew with the discovery of the Comstock

Lode in nearby Virginia City. The railroad arrived in 1868, and the city was renamed for the American Civil War General Jesse Lee Reno (1823–1862).

The University of Nevada-Reno was established soon afterward, in 1864. Now the seat of Washoe County, Reno was incorporated in 1879.

The city straddles the Truckee River, and civic leaders celebrate the revitalized downtown's Truckee River Walk with a festival in early June to begin the summer season and with a gala Christmas on the river in early December.

Mileage to Reno

Carson City 30	Elko 289
Fallon 60	Genoa 40
Heavenly Ski Resort 55	Incline Village 35
Jackpot 406	Las Vegas 440
Los Angeles 469	New York 2,711
Pyramid Lake 33	Sacramento 125
Salt Lake City 526	San Francisco 229
South Lake Tahoe 59	Sparks 3
Squaw Valley USA 50	Truckee 30
Virginia City 24	Yosemite National Park 137

The Econoguide to the Best of Reno

Hotels/Casinos
Reno Hilton
John Ascuaga's Nugget
Peppermill

Buffets
Eldorado
Peppermill
John Ascuaga's Nugget

Circus Circus	Comstock
Eldorado	Reno Hilton
Nevada Club	
John Ascuaga's Nugget	
Peppermill Hotel/Casino	

Point of reference. The Truckee River, which runs from Lake Tahoe to Pyramid Lake, travels from west to east as it passes through downtown Reno. The place where the river and Virginia Street intersect is the zero point for the street numbering of the city. Fourth Street, for example, is called West Fourth Street west of Virginia and (you figured this out, right?) East Fourth Street east of Virginia. The north-south roads are similarly split: the main drag of Virginia Street is called North Virginia on the north side of the river and South Virginia on the south side. The higher the number, the farther away from the heart of downtown at the river and Virginia.

Wheels and chains. If you are renting a car in Reno or Lake Tahoe, four-wheel drive vehicles and tire chains are usually available for an extra charge. If you are not familiar with how to use a 4WD car, or with the installation and use of chains, be sure to obtain instructions from the rental agency.

The early history of Reno, like Las Vegas, Carson City, and Genoa, was forged as a rest stop for travelers heading somewhere else. Many of the westward-bound settlers who chose a northern crossing of the Sierras followed the Humboldt-Carson trail; various branches of the trail crossed over at Carson Pass (north of Lake Tahoe) or a pathway through Truckee Meadows and over Donner Summit, named after the ill-fated expedition of the winter of 1846.

The wagon trains needed to find a place to cross the Truckee River, especially in the spring when the waters ran high, and several private entrepreneurs built private toll bridges in the area. A young New Yorker named Myron Lake bought one of the bridges and opened an inn for the travelers; his bridge crossed the Truckee at the spot that is today the heart of Reno: First and Virginia Streets. Lake expanded his operations when he obtained the franchise to collect tolls on the Sierra Valley Road (now Virginia Street) and made his fortune with the boom that came with the discovery of the Comstock Lode in Virginia City.

Lakes Crossing, as the enterprise was known, came to control much of the land that would become Reno. In 1868, Lake made a business deal with the Central Pacific Railroad, which was pushing its tracks through the area. He gave the railroad 60 acres of land; the CP agreed to use the town site as a freight and passenger depot.

Very much like what would happen 37 years later in Las Vegas, the railroad auctioned off 400 lots in May of 1868 and a town was born.

With its roots as a somewhat rough-and-tumble railroad city and trading post for the even-rougher mining men of Virginia City, Reno fulfilled the requirements of many of its clients for sin. The red-light district was on Lake Street and the gambling halls were semi-hidden on Douglas Alley.

Just as in Las Vegas, a power struggle over

gambling, liquor, and prostitution took place just after World War I; the push to tone down what had become known as the "biggest little city in the world" eventually came to a vote in the 1923 election for mayor. E. E. Roberts, backed by some of the political and economic forces who had the most to gain, ran for office on a platform promising to do away with or ignore all laws that affected "personal choice." He won easily and kept his word to close his eyes.

Reno, with its proximity to California, began to pick up a large trade in quickie divorces and marriages because of the liberal laws in Nevada. And the fact that there were other diversions in the town helped make it a very popular place with residents of the Golden State.

The casinos, though they were now legal, seemed stuck in the mold of the dark, hidden, illegal enterprise they had once been. This began to change with the arrival of Raymond "Pappi" Smith and his sons Raymond Jr. and Harold; their Harold's Club on Virginia Street was the first "carpet joint" in Reno, an attempt to swap sin for fun as an image. Smith dispatched bumper stickers, billboards, and other advertising devices all across the nation proclaiming "Harold's Club or Bust"; suffice it to say that Harold's Club did not go bust. He was followed by William Harrah, with a hotel/casino that bore his name.

About the Sierra Nevada

The Sierra Nevada mountain range lies mostly in California, reaching into Nevada near Lake Tahoe.

Bounded on the north by a gap south of Lassen Peak and by the Cascade Range, and on the south by Tehachapi Pass, the range runs from northwest to southeast for about 400 miles in a 40- to 80-mile-wide swath.

The tallest peak in the Sierra Nevada is Mount Whitney, which at 14,494 feet is the tallest peak in the lower 48 states.

According to geologists, the Sierra Nevada is made up of a single block

---

Fallen arches. The famous Reno Arch across Virginia Street was first installed in 1926 in commemoration of the Victory and Lincoln highways that crossed the continent; the Victory Highway climbed the Sierras to connect to Sacramento. The original slogan, "Reno Transcontinental Highway Exposition," gave way to the considerably more famous "Biggest Little City in the World." That slogan had itself been coined for Reno as part of the hoopla over the Jim Jeffries-Jack Johnson prize fight that took place in Reno in 1910.

Updated arches were installed in 1934, in 1963, and once again in 1987.

Namesake. Jesse Lee Reno, a native of Virginia, was a popular military leader in the U.S. Civil War and before that in the Mexican War. He was killed as he lead the 9th Corps at South Mountain in 1862.

So near. The Donner Party is one of the most famous tragedies of the American cultural consciousness.

Two families, the Donners and the Reeds, made up the largest portion of a group of 87 emigrants who left Sangamon County, Illinois, in 1846 for California.

Under the leadership of George Donner, they made a series of bad decisions and mistakes in choosing trails across the Great Salt Lake in Utah and then the Sierra Nevadas. They were trapped by unusually heavy snows in the mountains above Reno and were forced to camp for the winter at a small lake about 13 miles northwest of Lake Tahoe. They ran out of food and other supplies, and some of the members of the group resorted to cannibalism in order to survive—those few who would talk about their experience afterward claimed they ate only those who had died.

Come spring, 47 of the 87 emigrants were eventually brought to California by rescue parties, traveling over what is now known as Donner Pass.

of the earth's crust tilted upward toward the east. The predominant rocks of the range are granite, other igneous rocks, and metamorphic slate. Great quantities of gold have been found embedded in quartz, while silver has been mined on the eastern slope.

About Sparks

The town of Sparks was created in 1904 as the home of the Southern Pacific Railroad. It was named after cattle baron John D. Sparks who served as one of the first governors of Nevada.

Victorian Square downtown is a restored turn-of-the-century center.

The **Wild Island** family entertainment complex is open daily from May to October and includes a water park with water slides, a tide pool, and rafting.

Next door is **Adventure Golf,** a 36-hole miniature golf course and ice-skating facility. Call 359-2927 for information.

Among other events, Sparks is home of the International Whistle-Off in August and the Sparks Indian Rodeo in September.

Reno Area Annual Events

They love their festivals in Nevada, celebrating just about everything you can imagine. Of course, the fact that there are so many available hotel rooms and convention centers in the area, as well as the strong lures of the ski areas, golf courses, lakes, and mountains doesn't hurt.

If you're looking for an excuse to come to Reno, Sparks, or the surrounding area, here is a list of some of the major gatherings held annually. Check with (800) 367-7366 for exact dates or call the numbers where listed; all numbers are in area code 702 unless indicated.

March

California Gold Rush. Soda Springs. Cross-country ski marathon. (916) 426-3871.

Reno International Jazz Festival. University of Nevada, Reno. 784-4046.

Snowfest Winter Carnival. North Lake Tahoe/Truckee. (916) 583-7625.

April

Reno International Kite Festival. Rancho San Rafael Park. 827-7700.

May

Silver State Square Dance Festival. Reno-Sparks Convention Center. 359-2867.

Annual Sternwheeler Race. Lake Tahoe. Memorial Day weekend race between the *M.S. Dixie* and the *Tahoe Queen.*

Nugget All-American Suffolk Sheep Show and Sale. Reno Livestock Events Center. 323-3071.

Cinco de Mayo Celebration. Victorian Square, Sparks. Hispanic cultural celebration. 353-2284.

June

Annual West Coast Wine Tasting. Culinary and oenological festival at the Reno-Sparks Convention Center, featuring menu items from northern Nevada's finest restaurants and great vineyards of the west. 827-7636.

Annual Windjammers Southern Crossing. A 27-mile race down the length of Lake Tahoe opens the sailing season.

Kit Carson Rendezvous. The Old West comes alive in Carson City each year with a series of contests and demonstration of Indian and western arts, crafts, and skills. 687-7410.

Handshake Day and Chili Cook-Off. A downtown Carson City street fair. 885-0411.

Reno Rodeo. Reno Livestock Events Center. 329-3877.

Stewart Indian Museum Pow Wow. An annual arts and crafts festival in Carson City. 882-1808.

July Fourth Celebrations

Carson City. Parade, picnic, fair, fireworks. 881-1565.

Incline Village. Fireworks and air show. Hyatt Lake Tahoe Beach.

Reno. The Skyfire celebration at the University of Nevada-Reno. (800) 367-7366.

South Lake Tahoe. Timber Cove Pier. 588-6611.

July

Annual Sail Week. Lake Tahoe.

Capitol City Fair. County Fair in Carson City's Fuji Park. 882-4460.

Comstock Arabian Horse Show. Reno Livestock Events Center. 331-3300.

Nugget Jazz Festival. John Ascuaga's Nugget, Sparks. 358-2233.

Pacific Coast Cutting Horse Stakes. Reno Livestock Events Center. (916) 929-4144.

August

Basque Festival. Washoe County Fairgrounds. 323-3000.
Carson Indian Colony Pow-Wow. Carson City, Fuji Park. 885-9759.
Hot August Nights. Reno rock 'n roll and car show. 829-1955.
Nevada State Fair. Reno Livestock Events Center. 322-4424.

September

Genoa Candy Dance. Local celebration at the oldest permanent settlement in Nevada. 782-8144.
Great Reno Balloon Race. More than 100 balloonists compete in various events at Rancho San Rafael Park, Reno. 826-1181.
National Championship Air Races. Reno/Stead Airport. Planes of all descriptions compete in this famous event. 972-6663.
Nugget Best-in-the-West Rib Cook-Off. Food booths, entertainment at John Ascuaga's Nugget, Sparks. 353-2284.
Pacific Coast Quarter Horse Association Spectacular. Reno Livestock Events Center.
Virginia City International Camel Races. Honest! 847-7223.

Nevada Dept. of Wildlife.
Box 10678, Reno, NV 89520; 688-1500.

Pyramid Lake Fisheries.
Star Route, Sutcliffe, NV 89510; 673-6335.

Bureau of Land Management.
Box 12000, Reno, NV 89520; 785-6402.

October

Eldorado Great Italian Festival. Eldorado Hotel/Casino, Reno.
Mainstreet Chili Cook-Off. Carson City. 885-0411.
Nevada Day Celebration (Oct. 31). Old-time festival and celebration of Nevada's admission to the United States, in Carson City.

November

National Senior Pro Rodeo Finals. Reno Livestock Events Center. 323-3073.
Old Fashioned Christmas Faire. Carson City Community Center. 882-2111.

December

Festival of Trees. Reno. 786-7765.
Western Nugget National Hereford Show and Sale. Heifers and bulls take over for the showgirls at the Nugget's showroom. 356-3300.

The Best of Reno

Circus Circus Hotel/Casino

Yowzah, yowzah! It's Circus Circus, a smaller cousin of the Las Vegas original, but definitely a Reno must-see. With 1,625 rooms, it is downtown Reno's largest resort, quite a way from its start in 1978 when it had just 104 rooms. It is therefore the World's Second Largest Hotel and Casino with a Circus and Midway and a Shuttle Tram.

The midway and circus area was spruced up in 1993, pulling it out of a bit of the doldrums. Circus acts—including high-wire bicyclists, aerialists, gymnasts, and clowns—start about 11 A.M. and continue late into the night. The circus acts are introduced by a ringmaster and accompanied by a somewhat bored two-piece band. Each act is about 8 to 10 minutes long—the management doesn't want people to stay away from the tables too long.

The midway is a sure lure for children of all ages, offering coin toss, ring toss, shooting gallery, face painting, and other such carnival entertainment, plus a video arcade. Stands offer popcorn, food, and balloons.

Check out the shooting gallery that uses beams of light from the rifles; it's much better than your average mechanical ducks. We especially like the poor little canary atop the piano who will dance for you; hit the piano player in the behind and he'll provide the music.

And, of course, there is a casino, which is a pretty lively place at all hours. As you might expect, there do seem to be a few families with the youngsters dispatched upstairs to the circus and carnival and mom and dad downstairs gambling the dinner money.

The circus performers, according to the hotel, constitute a minor league for the major shows including Ringling Brothers and Barnum & Bailey Circus, the Moscow Circus, the Romanian State Circus, and other troupes.

During our visit, the stars included the Osorio Brothers. Working 30 feet above the spectators on the Circus Circus midway, they ran, jumped, skipped rope, and rode bicycles on the high wire. Romania's Cretu Troupe

Circus Circus, Reno

performed a set of amazing acrobatic stunts including a teeterboard act, propelling acrobats 20 feet into the air, and tricks atop a tall unicycle and a giant Russian Swing. Motorcycle daredevils the Jordans rode sideways and upside down in a 14-foot-diameter "Globe of Death" steel sphere.The Flying Morales performed their airborne acrobatics on the flying trapeze.

The **Three Ring Restaurant** is open 24 hours, offering specials, priced from about $3 to $6, such as Belgian waffles, Reuben sandwiches, and vegetable stir-fry. The **Big Top Buffet** is served beneath a red and white striped circus big top. Breakfast, offered from 7 A.M. to 11 A.M. for $2.29 includes fresh squeezed orange juice and ham carved to order. Lunch, available from 11 A.M. to 4 P.M. for $2.99 includes fried chicken, roast beef, and a build-your-own taco bar. Dinner is served from 4 P.M. to 10 P.M. for $3.99. A special Friday seafood buffet is $5.99.

The **Hickory Pit**, a dark brick wall room, is open for dinner from 5 P.M. to 11 P.M. with entrees from about $10 to $20. Specialties include 12-ounce filet mignon with béarnaise sauce, broiled salmon, and king crab legs with drawn butter.

Circus Circus Hotel/Casino, 500 N. Sierra Street; 1,625 rooms; 329-0711; (800) 648-5010.

▰ MUST-SEE ▰ Comstock

An eclectic casino worth a visit. The upper levels of the casino include western scenes, including an animated piano-playing couple named Lulabelle & Slim.

The casino floor includes a few real one-arm bandits (slot machines that point a six-shooter at the player) as well as a sprinkling of life-like dummies on the floor—some of which seem livelier than some of the players at the tables.

At the center of the casino is a stairway to **Amigo's Mexican Restaurant**, an inexpensive eatery that sweetens the offer with two-for-one Margaritas and combination platters.

Or, you can take an escalator down through a simulated mining tunnel to the **Miner's Cafe,** a 24-hour coffee shop that in the past has offered entrees including vegetarian burgers for $2.59 and vegetarian platter with cheese and salsa for $5.29. For meat-eaters, there's a create-your-own hamburger for about $2 plus 10 cents a topping and chili for $3; other specialties are

> **A dog's life.** Fantasia bills itself as a hotel so exclusive it doesn't accept humans. That is because it is a pet hotel, welcoming cats and dogs for stays at its heated kennels. The hotel even offers a "pet limo" service to pick up and deliver pets. Fantasia is located off North Virginia Street about equidistant between Reno and Sparks. Call 322-1199 for reservations.

fried chicken for $5.39 and Pick and Shovel Pasta Primavera for $4.29.

Within the Miner's Cafe is **Hop Sing's Kitchen,** which offers Asian specials from 11 A.M. to 11 P.M. Representative entrees included Mongolian beef for $6.29, almond chicken for $5.59, and sweet and sour pork for $5.29. Dinner specials are about $4 for lunch and $5 for dinner.

Comstock Hotel/Casino, 200 W. 2nd Street; 310 rooms; 329-1880; (800) 648-4866.

MUST-SEE Eldorado Hotel/Casino

The Eldorado is a very attractive, very classy modern casino worth a visit. It has a collection of some of the better hotel restaurants in town.

The lively casino includes what is billed as the world's largest roulette table, seating as many as 40 people.

A new 700-space parking lot was added in 1993. In true Las Vegas/Reno style, the 10-story structure is ringed with neon; it was lauded by civic officials as a new downtown gem.

Let's eat our way through the Eldorado.

First stop, near the entrance, is **Choices,** an all-in-one "express cafe" food court. Among the stands in the attractive open room decorated with glass brick and tile off the casino floor are **Chinatown,** which offers entrees for $4 to $5 including lobster Cantonese and roast duck, and appetizers including egg rolls and soup; **Little Italy,** offering pasta, pizza, and submarine sandwiches; **Virginia Deli,** with hot dogs, shrimp cocktail, and sandwich specialties; and the **American Kitchen,** featuring burgers, fried chicken, ham and eggs, and a steak and lobster special for about $10. The food court also offers a cheap shrimp cocktail with tiny, tiny shrimp.

Ristorante La Strada is a more formal room, serving dinner nightly from 5 P.M. Pizzas are prepared in a wood-fired brick oven. Pasta dishes range in price from about $11 to $16. Specials include *linguine del pescatore* (calamari, shrimp, scallops, and shellfish in tomato or white wine sauce), *tortellini alla panna* (veal-filled pasta in parmesan cream sauce), and *spiedini di gamberi*

A cuppa. If you thought that wine tasting was complex, consider the process used at the Eldorado for testing new shipments of coffee beans. A small amount of green beans is roasted in a special sample roaster and then ground and prepared with a precisely measured amount of water for "cupping." The grounds and water are mixed in a special cup and the grounds are then allowed to rise to the surface. Cracking this surface cap releases the aroma and allows the taster to judge the quality. Then the mixture is drawn across the palate. Based on the aroma and taste, the coffee roaster receives his instructions on temperature, time, and blend.

Mud in your eye. Coffees available at the Eldorado Coffee Company range in price from about $5 to $10 per pound and include products such as Ethiopian *Yergacheffe*, Mexican *Custepec*, Brazillian *Santos*, Guatemalan *Antigua*, and Swiss water decaf. You can also order by calling (800) 348-5966.

Visitor Centers in Reno/Sparks. For visitor information and room reservations call 827-7366 or (800) 367-7366.

Visitor centers are located at:

Reno Cannon International Airport;

Reno Downtown Visitors Center, 275 N. Virginia St.;

Reno-Sparks Convention Center, 4590 S. Virginia St.;

Sparks Downtown Visitors Center, Pyramid Way and Victorian Ave., Sparks.

al limone (marinated skewered prawns grilled and served with a lemon-basil sauce).

The dark, copper pot and fern-filled La Strada shares its space with the attractively understated **Grill and Rotisserie.** This dinner place, closed Wednesday and Thursday, offered on a recent visit specialties including blackened rib steak for $12, barbecued baby back pork ribs for $11, and grilled marinated scallops and prawn brochette for $14.

And the attractions go on and on: be sure to stop at **Tivoli Gardens,** a high-scale food court decorated with overhead arbors and lots of brass with offerings from around the world. You'll know things are a bit different when you come to the elaborate coffee roaster at the entrance.

According to the Eldorado, it is the only hotel in the country with such an elaborate coffee setup. The selection of beans is made by the restaurant's executive chef, choosing premium arabica green coffee beans from the high altitudes of Central America, Africa, Indonesia, and Hawaii.

The high-temperature Probat roaster, made in Germany, triggers a complex chemical reaction in which sugars and starches in the green beans are transformed into the volatile oils that give coffee its rich flavor and aroma.

Most of the coffee sold at the Eldorado is roasted to the "full city" stage. The temperature profile and roasting time varies, but the process usually takes about 16 minutes for a batch of 16 kilograms (about 35 pounds). Visitors can buy the fresh beans to take home, or they can drink a brewed cup at the restaurant.

In addition to regular coffee, the Eldorado roasts beans for espresso, using a secret blend of six beans. The espresso roast results in a darker color, and the grind is made using pressure rather than gravity. The same amount of beans go into a cup of espresso as in a regular cup of coffee, but the amount of water is much less: one and a half ounces versus six ounces.

Cappuccino, which is espresso with foamed milk, is also available, as is iced cappuccino, which is cold-water brewed using a coarse grind of the espresso blend.

Depending on your age, sex, and sweet tooth you may find the dessert carousel at Tivoli Gardens even more attractive than the cocktail waitresses, who, just for the record, wear some of the skimpiest outfits in town. The fabulous cakes cost a reasonable $2.25 or so for a slice.

Tivoli Gardens serves breakfast 24 hours a day. International specials, priced from about $5 to $9 and served from 11 A.M. to 3 A.M. include Oriental pepper steak, Vietnamese sliced beef soup, Italian rosemary chicken breast with fettuccine alfredo, Hawaiian pizza (bacon and pineapple), Thai chicken, and American liver and onions.

The Eldorado **Buffet** offers breakfast weekdays from 8 A.M. to 11 A.M. for $2.99 and lunch from 11 A.M. to 2 P.M. for $3.99. A prime rib dinner is offered Sunday to Friday from 4 P.M. to closing for $6.99. On Saturday, the special buffet has a western theme and is served from 4 P.M. to closing for $8.99. Finally, there is a Saturday brunch, served from 8 A.M. to 2 P.M. for $5.49 and a Sunday champagne brunch from 8 A.M. to 2 P.M. for $6.99. There is also a special **Seafood Buffet** served Friday and Saturday for $14.99 in the hotel's convention center.

And finally, there is **The Vintage,** a dark room with red velvet booths— your basic Nevada hotel hideaway. Specialties at the time of our visit included sole meuniere, finished tableside for about $16. The restaurant is closed Monday and Tuesday.

Eldorado Hotel/Casino, 345 N. Virginia Street; 800 rooms; 786-5700; (800) 648-5966.

Flamingo Hilton Reno

An attractive, quality hotel, nice enough to almost forget for a while you are in a casino. The Flamingo Hilton offers 604 rooms, including 66 suites. The hotel is actually located a block in from the Virginia Street strip but uses a street-level storefront (the former Paco's Casino) as a come-on to pedestrians. A series of escalators and a walkway connect you to the main hotel and casino.

> **Busy signal.** High-season at the Flamingo Hilton and much of Reno is generally from April to October, with the slowest period from December through February except for Christmas and New Year's Eve.

The hotel draws its lineage back to Del Webb's Sahara; it then became the Reno Hilton and then the Flamingo Hilton.

The longtime attraction at the 1,200-seat showroom is American Superstars, a rotating series of celebrity impersonators. Acts include Elvis, Roy Orbison, Sammy Davis Jr., Bette Midler, The Blues Brothers, and Madonna. There is one show Sunday through Thursday nights and two shows on Friday and Saturday nights; the theater is dark Tuesday. Tickets range from $12.95 to $14.95 and children are welcome; they may especially enjoy the confetti cannons at the conclusion of the show.

The premier restaurant is the **Top of the Hilton,** which offers gorgeous views of the surrounding mountains. The eatery is paneled in dark wood like a private club, with gray carpet and chairs; an even more private dining area near the bar is available by reservation to large parties. High rollers and local regulars have their own locked liquor storage bins by the bar.

Open for dinner only, it is closed Monday. Offerings, priced from about $18 to $25, have included various steaks, swordfish, shrimp scampi, and roast rack of lamb.

Standard rooms at the Flamingo Hilton are above average in quality; the suites on the top floor are quite impressive, but it is the Barron Suite, which includes two tubs and a large living room, that is most impressive. As in most Nevada casinos, the best rooms are generally reserved as comps for the high rollers.

Flamingo Hilton Reno, 255 N. Sierra Street; 604 rooms; 322-1111; (800) 648-4882.

Flamingo Hilton, Reno

Harold's Club

This lively place wins our vote as the friendliest place in town; the management seems to encourage its dealers to talk to the players and most of them have a spiel for each deal. Some even pretend to root for the players at their tables.

The sparkling casino has a small set of carousel horses in the center; a room-filling sound system plays instrumental music to pick up the pace. Near the front entrance is Bucky's Buckboard, one of a dozen contenders for the biggest slot machine in Nevada: this one has a bench that seats three players.

> **Home of the free.** Harold's Club is credited with introducing the concept of "comps" to casinos, rewarding regular customers with free meals and drinks. The club also organized the first junkets to bring in high rollers on all-expense-paid trips to Reno; all they had to do was spend their money at the tables.

The fun continues at the **Roaring Camp Bar** at Harold's. Clients at the bar can play a special, oversized slot called "Bust the Barrels." If you can line up four beer mugs, everyone at the bar gets a free drink. (It also pays off in coins.)

By the way, this place is advertised as "The World's Most Famous Casino." Did you know that? We suspect that Harold's is no longer on the tips of most people's tongues, but there was a time when bumper stickers and signs across the nation proclaimed "Harold's Club or Bust."

The advertising campaign was just one element of the change that Raymond "Pappi" Smith, a former carnival owner, brought to Reno when he opened his club in 1935. (Harold was his son, who ran the operation.) Today's Harold's Club maintains the original mission of the Smiths: to make the casino a fun place.

Harold's Club, 250 N. Virginia Street; 329-0881.

Harrah's Reno

There's nothing particularly wrong with Harrah's Reno; in fact, it's not a bad place at all. It's just that there is not much that is memorable here, either.

Harrah's is a mid-size hotel with your basic Nevada casino and a set of restaurants that range from a fine steakhouse to a McDonald's. It's history, though, reaches back to 1946 when it was the first major casino operation of William Harrah and one of the classiest joints in town; he had previously operated several tiny operations around Reno.

Today Harrah is part of the Promus Companies, which also operates Embassy Suites, Homewood Suites, Hampton Inns, and Bill's Casino.

Entertainment is presented in **Sammy's Showroom,** named after Sammy Davis Jr., who made more than 400 appearances there over 22 years. The early show is "Stagestruck," a salute to the best of Broadway. Things heat up later with "High Voltage," an adult revue of singers and dancers (the same singers and dancers from the earlier "Stagestruck" show, in fact).

Harrah's Skyway Buffet is an attractive, pleasant room with decent food and perhaps the only buffet room with a push-button cappuccino and espresso machine.

The **Garden Room** serves 24-hour breakfast in an unusually attractive coffee shop that features brass and wood with muted lighting. Specials, priced from about $5 to $15, at the time of a recent visit included corned beef hash and eggs, Belgian waffles, burgers, chicken fried New York steak, sirloin tips marsala, seafood kebabs, and shrimp scampi.

A section of the Garden Room is devoted to the **Oriental Garden,** serving middle-of-the-road Chinese meals with entrees from $6 to $13, and prix-fixe meals under $10. Specialties include seafood in black bean sauce and Chinese pepper steak.

Harrah's Steak House is an award-winning restaurant, decorated in muted reds and hidden a floor below and a world away from the jingle-jangle of the casino. Lunch is served 11 A.M. to 2:30 P.M. weekdays, and dinner is from 5 P.M. every day. Luncheon offerings, from about $6 to $14, include Caesar salad, warm teriyaki chicken salad, and *fettuccine frutti di mare* with lobster, scallops, prawns, and fish. The extensive din-

"Stagestruck" at Harrah's Reno

ner menu includes oyster, shrimp, and salmon appetizers and entrees priced from about $18 to $35 including veal chop, steak and lobster, broiled swordfish, chateaubriand, veal osso-bucca, and veal Oscar.

Cafe Andreotti is open for dinner at 5 P.M. from Thursday through Monday nights. The kitchen is open to view and is worth a peek. For an appetizer, you can create your own pasta misto. Pastas include spaghetti, linguini, cheese tortellini, and cheese ravioli, and sauces include tomato basil, white wine, and red or white clam. Entrees, priced from about $8 to $15, have included red snapper with fresh basil sautéed with scallops, mushrooms, and sweet peppers and veal saltimboca.

Harrah's Casino/Hotel Reno, 206 N. Virginia Street; 566 rooms; 786-3232; (800) 648-3773.

MUST-SEE Reno Hilton

At or near the top of the class in Reno, the Hilton was in the process of a major renovation project in 1994 that will make it even more of a must-see for visitors and gamblers, a remake into an indoor version of the Grand Canyon and Monument Valley. Plans include installation of the front desk within a Sequoia forest. The casino will feature a river running through it, Pony Express deliveries and the occasional gunfight.

The Reno Hilton was formerly a Bally's Hotel and before that the MGM Grand. At the time of our visit it still bore some of the Hollywood markings of the MGM.

It really is a city within a city, with 2,001 rooms and enough activities to entertain visitors for days at a time without venturing out the front door. The hotel includes a state-of-the-art 50-lane bowling alley with electronic scoring; the lanes were the site of a stop on the Ladies Pro Bowlers Tour in 1993.

Downstairs is a pair of high-tech movie theaters showing first-run features. (The back section of the theaters include love seats for those who are amorously inclined or who are generally more used to watching movies in the comfort of their living rooms or beds.)

The shopping arcade includes an electronic golf range where players

Goin' to the chapel. The Reno Hilton has an attractive wedding chapel for those who feel the urge or need for nuptials. Among the most unusual ceremonies performed there was the marriage of a pair of llamas who were in town for a rather sizeable convention of llama lovers. Emergency wedding cakes, gowns, and suits are available at stores in the shopping arcade; the llamas wore their own coats.

Parking lots. The Reno Hilton welcomes RV vehicles to park in a special camperland area, with rates of about $15 per night. There are spaces for 286 RVs.

drive their balls into projected images of famous courses around the world. Outside you can find **Hilton Bay Aqua Golf** on Lake Hilton, an artificial pond created during the excavation for the hotel. Using floating golf balls, players can test their swings on 100-, 150-, and 200-yard holes and hope to win prizes and free trips.

There is also one of the largest hotel health clubs we have seen, along with five indoor and three outdoor tennis courts, plus three hitting lanes.

Major changes due for the hotel include a massive expansion of the Sports and Race Book to include state-of-the-art electronics, two-level seating, and other accoutrements.

Marco Polo's offers a globe-trotting combination of Italian and Chinese entrees, priced from about $6 to $8 for lunch and a bit higher for dinner. Pizza is available by the slice or pie. Dinner includes a range of fiery Szechuan and more subtle Cantonese dishes.

The premier Italian restaurant at the Hilton is **Caruso's.** Appealing appetizers include *scampi alla livornese* (an appetizer of jumbo shrimp sautéed in olive oil with garlic, shallots, white wine butter sauce, and diced peppers) for $6.95. Entrees, priced from about $8 to $23, include *ravioli di gamberi* (raviolis filled with bay shrimps, fresh salmon mousse, and zucchini served in a light creamy tomato sauce), *tournedos al bardolino* (two petite filets mignons sautéed with mushrooms, rosemary, and garlic in bardolino red sauce), and *aragosta al pomodoro e basilico* (lobster tails sautéed with plum tomatoes and sweet basil). Desserts include *tiramisu* (lady fingers flavored with espresso, chocolate, and mascarpone cream sauce), and *creazione Caruso* (a house specialty cappuccino mousse cake). You can finish off the meal with espresso or cappuccino, available plain or spiked with anisette or brandy.

The **Patio Room** serves breakfast anytime, with specialties including corned beef hash served with two poached eggs for $5.25 or steak and eggs for $8.95. Non-cholesterol egg substitutes are available; other healthwise selections include marinated turkey breast served with steamed rice, snow peas, and carrots for $6.95. Other Patio Room specialties include baked lasagna with meat sauce and garlic bread for $6.25. A children's menu includes french toast fingers with two bacon strips, peanut butter and jelly sandwich, or hamburger with french fries for $1.95.

The **Reno Hilton Steakhouse** is open for lunch and dinner and features an English Tudor manor house setting. A salad bar is available at lunch and dinner. Light fare includes the Bagel Nosh (an open-faced smoked salmon and cream cheese bagel with potato salad or cole slaw) for $7.95, and croissant cordon bleu for $5.50. Dinner specialties include Pacific salmon for $16.95 and lamb chops with mint jelly for $24.50. Desserts include black bottom ice-cream pie. Homemade ice creams and sherbets are available with toppings including chocolate Kahlúa sauce, hot brandied fruits, vanilla hazelnut sauce, and butterscotch rum.

The hotel opened its newest restaurant, the **Grand Canyon Buffet,** in the summer of 1994. The southwestern-theme eatery has seating for 450 people for breakfast, lunch, and dinner.

Entertainment at the Reno Hilton centers around the **Hilton Theater,** the hotel's premier showroom, with 2,000 seats. Production shows including *Cats,* The Moscow Circus, and *Spellbound* and entertainers including Frank Sinatra, Liza Minelli, and Randy Travis have appeared here. And, would you believe, Dr. Ruth Westheimer? (We can only imagine the floor show.) The theater has one of the biggest showroom stages in the world. An interesting sidelight is the fact that when the showroom was constructed along with the hotel in 1978, the stage was built around a large mock-up of a jet plane that was used in the original long-running musical show at the hotel. The prop is so big—and the stage area so huge—that the plane was still there in 1993.

Nearby is the 250-seat **Just for Laughs Comedy Club,** a showcase for up-and-coming comics. There's music nightly at the **Confetti Cabaret** except Monday.

Reno Hilton, 2500 E. 2nd Street; 2,001 rooms; 789-2000; (800) 648-5080.

MUST-SEE Nevada Club

Our favorite, very strange and wonderful casino in Reno is The Nevada Club. It's not because of the millions spent on decoration; the casino is a barely improved storefront where you can all but smell the sawdust beneath the cheap carpet. The front of the building is an appropriately hideous purple, with signs and decorations that must have been all the rage in the 1950s.

> **Whoopie!** Many of the casino scenes of the film *Sister Act* with Whoopi Goldberg were shot in 1991 at the Nevada Club and at Fitzgerald's across the street.

It is, instead, the essential weirdness of the place, a sense of time warp and the evidence of a company that is miles away from the slick factories like those in Las Vegas.

The mystery tour begins at the right side of the front door where you can lay hands on what is rightfully labeled "The World's Ugliest Slot Machine." The so-called piggyback device was invented at the Nevada Club and consists of two standard machines mounted atop each other with one crummy handle. It was developed as a prototype but ended up in use for more than 25 years.

All around is a working collection of old mechanical slot machines; upstairs in a corridor is a section of penny slot and video poker machines.

Upstairs is Kilroy's Diner, a real old diner with counters, pie racks, antique coke signs, and waitresses in polyester uniforms.

And it just keeps on getting weirder. In the same club you'll find such attractions as a device that is said to be the world's largest pinball game; a hand-cranked Mutoscope nickelodeon that displays the slightly naughty antics of one Molly Malone in a display called "Birthday Surprise" filmed in 1910; and a circa 1916 Seeburg KT Midget Orchestrion, a coin-operated orchestra that includes a piano, mandolin, flute, tambourine, castanets, and triangle.

But wait: there's also the famed gun collection that features hundreds of priceless antiques from tiny pocket pistols to field pieces, from black powder wooden cannons to World War I machine guns.

In a case near the front of the main exhibit is a spectacular percussion shotgun by LePage-Moutier of Paris, with an ebony stock. All of the metal parts have been chiseled or sculptured. The hammers are carved steel dogs attacking foxes on the breech. The intricately carved steel trigger guard is formed by a pheasant eating grapes; there is also a rabbit feeding at the end of the guard. On the fore-end cap of the stock is a sculptured face of French President M. Paul Jules Grevy. The gun was made in 1860 and was presented to Don Manuel Gonzales, president of Mexico, by Grevy in 1879.

You'll also find a Gatling gun, capable of firing more than 400 .45- to .70-caliber shots per minute. The speed of firing was limited by the ability of the gunner to hand crank the barrel. The same basic design, with the aid of a motor, is used in modern combat aircraft. The Gatling gun is fully operational and is fired from time to time in promotional events. Finally, hawg fans should check out the 1917 Harley Davidson in army dress.

Nevada Club; 224 N. Virginia; 329-1721.

MUST-SEE Peppermill Hotel/Casino

The Peppermill is a thoroughly modern assault on the senses, including a riot of purple, green, and pink neon, and electronic signboards like those at a sports stadium. The Peppermill is a bit isolated from downtown, a few miles south; it is one of the more lively casinos in town.

The **Peppermill Island Buffet** is one of the nicest buffet settings we have seen in Nevada. Private booths sit among lush (fake) greenery. The serving line sits beneath a chandelier of lights. The food is not quite as extraordinary as the room, but still better than average.

The **Food Court** includes several serving sections including the **Italian Deli, American Diner, Chinese Wok,** and a **Mexican Taco Bar,** with offerings ranging from 99-cent tacos to shrimp scampi for $5 and Chinese offerings for $4 to $5.

Le Moulin offers dinner specialties including lobster linguine a la Roma (lobster sautéed with garlic and white wine, combined with a creamy Romano cheese) for $14.95, veal t-bone (a 14-ounce Provini t-bone, sautéed with button mushrooms and shallots) for $19.95, and an early bird special of prime rib and lobster for $9.95, served from 5 P.M. to 7 P.M.

Peppermill Hotel/Casino, 2707 S. Virginia Street; 633 rooms; 826-2121; (800) 648-6992.

Sands Regency Hotel/Casino

An older hotel-casino a few blocks off Virginia Street, the Sands is a strange jumble of slot machines, gaming tables, hotel desks, and donut counters. There's even a Baskin Robbins ice-cream stand directly opposite the registration desk.

The matriarch of the founding Cladianos family is honored with **Antonia's,** open for dinner only, nightly except Tuesday. It is, though, at heart a rather ordinary coffee shop. Specialties include roasted chicken for $5.99, and seafood linguine (shrimp, scallops, clams, and crab in a garlic and cream sauce) for $12.99.

There's a branch of the **Tony Roma's** chain, offering ribs for $7.95 to $9.95 and boneless chicken for $7.95. Appetizers include potato skins for $3.95 and chicken wings for $2.95. Special offers include a $7.77 ribs and barbecue chicken combo, and an all-you-can-eat Cajun or Carolina honey ribs dinner served Monday, Tuesday, and Wednesday from 4 P.M. to 10 P.M. Other franchise eateries at the Sands Regency include **Orange Julius, Winchell's Donuts,** and **Arby's.**

The **Palm Court** is a 24-hour coffee shop. Offerings include a veggie croissant (cucumbers, tomato, avocado, mushrooms, and alfalfa sprouts) for $4.79, a one-pound T-bone steak for $6.99; steak 'n lobster for $7.99, prime rib for $5.99, and chicken fingers for $3.99.

Sands Regency Hotel/Casino, 345 N. Arlington Avenue; 1,000 rooms; 348-2200; (800) 648-3553.

> **Family jewels.** At the entrance from the parking lot, check out the display of two old slot machines. The plaque identifies them as representing the original five machines bought in 1932 by Antonia and Pete Cladianos Sr., Greek immigrants who came to America penniless and unable to speak English. The hotel and casino they founded eventually became the Sands Regency in Reno, and the second and third generation of the family still operate the business.

> **Fishy business.** Be sure to check out the large salt water aquarium that sits behind the bar at Trader Dick's. The tank is home to more than 100 exotic fish, including clown, grouper, damsel, yellow tang, and lion fish.

Sparks

The urban sprawl of Reno now extends west into Sparks almost without interruption; at one time, though, Sparks was a self-sufficient railroad company town built around the Stone and Gates private bridge crossings over the Truckee.

Sparks was founded early in this century by the Southern Pacific Railroad as the site of switching yards and other facilities. By 1906, it was a company town of 3,500, and nearly all the residents had something to do with the railroad until the 1950s when the Southern Pacific closed down most of its operations and moved them west to California.

Today, in the great tradition of the state, Sparks is a thriving rest stop for truckers, with several large facilities just off I-80, and for busloads of visitors who come to the unusual Nugget hotel/casino.

Downtown is centered around **Victorian Square,** an attractive redeveloped area of gas lamps, ironwork, and improvements to the small strip of casinos, bars, and shops.

If you're interested in the history of the area, visit the **Sparks Museum** in downtown. Like the very best of museums, this place has an eclectic and constantly surprising collection of items, from railroad artifacts to remnants of ghost towns to elements of the great westward migration that passed through the area.

Located at 820 B Street. Open weekdays for several hours each day. Call 355-1144 for hours and information.

MUST-SEE John Ascuaga's Nugget

By now you should have guessed that our favorite hotels and casinos are those with a bit of quirkiness and individuality. By those criteria, John Ascuaga's Nugget qualifies as a must-see in the Reno Valley.

The large hotel and casino complex is actually located in Sparks, a small town that is within sight of Reno, just east of downtown. The place definitely caters to large bus tours, but it is certainly a step up from most of the downtown houses.

You'll know something is a bit odd when you cross the huge parking lot and see signs marking an elephant crossing. Yes, that's right, and their names are **Bertha and Angel,** the

> **Double room.** Bertha and Angel live in the Elephant Palace at the hotel, which includes a swimming pool and exercise area. Visitors are welcome to stop by between 10 A.M. and 2 P.M. to watch them as they get ready for work. Every night, they walk to the Celebrity Showroom where they open the show twice nightly, six nights a week.

> **One-man show.** The Nugget has been owned and operated by John Ascuaga since 1960, an unusual one-man history in Nevada gaming.

official goodwill ambassadors of the Nugget.

It all began back in 1962 when Bertha was hired to perform in the Nugget's showroom, known then as the Circus Room. Bertha was born in India in 1951 (a full-size Asian elephant, she tips the scales at a bit over four tons). Angel is a mere baby, born in captivity in Tampa, Florida in 1988.

And then there is the Golden Rooster, which may be the only member of its species ever to serve time in a federal lockup. The story is this: in 1958, the Nugget was preparing to open a new restaurant called the Golden Rooster and it was decided to decorate the place with an unusual work of art: a solid gold statue of a rooster.

Seven months after it went on display inside a fortified glass case, officials of the U.S. Treasury Department charged the Nugget with violation of the Gold Reserve Act which made it unlawful for a private individual to have more than 50 ounces of gold in his possession. Legal skirmishes continued until 1960 when the hotel was formally presented with a complaint entitled "United States of America vs. One Solid Gold Object in the Form of a Rooster." The statue was confiscated; the Nugget's offer to put up bail was denied.

Two years of captivity for the golden bird followed, until a jury trial was held in 1962; the government was unable to counter the arguments of the Nugget and art critics that the statue was a work of art, and the

John Ascuaga's Nugget, Sparks

rooster was sprung and returned to its perch at the restaurant. In 1987, the Golden Rooster Room was closed, but the bird eventually received a new place of honor behind the registration desk of the hotel. The 18-karat solid gold statue, weighing 206.3 troy ounces (14.1 pounds), is insured for $140,000.

The attractive, wide-open U-shaped casino is a bit on the loud side. There's a bingo room for the low rollers.

The Rotisserie combines a buffet and a la carte menu. **Trader Dick's,** a dark, lush tropical garden setting with palm fronds and grass thatching sits just off the main casino floor, serving South Sea and Polynesian lunch Monday through Friday and dinner every night. A prix-fixe dinner is available for $16.95; specialties include sesame chicken for $9.95; hoisin beef for $10.50; and a seafood luau with cold crab, shrimp, prawns, avocado, papaya, tomato, and asparagus for about $20. A soup and salad bar is offered for $4.95. At the center of the room is a large Chinese smoke oven.

At the far end of the casino are a few other casual eateries. The **Farm House** is a coffee-shop-like establishment, offering omelettes and pancakes for breakfast, a range of sandwiches and salads for lunch, and dinner specials including french fried deep sea scallops for $7.95, fried shrimp boat for $7.95, ranch-hand beef stew for $5.95, and liver and onions for $5.25.

Nearby is **John's Oyster Bar,** which carries a bit of a nautical theme including a ship's mast and yardarm overhead. Specialties include lobster surprise salad (topped with a remoulade sauce of mayonnaise, mustard, gherkins, chervil, tarragon, and capers with a touch of chablis) for $12.50, and a group of pan roasts in chablis, clam broth, cream, and butter: oyster or shrimp for $8.75 or both for $9.

The **General Store** is a dimly lit, open-space coffee shop with attractive ceiling fans. Specialties include deep fried catfish for $5.95 and nuggets of tenderloin (chunks of filet mignon breaded, seasoned, and fried) for $8.95. Other specialties include white sturgeon (8-ounce loin sautéed, topped with a fine wine and champagne sauce, and served with wild rice and vegetables) for $16.95.

John Ascuaga's Nugget, 1100 Nugget Avenue, Sparks; 750 rooms; 356-3300; (800) 648-1177.

A smaller, unusual Sparks joint worth checking out is **Baldini's Sports Casino.** This is not a place for the claustrophobic; in fact, it feels as if you have descended directly into the innards of a slot machine. There's a country-western dance floor and nearly-free food.

Baldini's is located at 865 S. Rock Boulevard; 358-0116.

Other Hotels and Casinos in Reno/Sparks

Cal-Neva Club. Earplugs are optional at this adult playroom. Some of the slots are built into colorful but not-all-that-realistic mockups of trains and western buildings. Food is served from a dining car lunch cart or at the Hofbrau restaurant.

Cal-Neva Club, E. Second and N. Virginia; 323-1046.

Fitzgerald's Casino-Hotel. The wearing of the green can become a bit wearing in this little piece of Ireland in Reno. The mirrored ceilings add to the visual overload.

But for a touch of the blarney, if not the bizarre, be sure to visit the "Lucky Forest" on the second floor. There has got to be something here that will improve your luck at the tables: four-leaf clovers, rabbit's feet, horseshoe, a wishing well, Asian gods—if there's a good luck charm not represented here, we'd like to know about it.

Fitzgerald's, located in the heart of downtown in the shadow of the Virginia Street arch, is named after Lincoln Fitzgerald, another of the early casino developers of Reno.

Fitzgerald's Casino-Hotel, 255 N. Virginia; 351 rooms; 785-3300; (800) 648-5022.

Riverboat Hotel & Casino. Relatively quiet, small, and ordinary. Specials at the restaurant include a prime rib dinner for $5.99, served from 4 P.M. to midnight.

Riverboat Hotel & Casino, 34 W. Second; 120 rooms; 323-8877; (800) 888-5525.

Virginian. A low-roller haven, lively but ordinary. It is one of the few casinos with a 25-cent minimum craps table, which may be an attraction to those who want to try the game without risking serious money.

Virginian Hotel-Casino, 140 N. Virginia; 329-4664.

Reno Hotel-Casino Listing

Reno

Adventure Inn. 3575 S. Virginia Street; 828-9000; (800) 937-1436.
Airport Plaza Hotel. 1981 Terminal Way; 348-6370; (800) 648-3525.
Americana Inn. 340 Lake Street; 786-4422.
Aspen Motel. 495 Lake Street; 329-6011.
Best Western-Continental Lodge. 1885 S. Virginia Street; 329-1001; (800) 626-1900.
Best Western-Daniel's Motor Lodge. 375 N. Sierra Street; 329-1351; (800) 528-1234.
Big 8 Motel. 795 W. 4th Street; 329-3420.
Bob Cashell's Horseshoe Lodge. 222 N. Sierra Street; 322-2178; (800) 843-7403.
Bonanza Casino. 4720 N. Virginia Street; 323-2724.
Bonanza Motor Inn. 215 W. 4th Street; 322-8632.
Cabana Motel. 370 West Street; 786-2977.
Capri Motel. 895 N. Virginia Street; 323-8398.
Carriage Inn. 690 W. 4th Street; 329-8848.
Cheers Hotel/Casino 567 W. 4th Street; 322-8181.

Circus Circus Hotel/Casino 500 N. Sierra Street; 329-0711; (800) 648-5010.
City Center Motel. 365 West Street; 323-8880.
Clarion Hotel/Casino. 3800 S. Virginia Street; 825-4700; (800) 723-6500.
Coach Inn. 500 N. Center Street; 323-3222.
Colonial Inn Hotel/Casino. 250 N. Arlington Avenue; 322-3838; (800) 336-7366.
Colonial Motor Inn. 232 West Street; 786-5038; (800) 255-7366.
Comstock Hotel/Casino. 200 W. 2nd Street; 329-1880; (800) 648-4866.
Crest Inn. 525 W. 4th Street; 329-0808.
Days Inn. 701 E. 7th Street; 786-4070; (800) 942-3838.
Donner Inn Motel. 720 W. 4th Street; 323-1851.
Downtowner Motor Lodge. 150 Stevenson Street; 322-1188.
Easy 8 Motel. 255 W. 5th Street; 322-4588.
El Ray Motel. 350 N. Arlington Avenue; 329-6669.
Eldorado Hotel/Casino. 345 N. Virginia Street; 786-5700; (800) 648-5966.
Executive Inn. 205 S. Sierra Street; 786-4050; (800) 648-4545.
Fantasy Inn. 2905 S. Virginia Street; 826-1515; (800) 662-8812.
Fireside Inn. 205 E. 4th Street; 786-1666.
Fitzgeralds Casino/Hotel. 255 N. Virginia Street; 785-3300; (800) 648-5022.
Flamingo Hilton Reno. 255 N. Sierra Street; 322-1111; (800) 648-4882.
Flamingo Motel. 520 N. Center Street; 323-3202.
Gatekeeper Inn. 221 W. 5th Street; 786-3500; (800) 822-3504.
Gateway Inn. 1275 Stardust Street; 747-4220.
Gold Dust West. Vine Street; 323-2211; (800) 438-9378.
Gold Key Motel. 445 Lake Street; 323-0731.
Harrah's Casino/Hotel Reno. 206 N. Virginia Street; 786-3232; (800) 648-3773.
Heart o' Town/Chalet Motel. 520 N. Virginia Street; 322-4066; (800) 628-3395.
Holiday Hotel Casino. Mill and Center Streets; 329-0411; (800) 648-5431.
Holiday Inn Convention Center. 5851 S. Virginia Street; 825-2940; (800) 722-7366.
Holiday Inn Downtown. 1000 E. 6th Street; 786-5151; (800) 648-4877.
Horseshoe Motel. 490 Lake Street; 786-5968.
Hotel El Cortez. 239 W. 2nd Street; 322-9161.
In Town Motel. 260 W. 4th Street; 323-1421.
Juniper Court Motel. 320 Evans Avenue; 329-7002; (800) 648-7366.
Keno Motel. 322 N. Arlington Avenue; 322-6281.
Keno Motel #2. 331 West Street; 322-4146.
La Quinta Inn. 4001 Market Street; 348-6100; (800) 531-5900.
Lakemill Lodge. 200 Mill Street; 786-1500; (800) 531-5900.
Lido Inn. 280 W. 4th Street; 322-3822.
Longhorn Motel. 844 S. Virginia Street; 322-2633.
Majestic Inn. 400 N. Virginia Street; 322-2868.
Mardi Gras Motor Lodge. 200 W. 4th Street; 329-7470.
Mark Twain Motel. 2201 S. Virginia Street; 826-2101.
Miner's Inn. 1651 N. Virginia Street; 329-3464.
Monte Carlo Motel. 500 N. Virginia Street; 329-2010.
Motel 500. 500 S. Center Street; 786-2777.
Motel 6 Reno Central. 866 N. Wells Avenue; 786-9852.
Motel 6 Reno North. 666 N. Wells Avenue; 329-8681.
Motel 6 Reno South. 1901 S. Virginia Street; 827-0255.
Motel 6 Reno West. 1400 Stardust; 747-7390.
National 9 Inn. 645 S. Virginia Street; 323-5411.
Nevada Inn. 330 E. 2nd Street; 323-1005; (800) 999-9686.
Olympic Apartment Motel. 195 W. 2nd Street; 323-0726.
Oxford Motel. 111 Lake Street; 786-3170; (800) 648-3044.
Park-N-Walk/Reno Royal Motor Lodge. 350 West Street; 323-4477.

Peppermill Hotel/Casino. 2707 S. Virginia Street; 826-2121; (800) 648-6992.
Pioneer Inn Hotel/Casino. 221 S. Virginia Street; 324-7777; (800) 879-8879.
Plaza Resort Club. 121 West Street; 786-2200; (800) 648-5990.
Ponderosa Hotel. 515 S. Virginia Street; 786-6820; (800) 228-6820.
Ponderosa Motel. 595 N. Lake Street; 786-3070.
Reno Hilton. 2500 E. 2nd Street; 789-2000; (800) 648-5080.
Reno Ramada Hotel/Casino. 200 E. 6th Street; 788-2000; (800) 648-3600.
Reno Riviera. 395 W. 1st Street; 329-9348.
Reno Spa Resort Club. 140 Court Street; 329-4251; (800) 634-6981.
Reno Travelodge Downtown. 655 W. 4th Street; 329-3451; (800) 255-3050.
Riverboat Hotel/Casino. 34 W. 2nd Street; 323-8877; (800) 888-5525.
Riverhouse Motel. 2 Lake Street; 329-0036.
Rodeway Inn. 2050 Market Street; 786-2500; (800) 648-3800.
RR Lodge. 500 Lake Street; 788-2000; (800) 648-3600.
Sands Regency Hotel/Casino. 345 N. Arlington Avenue; 348-2200; (800) 648-3553.
Savoy Motor Lodge. 705 N. Virginia Street; 322-4477.
Season's Inn. 495 West Street; 322-6000.
Shamrock Inn. 505 N. Center Street; 786-5182.
Showboat Inn. 660 N. Virginia Street; 786-7486; (800) 648-3960.
Silver Dollar Motor Lodge Six Gun Motel. 817 N. Virginia Street; 323-6875.
Six Gun Motel. 1661 E. 6th Street; 329-3426; (800) 648-3074.
Spring Hill Inn. 1450 Mill Street; 788-8040.
Stardust Lodge. 455 N. Arlington Avenue; 322-5641.
Sundowner Hotel/Casino. 450 N. Arlington Avenue; 786-7050; (800) 648-5490.
Swan Motel. 501 Lake Street; 786-1751.
Time Zone Motel. 448 Lake Street; 322-4666.
Town House Motor Lodge. 303 W. 2nd Street; 323-1821; (800) 438-5660.
Townsite Motel. 250 W. Commercial Row; 322-0345.
Town View Motor Lodge. 131 W. 3rd Street; 329-1560.
Truckee River Lodge. 501 W. 1st Street; 786-8888; (800) 635-8950.
University Inn. 1001 N. Virginia Street; 323-0321.
Uptown Motel. 570 N. Virginia Street; 323-8906.
Vagabond Inn. 3131 S. Virginia Street; 825-7134; (800) 522-1555.
Virginian Hotel/Casino. 140 N. Virginia Street; 329-4664; (800) 874-5558.
Washoe Inn. 75 Pringle Way; 328-5080.
White Court Motel. 465 Evans Street; 329-1957.
Windsor Hotel. 214 West Street; 323-6171.
Wonder Lodge. 430 Lake Street; 786-6840.

Sparks

Blue Fountain Motel. 1590 Victorian Avenue; 359-0359.
Emerald Motel. 145 15th Street; 358-5930.
Inn Cal. 255 N. McCarran Boulevard; 358-2222; (800) 446-2257.
John Ascuaga's Nugget. 1100 Nugget Avenue; 356-3300; (800) 648-1177.
McCarran House Inn. 55 E. Nugget Avenue; 358-6900; (800) 548-5798.
Motel 6 Sparks. 2405 Victorian Avenue; 358-1080.
Nendels Inn. 60 East Victorian Avenue; 356-7770; (800) 547-0106.
Pony Express Lodge. 2406 Prater Way; 358-7110.
Silver Club Hotel/Casino. 1040 Victorian Avenue; 358-4771; (800) 648-1137.
Sunrise Motel. 210 Victorian Avenue; 358-7010.
Thunderbird Resort Club. 200 Nichols Boulevard; 355-4040; (800) 821-4912.
Victorian Inn. 1555 Victorian Avenue; 331-3203.
Wagon Train Motel. 1662 Victorian Avenue; 358-0468.
Western Village Inn/Casino. 815 E. Nichols Boulevard; 331-1069; (800) 648-1170.

Bed and Breakfast

Bed & Breakfast South Reno. 136 Andrew Lane, Reno; 849-0772.

Deer Run Ranch. 5440 East Lake Boulevard, Washoe Valley; 882-3643.

Haus Bavaria. 593 N. Dyer Circle, Incline Village; 831-6122; (800) 468-2463.

Airlines Serving Reno

America West Airlines. (800) 247-5692.

American Airlines/American Eagle. (800) 433-7300.

Canadian Airlines International. (800) 426-7000.

Continental Airlines. (800) 525-0280.

Delta Air Lines. (800) 221-1212.

Northwest Airlines. (800) 225-2525.

Reno Air. 736-6247.

Southwest Airlines. 800-435-9792.

United Airlines. (800) 241-6522.

US Air. (800) 428-4322.

Bus Service

RTC/Citifare. For information on bus service, call 384-RIDE. Fares are adult, 75 cents; youth 18 and under, 50 cents; senior 60 and older with Citifare ID, 30 cents; disabled, 30 cents. Children ages 5 and under ride free; transfers are free.

Long Distance Bus Service

Aero Trans. Airport and Tahoe destinations. 786-2376.

Airport Mini Bus. Airport, Reno, and Lake Tahoe. 323-3727; (800) 235-5466.

Bell Limo Service. Airport, Reno, and Tahoe. 786-3700; (800) 235-5466.

Citifare. Scheduled service in Reno and Sparks. 348-7433.

Greyhound Lines West. Reno. 322-4511.

Sierra Nevada Gray Line. Daily ski shuttle to Alpine Meadows, Squaw Valley, and Northstar-at-Tahoe. 329-1147; (800) 822-6009.

Tahoe Casino Express. Scheduled service from Reno Airport to South Lake Tahoe. 785-2424; (800) 446-6128.

Car Rentals in Reno

Action Auto Rental. 324-2885.

Advantage Rent-A-Car. 5301 Longley Lane. 825-9191; (800) 777-5500.

Agency Rent-A-Car. 1105 Terminal Way; 786-3381; (800) 321-1972.

Alamo Rent A Car. 1120 Terminal Way; 323-8306; (800) 327-9633.

All American Auto Rental. 225 Telegraph; 323-0420.

Apple Rent A Car. Airport; 329-2137. 550 W. 4th, 329-2438.

Avis Rent A Car. Airport; 785-2727; (800) 331-1212.

Budget/Sears. Airport; 785-2545; downtown, 785-2880; (800) 527-0700.

Dollar Rent A Car. Airport; 348-2800; (800) 800-4000.

Enterprise Rent-A-Car. Airport; 329-3773; (800) 325-8007.

General Rent-A-Car. Airport; 785-2600. (800) 327-7607.

Hertz Rent A- Car. Airport; 785-2554. Flamingo Hilton downtown; 348-8860. Reno Hilton; 785-2605; (800) 654-3131.

Lloyd's International. 2515 Mill Street; 736-2663; (800) 654-7037.

Payless. 225 Telegraph Street; 333-6543; (800) 729-5377.

Thrifty Car Rental. 2697 Mill Street; 329-0096; (800) 367-2277.

Chapter 18

Eating Your Way Across Reno and Sparks

Reno-Sparks Buffets

Circus Circus. Big Top Buffet. Breakfast 6 to 11:30 A.M., $2.29; lunch 11:30 A.M. to 4 P.M., $2.69; and dinner 4:30 to 11 P.M., $3.89. Friday seafood buffet is $5.99.

Eldorado. Marketplace Buffet. Breakfast 7:45 to 11 A.M., $3.49; lunch 11 A.M. to 2 P.M., $5.49; and dinner 4 to 10 P.M., $7.49. Saturday night western buffet from 4 to 10 P.M., $9.99. Saturday brunch 8 A.M. to 2 P.M. for $5.49, and Sunday champagne brunch from 8 A.M. to 2 P.M. for $7.49. Special seafood buffet Friday and Saturday nights for $15.99 in the hotel's convention center.

Fitzgerald's. Breakfast 7 to 11 A.M., $2.99; lunch noon to 4 P.M., $4.49; and dinner 4 to 10 P.M., $4.99.

Flamingo Hilton. Breakfast 7 to 10:45 A.M., $3.49; lunch 11 A.M. to 3 P.M. weekdays for $4 and weekends for $5; and dinner 5 to 11 P.M. for $5.99.

Harrah's. Skyway Buffet. Breakfast 7 to 11 A.M., $4.74; lunch 11:30 A.M. to 3 P.M., $5.25; and dinner Monday through Thursday 5 to 9 P.M., $7.75. Friday seafood dinner buffet 5 to 10 P.M., $14.95. Saturday brunch 7 A.M. to 3 P.M. for $6.50; Saturday grille from 4 to 10 P.M., $8.99. Sunday brunch 7 A.M. to 3 P.M., $6.50; and dinner from 4 to 9 P.M., $7.75.

Nugget. Lunch Monday to Saturday 11 A.M. to 2 P.M., $6.95. Dinner 5 to 10 P.M.: Monday (fish), $11.95; Tuesday (chocaholic's dessert special), $10.95; Wednesday (ribs), $10.95; Thursday, $10.95; Friday (seafood), $13.95; Saturday, $13.95; and Sunday, $10.95. Sunday brunch 8:30 A.M. to 2 P.M., $8.95.

Peppermill. Island Buffet. Breakfast weekdays 7:30 to 11 A.M., $2.99; lunch weekdays 11:30 A.M. to 3 P.M., $4.99; and dinner Sunday through Thursday 4:30 to 10 P.M., $7.99. Friday seafood buffet dinner, 4:30 to 11 P.M., $14.99. Saturday breakfast, 7:30 to 11 A.M., $5.99; lunch 11 A.M. to 3 P.M., $6.99; and prime rib dinner, 4:30 to 11 P.M., $13.99. Sunday brunch, 9 A.M. to 3 P.M. for $10.99.

Reno Hilton. Breakfast 7 to 10:30 A.M., $3.99; lunch 11:30 A.M. to 3 P.M., $4.99; and dinner, 4:30 to 10 P.M., $7.95. Sunday brunch 10 A.M. to 2 P.M., $9.95. (The hotel's new buffet area, with new prices, was due to debut in the summer of 1994.)

Some of Greater Reno's Best Restaurants

(Be sure to also see listings for restaurants with major hotels in this section.)

Adele's Restaurant. Valley Bank Plaza, 425 South Virginia; 333-6503. Also, 1112 North Carson; 882-3353. Lunch and dinner. Reservations suggested.

Bagel Deli. 2600 South Virginia (across from Peppermill). 825-8866. Breakfast and lunch restaurant/bakery featuring 14 varieties of bagels, 18 choices of cream cheese, and Kosher-style deli meats. Open Tuesday through Saturday.

Bailey's Cafe. 4124 Kietzke Lane (across from the Convention Center); 825-6600. California cafe atmosphere and outdoor dining on garden terrace. Brunch-luncheon every day from 8 A.M. to 5 P.M.; dinner every evening from 5 P.M.

Bavarian World. 595 Valley Road (Valley Road & East 6th); 323-7646. Alpine cuisine from schnitzel to schweinebraten and more, including Munich draft beer and a German bakery. Open daily for breakfast, lunch, and dinner.

Bompi's. 300-A East Plumb Lane; 828-7300. Italian Tuscan food, plus pizza and pasta. Lunch and dinner daily. Reservations suggested.

Casanova's. 1695 South Virginia; 786-6633. Private curtained booths for fantasies of all sorts, including abalone, lobster, scampi, salmon, quail, pheasant, partridge, elk, and antelope, plus pasta dishes.

Colombo's Restaurant. 145 W. Truckee River Lane; 323-7004. New York-style Italian food in an art deco eatery. Open for dinner every evening.

Famous Murphy's Restaurant Grill and Oyster Bar. 3127 S. Virginia Street; 827-4111. The Grill serves sandwiches, burgers, salads, scampi, pan roasts, pasta, steamers, oysters, chowder, hot rocks, and more for lunch and dinner. The dining room serves steak, pasta, chicken, and seafood specialties. Lunch and dinner daily. Reservations suggested.

Galena Forest Inn. 17025 Mount Rose Highway; 849-2100. Six miles up Mount Rose Highway. Alpine cuisine combining Swiss, Austrian, northern Italian, French, and German specialties. Menu items include sweetbread fricassee with shallots, mushrooms, spices, and wine; sautéed frog's legs with tomato concassee and garlic butter; *escalope tessin* (veal scallops with prosciutto and emmentaler cheese); and rosette of beef with cognac morrels sauce. Dinner is served Wednesday through Sunday from 5 P.M. Reservations suggested.

The Reno Hilton

Gold Hill Hotel. Main Street, (Hwy. 342), Gold Hill; 847-0111. Built in 1859, this stone structure is Nevada's oldest hotel. Lavish accommodations decorated with period antiques and a fine French restaurant, the Crown Point.

Hooters Restaurant. 3665 South Virginia Street; 829-9464. Franchised fun including chicken wings, seafood, sandwiches, and salads with the accompaniment of '50s and '60s music on the juke box. Open daily for lunch and dinner.

Ichiban Japanese Steak House & Sushi Bar. 635 North Sierra Street; 323-5550. Teppen yaki tableside cooking including steak, lobster, shrimp, scallops, and chicken dishes. Traditional dishes such as sukiyaki, tempura, and yakitori are also served in private tatami rooms.

Kubla Khan Restaurant. 3702 S. Virginia Street; 829-8787. Barbecue your own chicken, beef, pork, or seafood on skewers at your table.

La Table Francaise. 3065 W. 4th Street; 323-3200. Chef Yves Pimparel's classic French restaurant, winner of the *Mobil Guide* Four-Star rating since 1979. Reservations necessary. Closed Sunday and Monday.

La Trattoria. 719 South Virginia; 323-1131. An Italian "little kitchen" cafe. Specialties include *ravioli de manzo* (steak ravioli in red wine sauce with carrots and onions) and *pasta 'n cacciata* (eggplant shell filled with penne pasta in marinara sauce). Open for dinner Monday through Saturday and lunch Monday through Friday.

Louis' Basque Corner. 301 East Fourth Street. 323-7203. Basque cuisine such as *tripas callos*, chicken, oxtails, shrimp, and *tonque a la basquaise, paella, lapin chasseur* (hunter's rabbit), and *veau panne* (breaded veal), served family style. Lunch Monday through Saturday from 11 A.M. to 2:30 P.M. Dinner each evening from 5:30 P.M. to 10 P.M. Monday through Saturday and 4:30 P.M. to 9:30 P.M. Sunday.

The Mandarin Restaurant. 5089 South McCarran Boulevard, Smithridge Plaza; 827-0222. Authentic Chinese cuisine.

Pyrenees Bar & Grill. 442 Flint Street; 329-3800. Located in one of the city's most beautiful and history-rich buildings, built in 1910 as a residence, the menu combines Basque specialties with American favorites.

The Basque Influence

The Basques, an adventuresome people with origins in the Pyrenees Mountains of France and Spain, came to Nevada in a circuitous route that began with migration to Argentina where they worked as shepherds. Many thousands moved north in the 1850s, lured by the California Gold Rush, and some then came over the Sierra Nevadas eastward to work in the mines of the Comstock and elsewhere in Nevada.

There are still remnants of the once-thriving Basque culture in and around Reno, including festivals and restaurants. Most Basque eateries are decidedly informal, serving dishes family-style. You will likely be served at a large table with strangers in a boisterous atmosphere; Basque restaurants are not the place for a romantic getaway, but they are a lot of fun and a lot of food for a reasonable price—usually in the range of $10 to $20 for a complete dinner.

Among Reno area restaurants worth checking out are Louis and Lorraine Erreguible's **Louis' Basque Corner** at 301 East Fourth Street, open for lunch Monday through Saturday, and every day for dinner. 323-7203.

A local favorite is the **Santa Fe Hotel,** at 235 Lake Street, next to Harrah's. Open every day for lunch and dinner. 323-1891.

The **Pyrenees Bar & Grill** at California and Flint, three blocks west of South Virginia Street, is by Basque standards a formal place. 329-3800.

The **Basque Restaurant** is at the Overland Hotel, 691 S. Main Street, Gardnerville, below Carson City on I-395, just below the cutoff to Route 207 on the southernmost route to South Lake Tahoe. Open for lunch and dinner; closed Monday, 782-2138.

The Nugget, Reno

Chapter 19
Reno/Sparks Area Attractions

Like Las Vegas, Reno is a lot more than casinos and showrooms. Here is a listing of some of the more interesting museums and entertainment areas, as well as sports and outdoor activities.

Be sure to also check listings in this book for Carson City, Virginia City, and Lake Tahoe. Information about ski areas at Mount Rose, Incline Village, South Lake Tahoe, and North Lake Tahoe, as well as other winter sports including sledding, skating, and snowmobiling can be found in the section about Lake Tahoe.

Call ahead of time to check on hours and fees which are always subject to change. All phone numbers are in the 702 area code unless otherwise indicated.

Museums

Wilbur D. May Museum, Arboretum, and Botanical Garden. A fabulous assortment of animal trophies and other items from the personal collection of Wilbur May, the founder of the department store chain that bears his name.

An indoor arboretum includes a three-story waterfall; a hands-on science room called the Sensorium was added in 1993. Located in Washoe County's Rancho San Rafael Park, 1502 Washington Street in Reno.

Hours and admission prices vary through the year; call 785-5961.

Boomtown RV Park.
I-80 at Garson Road, Verdi. 345-6000; (800) 648-3790. 230 sites. At Boomtown Hotel/Casino.

Chism Trailer Park.
1300 W. 2nd Street, Reno. 322-2281; (800) 638-2281. 50 sites.

Four Seasons RV Park. 13109 S. Virginia Street, Reno. 853-1423. 49 sites. 15 miles south of Reno.

Keystone RV Park.
1455 W. 4th Street, Reno. 324-5000. 104 sites. Free shuttle to downtown.

<table>
<tr><td>

Reno Hilton Camperland.
2500 E. Second Street. 789-2129; (800) 648-5080. 452 sites. Pool.

Reno RV Park.
735 Mill Street, Reno. 323-3381; (800) 445-3381. 46 sites.

River's Edge RV Park.
1405 S. Rock Boulevard, Sparks. 358-8533. 164 sites. On the Truckee River. Casino shuttle.

</td></tr>
</table>

Next door to the May Museum is the **Great Basin Adventure** theme park. Included are mining exhibits, gold panning, petting zoo, a dinosaur park, and more. Open summer months. Closed Mondays. Call 785-4319 for information. *Discount coupon in this book.*

E. L. Wiegand Museum of Art. An eclectic collection of modern and fine art, located at 160 W. Liberty Street. Open Wednesday through Sunday. Call 329-333 for hours and admission fees.

Nevada State Historical Society Museum. A well-stocked and presented collection of Indian artifacts, mining devices, and other elements of the Silver State's history, from prehistoric times to the Wild West to modern days. A research library includes many priceless manuscripts, records, maps, and other historical data. The gift shop is the answer to a history buff's prayer.

Located on the University of Nevada-Reno campus on Virginia Street near U.S. 395. Open Monday to Saturday. Call 688-1190 for hours.

Fleischmann Planetarium. Next to the Historical Society Museum on the UNR campus. A stargazer's fantasy: a fascinating planetarium show, there are films, a display of meteorites, and scheduled use of telescopes. Call 784-4811 for hours.

Mackay Museum of Mines. If a mining museum is what you're looking for, here is a fine example: an incredible collection of mineral wealth from Nevada, including gold and silver from the Comstock, as well as copper, lead, magnesium, and other rocks that shaped the state.

The collection was originally endowed by John Mackay, one of the men who made a fabulous fortune in the early days of Virginia City. On the UNR campus, within the Mackay Mining School. Call the school for hours and information at 784-6987.

National Automobile Museum. A simply spectacular collection of just some of the more than 1,000 vintage vehicles once owned by casino developer William Harrah. Most of the cars were auctioned off after Harrah's death (some were bought for the equally spectacular and quirky collection at the Imperial Palace in Las Vegas); about 200 were given to a foundation set up by his heirs. The collection was moved into an attractive new building in downtown in 1989; the architecture of the building is reminiscent of some of the chrome boats within.

Mill and Lake Streets. Open every day but Christmas. Call 333-9300 for hours and admission fees. *Discount coupon in this book.*

Amusement Parks

Amusement World offers go-carts, bumper boats, batting cages, a video arcade, and more. 12325 S. Virginia Street. Call 851-0961 for hours and fees.

Battle Born Splat World. The name just about sums it up, doesn't it? This is a paint ball arcade for those who feel they can reduce stress by firing paint-filled balloons at each other in mock warfare. Go figure. 555 Dermody Way, Sparks. 356-1864.

> **Shamrock RV Park.** 260 Parr Boulevard, Reno. 329-5222; (800) 322-8248. 121 sites.
>
> **Tiki Village Trailer Park.** 4055 S. Virginia Street, Reno. 825-1507. 66 sites.

Kiddie Playland at Idlewild Park is a small play area with trains, a merry-go-round, swimming pool, and rides. Call 329-6008 for hours and rates.

Wild Waters at Wild Island in Sparks offers a wave pool, water slides, and other wet entertainment in warm weather.

Also at Wild Island is **Adventure Golf,** a 36-hole miniature golf course, open year round weather permitting. Also at the park are three go-cart raceways and a video game arcade. 250 Wild Island Court (north from Sparks Boulevard exit of I-80). Call 331-9453 for operating days, hours, and rates. *Discount coupon in this book.*

Performing Arts and Theater Groups

Nevada Festival Ballet. 329-2552.
Nevada Opera Association. 786-4046.
Reno Little Theater. 329-0661.
Reno Philharmonic Association. 825-5905.
Sierra Arts Foundation. 329-1324.
UNR Performing Arts Series. 826-0880.
Washoe County Community Concert Association. 359-7670.

Major Hotel Showrooms

Flamingo Hilton. 322-1111.
Harrah's Reno. 329-4422; (800) 648-3773.
John Ascuaga's Nugget. 356-3304; (800) 648-1177.
Reno Hilton. 789-2285; (800) 648-3568.

Nightclubs

Baldini's. 865 S. Rock Boulevard, Sparks; 358-0116.
Cantina Los Tres Hombres. 7111 S. Virginia Street; 852-0202.
Casanova's. 1695 S. Virginia Street; 786-6633.
Catch a Rising Star Comedy & Music Club. Reno Hilton, 2500 E. Second Street; 354-4544.
Clarion. 3800 S. Virginia Street; 825-4700.
Easy Street Cabaret. 505 Keystone Avenue; 323-8369.
Hacienda del Sol. 2935 S. Virginia Street; 825-7144.
Lime Lite. 50 E. Grove Street; 829-0448.
Noizemakers at Garfields. 1537 S. Virginia Street; 323-1600.
Pink Pussy Cat. Non-stop topless shows. 195 S. Wells Avenue; 322-0388.
Sierra Stix. 2130 Oddie Boulevard, Sparks; 331-4083.

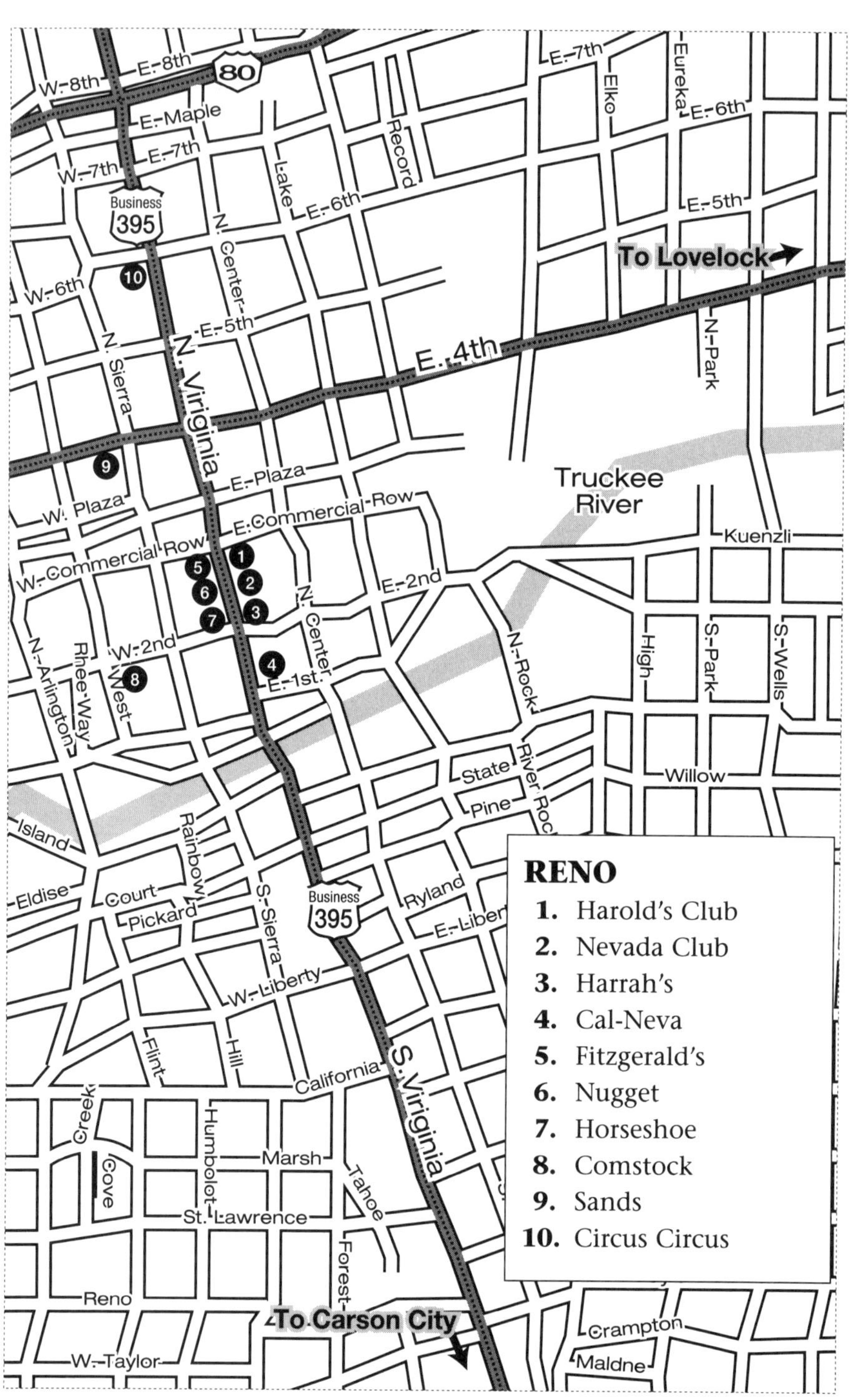

W-8th
E-8th
80
E-Maple
W-7th
E-7th
Business
395
N. Center
Lake
E-6th
Record
E-7th
Elko
Eureka
E-6th
W-6th
10
E-5th
E-5th
To Lovelock→
N. Sierra
N. Virginia
E-4th
N-Park
9
E-Plaza
W. Plaza
Truckee
River
Kuenzli
E-Commercial-Row
W-Commercial-Row
1
5
E-2nd
2
N. Center
6
3
E-2nd
7
N-Rock
High
S-Park
S-Wells
W-2nd
4
River Roc
Willow
8
N. Arlington
Rhee-Way
West
E-1st
State
Pine
Island
Eldise
Court
Rainbow
S-Sierra
Business
395
Ryland
E-Liber
Pickard
Flint
Hill
W-Liberty
California
Creek
Cove
Humbolot
Marsh
Tahoe
S. Virginia
St. Lawrence
Forest
Reno
To Carson City
Crampton
W-Taylor
Maldne

RENO
1. Harold's Club
2. Nevada Club
3. Harrah's
4. Cal-Neva
5. Fitzgerald's
6. Nugget
7. Horseshoe
8. Comstock
9. Sands
10. Circus Circus

Chapter 20

The Great Outdoors in Reno/Sparks

Golf Courses

Most Reno-area courses are open year-round or close to it; courses north and south may be closed in the winter. Call for hours and fees. Listed yardage is for championship or men's course.

Brookside Municipal Golf Course. 700 South Rock Boulevard, Sparks. 322-6009. 9 holes. Par 36; 2,930 yards. Year round. $5.

Lakeridge Golf Course. 1200 Razorback Drive, Reno. 825-2200. 18 holes. Par 71; 6,703 yards on championship course designed by Robert Trent Jones. Year round. Summer rates April 1 through October 31 $49 with cart; off-season $30 with cart.

Northgate Golf Club. 111 Clubhouse Drive, Reno. 747-7577. 18 holes. Par 72; 6,966 yards. Year round except December 15 through January 31. Summer rates April 1 through October 31 $37 with cart; winter rates $26 with cart; $13 without cart.

Rosewood Lakes. 6800 Pembroke Drive, Reno. 685-2893. 18 holes. Par 72; 6,661 for Gold course. Year round. $22 summer; $17 winter. Carts $16.

Sierra Sage Golf Course. 6355 Silver Lake Road, Reno. 972-1564. 18 holes. Par 71; 6,623 yards. Year round. Weekdays $18; weekends $21. Carts $18.

Washoe County Golf Course. 2601 S. Arlington Avenue, Reno. 785-4286. 18 holes. Par 72; 6,695 yards. Year round. Summer $21; winter $18. Carts $18. Built by the WPA in the 1930s.

Wildcreek Golf Course. 3500 Sullivan Lane, Sparks. 673-3100. 18 holes. Par 72; 7,105 yards. Year round except December 15 through January 31. Summer rates April 1 through October 31 $37 with cart; winter rates $26 with cart; $13 without cart.

Hunting Information

Contact the Department of Wildlife, P.O. Box 10678, Reno, NV 89520; or call 688-1500. Information is also available at most sporting goods stores.

Tennis Courts

Lakeridge Tennis Club. 827-3300.

Reno Hilton. 789-2145.

Reno Parks & Recreation Department. 334-2262.

Reno YMCA. 329-1311.

Sparks Recreation Department. 359-7930.

Washoe County Parks Department. 785-6133.

Foreign language assistance. Northern Nevada Language Bank can offer assistance on a 24-hour-a-day basis for non-English-speaking visitors. Contact the answering service operator, who can connect the caller with a volunteer who speaks the necessary language. 323-0500.

Parks and Recreation

City of Sparks Parks and Recreation. 353-2376.

Nevada State Parks Division. 687-4384.

Reno City Parks and Recreation. 334-2662.

United States Forest Service/Toiyabe National Forest. 355-5302.

Washoe County Parks and Recreation. 785-6133.

Chapter 21

Shopping, Getting Married, and Other Entertainment

Shopping Malls

Meadowood Mall.

Located off South Virginia Street near the intersection with South McCarran Boulevard, past the Reno Cannon International Airport and the Reno/Sparks Convention Center. Open Monday through Friday 10 A.M. to 9 P.M.; Saturday 10 A.M. to 7 P.M.; Sunday 11 A.M. to 6 P.M. 827-8450.

Citifare bus service is available from the following points to Meadowood: Downtown (4th and Center Streets), Reno Hilton (tour bus entrance at south doors), The Peppermill (Virginia Street), and Victorian Square in Sparks (11th and B Streets).

More than 75 stores in an attractive setting, including Macy's Reno, said to be the largest single department store in the state, JC Penney, The Gap, The Limited, and more.

Department Stores: JC Penney, Macy's.

Arts, crafts, hobbies, and toys: Clown's Closet, Docktor Pet Center, Prints Plus, World of Toys.

Athletic Wear and Sporting Goods: Champs, Copeland's Sports, Eddie Bauer, Foot Locker, Lady Foot Locker, Track 'n Trail.

Books and Cards: Amy's Hallmark, Waldenbooks.

Children's Clothing and Shoes: Champs, Clown's Closet, Foot Locker, Kinney Shoes, Lady Foot Locker, Limited Too, Miller Stockman, Track 'n Trail.

Electronics, Music, and Video: AT&T Phone Center, Fun-N-Games, Musicland, Radio Shack, Sam Goody, Suncoast Motion Pictures Company, Waldenbooks, Waldensoftware.

Food and Restaurants: Alamo Restaurant, Cindy's Cinnamon Rolls, GNC, Honey Treat Yogurt, McDonald's, Manchu Wok, Marie Callender's,

Mrs. Field's Cookies, Sbarro Italian Eatery, See's Candies, Spinnaker's.

Luggage: Eddie Bauer, Schillings.

Men's Fashions and Shoes: Champs, Copeland's Sports, County Seat, Dejaiz, Eddie Bauer, Florsheim Shoes, Foot Locker, Gap, J. Riggings, Kinney Shoes, Miller Stockman, Miller's Outpost, Structure, Track 'n Trail, Victoria's Secret.

Women's Fashions and Shoes: 9 West, Accessory Place, Benetton, Brooks Fashions, Caren Charles, Carimar, Casual Corner, Champs, Cobbie Shop, Connie Shoes, Contempo Casuals, Copeland's Sports, County Seat, Eddie Bauer, Express, FootLocker, Gantos, The Gap, Jean Nicole, Kinney Shoes, Lady Foot Locker, Lane Bryant, Lerner, Miller Stockman, Miller's Outpost, Naturalizer, Petite Sophisticate, Switzer's, The Limited, Track 'n Trail, Units, Victoria's Secret.

Park Lane Mall.

Across from the Peppermill Hotel, at Virginia Street and Plumb Lane. Open weekdays 10 A.M. to 9 P.M., Saturday from 10 A.M. to 9 P.M., and Sunday from 11 A.M. to 6 P.M. 825-7878. More than 90 stores.

Department Stores: Sears, Weinstock's, Woolworth's.

Women's Clothing: After Thoughts, Brooks Fashions, Career Image, Claire's Boutique, Clothestime, 5-7-9, Frederick's of Hollywood, Lizzie B, Modern Woman, Touch of Pizazz, Plenty Pretty.

Men's Clothing: Jeans West, KG Men's Store, Oak Tree.

Family Apparel: Hot Cats, Jay Jacobs, Kid's Mart, Miller's Outpost, Pro Sports Shoppe, Splatters Ink, T-Shirts Plus, Wilson's Suede and Leather.

Shoes: Athletic X-Press, Foot Locker, Huston's Shoes, Huston's Youngland, Kinney Shoes, Leeds Shoes, Lloyd Gotchy Shoes, Naturalizer Shoes, Payless Shoesource, Thom McAn, Wild Pair.

Toys, Hobbies, and Entertainment: Docktor Pet Center, Gordon's Photo Service, Jolly Time, Kay Bee Toy, Mirabelli's Music City, Radio Shack, Waldensoftware.

Food and Restaurants: Baskin Robbins, Bompi's, Carousel Snack Bar, Cinnamon Sams, Ethel M's Chocolates, Foxy Loxy, Great American Cookie Co. Great Earth Vitamins, Honey Treat Yogurt, Jia's Wok, Orange Julius, Pete & Jerry's, Pizza by Piece of the Pie, See's Candy, Swiss Colony, Taco Chips.

Gifts, Cards, and Books: Cartoon Junction, Crystal Island, Evans Art Company, Nicholson's Hallmark, Reno Gift & Souvenir, Rose Garden, Sierra Crystal Mines, Spencer Gifts, Things Remembered, Tinder Box, Waldenbooks.

Jewelry: Crescent Jewelers, Gordon's Jewelers, Helzberg Diamonds, J. Herbert Hall, JM Jewelers, Precision Diamonds, Time Square, Zales.

Factory Stores at the Parking Gallery.
A new collection of stores near downtown Reno, at the corner of Sierra and 1st Streets. **Adolfo II, Anne Klein, Carole Little, Mikasa,** and others.

Shopping in Sparks

Factory Outlets of Nevada.
Sparks Boulevard and I-80. 355-3200. An all-in-one factory outlet store with discounts on some 30 brands including **Aileen, Banister Shoe, Bass, Book Warehouse, Brass Factory, Bugle Boy, Cape Isle Knitters, Corning/Revere, Designer Brands, Earthly Creations, Fieldcrest Cannon, Gitano, Hawaiian Cotton, Home Again, Leather Loft, London Fog, Prestige Fragrances, Sierra Trading Post, Socks Galore, Toy Liquidators,** and **Van Heusen.**

Greenbrae Shopping Center.
Greenbrae Drive and Pyramid Way. 329-2233. 35 stores.

Silver State Plaza.
McCarran Boulevard and E. Prater Way. 825-4000. 42 stores.

Shopping in South Lake Tahoe and Stateline
A few miles over the border into California is a stretch of factory outlet stores offering clothing, accessories, and household items.

Factory Stores at the Y.
Intersection of Highways 50 and 89, South Lake Tahoe. (At the point where Highway 50 continues on toward the California coast and Highway 89 heads up along the western shore of Lake Tahoe.) The California number is (916) 541-8314; in Nevada call 265-2436. 12 stores, including **Bass Shoes, Capezio Shoes, Cape Isle Knitters, Geoffrey Beene, Great Outdoor Clothing Outlet, Home Again, Oneida Silver Company, Pfaltzgraff, Sierra Shirts,** and **Van Heusen.**

Tahoe Factory Stores.
2501 S. Lake Tahoe Boulevard. (916) 544-8784. **Book Warehouse, L'eggs/Hanes/Bali, Leather Loft,** and **Prestige Fragrance & Cosmetics.**
London Fog Factory Store. 2019 Lake Tahoe Boulevard, South Lake Tahoe. 541-8869.
Mikasa Factory Store. 2011 Lake Tahoe Boulevard, South Lake Tahoe. 541-7412.
Oneida Factory Store. 2014 Lake Tahoe Boulevard, South Lake Tahoe. 541-0826.

Van Heusen Factory Store. 960 Emerald Bay Road, South Lake Tahoe. 541-3820.

Harvey's Shopping Arcade.

Within Harvey's Resort Hotel, Stateline, Nevada. **David Grace Collections,** clothing for men and women; **The Sport Shop**, clothing for winter and summer sports; and **Jewelry Factory Gallery.**

Shopping in Truckee

Tahoe-Truckee Factory Stores.

I-80 to 12047 Donner Pass Road. (916) 587-5726. **Bass Shoe, Dansk, Fragrance Outlet, Gorham, Home Again, Izod, L'eggs/Hanes/Bali, Swank, Van Heusen,** and **Villeroy & Boch.**

Getting Hitched

Washoe County Recorder's Office, corner South Virginia and Court Streets, P.O. Box 11130, Reno, NV 89520. 328-3275. Hours: 8 A.M. to midnight, daily.

Wedding Chapels in Reno, Sparks and Nearby
  Adventure Inn. 825-1087; (800) 937-1436.
  Candlelight Wedding Chapel. 786-5355.
  Chapel of the Bells. 323-1375; (800) 872-2933.
  Church of the Ponderosa. 831-0691.
  Cupid's Chapel of Love. 323-2930; (800) 582-4737.
  The Dream Maker. 831-6419; (800) 252-3732.
  Heart of Reno Chapel. 786-6882.
  Incline Village/Crystal Bay Cal-Neva Lodge. 832-4000.
  Lady of the Lake. 832-0505.
  Nugget Hotel Wedding Chapel. 356-3300 ext. 3480; (800) 648-1177.
  Park Wedding Chapel. 323-1770.
  Reno Hilton Wedding Chapel. 322-5353; (800) 255-1771.
  Reno Wedding Chapel. 323-5818; (800) 248-6933.
  Riverside Wedding Chapel/Little Church of the Sierras. 322-3474.
  Silver Bells Wedding Chapel. 322-0420; (800) 221-9336.
  Starlite Wedding Chapel. 786-4949.
  Unity Church of Reno. 747-2207.
  Wedding Bells Chapel. 329-0909.

Chapter 22

Four Fabulous Day Trips from Reno

Top of the Lake and the Olympic Mountain

Reno to Mount Rose, Incline Village, Crystal Bay, Tahoe City, and Squaw Valley. To get to the north and upper west shores of the lake, and across the top of Lake Tahoe to Squaw Valley, Truckee, and Donner Lake, follow I-395 south out of Reno and drive to the intersection with Highway 431 and 341, about 10 miles from downtown Reno. (If you turn left onto route 341, you will climb Geiger Grade into Virginia City; see the Virginia City drive for details on that must-see tour.)

In wintertime, be sure to check with the Highway Patrol or Transportation Department for road conditions.

Turn right onto Highway 431 toward the imposing face of the mountains. From here you have a 25-mile twist-and-turn climb up Mount Rose (the road reaches an altitude of 8,911 feet; Mount Rose itself continues to a summit elevation of 10,338 feet). **Galena Creek Park,** on the slopes of the mountain, includes picnic areas, hiking trails, and other facilities for summer and winter recreation. The park is run by the Washoe County Department of Parks & Recreation; call 849-2511 for information.

A bit farther on is the **Mount Rose/Slide Mountain** ski area. The area, two facilities which combined into a single resort several years ago, has the region's highest base elevation at 8,250 feet, which is a pretty good guarantor of dependable snow. There is a 1,450 foot vertical drop with 27 trails served by a half dozen lifts. Call 849-0704 for information.

Still farther into the mountain pass is the proposed location for a large new ski complex, the Galena Resort, which may open in coming years if it can get past challenges from environmentalists. At the highest point on the road is a turnoff to the left to **Mount Rose Campground.** The road begins a gradual descent, and about six miles later you will enter Incline Village at the northern end of Lake Tahoe.

At Incline Village you can continue across the top of the lake to **Crystal Bay** and around the west edge of the lake. Route 267 branches off to the right at Crystal Bay toward Truckee and Donner Lake; if you don't want to drive back over Mount Rose to Reno, take this route up to Truckee and pick up Route 80 east which will return you to Reno.

To go to **Squaw Valley,** instead of taking Route 267 continue on around the lake a bit to Tahoe City and pick up Highway 89 which will enter the Olympic Valley. After it leaves Squaw Valley, Route 89 will meet up with Interstate 80 just west of Truckee. From here you can head east back to Reno, or take a short jog west to **Donner Lake** and the **Donner Memorial State Park.**

A complete round trip from Reno to Incline Village and back should take about two hours. A trip from Reno over Mount Rose to Crystal Bay and Truckee before returning on Interstate 80 should take about the same two hours. The extended trip through the Olympic Valley should take under three hours.

Forewarned. Pay attention to weather forecasts in the winter and spring, especially if you must cross one of the mountain passes. Rain at the "lower" elevations of Lake Tahoe or Reno may well be heavy snow in the passes. Highway 431 and Route 207 are regularly shut down in the winter because of storms. And Route 89 on the west shore of the lake is closed so often that there are permanent barriers that can be swung across the road to stop traffic at Emerald Bay.

Much of Route 89 on the California side and Routes 207 and 431 in Nevada have no guardrails to block the spectacular view—and the tremendous drop to the rocks below.

Over the Mountains and Around the Lake

Reno to Stateline, South Lake Tahoe, and Emerald Bay. There are four routes to the South Shore from Reno.

Route 1. The longest and most scenic route begins with the same plan followed above, using Highway 431 from I-395. In Crystal Bay, turn right on Route 28 and follow the outlines of the lake, passing through Tahoe Vista, Carnelian Bay, and Tahoe City, where you will pick up Route 89. Continue on 89 to Homewood, Meeks Bay, Rubicon Bay, Emerald Bay, and Camp Richardson. In Tahoe Valley, you will meet up with Route 50 coming from California. Make a left and drive into South Lake Tahoe and the casinos of Stateline. This route should take about two and a half hours.

Route 2. A shorter, less scenic route follows the east shore of the lake. Take I-395 to Highway 431 and up and over Mount Rose. In Crystal Bay, turn left on Route 28 and follow the outlines of the lake to Incline Village toward Spooner Lake where you will meet up with Route 50. Continue on Route 50 south through the

Cave Rock Tunnel to Zephyr Cove and into Stateline. This route should take about two hours.

Route 3. The most direct route to the south shore follows I-395 about 30 miles to Carson City where it joins Route 50. About three miles later, Route 50 splits off to the right to climb Spooner Summit (elevation 7,140 feet) and then continues along the east shore of the lake through the Cave Rock Tunnel and Zephyr Cover to Stateline. This route should take about 90 minutes in good weather.

Route 4. Another direct route, but one that involves some mountain switchback driving, following the old path of the Pony Express, and one that may not be pleasing to all drivers (and passengers). It starts with I-395 out of Reno, continues past Carson City, and goes on 11 miles past the point where Route 50 branches off. Just past the tiny Douglas County Airport, look for the signs to the historic settlement

Heavenly ski area, Lake Tahoe

of Genoa and turn right toward the imposing wall of mountains. At Genoa, turn left and follow the base of the mountains until you come to Route 207 (Kingsbury Grade). Head west, up and over Daggett Pass (elevation 7,334 feet), and then descend into Stateline. This path should take a bit less than two hours.

Back in Time

Reno to Virginia City, Gold Hill, Carson City, and back to Reno. Follow I-395 south out of Reno and drive to the intersection with Highway 431 and 341, about 10 miles from downtown Reno. Turn left onto Route 341 and begin the slow but steady climb up Geiger Grade into Virginia City. When you finally make it up the hill you will suddenly find yourself in **Virginia City** itself; there is no mistaking where you are, either. Every western movie ever made included a Hollywood version of this place. After you've visited the wonders of VC, continue on Route 341 to the point where it splits: take the right fork, marked as Route 342, to see the ruins of Gold Hill and Silver City, two of the mining outposts of the time. The road will soon join up with Route 341 again, which will eventually come to a T at Route 50. Make a right turn, west.

Route 50 will come to another T, at Interstate 395. Head south for a short jog to explore **Carson City,** or head north for the rapid return to Reno.

On your way back to Reno, you may want to branch off of the interstate at Route 429 to visit the historic **Bowers Mansion,** constructed by one of the original discoverers of the Comstock Lode, Lemuel Sanford Bowers. Bowers' new wife spent what was at the time a fortune—$400,000—on building and furnishing the house in 1864. Her husband, though, did not live to enjoy the house much, dying of miner's lung disease in 1867.

The trip from Reno to Virginia City is about 45 minutes. To make the full tour from Reno to Virginia City, continuing on to Gold Hill and to I-395 at Carson City before returning to Reno, allow about two hours. Add extra time to visit Virginia City, Carson City, and the Bowers Mansion.

A Desert Mirage

Reno to Pyramid Lake. A spectacular sea in the desert, Pyramid Lake is unlike any body of water in the world. Named for the distinctive rock formation that rises from its waters, Pyramid Lake is the largest remnant of a giant inland sea that once covered more than 8,000 square miles. Ancient petroglyphs depicting Paiute Indian life line the hills surrounding the lake, and its Anahoe Island (closed to the public) is a sanctuary for beautiful pelicans.

The west shore of the lake is a straight shot up Route 445 from Reno, about 25 miles.

Chapter 23

Virginia City: A Side Trip Back in Time

A century ago, Virginia City went from desolation to the richest place on earth and then back to desolation in the course of a few decades.

Today it is a living ghost town, a museum in place, and one of our favorite places to visit and dream. There are few places on earth that, by their mere existence, speak so eloquently of their history.

As you stand on C Street in Virginia City and feel the mass of Mount Davidson over your shoulder, you may think that you are on solid ground, but in fact you are perched atop a near-hollow shell. Millions of tons of rock have been removed from beneath your feet, and the hills around you are honeycombed with 750 miles of tunnel.

Mark Twain, under his real name of Sam Clemens, worked for a while as a reporter for the *Territorial Enterprise*. Years later he wrote about the town:

> *Virginia was a busy city of streets and houses above ground. Under it was another busy city, down in the bowels of the earth, where a great population of men thronged in and out among an intricate maze of tunnels and drifts, flitting hither and thither under a winking sparkle of lights, and over their heads towered a vast web of interlocking timbers that held the walls of the gutted Comstock apart.*

The money-making engine for Virginia City was the fabled Comstock Lode, a two-and-a-half-mile deposit that paid out some $500 million in silver and $700 million in gold. About 20 million tons of ore were brought out of the 750 miles of workings.

Discovered in 1859, the Comstock Lode began a wild 20-year boom that helped bring Nevada into the Union in 1864 and build San Francisco. There were seven major mines, several of which can be seen from C Street.

At boom time, Virginia City was home to 40,000 people, 100 saloons,

Bright lights, big city. When Ben Cartwright sent "the boys" to town for supplies or adventure in the television series *Bonanza,* he was sending them over the mountain ranges into Virginia City. A re-creation of the Ponderosa Ranch can be found in Incline Village at the north end of Lake Tahoe.

Namesake. Virginia City got its name from one of the first miners, James Finney, nicknamed "Old Virginny" after the state of his birth. Returning from a revelry, he supposedly dropped and broke a bottle of booze. Instead of crying over spilt whiskey, he christened the tent city on the slopes of Mt. Davidson "Old Virginny Town" in his own honor.

50 dry goods stores, four banks, and five newspapers. The local payroll reached $500,000 a month.

By the 1880s, though, most of the riches had been extracted, with the profits taken to San Francisco, New York, or overseas. Virginia City began a rapid decline and probably would have completely disappeared were it not for the birth of the tourist industry in the second half of the 20th century.

According to one version of many versions of the discovery of the riches of hills and valleys south of Reno, miners Pat McLaughlin and Peter O'Reilly discovered a small quantity of gold-bearing rock at the head of Six-Mile Canyon in 1859. Henry Comstock, another prospector, made a loud but dubious claim that the men were trespassing on his property, and the lucky-then-unlucky miners settled the dispute by giving Comstock a neighboring piece of land. It was there that the gigantic Lode was first found, and its riches were named after him and not its discovers.

The Carson Valley Rest Stop

Here's a story you've heard repeated in this book time and again: the early history of the Carson Valley was as a rest stop. In this case, it was a place for many of the emigrants heading west to California during the Gold Rush to stop for provisions or to spend the winter before making the treacherous crossing of the Sierras.

Some of the would-be California gold-seekers explored a bit on the eastern side of the mountains. In July of 1849, Abner Blackburn and the members of a Mormon wagon train spent some time on the banks of the Carson River and Blackburn found a few specks of gold in his pan near the present-day town of Dayton, but it was not enough to make them stay.

In the coming few years there were small discoveries among wagon trains waiting for the snows to melt in the mountain passes. One group panned its way up a small stream that flowed into the Carson River; they optimistically named the waterway Gold Creek. On June 1, 1850, one of the men discovered a gold nugget at an isolated rock formation now known as Devil's Gate.

Over the coming decade, many small finds were made, including, according to the legend, a major discovery in Gold Canyon by brothers Allen and Hosea Grosh. Unfortunately, both brothers died—one from blood poisoning because of an accident and the other as the result of severe frostbite suffered on a crossing of the Sierras on a trip to California to raise money to open a mine.

This brings us, then, to McLaughlin and O'Reilly and their grabby neighbor Comstock. They began to mine the area, grinding the rock in search of gold and casting aside the black rock that got in the way.

Early gold miners had complained about the sticky blue-gray mud that fouled their picks, clothing, and shovels. It wasn't gold—in fact, some thought it was low-value lead.

McLaughlin, O'Reilly, and the other miners, who had been earning about $876 per ton of the gold-bearing ore stopped complaining when the mud was assayed and discovered to be silver ore, worth $2,000 to $3,000 per ton.

Almost Everything You Wanted to Know About Mining

Dan DeQuille, whose real name was William Wright, headed west from Ohio with the news of the silver discoveries in the Comstock Lode. Failing as a miner, he became a journalist and in 1862 joined the staff of the *Territorial Enterprise* in Virginia City. In that same year, the newspaper also hired Sam Clemens (later to gain fame as Mark Twain) for a brief stint. In 1875, Clemens persuaded Wright to publish his remembrances of the wild times in Virginia City. The book was called *The Big Bonanza* and it paints a vivid picture of the difficulties and rewards of the time.

As rich as the Comstock Lode was, the Hollywood myth of miners carving out huge chunks of gold or silver rarely happened. Instead, there were tiny flakes of precious metal embedded in quartz or other rocks. There was much hard work involved in extracting the wealth. The first test of the worth of a piece of ore was usually done on the spot. DeQuille described the process:

Insert peg A into slot B. Several years into the boom, a German engineer named Philip Deidesheimer invented the square-set method of timbering that supported the crumbling rock and enabled shafts to be dug to depths of more than 3,000 feet.

The timbering of the mine had another effect: the near denuding of the forests for miles around. In fact, the search for more wood to timber the mines of Virginia City and Gold Hill extended over the Sierra Nevada. One of the more ambitious engineering schemes of the day took place in what is now called Incline Village, at the north end of Lake Tahoe. There a lumber company built a primitive tramway that lifted logs up the side of a mountain to a flume where they were tumbled back down to waiting wagons that transported them to Virginia City.

In gold-bearing quartz small specks of gold were often to be seen with the naked eye or aided by a small magnifying glass…If gold could be seen at all, with either naked eye or the glass, it was considered a good sign. In order to test the specimen further, it was then either beaten to a powder in a mortar or ground as fine as flour on a large flat stone, using a smaller stone for a muller. This pulverized ore was then placed in a "horn," a little canoe-shaped vessel made of the split horn of an ox, when it was carefully washed out, much as auriferous gravel is washed in a pan. The gold, in case the ore experimented upon contained that metal, was found lying in a yellow streak in the bottom of the horn, generally small particles of gold dust, almost as fine as flour.

The results of the test in the horn were generally enough to tell the miner whether to load up a larger sample and bring it into town to an assayer's office. There a determination would be made of the value of the ore by the ton.

If a specimen of ore was supposed to contain silver, it was pulverized in the same way as gold-bearing quartz, then was placed in the horn, and the lighter matter it contained washed out.…The heavy residuum was then washed from the horn into a matrass (a flask of annealed glass, with a narrow neck and a broad bottom). Nitric acid was then poured into the matrass until the matter to be tested was covered, then the flask was suspended over the flame of a candle or lamp and boiled until the fumes escaping (which are for a time red) came off white.

When the contents of the matrass had been allowed to cool and settle, the liquid portion was poured off into a vial of clear, thin glass, called a test-tube. A few drops of a strong solution of common salt was now poured into the test-tube. If the ore…contained silver, the contents of the test-tube would at once assume a milky hue.

Anyone who has worked in a darkroom has worked with the same basic set of chemicals, by the way. What the test produced was a silver salt, which is the basis of photographic film and paper. In fact, some miners would take the test tube out into the sun for a few minutes and observe the effect of strong light on the solution: if there was silver in the salt solution, the liquid would turn purplish-black.

Civic sites. The former red-light district was located on D Street, just below the Silver Dollar Hotel on D Street between Union and Sutton street. C Street has always been the commercial center, while B Street in "upper town" held many of the ornate mansions of the proprietors, a stretch called "Millionaire's Row."

Getting to Virginia City

I-395 South ends about 10 miles south of Reno and becomes a two-lane highway; continue until you come to a traffic light at the intersection of two of the most interesting roads most drivers will ever experience: Highway 341 and 431. Head left to Virginia City on 341 or right to Lake Tahoe.

Virginia City sits at 6,200 feet; Route 341 follows the Geiger Grade, which twists back and forth for 13 miles to its highest point of 6,799 feet before descending slightly as you reach the town. The trip is a total of 23 miles from Reno.

As you drive up the Geiger Grade, you will be assaulted by sign after sign proclaiming your approach to something called the "Suicide Table" at the Delta Saloon. It sounds a lot more sinister than it really is: the Suicide Table is an 1860 faro table that apparently was the source of lost fortunes for three of its owners, each of whom killed himself.

When you reach the town itself, find a parking space—a lot easier in the winter than the summer, when you may have to use an outlying lot—and walk to C Street. One good place to start is at the privately run **Visitor Center,** which in addition to selling knickknacks also has a continuous showing of an interesting video about Virginia City made a few years back as a promotional effort.

Virginia City: History Underfoot

Stop for a moment and absorb the history that surrounds you. The old buildings with their wooden walkways on C Street mostly date from about 1875, the year when fire nearly wiped out the town, destroying more than 2,000 structures. After the Great Fire, the entire town was rebuilt within six months, so strong was the faith that the underground riches would continue forever. Of course, this didn't happen,

Traffic report. In winter and especially the uncertain spring, pay attention to the altitudes listed in weather forecasts. It may be raining in Reno but sleeting or snowing in Virginia City.

We strongly recommend you come in from the Reno side of Highway 341, climbing the Geiger Grade; it is much more exciting and interesting than the approach from Carson City.

In the Reno area, tune your AM radio to 530 or 1610 to monitor road condition reports.

Dying to get in. Just below town is the Virginia City Cemetery. According to legend there were 88 violent deaths before someone spoiled it all by dying of natural causes.

Ink in his veins. William Wright joined the *Territorial Enterprise* in 1862 and was its leading writer until it shut down in 1893. His friend Mark Twain brought him back east in 1875 to write *The Big Bonanza,* but he returned after the manuscript was completed.

but there was just enough activity in the mines to keep the town alive.

In 1875, 30,000 people lived in town. The Fourth Ward School, built in 1876 and still standing, was one of the first commercial buildings with indoor plumbing west of the Mississippi. The six-story International Hotel had the west's first elevator, which they called a "rising room."

As befits a wild place with a lot of money, Virginia City quickly became home to celebrities, Shakespearean plays, opium dens, newspapers, competing fire companies, police precincts, and a red-light distinct.

The Old Courthouse is still open and used for government offices. Take a close look at the statue of Justice. What's wrong with the picture? Justice is not blindfolded, and the scales are in balance. It could be sloppy work; then again, it may be a message from the past.

The Combination Mine was the deepest mine in the region, going down 3,262 feet—half the way to sea level. These deep mines did suffer from a significant problem, that of flooding from underground springs. To make things even more difficult, the water was often hot and sulphurous. Mine owners were forced to install huge pumps like the Cornish pump at the Union Mine, which had a 45-foot flywheel and a pump rod that extended 2,500 feet down the shaft and could lift more than 1 million gallons of water to the surface each day.

The grandest scheme for removing the water from the mines, though, was that of businessman Adolph Sutro who came from Prussia in 1850 in search of wealth in California. He amassed his first fortune in retail and real-estate ventures in San Francisco, but he was drawn to Virginia City in 1860. He ran a successful reduction mill at Dayton.

Sutro saw the problems of ventilation and removal of water from the deep mines and came up with the idea of a deep tunnel that would run from three miles east of Dayton near the Carson River under the base of the mountains to link up with the mines of Virginia City. Mine operators would only have to drain their operations to the Sutro Tunnel and not to the surface. He expanded his concept to include the use of the tunnel as an emergency evacuation route for miners and as an underground transportation system that would bring the ore from the various mines to mills at the mouth of the tunnel.

It took more than eight years to secure all of the various permits and permissions, as well as financing, for the project. He even had to obtain a special act of Congress, the Sutro Tunnel Act of 1866, which granted him the land and the right to charge royalties to companies using the tunnel. Investors came from as far away as England and Germany.

Construction of the 3.8-mile tunnel began on October 19, 1869; it was July 8, 1878, when the tunnel connected with the Savage Mine at the 1,640 foot level. However, by the time the tunnel was completed, most of the major mines had gone far deeper than that. The tunnel did serve its original purpose as a means of getting some of the water out of the tunnels, but little more. Sutro eventually returned to California where he made more money in real estate and even served a term as mayor, from 1895 to 1897.

You can visit a portion of the **Ponderosa Mine** by descending an antique elevator from the back of the Ponderosa Saloon on C Street. A half-hour tour goes a few hundred feet into parts of the Belcher and Best works. In the summer, the **Chollar Mine** on D Street is also open for tours.

The **Ponderosa Saloon,** established in 1873, has some of its walls lined with old flume boards from the Virginia and Gold Hill Water Company. Iron pipes brought water from the High Sierras down across the Washoe Valley and up to a reservoir five miles from town. From there, wooden flumes brought water to Virginia City. The original system was used until 1957.

The front window of the **Red Garter** saloon celebrates the famous gift made by "Barbara," one of the most sought-after ladies of the night, to her new husband.

The inscription reads, "To Judge Orville Hardison from his loving wife Barbara on the occasion of her retirement and our marriage, July 23, 1893." The gift came from Barbara's personal collection of business tools: a .41-caliber ivory-handled Colt Derringer, a bone-handled dagger, and her red garter.

We suspect you will be unable to resist the insistent come-ons for the Suicide Table at the **Delta Saloon.** While you are there, check out the old nickelodeon at the back of the saloon, which features "Grandpa's Pin-Up Girls in 3D." The Delta also includes a great collection of old coin-operated devices including a gypsy fortune teller and an Electric Traveling Crane that can scoop up candy and trinkets.

The Castle on B Street is a local must-see, a snapshot of how the world came to Virginia City when it was at its peak. Built in 1868 for

> **Hands off.** Children can enter into the casinos and saloons of Virginia City, but as in other parts of Nevada they must stay away from gaming devices.

> **Low finance.** In 1869, John Mackay and James Fair bought an interest in the failing Hale and Norcross mines. Joined by James Flood and William O'Brien, a pair of San Francisco saloonkeepers turned stockbrokers, they bought the barren Consolidated Virginia Mine in 1872 for about $50,000.
>
> They sunk an even deeper shaft and eventually struck the "Big Bonanza" 1,167 feet down. That one lode brought out $135 million in ore; in today's money that is worth more than $2 billion.
>
> Mackay went on to lay the first Trans-Atlantic and Pacific telegraphic cable for a competitive company to Western Union. Fair became a U.S. Senator from the new state of Nevada. O'Brien and Flood spent their money.

Robert Graves, the superintendent of the Empire Mine, the 16-room mansion was furnished with the best money could buy. Furnishings include a 600-year-old Heidelberg sideboard, crystal chandeliers from Czechoslovakia, and elegant wallpaper from France. It is even more amazing when you consider that virtually everything in The Castle was sent by boat from Europe around the Horn to San Francisco, then overland through the Sierra Nevadas and into Virginia City. The Castle is open from May to November.

The **Territorial Enterprise Museum** on C Street commemorates the famous newspaper of the same name, as well as some of its most famous employees including Sam Clemens (Mark Twain) and Dan DeQuille.

The **Fourth Ward School,** which dates to 1876, was used for students until 1936. After sitting dormant for many years, it was restored by the Nevada State Museum and includes a fascinating exhibit about the history of the Comstock, including models of the mines and their works. The museum, at the end of C Street on the way out of town toward Gold Hill, is open from May to November.

For a decidedly offbeat view of old Virginia City, you might want to check out the **Red Light Museum** on C Street. (The sign out front warns that the exhibit is not for the "faint of heart.") We didn't see anyone being carried out on stretchers, but we did see an exhibit not often seen in museums: opium pipes and other drug paraphernalia, slightly risqué (by today's standards) French postcards, and leftovers from the local brothels were among the items on display.

The **Virginia and Truckee Railroad,** was built to serve the needs of the mines in 1869. The first track linked Virginia City to Carson City; in 1872, the line was connected to Reno, 30 miles north, directly linking Virginia City to the transcontinental line from the east to San Francisco on the West Coast.

Citizen Hearst. George Hearst, the father of newspaper magnate William Randolph Hearst, started the family fortune as a stockbroker in Virginia City. He claimed that his fortune was built entirely on commissions from sale of stock and that he never had any direct involvement in Comstock shares.

By 1938, traffic had diminished so much that the link to the state capital was discontinued, and in 1950 the last train was run to Reno. Parts of the line were rebuilt and restored in 1976 for the tourist trade and the railroad takes visitors on an interesting circuit through the mining areas in the summer months, pulled by a real steam engine.

In 1952, the celebrated *Territorial Enterprise* newspaper was purchased by former New York society columnist Lucius Beebe and his associate Charles Clegg. They came to town in great Eastern style, running the paper until 1961. Among the changes they brought to Virginia City were their ornately decorated railroad cars.

And now we come to one of the stranger elements of today's Virginia City: the **International Camel Races.**

It all began with the little-known fact that camels were used in some parts of the Wild West as pack animals; there was even a U.S. Army Camel Corps. They were brought to the Comstock to carry salt and general supplies in the early, disorganized days of mining. Once the major mines were functioning and the Virginia & Truckee Railroad was the main freight carrier the camels—not known as particularly affectionate pets—were turned loose in the hills and eventually disappeared.

In the 1950s, though, in the great tradition of Mark Twain, Dan DeQuille and other tongue-in-cheek writers for the paper, the *Territorial Enterprise* published a totally fabricated account of the result of a great camel race. In 1960, a race was held for real in a challenge that reached to San Francisco, with movie director John Huston winning the first race on a camel borrowed from the San Francisco Zoo. Quite logically, Ostrich Races were added in 1962.

Traditionally, the Camel Races are held on the weekend after Labor Day in Virginia City in an arena east of F Street, and in mid-May in Alice Springs, Australia, sister city to Virginia City.

Surrounding Towns

As you drive out of Virginia City toward Carson City you will immediately come to Gold Hill, site of other major discoveries. There are remains of former mines on the left and right as you traverse the switchbacks.

Gold Hill, just outside of Virginia City, was the actual location where the Comstock Lode was first found. By 1865, just six years after the first strike, Gold Hill had three foundries, two banks, two newspapers, and several thousand residents. The mines, though, petered out in the 1870s, and Gold Hill became a ghost town in the first half of the 20th century. Since then there have been sporadic attempts to bring out ore using modern methods, the most recent ending in 1983.

Dayton, at the location where the Gold Canyon empties into the Carson River, was a rest stop for travelers on their way to California. A permanent settlement and a tent trading post were established about 1851, just after Genoa was founded, for what was then called Chinatown because of the Chinese who populated the area left behind by railroad projects. After the gold discoveries on the other side of the range, the community was renamed as Dayton and with a population of about 2,500 was considered as a site for the state capital, which ended up a few miles west in Carson City. The town had great hopes when the Sutro Tunnel was being planned and constructed, but the boom never came.

Accommodations in the Virginia City Area

Remember: you're looking for historical ambiance and realism, right? You are not going to find the opulence of a Caesars Palace or the big-city hotel amenities of a Reno Hilton here in the hills. You will, though, find old-time bed-and-breakfasts, inns, and an antique hotel or two. (If you must have more modern facilities, continue on down the hill to Carson City.)

For general information about Virginia City, call 847-0311.

Chollar Mansion. A bed-and-breakfast within a former mansion and mine office built in 1861. The hotel includes rooms decorated with Victorian-era furnishings, an arched vault that once stored millions of dollars worth of silver and gold bullion, and the paymaster's booth. Rooms range from about $65 to $100 for a double. 565 South D Street, Virginia City. 847-9777.

Edith Palmer's Country Inn. A country home, built in 1862 by a prosperous wine merchant, now operating as a bed-and-breakfast. Five guest rooms are available, with double room rates from about $60 to $75. South B Street, Virginia City. 847-0707.

Gold Hill Hotel and Crown Point Restaurant. Nevada's oldest operating hotel, this a Victorian country inn built in 1859, less than a mile down the canyon from Virginia City in Gold Hill. There are 14 refurbished guest rooms, four with private fireplaces; a separate building offers three kitchen suites. The hotel's Great Room features a massive open hearth stone fireplace. Room rates range from about $40 to $150. Main Street, Gold Hill. 847-0111.

House on the Hill. A bed-and-breakfast overlooking the Comstock Mine and Gold Canyon. Three suites are available. Room rates range from about $45 to $95. Sky Lane, Gold Hill. 847-0193.

Silver Dollar Hotel. A Victorian relic with 14-foot ceilings. A Honeymoon Suite is available. Downstairs is the Silver Dollar Pub with a deck overlooking Silver Dollar Mountain. 11 North C. Street, Virginia City. 847-9051.

Comstock Lodge. A motel-like lodge just outside of downtown, with room rates of about $50 to $80 for a double. South C Street, Virginia City. 847-0233.

Virginia City Motel. Open year round. Room rates range from about $33 to $50. 675 C Street, Virginia City. 847-0277.

The RV Park. A 50-spot park designed to look like an old mining camp. Open year-round. Carson & F Streets, Virginia City. 847-0999.

Chapter 24

Carson City: A Capital Before There Was a State

Like the state for which it serves as capital, Carson City is a bit unusual. To begin with, it is one of the smallest capitals in the nation, with just 40,000 or so residents.

The site of Carson City lies in the Eagle Valley on the Overland Trail, over which stages and the Pony Express crossed the Sierras on the south side of Lake Tahoe to Sacramento, California. Once again, here is the story of a city—a state capital, even—that grew from a rest stop.

The commercial founder of Carson City was Abraham Curry, a businessman from Ithaca, New York, who arrived in Eagle Valley in 1858, just a year before the discovery of the Comstock Lode. Curry sought his riches as a merchant, buying an existing ranch and trading post to serve both the emigrants heading to California and, as it turned out, gold-seekers coming the other direction to the Comstock.

Though the idea of Nevada as a state was still a rather remote dream, Curry immediately began to develop the site as a future capital, even calling the "downtown" of his hardscrabble sand empire Capitol Square. He named the developing town Carson City after the famed guide Kit Carson, who was still alive at the time.

In addition to his skill as a merchant, Curry proved to be an able politician. He promoted his town site at every opportunity and also struck an alliance with the territorial governor, James Nye, another refugee from New York. The first territorial government was centered in Carson City, and in 1864, when statehood was granted, it became the capital.

The stone **Capitol**, first erected in 1871 and expanded in 1915, is distinctive for its huge log rafters within. It is set in a four-block, elm-shaded park—Abraham Curry's Capitol Square. The **Nevada State Museum** is housed in the old Carson City Mint Building, which operated from 1870 to 1893 and produced nearly 60 million coins, including the famous Carson City silver dollar. Fascinating exhibits range from a re-creation of an underground mine, old mint equipment, and a Nevada ghost town. The Environmental Gallery teaches about the animal and plant life of the state, from dinosaurs to today; the Earth Science Gallery explains the complex geology that formed not only the gold and silver deposits of Nevada but also the dramatic mountain ranges and deserts. Also on display is an impressive collection of artifacts of ancient Native American cultures. The museum is located at 600 N. Carson Street and is open every day. Call 885-4810 for hours and rates.

> **Map your course.** Stop at the cartographic mother lode in the State Department of Transportation at 1263 S. Stewart (Room 206) where you can purchase a full range of official maps of almost every description. Call 885-3449 for hours and information.

Another essential stop is the **State Capitol** on Carson Street between Second and Musser streets. The restored structure includes an amazing museum of official and unofficial state items.

Railroad buffs and children of all ages are not going to want to miss the **Nevada State Railroad Museum** which mostly commemorates the Virginia & Truckee Railroad, which ran from Carson City to Virginia City during the height of the mining boom. There are engines, passenger cars, and a display of model railroad cars that is definitely a cut above the old Lionel set you had as a kid. In the summer season, you can take a short ride around the museum property on an old engine. The museum is located south of Carson City on I-395 at Fairview Drive and is open weekends and a few days during the week. Call 687-6953 for hours and rates.

Yes, There Are Casinos

The **Nugget** is definitely a casino for the hardcore. How else to describe a place that was nearly packed with locals at noon on a drizzly Friday? At the time of our visit, The Nugget offered an eminently forgettable buffet with several varieties of indeterminate meat, poultry, and fish-like substances, tired salads, and scary Jell-O. 507 N. Carson Street. A newer casino is **Carson Station** farther south at 900 S. Carson Street. 883-0900.

Chapter 25

Lake Tahoe: Mountain Shangri-la

A Heavenly Emerald

As a travel writer and journalist, I have been to many spectacular places around the world, but on a stressful day at the keyboard, my mind regularly drifts back to a view of Lake Tahoe from Emerald Bay, with the Heavenly ski area towering over the casinos of Stateline.

Lake Tahoe is, without argument, one of the most breathtaking places on earth, and its natural beauty is complemented—for the most part— by resorts and developments to suit most tastes.

The lake itself covers the Nevada/California border, 58 miles southwest of Reno and 98 miles northeast of Sacramento. At 12 miles wide and 22 miles long, it is the largest alpine lake, and the third deepest lake in North America with an average depth of 989 feet and 1,645 feet at its deepest. Tahoe has a surface area of about 192 square miles, with a circumference around the lake of 72 miles.

The surface of Lake Tahoe is more than a mile above sea level, at 6,227 feet. In the summer, the top 12 feet of the lake warm to as much as 68 degrees. In winter months, and in the lower depths of the lake, the temperature remains at a constant—and life-threatening—39 degrees.

The highest peak rising directly from the shoreline is Mt. Tallac at 9,735 feet. The highest point in the basin is Freel Peak at 10,881 feet.

Like No Other Nevada Casinos

If you are going to Nevada to gamble, there is not a lot of difference between the major resorts of Stateline, Reno, or Las Vegas. They all have slot machines and 21 tables and myriad other ways to lose your money. The major resorts all offer lavish stage shows and headliner acts—admittedly, the headlines are larger in Las Vegas, but that doesn't necessarily mean the shows have more to offer you. The best of the restaurants in

Stateline, Reno, and Las Vegas are all satisfying.

But what you do get in Lake Tahoe that you get nowhere else is the combination of the excitement of the casinos and all they offer, and the tremendous range of outdoor activities available in the Tahoe Basin. Here are just a few: downhill skiing, cross-country skiing, ice skating, sleigh rides, sledding, dogsled rides, snowmobiling, horseback riding, and indoor and heated outdoor pool swimming in the winter; and waterskiing, lake and pool swimming, hiking, camping, horseback riding, ballooning, boating, and cruises in the summer, spring, and fall.

The Econoguide to the Best of Lake Tahoe

Hotel/Casinos
Bill's Casino
Caesars Palace
Harrah's
Harvey's

Buffets
Harrah's
Caesar's Palace

Places to Visit
Emerald Bay
Heavenly Tram
Lake Tahoe
Virginia City

Getting to Lake Tahoe from Reno

Lake Tahoe is an easy drive from Reno, less than an hour to Crystal Bay and about 90 minutes to South Lake Tahoe. *See the section on Driving Trips from Reno for guided tours from Reno to North and South Tahoe.*

If you have the time, make the great circle tour around the lake, using Routes 50 and 28 on the east shore and Route 89 on the west shore, for a round trip of about two hours.

Several bus and shuttle companies offer scheduled and on-demand service from Reno to South Lake Tahoe. One is **Tahoe Casino Express,** which has 14 departures in each direction, charging $15 per person.

Mileage to South Lake Tahoe

Reno 59   Sacramento 100   San Francisco 198

Lake Tahoe Weather

	High	**Low**			**High**	**Low**
Jan	**36**	**16**		Feb	**39**	**18**
Mar	**44**	**21**		Apr	**50**	**26**
May	**60**	**32**		Jun	**69**	**37**
Jul	**79**	**43**		Aug	**80**	**42**
Sep	**70**	**37**		Oct	**51**	**31**
Nov	**47**	**24**		Dec	**40**	**20**

Air Travel

More than 2 million passengers pass through the Reno International Airport each year, and in winter months about 25 percent of all travelers are destined for Lake Tahoe.

Reno Air offers non-stop jet service from the West Coast to Reno. Alpha Air serves the small Lake Tahoe Airport, seven miles from Heavenly with flights from California. Plans called for expansion of Southern California service from John Wayne Airport in Orange County. American Eagle offers service from San Francisco and other connections to Lake Tahoe.

Around the Lake

The Lake Tahoe Basin was a gathering place for three bands of Washoe Indians. Kit Carson and John Frémont "discovered" the lake in 1844.

The area now known as **Incline Village** in the northeast corner of Lake Tahoe near Crystal Bay was wilderness until the mid-1800s when loggers began using some of its timber to shore up the rich silver mines of Virginia City some 20 miles away on the other side of the easternmost mountain range.

On the mountain at Incline Village, behind the Ponderosa Ranch, lie the remnants of the Great Incline of the Sierra Nevada. Completed in 1880, this 4000-foot-long lift was constructed by the Sierra Nevada Wood and Lumber Company. A steam-powered cable railway carried cordwood and lumber 1,800 feet up. An engine on the summit pulled canted cars up a double track using 8,000 feet of wire cable. At the height of the enterprise, 300 cords of wood a day were moved from the mill at what is now Mill Creek.

Over and under. The U.S. Bureau of Reclamation controls the top 6.1 feet of the lake as a reservoir. The water is claimed to be 99.9 percent pure. The lake contains an estimated 39.75 trillion gallons of water, enough to cover the entire state of California to a depth of 14 inches.

Rocky row. Sand Harbor Beach State Recreational Area, about five miles south of Incline Village, offers a small but pretty sand beach on an inlet of Lake Tahoe. Rocks are piled on top of each other reaching out into the lake like little jetties. The beach sits at the base of an almost sheer cliff mountainside. In summer, there is an entrance fee of $2; the charge to launch a boat is $5.

Namesake. Crystal Bay was not named after the clear waters of Lake Tahoe, but rather after lumberman George Iweis Crystal who owned much of the area in the 1860s.

At the top of the mountain, the wood was loaded into a V-flume and tumbled down to the Washoe Valley where it was loaded onto wagons for use in the mines of the Comstock.

A small settlement was established in 1884, but the area did not gain much attention until 1927 when the first casino was built in Crystal Bay.

The **Cal-Neva Lodge** at Crystal Bay was famous for its swimming pool which sat atop the state border, allowing swimmers to start in California and end up in Nevada. Early guests included mobster Pretty Boy Floyd. The hotel was owned by singer Frank Sinatra during the 1960s and was one of the gathering places for the "Rat Pack" Hollywood crowd.

The development of the area for condominiums and homes also began in the 1960s, and included a spectacular 18-hole championship golf course designed by Robert Trent Jones Sr. and the development of a skiing area called Ski Incline. The ski area, greatly expanded, is now called Diamond Peak.Other major construction included what is now the Hyatt Regency Lake Tahoe Resort and Casino, a second golf course, beach facilities, and the Lakeside Tennis Resort.

Incline Village and Crystal Bay Area

Incline Village/Crystal Bay Visitors and Convention Bureau Lodging Information. (800) 468-2463; [(800) GO-TAHOE].

Reno/Sparks Visitor's Authority. (800) 752-1177.

Cal-Neva Lodge. Crystal Bay. 832-4000.

Hyatt Regency Lake Tahoe Resort & Casino. Country Club Drive and Lakeshore Drive, Incline Village. 832-1234.

Inn at Incline. 1003 Tahoe Boulevard, Incline Village. 831-1052.

Tahoe Biltmore Lodge & Casino. A big old-style hotel, with a group of small wooden motel units along the lake. Crystal Bay. 831-0660.

The **Ponderosa Ranch,** the mythical setting of the Cartwright family made famous in the *Bonanza* television series, has been brought to life in Incline Village in a mix of original artifacts from the show and re-creations in a historic setting along the shores of Lake Tahoe at an elevation of 6,350 feet.

The main attraction is the Cartwright home, the actual set used to film interior scenes with Ben Cartwright and his three sons, Hoss, Little Joe, and Adam. Visitors are taken on a guided tour, which includes antique furnishings and Hop Sing's kitchen, where the table is all set for Ben and his boys.

Just outside the home is a western theme park, including a general store, gambling hall, old-time photo parlor, and numerous shops. Other attractions include a shooting gallery, antique autos, one of the country's largest collections of farm and ranch equipment, a western memorabilia museum, and an 1870 church where old-fashioned weddings are celebrated. Children can visit a petting farm, gold panning slough, and Hoss' Mystery Mine.

Each morning from Memorial Day to Labor Day, visitors are invited to take the Haywagon Breakfast Ride, a tour that climbs through a rich pine forest to a scenic point high above Lake Tahoe. There an all-you-can-eat breakfast of scrambled eggs, sausage, pancakes, juice, and coffee is provided.

More than 300,000 people annually visit the Ponderosa Ranch. In 1994, the admission rate for adults was $8.50, and the rate was $5.50 for children ages 5 to 11. The Haywagon Breakfast Ride is an additional $2 per person. Hours are 9:30 A.M. until 5 P.M. daily from May to October.

Reruns. The original *Bonanza* series ran for 13 years on network television in the United States and has been seen in 85 other countries. It was the first major series to be regularly broadcast in color, making use of the surrounding area for many of its settings.

Ready when you are, C.B. Among the films made in and around Lake Tahoe are *Indian Love Call*, starring Jeannette McDonald, *The Godfather*, and *The Bodyguard*.

Tahoe North Visitors and Convention Bureau. Box 5578, Tahoe City, CA 95730. (916) 583-3494; (800) 824-6348.

Kings Beach, across the border into California, sits at the absolute "top" of the lake, and affords a spectacular view down its length. On a clear day—and there are many—you will be able to see the Heavenly ski resort 22 miles away, towering over the casinos of Stateline. Kings Beach, which includes some lovely beaches and marinas for boating and other water sports, was self-named by Joe King, a gambler who supposedly won the property in a poker game in 1925.

The next settlement westward around the lake is **Tahoe Vista,** which overlooks Agate Bay. It was named after a spectacular hotel of the early 1900s, which sat up on a hill overlooking the lake.

Carnelian Bay takes its name from the reddish semi-precious stones called Carnelian which were found on its beach by the Whitney Survey party in 1860s. An early establishment there was Dr. Bourne's health resort.

Tahoe City was established as a lumbering camp and as a port for freight traffic on the lake. Today it sits at the northern end of man's intrusion on the beauty of the lake; from Tahoe City south to Camp Richardson near South Lake Tahoe there is little in the way of development save a few cottages here and there and the Alpine Meadows and Ski Homewood ski areas.

In the summer, special events at Incline Village include the **Shakespeare at Sand Harbor** festival, with plays presented from the end of July through August. Call (800) 468-2463 for information.

Hotels and Casinos in South Lake Tahoe

The state border runs more or less down the middle of Lake Tahoe, dividing Nevada from California and demarking the line between two rather different cultures.

The Nevada villages of Crystal Bay, Incline Village, and Stateline each feature small-scale versions of Reno or Las Vegas casino resorts, with all that entails: gambling, glitzy shows, buffets, and fine dining. The largest collection of casinos can be found in Stateline, along both sides of a half-mile stretch of Highway 50. The very last casinos sit directly on the borderline.

On the other side of the border, the hotels in California must find different lures. They generally go for high luxury or low price; either way, they do not have casinos to subsidize the room rates.

Three miles into California on Route 50, you'll find a tiny amusement park called the Magic Carpet Golf and Arcade on the lake side of the road. Rides include bumper cars, a small ferris wheel, and a slide. The park is closed during the winter.

Tahoe resorts are generally more expensive than their equivalents in Reno and some Las Vegas resorts, partly because of the additional appeal of winter and summer recreation.

High-season in Lake Tahoe is generally mid-June to Labor Day and into September. Low-season is April and May, and November into early December. New Year's and Christmas are

> **Someone has to do it.** Yes, that really is a U.S. Coast Guard station just north of Tahoe City. Because of its size and the fact that it is an interstate navigable waterway, it falls under the supervision of the federal Coast Guard in what must be one of the most desirable assignments in the service.

> **Econoguide alert.** You'll find most of the major fast-food chains on the California side, along with a large assortment of factory outlets and discount stores. You will also find cheaper ski rental and equipment stores past the entrance to the Heavenly resort, toward California.

busy times. The "shoulder" or middle season is February and March, when ski and winter sports fans sell-out the hotel on weekends.

Harvey's Lake Tahoe. The attractive lobby is a floor away from the casino, and nicely insulated; it is possible to forget that there is a world of blinking lights, bouncing coins, and shuffling cards.

Rest assured, though, that there is a full-featured casino at Harvey's including the Land of the Giants, five seven-foot-tall slot machines against the wall between the California Bar and Sage Room. Harvey's has a Vegas-sized casino, at 88,000 square feet, offering 2,300 slot machines, 121 table games including blackjack, red dog, fast action hold'em, poker, pai gow, baccarat, craps, and roulette plus a race and sports book.

The 740 rooms and suites are among the nicest in Lake Tahoe. The prime Lake Suites include a Jacuzzi, private lakeview balcony, two color TVs, and a marble bath and dressing area. Hotel facilities include a heated outdoor swimming pool, health club, wedding chapel, and four tennis courts.

Downstairs in an arcade is the Orbitron, an Ultra Gravity Simulator that propels riders through a fighter jet ride, re-creating all of the G-force sensations of flight without ever leaving the ground.

Tickets for the four-minute trip are about $3.50 and are restricted to those taller than 42 inches and over the age of seven. Pregnant women and those with health problems are advised not to take the journey.

Just slightly less adventuresome are arcade challenges like the four-seat Namco Endurance Championship Race, which permits head-to-head motorcycle racing. Nearby is a Galaxy Force machine, a moving fighter-pilot simulator. At the rear of the arcade is a shooting gallery with a room full of animated Smurf-like creatures; the targets may be a bit too realistic for the tastes of some parents.

More traditional amusements include a wide variety of video games and a skee-ball bowling alley.

Restaurants at Harveys include the **Seafood Grotto,** a somewhat ordinary room with open windows toward the slot machines. Lunch sandwiches and salads range from $7 to $11 and include the Clipper Salad

---

Orbitron advice. Professional thrill-riders recommend you keep your eyes straight ahead on the screen and avoid looking from side to side; there is also an emergency stop button at each seat.

More State and National Parks.

Death Valley National Monument.
Death Valley, CA 92328.
(916) 786-2331.

Great Basin National Park.
Baker, NV 89311.
234-7331.

Humboldt National Forest.
976 Mountain City Highway, Elko, NV 89801.
738-5171.

(greens with shrimp, crabmeat, avocado, asparagus, cucumber, tomato, and onion).

Dinner entrees range from about $13 to $25 and include a Pacific clambake for two (lobster, prawns, chicken, corn on the cob, and potatoes steamed with wine and herbs), broiled New York steak teriyaki, and bouillabaisse Marseilles.

At **Llewellyn's,** a stunning rooftop restaurant with wraparound windows, you'll find dishes priced from about $16 to $25 such as mesquite broiled quails with creamy polenta and wild rice; salmon involtini, stuffed with asparagus, leeks, and carrots wrapped in phylo dough with sun-dried tomato butter; and lamb Gilroy, in caramelized garlic with couscous and ratatouille.

Llewellyn's is open for lunch from Wednesday through Saturday from 11:30 A.M. to 2:30 P.M., and for dinner daily. A champagne brunch is offered Sunday from 10 A.M. to 2 P.M. for about $17.

El Vaquero is a pleasant den-like setting decorated in Santa Fe reds and blacks; don't back into the cacti in the dark. Specialties include enchiladas Acapulco (flour tortillas filled with your choice of shrimp or crabmeat or both, covered with ranchero sauce and covered with melted cheeses and sour cream), for about $12. For lunch, offerings include sautéed red snapper topped with a tomatillo sauce and served with black beans, for about $8. Open for dinner every night, and for lunch from Wednesday to Sunday. El Vaquero also offers karaoke parties in the lounge Friday and Saturday nights at 10 P.M.

The Carriage House is an attractive 24-hour coffee shop that has a variety of standard offerings, plus a special breakfast and lunch on-the-run deal for skiers and travelers: for about $8, you get an egg or pancake breakfast and leave the restaurant with a box lunch of fried chicken or ham and cheese sandwich, with fresh fruit, cookie, and granola bar.

The **Garden Buffet** offers a Friday night seafood dinner, served from 4 P.M. to 10 P.M. for about $16. Included are two broiled lobster tails, mussels with clam sauce, seafood Newburg, and champagne. The Saturday Brunch, offered from 7 A.M. to 2 P.M., includes scrambled eggs, top round, and baked ham.

The **Sage Room** steak house, open for dinner from 6 P.M., features entrees from about $16 to $22, including peppercorn steak filet mignon with sauce béarnaise; roast duckling "bigarrade" (Long Island duckling topped with an orange sauce and flambéed with Grand Marnier).

Harvey's **Peak Lounge,** a small room alongside Llewellyns, offers light fare including chilled prawns or crab, minted split pea soup with lobster, soufflés and hot spiced wine.

Harvey's Resort/Hotel, Highway 50, Stateline. 588-2411.

Bill's Lake Tahoe Casino. This is a high-fun, low-roller joint, the self-proclaimed "Quarter Capital of Nevada." Bill's, which is part of the same company that owns the next-door Harrah's Casino, has gone out of its way to encourage its young staff of dealers and attendants to be friendly to its crowd of skiers, summer vacationers, and party-goers. The serious gamblers are elsewhere.

They even encourage the taking of photographs on the casino floor.

Bill's includes a McDonald's and a Bennigan's within its walls. Along the streetfront it includes a large collection of older mechanical slot machines. And there is "Billie Jean," described as the World's Largest Free Pull Slot Machine.

Bill's Lake Tahoe Casino, Highway 50, Stateline. 588-2455.

Harrah's Casino Hotel Lake Tahoe. Harrah's is one of the class acts of South Lake Tahoe, and it is due for a facelift to make it even more attractive. The 18-story, 534-room hotel begins with one of the best views of the mountains and the lake. By Nevada standards, it is one of the more understated and elegant hotels in town.

A major remodeling of the lobby converted its look to an alpine lodge, with slate tile floors and Persian rugs, wood and brass, a natural stone fireplace, and a waterfall. A large L-shaped casino, it is relatively muted compared to some of the other casinos in town. Harrah's draws a lively mix of skiers, lake visitors, and gamblers. It offers a set of nice restaurants tucked away from the casino floor.

Guests staying at the nicely appointed rooms have access to a dome-covered swimming pool and spa and health clubs.

The hotel's Value Season runs from January 1 to mid-June and from

Payment due. Some casinos will advertise their "overdue" jackpots on progressive machines, giving the implication that your chances of winning are higher if you play on one of them. Actually—assuming as you must that the machines are honest—the chances of winning on an overdue machine are the same if it has been 10 years since it has paid off or if the machine just paid off five minutes ago.

Think of it this way: if you flip an honest quarter 49 times and it comes up heads every time, the odds of it coming up tails on the 50th toss are still 50-50.

Old money. While you're in the registration area, look for the display of antique slot machines, including a circa 1902 Mills Duplex Ten-Way and a Caille's Centaur double, fitted out in oak and chrome.

mid-September through mid-December with room rates starting at $119 ($20 higher on weekends). The Summer Season occupies the middle of the year, with rooms starting at $139 in midweek.

One Harrah's service we haven't seen duplicated elsewhere was an offer from "The Ski Renter" for fittings of boots and equipment in your room.

The exquisite **Summit Room** is on the 16th and 17th floors, not quite the summit of the High Sierras, but still a highly recommended gourmet experience for dinner; reservations are necessary. The two-story windows offer spectacular views.

The menu changes, but a recent visit featured an appetizer selection that included ragout of wild mushrooms in puff pastry, Chesapeake blue crab timbale, and marinated grilled quail with apple fritters; soups included spicy black bean soup, and lobster bisque laced with Armagnac and crème fraîche.

Family tree. Harrah's is part of the Promus Companies, which also operate Embassy Suites, Homewood Suites, Hampton Inns, and Bill's Casino; in fact the hotel is sandwiched between a new Embassy Suites on the California side and Bill's on the Nevada side. (Guests at Embassy Suites can use some of the health club facilities at Harrah's, and when Harrah's is oversold, some of its guests are put up next door in California.)

Entrees, priced around $30 at the time of our visit included Jamaican thresher shark steak with plantains, slow-smoked game hens with wild rice pancakes and lingonberry relish, grilled venison with kiln dried cherries and melted Brie; and filet of Black Angus beef Gilroy for $29.

And, of course, there are some fabulous desserts including Grand Marnier soufflé, mango mousse, and crème brûlée.

A full six-course meal could be expected to cost about $60 to $70 per person; a daily chef's selection that includes appetizer, salad, intermezzo, entree, and dessert costs about $50.

Another fine restaurant is **Friday's Station Steak & Seafood Grill** on the 18th floor. Named after a famous stop on the Pony Express that used to be located near Stateline, Nevada, it offers views of Lake Tahoe and the Sierras matched only by the food.

Offerings, which range from about $20 to $30, include Black Angus beef; pan-fried sea scallops and prawns in brown butter and lemon thyme; cheese battered Alaskan halibut in pesto cream with bay shrimps and asparagus; a mixed grill of lamb chops, filet of beef, smoked quail, and Andouille sausage and peppered filet mignon in green peppercorn sauce with brandy.

We were especially impressed with the offer on the menu to broil, poach, sauté, steam, or blacken most seafood entrees to taste.

An attractive, reasonably priced Italian restaurant is **Cafe Andreotti,** with entrees priced from about $10 to $20. Specialties include an antipasto plate of Italian meats, cheese, marinated vegetables, olives, and bread sticks; and *pollo picatta* (chicken breasts dipped in parmesan egg batter, sautéed with mushrooms and capers in lemon butter).

The 24-hour **Sierra Restaurant** features sandwiches from $4 to $10 and burgers, fish, and chips. Breakfast omelettes range from $5 to $9.

Asia, the newest eatery at the hotel, offers a variety of Oriental specialties for dinner. On one visit, appetizers included Vietnamese calamari with spicy dipping sauce, *kim chee* (Korean pickled cabbage), Chinese pot stickers, and Thai chicken wings braised with chilies.

Entrees, which range from about $7 to $15, included Szechuan scallops, Thai coconut shrimp, Mongolian beef, Thai ginger beef, and Chinese *kung pao* chicken.

The **North Beach Deli** offers San Francisco decor and specialties, including pasta, submarine sandwiches, espresso and desserts 24 hours a day. Entrees start at about $7. One of the specialties is San Francisco Bay dilled shrimp with lettuce and tomato on sourdough baguette. Skiers and travelers can order sandwiches to go.

INDIAN COUNCILS

Battle Mountain Band Council
35 Mountainview Drive, #138-13
Battle Mountain, NV 89820; 635-2004

Carson Indian Community Council
2900 South Curry Street
Carson City, NV 89701
883-6431

Duck Valley Shoshone-Paiute Tribes
P.O. Box 219
Owyhee, NV 89832
757-3211

Duckwater Shoshone Tribe
P.O. Box 68
Duckwater, NV 89314
863-0227

The **Skyway Buffet** offers eggs cooked to order for breakfast and prime rib every dinner. On Friday night there's a special seafood buffet, and brunch is served on Saturday and Sunday.

The **Forest Restaurant** offers a breakfast buffet Monday through Saturday and a Sunday brunch including french toast, Canadian bacon, and cheese blintzes. Lunch and dinner buffets are offered Saturday through Thursday; the Saturday seafood buffet includes caviar, smoked salmon, and scallops.

The 800-seat **South Shore Room** has been the home of regular headline entertainment including Hollywood and Broadway-theme productions. It also features late-night "Nevada adult entertainment"; in other words, near-naked women and men in dance, music, and comedy routines with titles like "Beyond Bare Essence" and "E*ROCK*TICA."

A new lounge, the **Center Stage,** was due to open late in 1994. A new **Family Entertainment Center** was also under construction.

A special enclosed **Children's Arcade** allows parents to register their children, ages 5 to 14, and leave them with an attendant for up to five hours. The kids can enjoy games, a video room, coloring books, and beverage and snack machines. The charge for up to five hours is $6. An attendant is on duty from 9 A.M. to midnight every day; on Saturday the attendant is on duty until 1 A.M.

The hotel also rents pagers to the parents so they can be reached at any time.

Harrah's Casino Hotel Lake Tahoe, Highway 50, Stateline. 588-6606; (800) 648-3773.

Elko Band Council
P.O. Box 748
Elko, NV 89801
738-8889

Ely Shoshone Tribe
16 Shoshone Circle
Ely, NV 89301
289-3013

Fallon Paiute Shoshone Tribe
8955 Mission Road
P.O. Box 1650
Fallon, NV 89406
423-6075

Fort McDermitt Indian Reservation
P.O. Box 457
McDermitt, NV 89421
532-8259

Caesars Tahoe. Smaller than the Las Vegas landmark and considerably less opulent, Caesars Tahoe nevertheless carries through its Roman theme pretty well. Among the touches of Vegas transported to the lake is the legion of cocktail waitresses in off-the-shoulder togas. Unlike the Vegas floor, though, the skimpy costume does not include cone-headdresses.

Many of the 440 suites and rooms offer circular bathtubs for those who like to bathe in the round. Other facilities include an indoor pool, health spa, racquetball, and tennis courts.

The casino is attractive but a bit cramped. Top headliners perform in the 1,600-seat Circus Maximus Showroom. Music, magic, and comedy are presented in the 300-seat Caesars Cabaret, and there is live music and dancing at Nero's 2000 Nightclub.

The highest-tone Chinese restaurant in town is the **Empress Court,** a small, dimly lit room decorated in Oriental blues and reds with gold accents. Prix-fixe meals are available in the range of $12.95 to $19.95. Specialties include sautéed scallops and shrimp in black bean sauce for $18.50, crystal prawns with glazed walnuts for $18.50, and slowly roasted imperial Peking duck for $38.

The **Broiler Room** is an unusual cubbyhole, with dark brick walls and dim candelabras and sconces. The menu includes meat dishes such as New York steak for $18.95, veal piccata for $22.95, and T-bone steak for $26.95. Seafood specialties include Spanish gambas (jumbo prawns marinated in olive oil and herbs, broiled, and served with garlic croutons and sauce Catalan) for $19.95.

Also on the menu is a selection of spicy Creole foods using seasonings and recipes from the famed K-Paul's Louisiana Kitchen in New Orleans. Offerings include Louisiana seafood gumbo for $5.95, K-Paul's favorite blackened prawns for $19.95, and jambalaya (plump shrimp and spicy Andouille sausage) for $16.75.

The **Pisces Bar** lives up its name with offerings including clams on the halfshell for $1.65 each, and sea scallops "Pisces" for $18. Other specialties include angel hair pasta pomodoro in tomato-basil sauce for $11.

The **Cafe Roma** features the Cafe Roma burger (ground beef with melted cheese and a strip of bacon on a freshly baked bun) for $5.25, two eggs any style with pancakes for $2.95, and *huevos con chorizo* (Mexican pork sausage scrambled with eggs and garnished with fresh tomatoes and green onion, served with breakfast potatoes) for $5.95. The Cafe is a large, open space with wall murals and Roman columns.

Caesars Tahoe, Highway 50, Stateline. 588-3515; (800) 648-3353.

Horizon Casino Resort. A very lively and busy casino with a big collection of nickel slots; we'd recommend dark glasses. The mirrored ceiling makes you feel like you're inside a huge powder room turned sideways. There are 539 rooms and suites, many with lakeview balconies. Facilities include a large outdoor pool and hot tubs.

Entertainment, featuring headline acts, is presented in the 1,200-seat **Grande Lake Theatre.** Shows and revues are offered in the 200-seat **Golden Cabaret,** and there is live music nightly in the **Aspen Lounge.**

Josh's restaurant, a rather ordinary setting, offers a special lobster dinner for $10.95 every night but Saturday. Other entrees include shrimp scampi for $15.50, fillet of petrale sole sauté Veronique (a grape and almond butter sauce) for $13.75, blackened red snapper for $13.95, and Kansas City rib eye steak for $14.95. Two cuts of prime rib—big and bigger—are offered for $13.95 or $15.50.

The 24-hour **Four Seasons** coffee shop includes burgers for $5 to $6, chicken fajita salad for $7.75, shrimp Louie for $8.95, and cold deli sandwiches for $4.25 to $6. A New York steak special is priced at $7.99.

The **LeGrande Buffet** offers a weekday brunch buffet for $2.99; Saturday and Sunday brunches are priced at $4.99; the dinner buffet is $4.99 every night but Saturday, when it is priced at $6.99.

Horizon Casino Resort, Highway 50, Stateline. 588-6211; (800) 648-3322.

Embassy Suites Resort. A new all-suites hotel with 400 rooms, just across the state line into California and sharing some of its facili-

Moapa Tribal Store
P.O. Box 340
Moapa, NV 89025
865-2787

Pyramid Lake Paiute Tribe
P.O. Box 256
Nixon, NV 89424
786-5626

Reno-Sparks Indian Colony
98 Colony Road
Reno, NV 89502
329-2972

Stewart Indian Museum
5366 Snyder Avenue
Carson City, NV 89701
882-1808

ties with its corporate and geographic neighbor, Harrah's. Offers an indoor pool, whirlpool spa, and work-out room.

Entertainment is presented at the Turtles Sports Bar & Dance Emporium. Restaurants include Zackary's, Pasquale's, Julie's Deli, and the Turtles Sports Bar.

And guess what? No casino. That is, unless you want to walk a few feet into Nevada.

Embassy Suites Resort, Highway 50, South Lake Tahoe, CA. (916) 544-5400; (800) 362-2779.

Telephone Numbers for Lake Tahoe Region Hotels and Casinos

(Note: All phone numbers are in area code 702 unless noted.)

Lake Tahoe Visitors Authority. Lodging referral service. (800) 288-2463.

Heavenly Central Reservation. P.O. Box 2180, Stateline, NV 89449. (800) 243-2836.

Lake Tahoe Accommodations. 2048 Dunlap Drive #4, South Lake Tahoe, CA 96150. (916) 544-3234; (800) 544-3234.

Cabins and Campgrounds

Cabins to Castles	(916) 544-5397; (800) 422-2467
Carney's Cabins	(916) 542-3361
Carson Valley Inn RV Park	782-9711
Echo Creek Ranch	(916) 544-5397; (800) 462-5397
KOA Campground	(916) 577-3693
Lakeside RV Park	588-4220
Michelsen Vacation Rentals	588-4811; (800) 568-2463
Pine Cone Resort	588-6561
Reservation Bureau	(916) 544-4244; (800) 422-2467
Richardson's Resort	(916) 541-1801; (800) 544-1801
Sorensen's Resort	(916) 694-2203; (800) 462-5397
Tahoe Pines Campground	(916) 577-1653
Tahoe Valley Campground	(916) 541-2222
Walley's Hot Springs Resort	782-8155
Zephyr Cove Lodge and Campground	588-6644

Hotels

Caesars Tahoe	588-3515; (800) 648-3353
Carson Valley Inn	782-9711
Ed's Tahoe Nugget	588-7733
Embassy Suites Hotel	(916) 544-5400; (800) 362-2779
Gold Hill Hotel	847-0111
Harrah's Tahoe	588-6611; (800) 648-3773
Harvey's Resort Hotel/Casino	588-2411; (800) 648-3361
Inn by the Lake	(916) 542-0330; (800) 877-1466
Lake Tahoe Horizon Casino Resort	588-6211; (800) 648-3322
Lakeside Inn & Casino	588-7777; (800) 624-7980
The Ridge Tahoe	588-3553; (800) 334-1600
Tahoe Beach & Ski Club	(916) 541-6220; (800) 822-5962
Tahoe Seasons Resort Hotel	(916)541-6700

Motels

Cedar Lodge	(916) 544-6453
Elm Inn	(916) 541-7900
Fantasy Inn	(916) 544-6767; (800) 441-6610
Heavenly Valley Motel & Spa	(916) 544-4244; (800) 422-2467
LaBaer Motor Lodge	(916) 544-5232
LeGeraniums Bed & Breakfast	(916) 544-6450
Nendel's Blue Jay Motel	(916) 544-5232
Richardson's Resort	(916) 541-1801; (800) 544-1801
Riviera Inn	(916) 544-3448
Royal Valhalla Motel	(916) 544-2233
Sierra Cal Lodge	(916) 541-5400; (800) 541-0202
Sorensen's Resort	(916) 694-2203; (800) 423-9949
Station House Inn/Best Western	(916) 542-1101; (800) 822-5953
Super 8 Motel (Carson City)	883-7800
Tahoe Chalet Inn	(916) 544-3311; (800) 821-2656
Tahoe Marina Inn	(916) 541-2180; (800) 448-4577
Tahoe Sands Inn	(916) 544-3476; (800) 237-8882
Tahoe Tropicana Motel	(916) 541-3911
Tahoe Valley Motel/Condominium	(916) 541-0353; (800) 669-7544
Tahoe Villa	(916) 544-3041
Thunderbird Motel	(916) 544-5741
Travelodge-Casino Area	(916) 541-5000; (800) 255-3050
Travelodge-South Tahoe	(916) 544-5266; (800) 255-3050
Travelodge-Stateline	(916) 544-6000; (800) 255-3050
Viking Motor Lodge	(916) 541-5155; (800) 288-4083
Walley's Hot Springs Resort	782-8155
Zephyr Cove Lodge	588-6644

Getting Around in Lake Tahoe

Airports

Tahoe Valley Airport. South Lake Tahoe, CA. (916) 541-4080

Truckee-Tahoe Airport. Private and corporate. Truckee, CA. (916) 587-4119.

Carson Airport. Private and corporate. Carson City, NV. 882-1551.

Douglas County Airport. Charter service. Minden, NV. 782-8277.

Car Rentals

Action Auto Rental. 885-2885.

Adventure Sport Vehicle Rentals. South Lake Tahoe. (916) 541-7155; (800) 223-2999.

Avis Rent A Car. Tahoe Valley Airport: (916) 542-5638. Embassy Suites hotel, South Lake Tahoe: (916) 542-5710; Nationwide: (800) 331-1212.

Budget/Sears. Caesars Tahoe, Stateline: 588-5145. South Lake Tahoe Airport: (916) 541-5777; (800) 527-0700.

Dollar Rent A Car. Horizon Casino Resort, South Lake Tahoe: 588-4849; (800) 800-4000.

Enterprise Rent-A-Car. South Lake Tahoe: (916) 544-7788; (800) 325-8007.

Hertz Rent A Car. Harrah's Stateline: 588-4911. South Lake Tahoe Airport: (916) 544-2327. Incline Village: 831-4371. Nationwide: (800) 654-3131.

Tahoe Rent-A-Car. Tahoe Valley Motel, South Lake Tahoe: (916) 544-4500.

Bus Service

Dial-A-Ride/Lake Tahoe Transportation System. South Lake Tahoe area. (916) 577-7000.

Five Star Enterprises Limo Service. Airport to Reno and North Lake Tahoe. (916) 587-7651; (800) 782-4707.
Greyhound Lines West. South Lake Tahoe: (916) 544-2351. Truckee: (916) 587-3822.
STAGE (South Lake Tahoe Area Ground Express). South Lake Tahoe area. (916) 573-2080.

Ski Area Shuttle Buses

The following ski areas provide shuttle services; call for schedules and pickup locations:

Alpine Meadows. (916) 583-4232.

Diamond Peak. 832-1177.

Northstar. (916) 562-1010.

Squaw Valley. (916) 583-6985.

Sugar Bowl. (916) 426-3651.

Mount Rose. 849-0704.

Lake Tahoe Health

Altitude Sickness. Feeling a bit faint, tired, nauseous, headachy, or short of breath? Having trouble sleeping, or does the fabulous spread of a casino buffet hold no particular appeal? You may be suffering from a mild case of altitude sickness. Lake Tahoe sits at about 6,235 feet above sea level; if you have come from an East or West Coast city, you are living more than a mile higher than you are used to.

The cure is to avoid overexertion, get plenty of rest, and drink plenty of fluids. You also should eat lightly and cut down on alcohol consumption. The ultimate cure is time: your body should adjust within two or three days.

If your symptoms are especially severe, or if they don't seem to pass, you should see a doctor. Persons with heart conditions or high blood pressure should check with their doctor at home before heading for the mountains.

White stuff. Snowfall at alpine skiing elevations averages 300 to 500 inches per year. At the lake level, the average is about 125 inches. At high elevations, it has been known to snow in any month of the year. On December 28, 1992, snow began to fall at South Lake Tahoe, eventually reaching rates of up to six inches per hour. Over the next 48 hours, the ski resort received more than nine feet of snow, one of the largest recorded snowfalls ever.

Frostbite. It gets very cold up in the hills. Cover all exposed parts of the body, and come in frequently in cold weather.

Frostbite occurs when the water in your body cells literally freezes. Superficial frostbite usually involves the fingertips, ears, nose, toes, and cheeks; symptoms include a burning sensation, tingling, or numbness, and a whitish discoloration of the skin. Deep frostbite is more serious and can result in the death of the cells and even open wounds susceptible to infection. If you develop frostbite, find warm shelter immediately. Do *not* rub frostbitten skin; instead, immerse the affected parts of the body in *lukewarm* (not hot) water. If the skin does not return to its normal color, or if blisters, swelling, pain, or numbness develops, seek medical attention.

Hypothermia. This serious condition results when the body's core (internal) temperature drops below the normal range of about 98.6 degrees and the body is unable to restore the proper temperature. Left untreated, hypothermia can lead to organ malfunction, damage, and eventual death. Symptoms include fatigue, mood changes, and impaired motor skills. Wear warm, layered, dry clothing including hats and gloves; avoid alcohol and take indoor breaks.

Sunburn. The higher elevation of mountainous areas increases your risk of sunburn; ultraviolet rays are about five times as strong as at sea level. Doctors generally recommend use of a sunscreen with a rating of 15 or 20, including PABA; lip balms with PABA or zinc oxide are also suggested. Sunglasses are also recommended to protect your eyes.

If you receive a sunburn without blisters, apply cool compresses to the affected area and take aspirin for pain and Benadryl to relieve itching. Blisters are a sign of a second-degree burn. Do not pop blisters, and stay out of the sun to avoid further damage. You should see a doctor for any facial blisters or blisters with cloudy liquid, or for severe pain.

Road and Weather Information
California Highway Conditions. (916) 581-1400

California Highway Patrol. (916) 587-3510.

Caltrans Road Information. South Lake Tahoe: (916) 577-3550. Truckee: (916) 587-3806. Reno: 793-1313.

Nevada Highway Patrol. 793-1313.

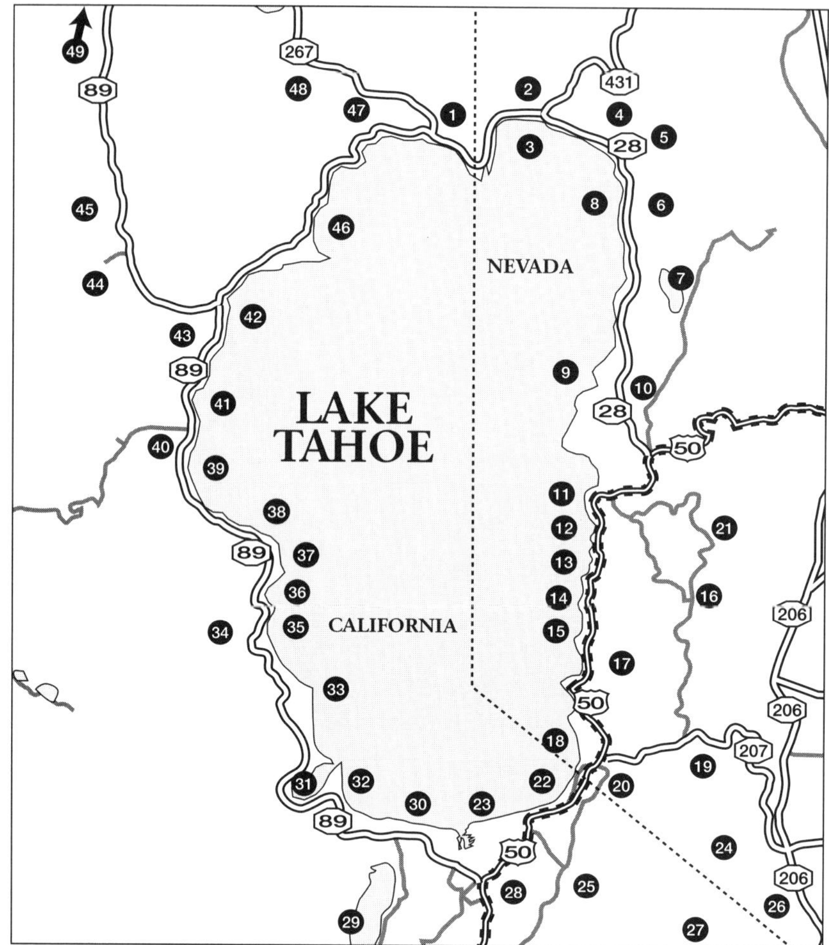

LAKE TAHOE

 1 Kings Beach
 2 Incline Village
 3 Crystal Bay
 4 Diamond Peak
    Ski Area
 5 Ponderosa Ranch
 6 Lake Tahoe
    Nevada State Park
 7 Marlette Lake
 8 Sand Harbor
 9 Secret Harbor
10 Spooner Lake
11 Glenbrook
12 Logan Shoals
13 Cave Rock
14 Skyland
15 Zephyr Cove
16 Genoa

17 Round Hill
18 Nevada Beach
19 Kingsbury Grade
20 Stateline Hotels/Casinos
21 Mormon Station
22 El Dorado
23 Regan Beach
24 Monument Peak
25 Heavenly
    Ski Area & Tram
26 Job's Sister
27 Freel Peak
28 South Lake Tahoe
29 Fallen Leaf Lake
30 Pope Beach
31 Emerald Bay
32 Baldwin Beach
33 Rubicon Point

34 Sugar Pine Point
    State Park
35 Tahoe Hills
36 Meeks Bay
37 Sugar Pine Point
38 Tahoma
39 Homewood
40 Homewood Ski Area
41 Sunnyside
42 Tahoe Tavern
43 Tahoe City
44 Alpine Meadows
    Ski Area
45 Squaw Valley Ski Area
46 Carnelian Bay
47 Tahoe Vista
48 Northstar Ski Area
49 Donner Memorial
    State Park

Chapter 26

Winter and Summer Sports in the Lake Tahoe Region

Ski Areas

Heavenly Lake Tahoe. The Queen of Lake Tahoe ski areas is Heavenly, a massive resort whose lower slopes can be seen from Stateline/South Lake Tahoe, and from much of the lake itself.

Heavenly opened in 1955 with one chair lift and a small hut on U.S. Forest Service land on the south shore of Lake Tahoe. Today it includes 25 lifts, six day lodges, 4,800 acres of terrain, 700 acres of snowmaking, and parts of two states.

What you see from the road in South Lake Tahoe or Stateline is perhaps one-third of just one face of the mountain.

Sixteen of its lifts lie in California, and nine are in Nevada, including an aerial tramway, two detachable quads, eight triple chairs, eight double chairs, and six surface lifts. There are 68 runs—20 percent beginner, 45 percent intermediate, and 35 percent advanced/expert.

The vertical drop is 3,500 feet, with the top elevation at 10,040 feet. The base elevation in California is at 6,540 feet, and in Nevada it is at 7,200 feet. The longest mountain descent is five and a half miles.

Heavenly receives an average annual snowfall of 300 inches, and in recent years has put down an additional 120 inches of machine-made snow. The season usually runs from mid-November through April. Area hotels usually offer packages based on three seasons, running from least crowded to busiest.

Value Season: Just after Thanksgiving to just before Christmas, or approximately November 29 to December 17.

Regular Season: Thanksgiving and January through the end of March, except for the President's Week holiday, or approximately November 25 to 28, January 3 to February 11, and February 15 to March 31.

Holiday Season: Christmas through New Year's and President's Week, or approximately December 18 to January 2 and February 12–14.

Ski lift tickets for Heavenly are about $40 for an adult day pass and $20 for a child or senior.

Also available were interchangeable five- or six-day tickets usable at Heavenly, Squaw Valley USA, Northstar at Tahoe, Alpine, and Kirkwood. Note that the multi-day tickets represent only a small discount from Heavenly's ticket price and may actually be more expensive than individual tickets if you visit the smaller Northstar, Alpine, and Kirkwood resorts. And, the tickets are definitely more expensive if you end up choosing to miss one of your prepaid days of skiing for other activities.

In 1991, the Mott Canyon lift opened up 800 acres of double black diamond skiing, the most difficult rating on the mountain. In 1992, a new high-speed detachable quad lift was added from Sky Meadows to the top of the mountain, replacing an older lift and reducing travel time by half.

Heavenly Ski Resort is a member of the Kamori International group, a Japanese company that includes among its properties the Steamboat Ski Resort in Colorado, Rusutsu Ski Resort in Japan, Tignes Ski Resort in France, Saba Point Country Club near Orlando, Florida, and Lone Pine Koala Sanctuary in Australia.

With optimum conditions (0 to 20 degrees, no wind, and 20 percent humidity) Heavenly can make snow at the rate of 3.6 feet per acre in one hour. Machine-made snow is just like natural snow, only more so. Water and air are pumped through a network of more than 100,000 feet of pipe

Heavenly ski area, Lake Tahoe

to the snowmaking guns. The water is atomized by the air and then shot out into the cold atmosphere where the droplets crystallize and form snowflakes. Water and air settings can be adjusted to achieve a particular type of snow—early in the season, snowmakers make heavier snow to build the base; after the base is in place or after natural snowfall, snowmakers use less water to make a light, dry snow for best skiing.

The **Monument Peak Restaurant** is located at the top of the Heavenly Aerial Tram, 2,000 feet above Lake Tahoe, serving Italian food and spectacular vistas to skiers as well as visitors who ride the lift. Lunch is served from 11 A.M. to 2 P.M. Breakfast and dinner are available Thursday, Friday, and Saturday during the skiing season. Dinner entrees include *bistecca di filetto* (charbroiled filet mignon with light mushroom marsala sauce), *saltimbocca alla Romana, scampi alla Anna* (shrimp sautéed with white wine, garlic, concasse of tomatoes, and finished with a light *fume* sauce), and *petti de pollo Florentina* (breast of chicken stuffed with fontina cheese, sautéed with white wine and spinach).

Facts and Figures on Lake Tahoe Skiing

*N-I-A is Novice-Intermediate-Advanced

Heavenly. P.O. Box 2180, Stateline, NV 89449. (916) 541-1330; (800) 243-2836.

Vertical	Elevation	Lifts	Rating (N-I-A)*
3,600	10,100	24	25-50-25

Longest trail: 5.5 miles. Lifts: 1 tram, 1 detachable quad, 7 triples, 9 doubles, and 6 surface lifts. Complimentary shuttle throughout South Lake Tahoe. Location: South Lake Tahoe, on the California/Nevada border, 55 miles southwest of Reno and 180 miles east of San Francisco.

Alpine Meadows. Tahoe City, CA. (916) 583-4232.

Vertical	Elevation	Lifts	Rating (N-I-A)*
1,800	8,6371	22	5-40-35

Longest trail: 2.5 miles. Base: 6,840 feet. Summit: 8,637 feet. Lifts: 1 high-speed quad, 2 triples, 8 double chairs, and 1 surface lift. Call for information on daily and multiple-day tickets and interchangeable multi-day tickets for other North and South Lake Tahoe areas. Complimentary shuttle bus from South Lake Tahoe/Stateline and from North Shore of Lake Tahoe. Location: 6 miles northwest of Tahoe City on State Route 89.

Boreal Ridge. P.O. Box 39, Truckee, CA 96160. (916) 426-3666.

Vertical	Elevation	Lifts	Rating (N-I-A)*
600	7,800	10	30-55-15

Longest trail: 1 mile. Base: 7,200 feet. Summit: 7,800 feet. Lifts: 1 quad, 2 triples, and 7 doubles. Location: 10 miles west of Truckee, 90 miles east of Sacramento.

Diamond Peak. 1210 Ski Way, Incline Village, NV 89451. (702) 831-3211; (800) GO-TAHOE.

Vertical	Elevation	Lifts	Rating (N-I-A)*
1,840	8,540	7	18-49-33

Longest trail: 2.5 miles. Base: 6,700 feet. Summit: 8,540 feet. Lifts: 1 quad, 6 doubles. Complimentary shuttle service within Incline Village. Pickup by reservation for groups of 10 or more from Reno or South Lake Tahoe. Lift Rates: call for information. First time beginner packages available. Location: Northeast shore of Lake Tahoe in Incline Village.

Donner Ski Ranch. (916) 426-3635.

Vertical	Elevation	Lifts	Rating (N-I-A)*
720	7,751	5	25-50-25

Base: 7,031 feet. Summit: 7,751 feet.

Granlibakken. (916) 583-4242.

Vertical	Elevation	Lifts	Rating (N-I-A)*
280	6,480	2	50-50-0

Base: 6,200 feet. Summit: 6,480 feet.

Ski Homewood. Homewood, CA. (916) 525-7526.

Vertical	Elevation	Lifts	Rating (N-I-A)*
1,650	7,880	10	15-50-35

Longest run: 2 miles. Base: 6,230 feet. Summit: 7,880. Lifts: 5 surface lifts, 2 double chairs, 2 triple chairs, 1 quad chair. Location: on Highway 89 along the west shore of Lake Tahoe, 6 miles south of Tahoe City and 19 miles north of South Lake Tahoe.

Kirkwood. Kirkwood, CA. (209) 258-6000; (209) 258-7000; (800) 545-2034.

Vertical	Elevation	Lifts	Rating (N-I-A)*
2,000	9,800	11	15-50-35

Longest trail: 2.5 miles. Base: 7,800 feet. Summit: 9,800 feet. Lifts: 4 triples, 6 doubles, and 1 surface lift. Ski shuttle from major South Lake Tahoe resorts. Location: 35 miles south of South Lake Tahoe, Highway 88 at Carson Pass.

Mount Rose. 22222 Mount Rose Highway, Reno. 849-0704.

Vertical	Elevation	Lifts	Rating (N-I-A)*
1,440	9,700	5	30-35-35

Longest trail: 2.5 miles. Base: 8,260 feet. Summit: 9,700 feet. Lifts: 1 quad, 3 triples, 1 double. Location: 22 miles southwest of Reno, on State Route 431, 11 miles from Incline Village.

Northstar-at-Tahoe. (916) 562-1010; (800) 533-6787.

Vertical	Elevation	Lifts	Rating (N-I-A)*
2,200	8,600	11	25-50-25

Longest trail: 2.9 miles. Base: 6,400 feet. Summit: 8,600 feet. Lifts: 1 gondola, 2 express quads, 3 triples, 3 doubles, and 2 surface lifts. Interchangeable tickets with other Lake Tahoe resorts available. Complimentary shuttle bus between Incline Village/Kings Beach and Northstar. Reno airport pickup for groups. Shuttle to South Lake Tahoe runs twice weekly. Location: 40 miles southwest of Reno on California Highway 267 and 196 miles northeast of San Francisco.

Sierra at Tahoe. (Formerly Sierra Ski Ranch.) 9921 Sierra Ski Ranch Road, Twin Bridges, CA. (916) 659-7535.

Vertical	Elevation	Lifts	Rating (N-I-A)*
2,212	8,852	8	20-60-20

Longest trail: 3 miles. Base: 6,640 feet. Summit: 8,852 feet. Lifts: 2 detachable quads, 2 triples, and 4 doubles. Complimentary shuttle bus from South Lake Tahoe/Stateline casino area. Location: 12 miles west of South Lake Tahoe on Highway 50, 72 miles west of Reno.

Soda Springs. (916) 426-3666.

Vertical	Elevation	Lifts	Rating (N-I-A)*
650	7,352	2	30-55-15

Base: 6,702 feet. Summit: 7,352 feet.

Squaw Valley USA. Squaw Valley, CA. (916) 583-6985.

Vertical	Elevation	Lifts	Rating (N-I-A)*
2,850	9,050	32	25-45-30

Longest trail: 3 miles. Base: 6,200 feet. Summit: 9,050 feet. Lifts: 120-passenger cable car, 1 gondola, 3 detachable quad chairs, 7 triple chairs, 16 double chairs, 4 surface lifts. Shuttle services from various North Lake Tahoe and South Lake Tahoe locations. Location: 50 miles west of Reno, 200 miles east of San Francisco.

Sugar Bowl. Norden, CA. (916) 426-3651.

Vertical	Elevation	Lifts	Rating (N-I-A)*
1,500	8,383	9	20-30-50

Longest trail: 2 miles. Base: 6,883 feet. Summit: 8,383 feet. Lifts: 1 gondola, 1 quad, and 7 doubles. Location: Near Soda Springs, 44 miles from Reno.

Tahoe Donner. (916) 587-9400.

Vertical	Elevation	Lifts	Rating (N-I-A)*
600	7,350	3	15-80-5

Base: 6,750 feet. Summit: 7,350 feet.

Children's Ski Programs

Alpine Meadows. Snow School for children ages 4 to 6.
Boreal. Animal Crackers Children's Ski School for children 4 to 10.
Diamond Peak. Bee Ferrato's Child Ski Center. First-time Beginner's Special for chil-

dren 7 and older; Second-time course for experienced young skiers. The Sierra Scout Adventure lesson for ages 7 to 12.

Heavenly. L'il Angels for children 3½ to 8. Junior Mountain Adventure for children 8 to 12.

Homewood. Ski and Play for children ages 4 to 12.

Kirkwood. Mighty Mountain for children 4 to 12.

Northstar. Ski Cubs for children 3 to 6 is an introduction to snow sports. Children 4 to 6 can enter Super Ski Cubs. Experienced young skiers from age 5 to 12 can enter StarKids.

Squaw Valley. Children's World at Papoose for children 3 to 12.

Sugar Bowl. PowderKids is for children 6 to 12. For the youngest visitor, there's the Sugar Bears Child Care program.

Lake Tahoe Region Cross-Country Ski Areas

Diamond Peak Cross-Country. 1210 Ski Way, Incline Village. 832-1177. 8 trails, 35 km of track.

Northstar-at-Tahoe Cross-County & Telemark Center. Truckee, CA. (916) 562-2475. 38 trails, 65 km of track.

Royal Gorge Cross-Country Ski Area. Soda Springs, CA. (916) 426-3871; (800) 634-3086. 81 trails, 317 km of track. For shuttle service call (916) 426-3871.

Spooner Lake Cross-Country. Glenbrook, NV. 887-8844. 21 trails, 101 km of track.

Squaw Creek Cross-Country Ski Area. Olympic Valley, CA. (916) 581-1946. 11 trails, 30 km of track.

Tahoe Donner Cross-Country. Truckee, CA. (916) 587-9484. 32 trails, 65 km of track.

Tahoe Nordic Center. Tahoe City, CA. (916) 583-0484. 12 trails, 65 km of track.

In addition to day passes, the above seven North Tahoe cross-country ski resorts are members of a cooperative selling an interchangeable trail pass good at any of the areas for a total of 678 kilometers (420 miles) over 203 forest and lake view trails. Call (800) 824-6348 for information.

Other cross-country centers in the Lake Tahoe region include:

Alpenglow. Tahoe City. 583-6917.

Bijou Park. South Lake Tahoe Parks & Recreation Department, Glenwood Avenue, South Lake Tahoe. (916) 541-4611.

Hope Valley Cross-Country at Sorensen's Resort. Highway 88 in Hope Valley. (916) 694-2266; (800) 423-9949.

Kirkwood. Highway 88, 30 miles south of Lake Tahoe, adjacent to Kirkwood Ski Resort. Kirkwood, CA. (209) 258-8864. Snow conditions: (209) 258-3000. 80 km of track.

Lake Tahoe Basin. Various trails maintained by the U.S. Forest Service. (916) 573-2600.

Spooner Lake Cross Country Ski Area. Highway 28, 11 miles north of South Lake Tahoe, 12 miles south of Incline Village. 749-5349. Snow conditions: 887-8844.

Sugar Pine Point State Park. 20 miles north of South Lake Tahoe on Highway 89, Tahoma, CA. (916) 525-7982.

Sunset Ranch. Tahoe Airport Highway 50, South Lake Tahoe. 541-9001.

Tahoe Paradise Sports. Highway 50 at Meyers, CA. (916) 577-2121.

U.S. Forest Service Trails. Contact Forest Service for Sno-Park and wilderness permits, snow conditions, and trail safety information at (916) 573-2600.

Snowmobiling

Lake Tahoe Winter Sports Center. 3071 Highway 50, Tahoe Paradise, CA. (916) 577-2940.

Mountain Lake Adventures. Kings Beach, CA. 831-4202, (916) 583-9131.

Tahoe Paradise Sports. Highway 50 at Meyers, CA, 3 miles south of Lake Tahoe Airport. (916) 577-2121.

United States Forest Service. Snowmobiling is open in most of National Forest lands within the Lake Tahoe Basin, provided there are at least 6 inches of snow on the ground. Recommended areas include Spooner Summit, Hell Hole, and Blue Lakes Road in Hope Valley. Contact USFS for maps. (916) 573-2600.

Zephyr Cove Snowmobile Center. 760 Highway 50, Zephyr Cove, NV. 588-3833.

Snow Play Areas

The California Department of Parks requires purchase and display of a permit to use Sno-Park parking areas during the season. Call (916) 653-8569 or (916) 573-2600 for information. Permits may also be obtained at many sporting goods stores, ski rental and snowmobile shops, automobile clubs, and the South Lake Tahoe Chamber of Commerce.

You don't need a lot of facilities to go sledding—a patch of snow and a saucer, sled, or cardboard box will do—but some places are nicer than others. Here are some designated sledding spots in the Lake Tahoe region.

Boreal Ski Area. Off I-80 in Donner Pass. Snowplay area; plastic disk use only. Fee includes rental. Open weekends and holidays. (916) 426-3666.

Granlibakken Ski Area. Hill for saucers only; day use fee. Saucers available for rent. (916) 583-9896.

Hansen's Resort. 1360 Ski Run Boulevard, South Lake Tahoe, CA. (916) 544-3361.

Mt. Rose. Undeveloped area eight miles up Mt. Rose Highway (Highway 431). Bring your own equipment.

North Tahoe Regional Park. At the end of National Avenue in Tahoe Vista, CA. Snow hill for toboggans, saucers, and inner-tubes. No charge for play area; equipment rentals available. (916) 546-7248.

Old MacDonald's Enterprise. 1060 Ski Run Boulevard, South Lake Tahoe, CA. (916) 544-3663.

If you choose to go sledding in an "unofficial" area be sure to follow common sense rules. For example, never sled alone. Don't sled onto bodies of water or across roads or trails.

Sleigh Rides/Horseback Riding

Northstar. Sleigh rides from the Basque restaurant through the Martis Valley. Operates when snow conditions and weather permits. Horseback trail rides open all year. (916) 562-1230.

Ice Skating

Resort at Squaw Creek. Ice Skating Pavilion and Sports Activity Center at Squaw Valley. Rental shop. Open daily from Thanksgiving to spring. (916) 583-6300.

Squaw Valley USA. Olympic-size outdoor ice rink at the High Camp Bath and Tennis Club. Rental shop and lessons. Open year round. (916) 583-6985.

Cruises

M.S. Dixie. Cruises Lake Tahoe daily, from April to November. Zephyr Cove. 588-3508.

North Tahoe Cruises. Year-round cruises on the *Sunrunner.* Departs from Tahoe Yacht Harbor, Tahoe City, CA. (916) 583-0141.

The Tahoe Queen. Scheduled cruises to Emerald Bay, including dinner-dance cruise. Ski shuttle cruises run Tuesday through Friday. Boats depart from the Ski Run Marina in South Lake Tahoe. Call for reservations. (916) 541-3365; (800) 238-2463.

Woodwind Sailing Cruises. Five departures a day including a sunset champagne cruise each night on a 41-foot catamaran with glass bottom. Departs from Zephyr Cove. 588-3000. Day trips: adults, $14; children 2 to 12, $7. Evening cruises $20 for adults.

South Lake Tahoe Attractions

Please call the numbers listed for hours of operation, ticket prices, and use fees. All phone numbers are in the (702) area code unless otherwise noted.

Heavenly Aerial Tram. Available for sightseeing trips and for dinner at the mountainside restaurant. Summer: (916) 544-6263, Winter: 586-7000. Dinner reservations: 586-7000 ext. 6347. Heavenly Ski Resort, South Lake Tahoe, CA.

Lake Tahoe Historical Society Museum. (916) 541-5458. 3058 Lake Tahoe Boulevard, South Lake Tahoe, CA.

U.S. Forest Service Lake Tahoe Visitor Center. June to September, 8 A..M. to 6 P.M.; interpretive center, stream profile chamber. (916) 573-2600; (916) 573-2674. Highway 89, South Lake Tahoe, CA.

Washoe Indian Cultural Foundation Exhibit. (916) 573-2600. McGonagle Estate, Tallac Historic Estates, Highway 89 South Lake Tahoe, CA.

Emerald Bay State Park. If you've got a camera, this is the place to take it for breathtaking views of Lake Tahoe; if you didn't bring a camera, buy one and bring it here. Highway 89, South Lake Tahoe, CA. (916) 525-7277. Within the park is **Vikingsholm Castle** at the head of the bar near Eagle Falls and Creek. Tours are offered June through September, 10 A.M. to 4 P.M. (916) 525-7277; (916) 541-3030. Emerald Bay State Park, Highway 89, Emerald Bay, CA.

D. L. Bliss State Park. (916) 525-7277. Highway 89, South Lake Tahoe, CA.

Ehrman Mansion. Tours 11 A.M. to 4 P.M. July through September. (916) 525-7982. Sugar Pine Point State Park, Highway 89, Tahoma, CA.

Gatekeeper's Log Cabin Museum. (916) 583-1762. 130 West Lake Boulevard, Tahoe City, CA.

Donner State Park. Memorial to the ill-fated Donner Party of 1846. Open Memorial Day to mid-October, weather permitting. (916) 587-3841. Highway 40, Truckee, CA.

Ponderosa Ranch. Open from May through October, 9:30 A.M. to 5 P.M. Site of some of the scenes of television's *Bonanza* series. 831-0691. Highway 28, Incline Village, NV.

Boating Activities

Lake Tahoe Sailboat Sales & Charters. (916) 541-5053. Tahoe Keys Marina, South Lake Tahoe, CA.

M.S. Dixie. Sternwheeler cruises. 588-3508. Zephyr Cove Marina, 760 Highway 50 at Zephyr Cove, NV.

Tahoe Para-Dice. (916) 541-7499. Anchorage Marina, South Lake Tahoe, CA.

Tahoe Queen Sternwheeler. (916) 541-3364; (800) 238-2463. Ski Run Marina, South Lake Tahoe, CA.

Woodwind Sailing Cruises. 588-3000. Zephyr Cove Marina, 760 Highway 50 at Zephyr Cove, NV.

Zephyr Cove Resort & Marina. Boating and snowmobiling. 588-3833. 760 Highway 50, Zephyr Cove, NV.

Fishing

All of Lake Tahoe and most of the hundreds of smaller back country lakes are open for fishing year-round. Certain exceptions apply to tributaries of Lake Tahoe on both the California and Nevada sides—obtain a copy of fishing regulations from sporting goods stores in the area.

Game fish in the region include mackinaw (lake trout), kokanee salmon, brown trout, rainbow trout, eastern brook trout, golden trout and cutthroat trout, as well as white fish.

Here are some fishing services and resorts catering to anglers:

Caples Lake Resort. (209) 258-8888. Highway 88, Kirkwood, CA.
First Strike Sportfishing. (916) 577-5065.
The Outdoorsman. (916) 541-1660. 2358 Lake Tahoe Boulevard, South Lake Tahoe, CA.
Rich's Fishing Charters. (916) 541-3565; (916) 541-5550.
Sorenson's Resort. (916) 694-2203; (800) 423-9949. Highways 88 and 89, Hope Valley, CA.
Tahoe Sportfishing Company. (916) 541-5448; (800) 696-7797. Ski Run Marina, South Lake Tahoe, CA.
Tahoe Trout Farm. (916) 541-1491. 1023 Blue Lake Avenue, South Lake Tahoe, CA.
Woody's Sportfishing. (916) 544-3086. Lakeside Marina at Stateline, NV.

South Shore Boat Rentals/Launching/Marinas

Call first to check on hours, rates, and conditions.

Action Watersports of Tahoe. Boating, waterskiing. (916) 544-5387; (916) 544-0200.
American River Rafting. (916) 635-4479.
The Anchorage Marina at Camp Richardson. (916) 541-1777. Highway 89, South Lake Tahoe, CA.
Cave Rock. 831-0494. Cave Rock, NV.
Club Nautico. (916) 541-8405. Tahoe Keys Marina, South Lake Tahoe, CA.
The Diving Edge. Scuba Diving. 588-5262.
El Dorado Recreation Area. (916) 541-4611.
Kayak Tahoe. (916) 544-2011.
Lakeside Marina. (916) 541-6626. End of Park Avenue, South Lake Tahoe, CA.
O.A.R.S. Inc. (209) 736-4677; (800) 346-6277.
Ski Run Marina. (916) 544-0200. 900 Ski Run Boulevard, South Lake Tahoe, CA.
Tahoe Keys Marina. (916) 541-2155. Venice Drive East, South Lake Tahoe, CA.
Timber Cove Marina. (916) 544-2942. 3411 Highway 50, South Lake Tahoe, CA.
Tributary Whitewater Tours. (916) 346-6812.
Whitewater Connection. (916) 622-6446; (800) 336-7238.
Zephyr Cove Marina. 588-3833. 760 Highway 50, Zephyr Cove, NV.

North Shore and Surrounding Area Boat Rentals/Launching/Marinas

North Tahoe Marina. (916) 546-8248.
Homewood High & Dry. (916) 525-5966. Homewood, CA.
Meeks Bay Resort & Marina. (916) 525-7542. Meeks Bay, CA.
Sand Harbor. 831-0494. Sand Harbor, NV.

Campgrounds

Mount Rose Campground. 20 miles southwest of Reno on slopes of Mount Rose. 24 sites for tents and trailers up to 16 feet. Elevation 8,900 feet. Open July to mid-September. Route 431. 687-4384.

Warrior Point Park. 40 miles north of Reno. Fishing, beach, waterskiing, boating. Route 445, past Sutcliffe 9 miles to the end of the pavement. 476-1155.

Washoe Lake State Park. 25 miles south of Reno. 25 sites for tents and trailers up to 30 feet. Equestrian area, swimming, fishing, boat launch. Highway 395, Washoe Lake State Park exit. 687-4319; 687-4384.

Beaches, Picnic Areas, and Campgrounds

D. L. Bliss State Park. (916) 525-7277. Highway 89, north of Emerald Bay.

Emerald Bay State Park. (916) 525-7277. Highway 89, Emerald Bay.

Grover Hot Springs State Park. (916) 694-2248. Highway 89 South, 3 miles west of Markleeville, CA.

Sugar Pine Point State Park. (916) 525-7982. Highway 89.

Lake Tahoe Nevada State Parks. 831-0494.

South Lake Tahoe Parks & Recreation Department. (916) 541-4611.

U.S. Forest Service, Lake Tahoe Basin. (916) 573-2600.

Camp Richardson. (916) 541-1801. Highway 89, South Lake Tahoe, CA.

Echo Lakes. Echo Chalet, a privately leased USFS resort. (916) 659-7207. Echo Summit Road off Highway 50.

Davis Creek Park. 20 miles south of Reno. Sites for tents and trailers up to 26 feet. Fishing. Open all year. Take Highway 395 to Bowers Mansion exit. 849-0684.

Golf Courses

Lake Tahoe South Shore

Bijou Municipal Golf Course. South Lake Tahoe, CA. 9 holes, 2,685 yards. Open daily 7:30 A.M. to 7 P.M. 3464 Fairway Avenue. (916) 544-5500.

Edgewood Tahoe Golf Course. Adjacent to the Horizon Casino Resort. 18 holes, 7,491 yards. Rated as one of the top courses in the country. Open May through October. Rates $100 per player, with cart. 588-3566.

Glenbrook Golf Course. 9 holes, 2,577 yards. Mid-April to mid-October. About $30 to $35 per player. Oldest course in Nevada. Highway 50, Glenbrook, NV. 749-5201.

Lake Tahoe Golf Course. 18 holes, 6,707 yards. Highway 50, Meyers, CA. (916) 577-0788.

Tahoe Paradise Golf Course. 18-hole course, 9-hole executive course. Driving range. Highway 50, Meyers, CA. (916) 577-2121.

Lake Tahoe North Shore

Carson Valley Golf Course. 18 holes, 5,700 yards. 265-3181. Carson Valley, NV.

Incline Village Championship Golf Course. 18 holes, 7,138 yards. Designed by Robert Trent Jones, Jr. Open May 1 to October 15. Fees $75 to $85 with cart. Incline Village, NV. 832-1144.

Incline Village Executive Golf Course. 18 holes, 3,200 yards. May 15 to September 30. $45 with cart. Incline Village, NV. 832-1150.

Northstar-at-Tahoe Resort Golf Course. 18 holes, 6,897 yards. Driving range. May through October. $48 with cart. Highway 267 between Truckee and North Lake Tahoe. (916) 562-2490.

Tahoe Donner Golf Course. 18 holes. 6,961 yards for championship course. Mid-May through mid-October. $65 with cart. 12850 Northwoods Boulevard, Truckee. (916) 587-9440.

Hiking Areas

Tahoe Rim Trail. A hiking and horseback riding trail through National Forest lands surrounding Lake Tahoe. Built entirely with donations and volunteer labor, 107 miles of a planned 150-mile circle have been completed, including 50 miles of the existing Pacific Crest Trail. The trail passes high mountain lakes, streams, and meadows and offers views from as high as 10,000 feet at Freel Peak and Alpine Meadows. The trail does not exceed a 10 percent grade and is suitable for beginner through advanced hiking. For information, call (916) 577-0676. Camping is allowed along the trail; contact the U.S. Forest Service for camping information at (916) 573-2600.

Desolation Wilderness Area. Intermediate and advanced trails along the west shore of the lake on U.S. Forest Service land off Highways 50 and 89. The trail encompasses 63,469 acres, 80 small lakes, many streams, alpine, and sub-alpine terrain. There are five primary trailheads on the south and west shores. California permit required; call (916) 573-2600 for information.

Kirkwood. Highway 88 at Carson Pass. Along the south shore, 8,000 acres with trails for all abilities. Passes high country lakes and streams with access to Pacific Crest and Mormon Emigrant Trails. Call (209) 258-6000 for information.

Meiss Lake Country. U.S. Forest Service land south of South Lake Tahoe, CA. The trails encompass 10,000 acres, at intermediate and advanced levels, and pass several high country lakes. Access off Highway 89, 5 miles south of Highway 50 in Meyers, CA. Call (916) 573-2600 for information.

Pope-Baldwin Recreation Area. The Fallen Leaf Trail System leads to the south shore of Fallen Leaf Lake. Access from the U.S. Forest Service Lake Tahoe Visitors Center on Highway 89. Call (916) 573-2600 for information.

Nevada Lake Tahoe State Park. On the East Shore, off Highway 28. Trail to Sand Harbor, Marlette Lake, and the upper elevations of the Carson Range. Access from Spooner Lake at the intersection of Highways 50 and 28. 831-0494; (916) 573-2600.

Bicycle or Moped Rentals

Adventure Sport Vehicle Rental. 2513 Lake Tahoe Boulevard, South Lake Tahoe, CA. (916) 541-7155.

Anderson's Bicycle and Skate Rentals. 645 Emerald Bay Road, South Lake Tahoe, CA. (916) 541-0500.

Don Cheepo's Adventures. 3349 Highway 50, South Lake Tahoe, CA. (916) 544-0356.

Lakeview Sports. 3131 Highway 50, South Lake Tahoe. (916) 544-0183.

Olympic Bike Shop. 620 North Lake Boulevard, Tahoe City, CA. (916) 581-2500.

Porter's Ski & Sport. Tahoe City: 501 North Lake Boulevard; (916) 583-2314. Truckee: (916) 587-1500. Incline Village: 885 Tahoe Boulevard (916) 831-3500.

Richardson's Resort Bicycle Rentals. Highway 89, Camp Richardson. (916) 541-7522.

Sierra Cycleworks. North Shore (Kings Beach): (916) 546-7992. South Shore (South Lake Tahoe): (916) 541-7505.

Tahoe Gear. 5095 West Lake Boulevard, Homewood, CA. (916) 525-5233.

Tahoe Sports Ltd. Crescent V Center, Stateline, NV. (916) 542-4000. South Y Center, South Lake Tahoe, CA. (916) 544-2284.

Horseback Riding and Carriage Rides

South Shore

Borges Carriage & Sleigh Rides. Highway 50 and Lake Parkway, South Lake Tahoe, CA. (916) 541-2953

Camp Richardson Corral. Trail rides, wagon rides, sleigh rides in winter. Overnight and extended pack trips. Emerald Bay at Fallen Leaf Road, South Lake Tahoe. (916) 541-3113.

Sunset Ranch. Ride through the open meadows of the Upper Truckee River, with or without a guide. Children's pony rides and petting zoo. Hayrides and sleigh rides in season. Open year-round. Highway 50, South Lake Tahoe. (916) 541-9001.

Zephyr Cove Stables. Zephyr Cove Resort, Highway 50, Zephyr Cove, NV. 588-5664.

North Shore

Alpine Meadows Stables. Open daily June through October. (916) 583-3905.

Northstar Stables. Open year round. Trail rides in winter and summer, sleigh rides in season, pony rides. Located at Northstar-at-Tahoe ski area. Northstar, CA. (916) 562-1230.

Squaw Valley Stables. Ride the site of the 1960 Winter Olympics. Guided rides, rentals, pony rides. Squaw Valley, CA. (916) 583-7433.

Tahoe Donner Equestrian Center. Truckee. 587-9400.

Balloon Rides

If you've got the nerve, we can't think of very many more thrilling ways to explore the Lake Tahoe or Carson valley than from a hot air balloon at 5,000 feet. There are several companies offering tours; most offer a one- to two-hour trip and charge between $100 and $200 per person. The trips leave early in the morning, before the air heats up and makes things even more unpredictable. The balloon pilots, by the way, have only a limited ability to steer their bags of air and they are chased by ground crews that will retrieve the equipment and passengers and bring them back to the base.

Aerovision Balloons, Inc. 265-5177; (800) 468-2476.

Alpine Adventures Aloft. Minden, NV. 782-7239; (800) 332-9997.

Mountain High Balloons. Truckee. (800) 321-6922.

Soaring

Soar Minden. 782-7627; (800) 345-7627.

Soar Truckee, Inc. (916) 587-6702.

IV
Gambling:
Nevada's Leading Industry

Chapter 27

Gambling Is Not a Sport: A Cautious View

The Business of Playing

A quarter here, a dollar there, a hundred dollar chip on the craps table, and a nickel in the slot of a sawdust joint downtown: it all adds up very quickly.

Casino gambling is big business, with U.S. revenues in 1992 of $12.9 billion. That's an increase of 50 percent since 1990, with much of the growth coming from new casino destinations including riverboats, Indian reservations, and low-stakes casinos.

According to Harrah's, 27 percent of all U.S. households (28 million households) made visits to casinos in 1993. In 1993, U.S. households made 92 million visits to casinos, nearly twice the number from 1990.

And just to put this in perspective, with 92 million annual visits, casinos as an entertainment ranks ahead of Major League Baseball, arena concerts, and Broadway shows.

Nevada, which once had nearly all of the legal gambling in the country, now represents a bit more than half of the industry. Here are the estimated revenues from 1993:

| Las Vegas | $4.5 billion | Reno | $840 million |
| Laughlin | $519 million | Lake Tahoe | $320 million |

Someone's Got to Pay for the Marble

Let's start with two very important points: the fabulous resorts of Las Vegas, Reno, Lake Tahoe, Laughlin, and everywhere in between were not built as exotic gifts by eccentric multimillionaires. Exotic they are, and eccentric be their developers, but every one was built as a business.

Point number two: the business of the fabulous resorts of Nevada is based on the fact that nearly every visitor can be counted upon to *lose* money at gambling tables and slot machines. Some will lose more than others, and a few will even come away with an occasional small or large or huge win, but always remember that the streets of Nevada are paved by the losers.

Before you even *think* about making money gambling, take a good look around you. Do you see those huge casino buildings with their spectacular come-ons outside and opulent decorations within? Do you see those cheap-to-free meals and drinks? Do you see the hundreds of dealers, supervisors, cocktail waitresses, change clerks, keno runners, gladhanders, and assorted others in the cast?

Someone has to pay for all of this. Guess who?

Playing Smart

It is not the purpose of this book to teach you to become a professional gambler. There are any number of detailed tomes that purport to do just that. And, we are not going to attempt to preach at you about the evils of risking your family's rent money at the tables. If that is a problem, you should seek the help of a professional counselor or a 12-step program. (In fact, Nevada has quite a collection of counseling services and organizations, which says something about something.)

Instead, we are going to attempt to explain some of the more popular games played at the casinos and help you have a bit of fun as you lose the money you brought with you. If you win, perhaps you'd like to send an offering to the author.

Rule Number One of Gambling: Do not bet more than you can afford to lose.

Corollary to Rule Number One of Gambling: Do not bring with you to the table (or with you to the hotel) more money than you can afford to lose.

Second Corollary to Rule Number One of Gambling: Don't beg, borrow, or steal more money than you can afford to lose. The casinos will make it very easy for you to tap into credit cards or savings accounts and may even offer unsecured loans. Whatever the source, it will still be a debt.

The House Always Has an Advantage

I am indebted to one of Las Vegas' leading characters, Bob Stupak, for some of the analysis of the business aspects of gambling. Stupak, the founder and personification of Bob Stupak's Vegas World on The Strip, published his own book, called *Yes, You Can Win!* (Galaxy Publishing, Las Vegas) which actually explains how you will most often lose. The book, which is often given away to acolytes at Stupak's house of gambling, is part instruction, part self-promotion.

Let's start with a very basic concept, that of the House Advantage.

The simplest form of gambling might be a bet between two individuals over whether the next flip of a coin would come up heads or tails. If the coin and the person doing the flipping are both honest, the odds of the coin coming up heads or tails are exactly even. This means that the true odds are 1:1, also called even money. If you bet $5 on the flip of the coin and won, you would receive your $5 back plus $5 in winnings.

If a casino (the house, in gambling parlance) was to pay off at those odds, over the course of time both the player and the casino would break even. (Which, in the case of the casino, means it would lose a lot of money, since it costs a lot for the fancy building, the dealers, the free drinks…you get the idea.)

The way the casino makes its money is to charge a commission on winning bets. The house will try to take as much as it can get, although as in any pricing scheme, there comes a point at which the consumer refuses to buy. The typical range of commission on betting is between 2 and 10 percent.

In our fictional example, if the house were to charge a 5 percent commission, a $100 winning bet on a coin toss would receive $195 back instead of $200. (The wager of $100 is returned untouched, and the commission is applied to the winnings.)

If the bet is a loser, the house does not charge a commission, but keeps the entire amount. That money, though, goes to pay off winners.

One way to look at the operations of a casino—and it is only one of many ways—is this: over the long term, a casino makes money only on winning bets.

The poker room at the Palace Station, Las Vegas

Even if a player strikes it rich on a particular bet, the casino can count on the law of averages rebuilding the pot over time. Among other things, most winners stick around and proceed to lose their winnings. The worst possible player for a casino is someone who comes in and wins quickly (paying very little commission along the way) and then leaves ahead of the game (contributing little or nothing to the pot for other winners).

The House Percentage

Now that we have explored the statistical advantage the casino has over the very best gamblers, whether they win or lose, there is one more number to understand.

How, you may ask, does a huge and expensive operation like a major casino make much money if it is able to hold on to only 5 or so percent of the action at the table?

Well, first of all, there is a *lot* of action at most casinos, and so those nickels on the dollar add up very quickly.

Second, though, and more important, there is the fact that the vast majority of gamblers are just not very good at what they do. They'll play hunches, they'll use faulty "systems," and they'll just plain make costly mistakes at the tables. The costliest error of all for many gamblers is this "chasing": throwing good money after bad when they are losing, or perversely throwing away their winnings when they are ahead.

The true winning percentage at most casinos is in the neighborhood of 20 percent.

Everybody Has a System

Some of us like to bet on our birthdate (which in the case of roulette freezes you in time at age 36; the keno game is a bit more accommodating, up to 80). These schemes are harmless, so long as you realize that the odds of a particular number coming up are the same on each spin of the wheel.

More complex and sometimes dangerous betting systems are those that are based on some sort of betting scheme. The most popular of these is a "doubling" strategy, which sounds logical—and is, over time—but rarely works for most bettors with limited resources.

Put another way, doubling is not a very good strategy unless you have a lot of money and a lot of time. Make that an almost unlimited amount of money or an infinite period of time, unless you run into a nice streak of luck—and luck is not an element of strategy.

Doubling works like this: let's say your basic bet is $10. If you bet $10 and lose, your next bet is for $20; if you lose again, you double again to $40 and so on. At some time the bettor will win and at that point will be slightly ahead.

Let's assume you are wagering an even-money bet, which means that when you win your $10 is returned as $20. If you win 10 times in a row, you will be $100 ahead of the game.

Now, let's consider what happens when you lose. Remember—you are planning to double your bet with each loss. As any school kid who has had to work on math tables can tell you, doubling a simple number can quickly lead to a huge value. For example, if you were to lose 10 times in a row, your $10 bet would have risen to $10,240, and you will be out-of-pocket $20,470 at that moment, which just may be beyond your budget for spending money. And, you may run into the table limit, which is yet another way for the casino to increase its chances of cleaning you out.

But let's say you win that even money bet of $10,240. The crowd will gasp, the dealer will smile and you will feel greatly relieved as you are handed a stack of chips worth $20,480. You and the dealer may be the only ones who realize that the net profit on your huge bet will be $10!

Casinos make out quite well on doublers, because the fact is that sooner or later most run out of money or nerve and drop out before they make their small profit.

Gambling professionals—and remember that there are very few who consistently make money at the "game"—say that the classic doubling scheme is exactly backwards. They suggest you increase the size of your bet when you are winning and reduce your bets when you lose. This way you take advantage of your streaks rather than work against them.

In other words, don't chase your losses.

If you just continue to play at the same level, without changing the amount you bet, over a period of time the house's advantage is almost sure to eat away your bankroll.

Slot Machines

At one time, the conventional wisdom may have been that table games—from roulette to 21 to baccarat—were where the real action was at a casino. Slot machines were looked down upon as the province of the low roller.

Today, the average bet at the tables is still considerably higher than at the slot machines, but don't make the mistake of assuming that casinos look down on slot machines as being less interesting than the table games. According to Nevada's Gaming Control Board, in the one-year period ending June 30, 1992, slot revenue totalled about $966.7 million, or 48.6 percent of the market. By the way, the ratio

Some are more equal than others. At Vegas World, as at some other casinos, it is worth your while to pay attention to the payoff rates promised on slots and video poker machines. Some machines in the same casino will have different payouts. One way to check this is to look at the payout for a full house in poker; one bank of machines offered a standard 40:1, while another set of machines promised 50:1.

in Atlantic City crosses the halfway mark.

In any case, here is the rap on slots: they are dumb, require no skill, and provide no human interaction. They are pure exercises in luck, and like other casino bets they ask the player to put aside the knowledge that the casino is almost sure to win over time.

The easiest game in town has just two requirements—coins of the right denomination and a strong arm. Actually, most modern slot machines don't even require you to pull the handle; there's a button you can press to let the machine do the work.

The sexy thing about slot machines is that they can pay off with astronomical amounts; the highest of the high—progressive machines—can return millions of dollars on a bet of $3 or $5.

On slot machines, the house edge is expressed as a "payback" percentage. A particular machine may claim 98 percent payback, meaning that over time the machine pays back 98 percent of the money put into it. The casino keeps 2 percent as its advantage, which can add up over time.

Some casinos will advertise that their machines are "loose," meaning that they pay back higher than others; no casinos that we know of will announce that their machines are "tight" with your money. However, in general the small change machines (nickels and quarters and the rare penny machines) are tighter than the larger denomination slots.

The odds against winning are based on the number of reels (rolling sets of symbols) and the number of symbols on each reel. The highest payoff five-reel machines may work out to a chance of 1 in 3.2 million pulls for the jackpot.

Most slot machines pay better jackpots to bettors who play the maximum number of coins on a pull. So, if you are willing to bet about $1 per pull, you generally would be better off at a quarter machine putting in five coins at a time ($1.25 per pull) than putting in a single dollar token at a dollar machine.

As we've noted, the biggest payoffs are to be found at "progressive" machines, which are slots tied into an electronic network within the same casino, across a group of casinos under the same ownership, or even as part of a statewide network run by an independent slot company. The potential payoffs are huge—millions of dollars in some cases—but the odds against winning can be astronomical.

One other point to be aware of is the payoff scheme for a particular jackpot. Most systems pay off their huge jackpots with an annuity: if you win what is advertised as a $1 million prize, what you may receive are 20 annual checks of $50,000 each, which costs the casino less and is worth less to you. A few casinos, always seeking some new lure, advertise full payoffs at the time of winning.

Every Slot Machine Is Not the Same

Understand this: slot machines are fixed. Technicians can set the rate of payout over time. It's all legal, and it's all under the supervision of state gaming authorities.

Another thing: not all slot machines in the same state, same city, or even the same casino are set at the same payoff rate.

According to a survey published in *Casino Player* magazine in April of 1994, on average the best slot payoffs in Nevada are generally found in downtown Las Vegas, with an average payout of 95.8 percent, about 1 percent better than found on The Strip. The best payout percentage could be found on the higher denomination machines, especially the $5 slots.

What does it mean when a machine pays off at a 95.8 percent rate? Well, it could mean that a bettor putting $100 into the machine will walk away with about $95.80 and a sore arm. Or, it could mean that the same bettor could lose every penny of his or her stake, and the next player could leave with $191.60 for $100 bet. Even more likely, 99 bettors could lose every penny and the one hundredth could hit a $10,000 jackpot. In every case, over time, the house will earn a profit. And over time, every player but the most lucky will lose.

Slot machines at the Las Vegas Hilton

Bigger than life. At various times, Vegas World has claimed it offers more than 100 percent payout on some video poker machines. What does that mean? It means that if played properly, over the long haul, they will pay out more than they collect from an individual player. It does not mean that a bad player—or even an average player—will win anything at all.

Video Poker

Among the hottest types of gambling machines are video poker devices. There are dozens of different formats, but most of them come down to versions of Stud Poker. The machine will deal you five cards and you can choose to hold any or all of them or draw from one to five new cards. After the second round of cards the hand is evaluated and winning hands are paid off.

Most machines pay off only on a pair of jacks or better. In addition, the relative payoffs are much higher for the best hands. Therefore, professional video poker players generally recommend throwing away any low hands and always making a play for the high-payoff hands. For example, in standard poker you would almost never draw to an inside straight (seeking to fill out a straight with a gap in the middle, as in 9-10-Q-K), but in video poker it might be worth a chance.

One area worth paying attention to are the listed payouts on video poker machines. Some casinos pay off considerably better than others; there may even be a noticeable disparity among machines in the same casino.

Circular Logic: Roulette

Round and round she goes, where she stops nobody knows. Some historians track the roulette wheel back to the ancient Chinese or Tibetans of 1,000 years ago; the famous French scientist and mathematician Blaise Pascal is credited with adapting the wheel to a casino game in 1655.

Of the four major table games (roulette, craps, blackjack, and baccarat), roulette offers the poorest odds to the player. The American game, as played in Nevada with the 0 and 00 numbers added to the layout, gives the house a 5.26 percent advantage on most bets; the worst gamble for the player is the five-number bet, which gives the house an advantage of more than 7 percent. It is, though, one of the simplest of games to play. In the standard Nevada game, the wheel is divided into alternating red and black compartments that are numbered from 1 to 36; in addition, one compartment is numbered 0 and another 00. A player can bet on any of the 38 numbers directly, and is paid off at 35:1. (Here is the House Advantage presented about as clearly as possible: there is a 1 in 38 chance of a particular number coming up, and the winning payoff is 35:1.

The 0 and 00 are excluded from the payoffs on red/black, odd/even, columns, or rows. In other words, the casino wins all bets on color, odd/even, or groups of numbers if 0 or 00 comes up.

(There are a handful of smaller casinos in Nevada that may offer roulette wheels with only a single 0, which improves the player's odds somewhat.)

The roulette table, usually made of green felt, includes boxes colored and numbered to correspond to the colors and numbers of the compartments of the wheel. The numbers are divided into 12 rows and three columns; there are also betting boxes for group bets including red or black, odd or even, 1-12, 1-18, 13-24, 19-36, and 25-25. There are also boxes for each of the three columns. Finally, there are betting boxes for 0 and 00.

After a period of time to place bets, the dealer starts the wheel spinning in a counterclockwise direction and then sends the ball in the opposite direction. Players can continue to place bets until the ball is about to fall off its track and onto the wheel; the dealer will indicate when bets are closed.

At most casinos, you will use special chips to play roulette, cashing in your casino markers for a special set of colored chips in various denominations. The reason for the change is that the player is able to place as many bets as he or she wants, all over the table; the color-coded chips allow the dealer to keep track of which bets belong to which player.

Here is the typical payoff schedule for roulette wheels in Nevada. At most casinos you will find the payoffs listed on the felt surface of the table itself.

Single number	35:1	**12 numbers or**	
Single 0	35:1	**section bet**	2:1
Double 00	35:1	**2 numbers/split**	17:1
0/00 Split	17:1	**3 numbers**	11:1
5 numbers	6:1	**4 numbers**	8:1
Black/Red	1:1	**6 numbers**	5:1
Odd/Even	1:1	**Column bets**	2:1
1 to 18/19 to 36	1:1		

As we have noted, at most casinos the house has an edge of 5.26 percent on all roulette bets except for the five-number bet of 0-00-1-2-3 which is even less advantageous to the bettor with an edge of 7.89 percent. Put another way, the five-number bet, with payoff odds of 6 to 1, is the worst bet in roulette.

Since no one bet in roulette is theoretically better than another (with the exception of the five-number parlay), it may make sense to concentrate on one type of bet and hope that your luck over the short term is better than the house advantage's chomp at your bankroll.

Blackjack (21)

Blackjack, also called 21, is one of the more popular casino games and—on one level—one of the easiest to play. All you have to do is request cards from the dealer, one at a time, until you get as close to a card value of 21 as you can. If you get closer to 21 than the dealer, you win; if you go over 21 or if the dealer is closer to that magic number you lose. If you and the dealer tie, your bet is returned to you.

Betting is relatively simple, too. You are always betting against the dealer, always betting that your card value will be better than his or hers. There are only a few variations in betting schemes, including doubling down and splitting, which we will explain in a moment.

But, as we said, although blackjack is easy to play, it is not easy to win. It is, though, one of the few games at the casino that can be consistently beaten, or at least fought to a draw, by a careful player.

A player who understands the basic strategy and bets conservatively can expect to win about 1 percent of total action over the course of time which doesn't sound like much but can quickly mount up into serious money. Players who can count cards and adjust the levels of betting and strategies based on the current condition of the deck can expect to win much more. The line between winning and losing is always slim, and the casino always stands to benefit from a mistake by the player.

Numbered cards, from 2 to 10, are counted at face value. Face cards (jacks, queens, and kings) count as 10. An ace counts as 1 or 11, whichever suits your purposes.

Place your bet in front of you prior to the deal. The dealer will then work his way around the table twice, dealing two cards to you and two cards to himself. In the standard game, the player's cards are dealt face up and the dealer's cards are dealt one down and one up.

If you score 21 (an ace together with a king, queen, jack, or 10) with your first two cards, turn them over immediately and collect one and a half times your bet. If your first two cards don't total 21, you can either "stand" (refuse additional cards) or request a "hit" (an additional card). You can request as many hits as it takes to either approach a total of 21 or be "busted" (to exceed 21 and lose).

Watch the players at the table, or ask the dealer about the protocol for indicating whether you want to hit or stand. Some casinos are more picky than others about hand signs used at the table. In most casinos, you indicate that you want another card by scratching your current cards toward you on the felt or by waving at the dealer with a "come to me" gesture. (Looser dealers will permit you to nod your head "yes" or perform some other positive signal.) To indicate you want to stand, you can slip your cards, face down, under your bet or give some sort of a "wave off" signal.

The reason casinos are sometimes picky about the signals used is that they don't want a bettor to ask for his money back on a losing bet because of any ambiguity about betting intentions. Other casino protocol: handle the cards with one hand only; don't take the cards off the table, and don't touch your bet once cards have been dealt.

If you are busted, turn over all your cards and watch the dealer take away your bet.

If you stand with your current card total, action passes to the next player at the table and so on until it reaches the dealer.

Although you are free to do just about anything at the table, the dealer must follow some very specific rules. The basic rules are these:

• The dealer must stand with cards totaling 17 or more, and must hit for any total under 17.

• At many casinos, the dealer must also hit on a "soft" 17, which is a card that can be valued as 7 or 17 depending on whether the ace is counted as a 1 or an 11.

If the dealer busts, all players still in the game win. If the dealer does not bust and your cards are closer to 21 than the dealer's you will win your bet; if the dealer's cards are closer to 21, you will lose your bet. And if your card value is the same as the dealer's it is a "push" and your bet is returned to you.

That's all there is to the game. Now, of course, you have to figure out the way to stay a step ahead of the dealer. As we have noted, the dealer has no choice in his or her actions.

There are two steps to becoming a good blackjack player. First is to understand basic playing strategies that will change based on the cards you have drawn and the face-up card displayed by the dealer. The second step, which is for only the most advanced players blessed with extraordinary attention to details and memory, is called "card counting."

We're not going to go into details on card counting—there are many books about the subject if you've got a few months you want to devote to practicing this art. Basically, the purpose of card counting is to determine the balance of the deck to improve your chances at figuring whether cards you may draw are likely to be high-value or low-value cards. A good card counter can all but guarantee a winning margin at the table.

Before you give up those months to study, though, you should be aware that most Nevada casinos look very unfavorably on card counters. If the pit boss or the dealer suspects a player is counting cards, he may order constant shuffling of the deck which disrupts the system or he may try other distractions. The Nevada authorities even cooperate with casinos in barring card counters from their casinos. Obviously both the casinos and the state much prefer losing players to those with a fighting chance at winning.

Blackjack Bets

The standard payoff for winning hands in blackjack is 1:1 (your bet is returned with an equal winning amount). If you draw a blackjack (two cards that total 21, such as an ace and a jack or other face card or an ace and 10) you will be paid 1.5:1.

There are also a few special bets you can make once play begins. They include:

Doubling Down. If you think you have a strong hand with the first two cards you draw (usually a pair of cards totaling 9, 10, or 11) you can double your bet and hope for a winning hand with the third card you are drawn. You will automatically stand with the hand you have.

Splitting Pairs. You can split two same-value cards into two hands each with its own bet. The dealer will give you an additional card on each half of the pair and can stand or continue drawing on each hand. At most casinos, though, the payoff on a winning split hand is just 1:1.

Insurance. If the dealer shows an ace as his "up" card, you can bet half of your original wager as insurance against the chance that the dealer will have a card worth 10 as his "hole" card. In other words, protection against the dealer having a blackjack. If the dealer does score 21, you lose your original bet but are paid 2:1 on your insurance bet.

As we've said, there are entire books on blackjack strategies. We'll only touch the surface in this book with a simple summary.

First of all, you should always draw a card if you have a hand worth 11 or less; there is no possible way to go over 21.

From there on it gets a bit more complex. First let's define two types of hands:

A **hard total** is any hand of any number of cards that adds up to 12 or more without an ace, or any hand in which the ace is valued as 1 and not 11. (If the ace were valued as an 11, the hand would go over 21 and therefore bust the bet.)

A **soft total** is any hand of any number of cards in which an ace can be valued at either 1 or 11 without busting the hand. When the ace is valued at 11, the hand is called a soft hand. A soft total can change to a hard total based on the values of other cards drawn. For example, if you held an ace and a 5, the total can be either 6 or 16. If you were to draw a jack or other 10-value card, your hand would now be a hard total of 16 since counting the ace as an 11 would bust the hand.

The player in blackjack has some significant advantages over the dealer because the dealer must follow the house rules without exception, always drawing on a 16 and standing on a 17. The player can adjust strategy based on the latest run of cards or the up card shown by the dealer. The one advantage held by the dealer, and it is a very large one, is the fact that the dealer goes last. If a player busts before the dealer draws a card—even if the dealer busts—the player loses his or her bet.

The strategies are based on statistical analyses that show that the dealer is most likely to bust his hand when he has a low value card, from 2 to 6, showing. This is called a "bust hand." The dealer will have to draw another card unless he has a 6 showing and an ace hidden. When the dealer shows a bust hand and you have a decent hand yourself, you will be best off standing pat and not drawing another card.

At the other end of the scale, the dealer is likely to have a "pat hand" when a 7 through ace is showing, and unless you have a strong hand already it will be worth taking a chance to draw another card.

Here are two charts that show common strategies for hard and soft totals.

Hard Total	Dealer's Up Card	Strategy
17	Any card	Stand
16, 15, 14, or 13	2, 3, 4, 5, or 6	Stand
16, 15, 14, or 13	7 through ace	Hit
12	2 or 3	Hit
12	4, 5, or 6	Stand
12	7 through ace	Hit

Soft Total	Dealer's Up Card	Strategy
Ace and 9	Any card	Stand
Ace and 8	Any card	Stand
Ace and 7	9 or 10	Hit
Ace and 7	2, 3, 4, 5, 6, 7, 8, or ace	Stand
Ace and 6	Any card	Hit

Why should you always hit against an ace and 6? Blackjack players consider a 17 a useless hand, since the only way you can win with it is for the dealer to bust his hand. You may as well try to improve your hand until it is greater than 17 or you reach a stand-pat hard total.

Strategies for other kinds of bets can become increasingly complex and will not be covered here.

Craps: Where the Action Is

Craps is one of the more exciting games at the casino, one where the players and even the various casino employees are encouraged to yell, shout, and otherwise encourage the little cubes of plastic to come up properly.

We'll cover the basic mechanics of the game and how to bet; if you are serious about the game, you should read a specialized gambling book.

The thrower (called the shooter) makes a money bet, covered by one or more opponents. The shooter throws the two dice against the far wall of the craps table. (This is an important rule of the casino; the boxman or pit boss may halt the game if they don't feel you are throwing the dice with enough force to ensure an honest tumble.) If the first throw totals 7 or 11, the player wins, but if 2, 3, or 12 is thrown, the player loses. In any of these cases betting and throwing are repeated.

If the throw totals 4, 5, 6, 8, 9, or 10, that number becomes the player's point, and throwing is continued until the same point is made again or a 7 is thrown. If the point is made, the player wins, but if a 7 is thrown, the player loses both the bet and the right to throw again.

So far, so good: now let's talk about the betting protocol for craps which is a bit more difficult to understand than the game itself. First of all, there are some variations from casino to casino; most casinos offer classes at quiet times or may have a printed summary of rules and payoff odds. Some casinos pay off better than others, too.

Pass Line. A bet placed on the Pass Line means you are betting with the dice and the shooter. If the shooter rolls 7 or 11 (a natural) on the first roll, you win and are paid even money (one chip for each chip you have bet).

If the shooter rolls 2, 3, or 12 (craps), you and the shooter lose. Any other number (4, 5, 6, 8, 9, 10) is a "point" number and the bet rolls over. If the shooter rolls a point number again before a 7, you both win.

Casino gaming lessons at Caesars Palace, Las Vegas

Don't Pass Line. A bet on the Don't Pass Line means you are betting against the dice and the shooter, and the reverse of the pattern for the Pass Line applies.

You will lose your bet on a 7 or 11 on the first roll, and will win on a 2 or 3. A 12 is a "standoff" with no winner or loser. If a 7 is rolled before the shooter makes his point, you win; if a point number is made before a 7 is rolled, you lose.

Come. After the shooter has rolled a point number, you can place a bet on the Come line.

You will win your bet if the shooter rolls a 7 or 11, and you will lose if a 2, 3, or 12 comes up. Any other combination is a "come" point; if the come point appears before a 7, you win.

Don't Come. After the shooter has rolled a point number, you can bet on the Don't Come line. You win if a 2 or 3 is rolled. A 7 or 11 is a loser, and 12 is a standoff. If a come point is rolled before a 7, you lose.

Proposition Bets. Most craps tables allow specific bets on the next roll of the dice; consult the stickman for how to place your bets. These include **Any Craps** (2, 3, or 12), which pays 7:1; **Any Seven,** which usually pays 4:1; a bet on **2** or **12,** which pays 30:1; or a bet on **3** or **11,** paying 15:1. These bets are not recommended by experts.

Place Bets. Ask the dealer for the way to place this bet in one of the numbered boxes on the felt. Before any roll, you can bet on 4, 5, 6, 8, 9, or 10. If your number comes up before a 7 you win. Typical odds are 7:5 for a 5 or 9, 7:6 on a 6 or 8, and 9:5 for a 4 or 10.

Field Bet. Bet on the next roll of the dice by placing a chip in the Field box. You will be paid even money if a 3, 4, 9, 10, or 11 is rolled; a 2 pays 2:1 and a 12 pays 3:1.

Big 6 or 8. Some casinos include a separate betting box for this wager; you will be paid even money if a 6 or 8 is rolled before a 7. Craps experts consider this one of the least attractive bets on the table.

Horn Bet. A four-unit bet that the next roll will come up 2, 3, 11, or 12; even if you win, the house will keep three out of the four units as losing bets. An especially unattractive gamble, according to the experts.

Baccarat: The High Roller's Game

The ancient game of baccarat (pronounced bah-kah-rah), is derived from a French card game dating from the 15th century. In Europe, a very similar game is called "chemin de fer" which means road of iron, better known as a railroad.

Baccarat is a fairly difficult game to understand, but it is very easy to play since the dealer will handle all of the work. All you need to do is make your bet. And the house advantage is rather low, just over 1 percent on bank and player bets.

In the version of baccarat played in most Nevada casinos, the game is played with a set of eight decks of cards shuffled and placed in a "shoe." The casino will provide a printed copy of the rules or a wall plaque with rules; in any case, it is the dealer who makes all of the decisions.

The object of the game is to wager on the hand which the player believes will come as close to nine as possible (without going over) with two cards (and a possible third). Ties are replayed. The players may bet a total of any amount equal to or less than the amount of the bank.

You can bet at any time on the player's hand or the bank's; you can also bet on a tie. Standard bets are paid even money, minus a 5 percent commission on all winning bank bets. Tie bets pay 9 to 1 odds.

The player keeps control of the shoe as long as the bank hand wins; when the bank hand loses, the shoe moves to the next player to the right. A player can voluntarily pass the shoe after any hand.

Although only two players—the "banker" and the "player"—are actually dealt cards from the shoe by the banker, all players (including the banker) can bet either on the banker's hand or the player's hand. The "player" is the player with the largest bet on the player's side.

The highest hand in baccarat is nine and the lowest zero. An ace counts as 1, a deuce as 2, and so on. Face cards and 10s, or any combination of cards totaling 10 have no value.

The last digit of the total is the hand value; a 7 and a 7, for example, may equal 14, but the value of the hand is 4; the value of a 9 and 4 is 3.

Keno: The Unglamorous Game

Keno is bingo with gambling on the odds of particular combinations of numbers being called. In some places, it is sort of the background music of the casino, with keno cards and display boards almost everywhere, from the casino floor to the restaurants and sports books.

The game consists of gambling on the likelihood of any 20 of 80 numbers being drawn at one session. The more numbers you mark the higher the possible payoff (and the lower the chances of winning).

To play the game, obtain a blank keno ticket from a keno writer or from the tabletop holder in many restaurants or lounges and put an X through the numbers you want to bet on. Give your bet to the runner and retain the duplicate ticket he or she will give to you.

Depending on the time of the day and the size of the casino, the keno game will be conducted as often as two or three times per hour; some casinos even run multiple games at the same time, using color-coded cards.

The casino selects 20 of the 80 numbers at random. Compare these with the numbers you selected; it isn't hard to figure out if you've won or lost. There are no guaranteed winners in a game; if all of the players lose, the house wins all of the money. When there is a large payoff it will almost certainly be larger than the amount bet in the current game, but it will come out of the pool of money from previous losing sessions.

The simplest bet in keno is just to select a few numbers and bet on them coming up. At some houses the highest payoff is a fixed amount, while at others the top payment is part of a progressive pool shared with other casinos. If the pool is large, the payoff will be large; if someone has tapped it lately, the payoff will be less. You should also be aware that most keno games limit the total payout per game; if you have the good luck to win a high-payoff bet you might also have the bad luck to do so in the same game as someone else's winning play.

Here are some randomly selected payoff schedules in effect at several Nevada casinos on one of our visits; they are subject to change, of course.

Standard Game. Mark 10 numbers and bet $5.

Hit	Harrah's Reno	Rio Vegas	Bally's Vegas	Harrah's Tahoe
5	$10	$5	$5	$10
6	$100	$100	$100	$100
7	$625	$750	$750	$700
8	$5,000	$5,000	$5,000	$4,500
9	$22,500	$25,000	$22,500	$20,000
10	$250,000	Progressive	$50,000	$100,000

Keno is a game at which the casino has a huge advantage, as much as 40 percent on some bets. The large payoffs for small investments and its slow pace make it a sometimes enjoyable pastime when you are too busy eating dinner to stand at the tables.

Be sure you read and understand the rules of the game at each casino. At most establishments, for example, you must immediately cash in winning tickets before the next game is begun; in other words, a ticket that is worth $250,000 drops to $0 if not collected within minutes. Obviously, you don't want to be sitting in a show, up in your room, or otherwise distracted if you have a live keno ticket. Some casinos have introduced series tickets that are valid for extended periods of time across multiple games; study the rules and the fine print.

Pai Gow

A game that originated in ancient China and is sometimes called Chinese dominoes, pai gow is increasingly popular in Nevada because of the influx of Asian gamblers. Similar to baccarat, the house collects a commission of 5 percent on all winning bets.

Pai gow is a rotating bank game that uses a standard set of 32 Chinese dominoes. The dealer mixes or shuffles them and they are then placed in eight stacks of four tiles. The dealer and up to seven players are each given one stack.

The object of the game is to divide the four tiles in your stack into the best two pairs; if your rankings are higher than those of the banker, you win. If the banker's rankings are higher or the same as the player's, the player loses the bet.

Pai Gow Poker

One way in which pai gow has been simplified for western players is pai gow poker, which combines elements of the ancient Chinese game with the American game of poker. The game is played with a standard deck of 52 cards plus a single joker.

The joker is a not a true "wild" card. It can be used only as an ace, or as wild card to complete a straight, flush or straight flush.

Each player is dealt seven cards. The player's task is to arrange the cards into two hands: a two-card (low) hand and a five-card (high) hand. The object of the game is to arrange your cards so that both of your hands rank higher than both of the banker's two hands.

The Sports and Race Book

One of the more interesting areas of major casinos is the sports and race book, where you can place bets on almost every major sporting event. Satellite dishes feed multiple TV screens showing horse racing from around the country as well as professional and collegiate basketball, hockey, baseball, and football. You can also bet on far-distant events, such as picking the winner of the Super Bowl, the Stanley Cup, the NBA Championships or the World Series at the start of a season.

Football

To place a bet, all you need to do is pick a team and determine how much you want to wager.

In order to win a straight football bet, though, your chosen team must "cover the spread" by either winning or not losing by the indicated number of points.

The point spread is determined by oddsmakers, who choose one team as the favorite; then a guess is made of how many more points that team is likely to score than the underdog team. It is then said that the favorite *gives* a certain number of points to its opponent.

For example, if Team A is listed as a 14 point favorite over Team B, to win a bet on Team A it must be victorious by more than 14 points in order for you to win. If you bet on Team B, the underdog, you will win if they win or if they lose by less than 14 points.

Point spreads may change before a game begins and even while the game is underway. However, all bets stand as written; the point spread in effect at the time you place your bet is the one that will be used in determining whether your particular bet wins or loses.

Here is the way an available football bet might appear on the boards:

    101 New England Patriots   (ov/un 42)
    102 San Francisco 49ers   -14

In this case, the teams are identified by a betting number. The bottom team is always the home team, unless indicated. The 49ers are listed here as a 14-point favorite, meaning that they must win the game by no less than 15 points for you to win your bet. If you were to take the Patriots, a 14-point underdog, you will win your bet if they win the game or if they lose by no more than 13 points.

The *ov/un* listing is the estimation of the total number of points that will be scored in the game. You can bet that the final score (including overtime) will add up to more or less than this amount; the point spread has no effect on the bet. This bet pays off at 10:11.

Straight Bet. This is a wager on one event whose outcome for betting purposes is determined by a point spread or money odds. The standard betting odds on a point spread bet are 11 to 10, meaning that you can win $10 for each $11 you wager. (If you bet $11 and win, you will be paid a total of $21.)

Parlays. Two or more team events or propositions can be tied together to make one wager. All teams must win by the listed point spread. Parlays are more challenging to win than straight bets, but the return on the money is much more attractive. The payout odds progress as the bettor picks more teams. Parlay payoff odds differ from casino to casino; consult the rules of the sports book.

Teasers. Some sports books offer a wager in which additional points are either added to the underdog, or subtracted from the favorite. Teaser points and payoff odds are posted.

Horse Racing

You can bet on any horse to win, place (come in first or second), or show (come in first, second, or third) as well as wager on combinations of horses or combinations of races.

Horses are assigned a betting number on the display boards and scratch sheets, and bets are placed by specifying the amount of the bet, the type of the bet, and the horse number.

Winning bets are paid off based on the odds in effect at the time the race begins. You are not betting against the casino, but instead against all other bettors in the parimutuel pool. Here are the approximate pay-offs for horse racing odds, based on a $2 bet; multiply the payoff times the appropriate factor for a larger bet:

Odds	Pays on $2 bet	Odds	Pays on $2 bet
1-5	$2.40	8-5	$5.20
2-5	$2.80	9-5	$5.60
1-2	$3.00	2	$6.00
3-5	$3.20	5-2	$7.00
4-5	$3.60	3	$8.00
1	$4.00	7-2	$9.00
6-5	$4.40	4	$10.00
7-5	$4.80	9-2	$11.00
3-2	$5.00	5	$12.00

Check the house rules for payoffs. Here is some of the fine print from Harvey's at Lake Tahoe: full track mutuels are paid up to $100 across the board on all straight winners; after that the maximum odds are 20:1 to win, 8:1 to place, and 4:1 to show. Daily doubles, exactas, parlays, and house quinellas are subject to a 150:1 maximum limit, not to exceed $5,000 on an single wager.

Straight Wager. A single bet on one horse in one race. Pays off at parimutuel odds.

Daily Triple. A single bet in which you attempt to pick the winners of three designated races. Payout is limited to 299:1 at many casinos.

Trifecta. A single bet that predicts the win, place, and show horse in a single race. Payout is limited to 299:1 at many casinos.

Daily Double. Pick the winner of the first two races at a track or (at some tracks) two other races. If one of the horses is scratched, the bet is converted to a straight wager on the remaining horse. Odds are based on the betting pool at the track.

Exacta. Select one horse to win and another to place in a particular race. Paid based on track odds.

Basketball

Similar to football betting, there is both a point spread and an over-under bet available.

There are also **basketball parlays** that combine various games; all teams in a parlay must cover the point spread to win the bet.

Baseball

There is no point spread in the standard baseball bet; instead the betting "units" are adjusted to represent the estimation of the oddsmakers of the chances of either of the two teams.

A baseball betting option is presented like this:

```
601NY METS    +1.20   7        ov       -1.10
602CHI CUBS   -1.35   7        un       -1.10
```

The minus (–) on the board indicates the favorite, while the plus (+) indicates the underdog.

In the above example, the Cubs are the favorite at –1.35. To bet on the Cubs, you must bet 1.35 units for each one you hope to win; for example, you would have to put up $13.50 to win $10 for a total of $23.50. If you bet on the hapless Mets and they win the game, you will be paid 1.20 units for each unit you wager; for example, you would be paid $12 for a $10 bet for a total of $22.

The next number is the total or over/under number, the estimation of the combined score of both teams. Also indicated are the over and under odds, in this case 1.10, meaning you would have to put up $11 in hopes of winning $10 more.

Some casinos will offer a run line bet, which is similar to a point spread in that it requires the favorite to win by the specified number of runs. Or, if you bet on the underdog, that team receives extra runs added to the final score. The run line uses the same sort of unit wagering as other baseball bets.

Some sports books permit you to qualify your bet so that it only applies if the listed pitcher starts the game; if a different pitcher is used, the bet is scratched and your money will be refunded.

Hockey

Hockey bets follow the same model as baseball, with a point or "puck line" defining the difference, plus an over/under bet for total goals.

Boxing

To bet on a boxing match, you either lay odds or take money odds. Here is the way a boxing bet might be listed:

```
101       P. Herman      +4.50
102       Ali            -6.00
```

In this case Ali is the clear favorite, and bettors must put up six units to win one. For example, a $600 winning bet would return $100 in profit, or a total of $700.

A bet on Peewee Herman would pay off 4.5 units to 1 bet. For example, a $100 winning bet would return $450 in profit for a total of $550.

Other bets on major bouts include wagering on whether a match will go above or below a specified number of rounds.

Bingo

You know, just like the game the church ladies offer Thursday nights. Some of the low-roller joints offer games with fees as low as 10 cents; anything to bring in a buck.

Among the hotels with bingo games are:

Strip and nearby: Aladdin, Gold Coast, Harrah's, and Palace Station.

Downtown and out of town: Arizona Charlie's, Binion's Horseshoe, Ellis Island, Gold Spike, Jerry's Nugget, Sam's Town, and Western.

The bingo room at Palace Station, Las Vegas

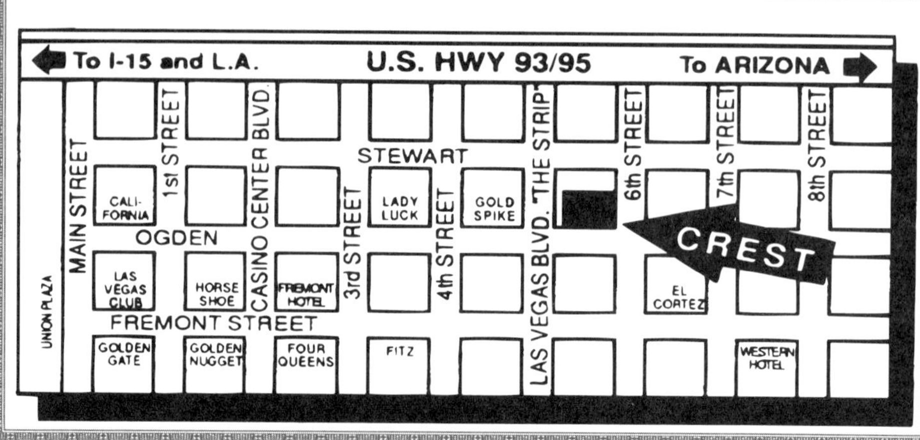

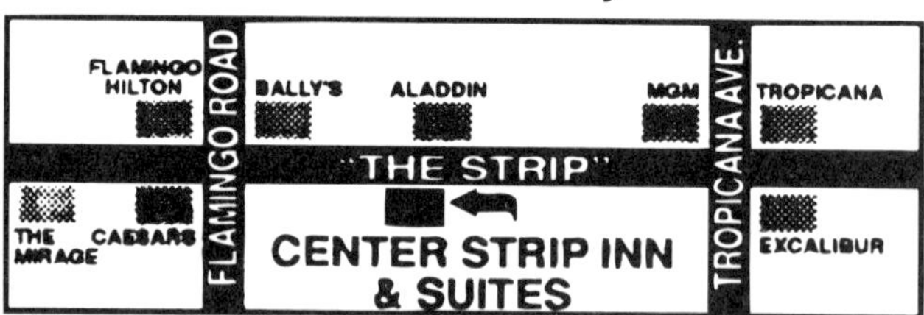

"*Located in the ♥ of the Strip*"

Las Vegas, Reno, and Lake Tahoe

Word Association, Inc.
Box 2779 Nantucket, MA 02584

Valid thru Sept. 1995
Present to ticket window (Las Vegas Park only) for your discount. Coupon is good for up to six people. Not to be used in conjunction with any other offer, discount or afternoon pricing. Not for sale.

For general information call (702) 734-0088.
GPLU #121   CPLU #122

WALK TO THE "GLITTER GULCH" GAMBLING HALLS

DOWNTOWNER INN

129 North 8th Street, Las Vegas, NV
702-384-1441 • 800-777-2566

Only steps away from Binions Horseshoe, El Cortez, 4-Queens

$24.00 * 1-4 persons

- **Free complete breakfast**
  Bacon/eggs or hotcakes each morning
- **Free pastries, snacks, coffee**
- **Free local calls and fax, TV/VCR and refrigerator in each room**

$5.00 discount with this coupon

*Midweek, excluding holidays and special events. No other discounts apply— subject to availability—rates subject to change without notice.

Expiration: 12/31/95

Sundance Helicopters
1-800-653-1881
Las Vegas, Nevada

• 10% Discount •
Discount to be used on next Grand Canyon adventure.

Direct Bookings only. Coupon must be presented at time of reservation.
Offer expires 12/31/95

Econoguide

Las Vegas, Reno, and Lake Tahoe

Word Association, Inc.
Box 2779 Nantucket, MA 02584

Las Vegas, Reno, and Lake Tahoe

Word Association, Inc.
Box 2779 Nantucket, MA 02584

ECONOGUIDE
1995
Las Vegas, Reno, and Lake Tahoe
Word Association, Inc.
Box 2779 Nantucket, MA 02584

ECONOGUIDE
1995
Las Vegas, Reno, and Lake Tahoe
Word Association, Inc.
Box 2779 Nantucket, MA 02584

ECONOGUIDE
1995
Las Vegas, Reno, and Lake Tahoe
Word Association, Inc.
Box 2779 Nantucket, MA 02584

ECONOGUIDE
1995
Las Vegas, Reno, and Lake Tahoe
Word Association, Inc.
Box 2779 Nantucket, MA 02584

Las Vegas, Reno, and Lake Tahoe

Word Association, Inc.
Box 2779 Nantucket, MA 02584

CACTUS JACK'S

FREE LAUGHLIN TOUR!

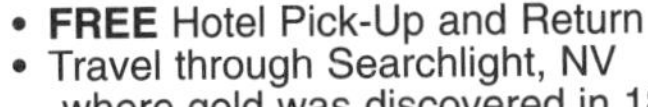

TOUR INCLUDES
- **FREE** Hotel Pick-Up and Return
- Travel through Searchlight, NV where gold was discovered in 1890
- Buffet Luncheon **INCLUDED**
- **FREE** Coffee and Donuts at a.m. Check-in
- **FREE** Funbook from your Host Hotel on the Colorado River
- **FREE** Las Vegas Fun Pak

Daily Departures
24 Hr. Reservations
Call Now!

HOOVER DAM DELUXE
- All Transfers
- Hoover Dam Lunch
- Liberace Museum
- Ethel M's Choc. Factory

Save $10 ONLY $22.95 P.P.
Express Tour Only $12.95 P.P.

THE LAND/AIR
- Hoover Dam
- Grand Canyon All Transfers
- Aerial Air Tour of Grand Canyon
- Hoover Dam Lunch
- Ethel M's Choc. Factory

Save $20 Only $99.95 P.P.

HOOVER DAM CRUISE
- All Transfers
- One Hr. Cruise on Lake Mead
- Lunch • Ethel M's Choc. Factory
- Hoover Dam

Save $5 Only $29.95

EXPIRATION: 12/31/95

Cactus Jack's Wild West Tour Co. (702) 731 9400

"VIVA LAS VEGAS" SHOW

Buy 1 and get 1 free show ticket

Performances Monday thru Friday 1:00 & 3:30 p.m.

Present this coupon at the Sands Show Reservations Booth to purchase your show ticket at the price of $10 and receive one free ticket. One standard drink and tax included. Not valid with any other offer. No cash value. Management reserves all rights.

Expires 12/30/95

3355 Las Vegas Blvd. So., Las Vegas, NV 89109 (702) 733-5000

MANFREDI'S 2 FOR 1

RENAISSANCE CENTER
TROPICANA & EASTERN

Bring this coupon in for a **FREE ENTREE** with the purchase of **ANY ENTREE** of equal or greater value.
Must present coupon before ordering.
Not valid with any other coupon. Not valid holidays.
No separate checks. Minimum $20 credit card.
Coupon can be cancelled any time.

739-1410

EXPIRATION:
12/31/95

CASINO
BOARDWALK

3750 Las Vegas Blvd. So.
Across from the MGM
"So close you can hear the lion roar"

(702) 735-2400 (800) HOLIDAY
(465-4329)

Good for choice of:
Frozen Margarita or Bloody Mary and One Castle Burger

Must present coupon when ordering.
Limit one coupon per person. Must be 21.
Valid 24 hours a day. Expires 12/31/95

ECONOGUIDE
1995
Las Vegas, Reno, and Lake Tahoe
Word Association, Inc.
Box 2779 Nantucket, MA 02584

ECONOGUIDE
1995
Las Vegas, Reno, and Lake Tahoe
Word Association, Inc.
Box 2779 Nantucket, MA 02584

ECONOGUIDE
1995
Las Vegas, Reno, and Lake Tahoe
Word Association, Inc.
Box 2779 Nantucket, MA 02584

ECONOGUIDE
1995
Las Vegas, Reno, and Lake Tahoe
Word Association, Inc.
Box 2779 Nantucket, MA 02584

ECONOGUIDE 1995

Las Vegas, Reno, and Lake Tahoe

Word Association, Inc.
Box 2779 Nantucket, MA 02584

ECONOGUIDE 1995

Las Vegas, Reno, and Lake Tahoe

Word Association, Inc.
Box 2779 Nantucket, MA 02584

ECONOGUIDE 1995

Las Vegas, Reno, and Lake Tahoe

Word Association, Inc.
Box 2779 Nantucket, MA 02584

ECONOGUIDE 1995

Las Vegas, Reno, and Lake Tahoe

Word Association, Inc.
Box 2779 Nantucket, MA 02584

ECONOGUIDE 1995

Las Vegas, Reno, and Lake Tahoe

Word Association, Inc.
Box 2779 Nantucket, MA 02584

ECONOGUIDE 1995

Las Vegas, Reno, and Lake Tahoe

Word Association, Inc.
Box 2779 Nantucket, MA 02584

ECONOGUIDE 1995

Las Vegas, Reno, and Lake Tahoe

Word Association, Inc.
Box 2779 Nantucket, MA 02584

SOUTH SHORE PARASAILING

$5. off per flight

Take off and land on the back of the boat.
The only way to see Lake Tahoe.

Two Locations in Lake Tahoe
Camp Richardson: 916-541-PARA (7272)
Ski Run Marina: 916-544-0200

Expiration: September 1996

250 Wild Island Ct., Sparks–
Located at 1-80 East Sparks Blvd

$3.00 off General Admission
$2.00 off Junior Admission

(Limit six guests per coupon, admission prices based on height)

Splash into a Real Cool Deal! Experience the tropical adventures of an action-packed waterpark featuring a motion-of-the-ocean wave pool, children's lagoon, lazy river, speed slides, or dare to ride our newest attraction, the "Black Widow." Open Memorial Weekend through August, 1995.
Call for operating hours 702-331-WILD.

Not valid with any other discount offer. No cash value. Non-transferable. Must be presented to cashier at time of purchase. EXPIRES ON THE LAST OPERATING DAY IN 1995. G912/J913

NATIONAL AUTOMOBILE MUSEUM

10 Lake Street South,
Corner of Lake & Mill
Reno, Nevada 89501

Phone: **702-333-9300**
Hours: 9:30 am–5:30 pm

$1 off Regular Adult and Senior Admission

50 cents off Juniors (6-18)

Expiration:
12/31/95

#12

ECONOGUIDE
1995
Las Vegas, Reno, and Lake Tahoe
Word Association, Inc.
Box 2779 Nantucket, MA 02584

ECONOGUIDE
1995
Las Vegas, Reno, and Lake Tahoe
Word Association, Inc.
Box 2779 Nantucket, MA 02584

ECONOGUIDE
1995
Las Vegas, Reno, and Lake Tahoe
Word Association, Inc.
Box 2779 Nantucket, MA 02584

Buy one meal in our 24 hour restaurant and get another meal of equal or lesser value for

Free

Present this ad to food server.
*Not valid on $1.49 breakfasts or steak meals.
*Not valid with any other coupons.

329-4664

800-874-5558

EXPIRATION: 12/31/95

Free Valet Parking Through Lincoln Alley

Center		
2nd	Lincoln Alley	1st
Virginia		

GREAT BASIN ADVENTURE

Splash down the log flume, ride a pony, pet a pig–Discover these adventures at the:

Wilbur D. May Great Basin Adventure
1502 Washington St., Reno, NV 89503

702-785-4319

2 FOR 1 ON THE SAME PRICE ADMISSION.

Limit 6 guests per coupon. Open Memorial Day–Labor Day, 10 am–5 pm.
Valid May 27, 1995 through September 4, 1995
A division of Washoe County Parks and Recreation.

There are a lot of good reasons to rent a car.
Here is one good reason to rent from Budget.

$5 Off*
1-4 day rental
Economy through
luxury cars

$10 Off*
5-7 day rental
Economy through
luxury cars

Whether it's for vacation, replacement car or friends in town, Budget has the right car for you.

Offer valid at participating locations if presented at start of rental. One coupon per rental. Discount applies to time and mileage. Taxes, refueling services, and optional items are extra. Normal rental requirements apply. Offer not available in conjunction with any other promotion or discount. For information and reservations, **call 702-785-2690.**

*Discounts valid in Reno only.
EXPIRATION: 12/31/95

The Mandarin Restaurant

5089 S. McCarran Blvd. • Smithridge Plaza • Reno, Nevada 89502

702-827-0222

With this coupon, you are entitled to 20% off on any family dinner or entree you order. (One coupon per table.)

We serve the best Authentic Chinese cuisine in Reno with a house-prepared special sauce. The National Food Critics Association selected us as one of the best restaurants in the country. Western style decor with soft romantic lantern lights enhance each comfortable booth. EXPIRATION: 12/31/95

ECONOGUIDE
1995
Las Vegas, Reno, and Lake Tahoe
Word Association, Inc.
Box 2779 Nantucket, MA 02584

ECONOGUIDE
1995
Las Vegas, Reno, and Lake Tahoe
Word Association, Inc.
Box 2779 Nantucket, MA 02584

ECONOGUIDE
1995
Las Vegas, Reno, and Lake Tahoe
Word Association, Inc.
Box 2779 Nantucket, MA 02584

ECONOGUIDE
1995
Las Vegas, Reno, and Lake Tahoe
Word Association, Inc.
Box 2779 Nantucket, MA 02584

Quick-Find Index to Attractions

(See also the Contents)

RENO, VIRGINIA CITY, AND LAKE TAHOE

The Bests